BRAZIL 1980:

THE PROTESTANT HANDBOOK

BRAZIL 1980:

THE PROTESTANT HANDBOOK

William R. Read &
Frank A. Ineson

THE DYNAMICS OF CHURCH GROWTH IN THE 1950'S AND 60'S AND THE TREMENDOUS POTENTIAL FOR THE 70'S.

MARC
919 WEST HUNTINGTON DRIVE, MONROVIA, CALIFORNIA 91016
A DIVISION OF WORLD VISION INTERNATIONAL

Grateful acknowledgement is made to the following for copyright material:
Attic Press for material duplicated from William Carey's *Enquiry.*
The Organization of American States for use of maps of the Amazon region.

Missions Advanced Research & Communications Center

ISBN 0-912552-04-2
Library of Congress Catalog Card Number, 73-848879
Printed in the United States of America

Table of Contents

List of Figures

List of Tables

Foreword

One way of approaching the challenge of world evangelism is to understand the "force for evangelism" that is available in each country of the world and then attempt to understand God's strategy for that land. What is He doing? Where is His Spirit leading? People usually come to Christ one at a time, but sometimes families are saved and great movements toward God seem to take place when Spirit-filled men take advantage of the times they are in.

The Brazil 1980 effort is part of the attempt to reach the untold two billion of the world by 1) discovering the strength and weakness of the national church and missionary force in a single country, 2) analyzing what God seems to be saying in light of the opportunities and the obstacles for evangelism, and 3) finding ways of sharing with the existent "force for evangelism" what has been discovered in the confidence that the Holy Spirit will use this to bring the Church in that country to see their role in God's plans.

Five years ago, Brazil was prayerfully chosen as the first real test case for this concept. Brazil was selected because of the availability of the unusual Brazilian religious census data, the diversity and regionalism of the country, the existence of the Missionary Information Bureau, and the helpful studies and research findings about church growth that were available for this country. Here was a place where God had evidently placed the needed information and the tools.

Brazil is a country which has tremendous potential for its own foreign mission effort. Because of the large number speaking German, Italian, Japanese and other foreign-languages, there are many people who can easily move from the Brazilian culture to another culture to proclaim Jesus Christ.

William R. Read, who had served as a missionary in Brazil under COEMAR for seventeen years and has been engaged in church growth research in this country, was invited to participate in this Brazil Project. In God's timing he was able to go on leave of absence to become a member of the MARC Staff and take the responsibility for the Brazil Project, that shortly thereafter was named BRAZIL 1980.

At the same time, Frank Ineson, former executive secretary of Missionary Information Bureau in Brazil, and presently director of International Intecessors at World Vision International, joined the BRAZIL 1980 team. As a team Read and Ineson brought together in one place, more knowledge, insight and understanding of the situation and status of the churches and missions in Brazil than any other possible combination of personnel. They have been working together for almost three years and their efforts have taken them through the first and second phases of the Project into the all important Phase III.

Phase I

Phase I involved gathering the information about the missions and the church. Today we know more about the numerical disposition of Protestant forces in Brazil than in any other country of the world (including the United States).

The government statistical data for the Protestant churches of Brazil has now been computerized and is in the process of being transferred to Brazil to be used by Brazilian leaders for "in depth" studies of their local churches so they can analyze the larger growth potential around them. This information will be available for both church and mission leaders.

The BRAZIL 1980 effort produced a special survey that will measure the methods of evangelism and analyze how people have been converted to Jesus Christ. Originally this survey was administered by the local pastor. It gave the pastor and his people the means to examine what God is doing among them and to understand what needs to be done. It has now been revised and a nation-wide survey is in process to obtain the larger picture of how God is calling individuals to Himself.

Phase II

Phase II saw the sharing of this information and its interpretation with both mission and church leaders in the United States and Brazil.

An analysis of the dynamics of church growth was made. The results of this study were distributed to church and mission leaders, both in Brazil and in the United States as Interpretive Bulletin #1 entitled *Continuing Evangelism in Brazil*. This bulletin was first sent out for comment by a great number of those involved in the actual task, and many observations, corrections, and additions were received. This bulletin has been incorporated into *BRAZIL 1980: The Protestant Handbook*.

An historic meeting was held in Brazil between Dr. R. C. Halverson, Chairman of the World Vision International board, and myself as Director of MARC, and eighteen church leaders who represented almost eighty-five percent of the Protestants in Brazil. This was the first time that such a meeting had ever been held with these traditionally separatist groups. These men were excited about the information contained within *Continuing Evangelism in Brazil* and the suggestion was made that they create for themselves a Church Information/Research Center for the churches in Brazil.

A committee was appointed by these church leaders, and it interacted with various proposals that came from MARC. Tentatively, they agreed to bring selected people from each of their denominational groups for special two-week seminars on strategy, church growth ways and means, communication and management.

The BRAZIL 1980 team made contact with the Overseas Crusade (SEPAL) team in São Paulo and presented them with the challenge of this type of program. The correspondence that ensued resulted in the setting up of a second meeting to work out the details for organizing a special type of Information/Research Center that would function as an agency to continue in Brazil as the servant of the national church and missions leadership who felt the need of these specialized research-oriented ministries.

In May of 1972 a second meeting with twenty-four top Evangelical leaders was held in Brazil to discuss the best ways to implement everything that has been produced in the BRAZIL 1980 project to date.

It was agreed to initiate a series of training institutes, having the goal of training key men in each denomination to do church growth research for their own churches. A conversion survey was officially introduced to the churches and enthusiastically adopted as a tool to measure and evaluate local church performance and evaluate local church ministries.

The publication of a bimonthly newsletter was approved. In this way research activities could be coordinated and results immediately made available to other pastors who can be aided by them. Representatives of the Overseas Crusades team in Brazil were introduced to these Brazilian leaders and were well received. The idea of the establishment of a research and communication center in São Paulo to be called CASE (Center for Advanced Studies in Evangelism), a cooperative venture between these national church leaders, MARC, and Overseas Crusades, came out of this meeting. The last important resolution of the meeting was the planning of two extensive trips by Harmon Johnson and Paul McKaugan, of CASE, to each of the denominational headquarters to select key men from each church who would benefit from the training seminar which was held in February and March 1973.

Phase III

MARC accepted the responsibility of completing and transferring the massive computer analysis of church growth in Brazil for a twelve-year period county-by-county. When finished, this would constitute the basic information and data needed for the CASE research and communication center that will be in a position to serve all Church and Mission organizations in Brazil. This was decided through a special agreement and cooperative plan between MARC and SEPAL, the field unit of Overseas Crusade, who are in Brazil and maintain the close contact with these churches. SEPAL agreed to take the field responsibility for the maintenance and dissemination of the vital church growth information on behalf of all the national church denominational groups and mission organizations who might be interested.

As the BRAZIL 1980 effort entered the all important Phase II, it was decided that a definitive publication was needed to document the Brazil 1980 effort. The result was the writing of *BRAZIL 1980: The Protestant Handbook*.

For the first time in history, a detailed analysis has been made of the growth of the Protestant church in an entire country, county-by-county, denomination-by-denomination. Such a study was never previously possible. Not only was the data not available, but the tremendous amount of manhours that would be needed to analyze all of the details, if they were there, would have made the cost prohibitively high. But through the use of modern data processing techniques, combined with years of missionary research expertise, we now have before us an overall picture of a country that permits us to see what God has been doing, and what doors of opportunity stand open for the future.

Whether it is the local pastor who has wondered how to interpret the tremendous task of missions to his church, a mission executive with a responsibility in Brazil, or a mission or church leader struggling with the magnitude of the problems of world evangelization, this book will cast new light and give new insights on how to advance in the days ahead.

The timing is right. This book may be used and studied by different churches and missions through the world. Five years of practical research has been brought together to be used either as a handbook for particular studies, or used as an overall introduction to an in-depth country analysis.

The book will be translated into Portuguese and made available through both the Missionary Information Bureau (MIB) and the Center for Advanced Studies in Evangelism (CASE) in São Paulo, Brazil. It is heavily indexed, and has extensive appendices. The appendix on *conversion profiles* of congregations will be of interest to local pastors and mission executives.

The Protestant Handbook written by colleagues William R. Read and Frank A. Ineson, if read, studied, and discussed frankly with associates should arouse some warm discussion. Here is a book that can be an instrument to stimulate your thinking about the new horizons of evangelistic opportunities and give some new insights and a greater understanding about the social dynamics involved in the emergence of new, ripe harvest fields for Gospel proclamation not only in Brazil, but in other parts of the world.

Edward R. Dayton

Preface

Three individuals representing different organizations and interests began working separately on diverse aspects of the Protestant situation in Brazil, some of their earliest efforts dating back into the early 1960's. When the time was right there was a remarkable coming together -- a merging of these different people into a cooperative entity and the results of their labor were united into the research project that soon became known by the name, BRAZIL 1980. This name became the vehicle for the expectations held by each of these team members that their findings would make a substantial difference in the evangelistic outreach and church growth activities of the Protestant Churches of Brazil during the challenging period of the 1970's.

Two of these team members were the authors; the third, Edward Dayton, Director of MARC, whose constant encouragement and astute management has led to the publication of this volume.

The authors feel that BRAZIL 1980: THE PROTESTANT HANDBOOK comes at a time when all Protestant leaders need to vigorously grapple with these facts, determine what they mean, and forge ahead toward 1980 with a renewed determination to evangelize and plant churches based on enthusiastic plans and a strategy commensurate with the expanding opportunities.

WILLIAM R. READ
FRANK A. INESON

Acknowledgements

The BRAZIL 1980 MARC/MIB project captured the interest and imagination of hundreds of people who were willing to give themselves in generous effort, time, and substance to assist the research team attain its ambitious goals. This generous contribution of help covered a wide spectrum of activities and used so many of our contributors' special talents and gifts in the job of field work, data collection, compiling, and transcription of data onto hundreds of special forms that now fill file cabinets and book cases. The job of correspondence steadily increased. There was continuous search for creative, technical advice and dedicated secretarial help. A heavy load of art and graphic work was undertaken. Planning sessions and management meetings were scheduled each week. Card punching, computer programming, and scheduling of computer runs became a way of life. Funds had to be raised and accounted for. The ability of such a project to use large sums quickly was fantastic. Meetings involving long trips to South America were held with national church leaders in Brazil. There were interviews with mission leaders in the USA and in Brazil. It is impossible to mention all of the people by name who were involved in one way or another in these different phases of the work, but some must be mentioned here and given special recognition and acknowledgment.

Rev. Robert C. Whitaker, Minister of Evangelism and Mission of Glendale Presbyterian Church made the initial contacts in Brazil which eventually led this church, under the pastoral leadership of *Dr. Bruce Thielemann,* to approve substantial financial support to guarantee the major financing of the first two years of the BRAZIL 1980 effort.

Dr. Ted W. Engstrom, as Executive Vice President of World Vision International, gave World Vision support to an infant pilot project. World Vision's initial commitment in resources and manpower was the foundation on which BRAZIL 1980 was built.

Mr. John Grove, former elder of Knox Presbyterian Church of Pasadena, California, and presently Registrar of Sterling College in Kansas, was the first computer programmer of the project, along with *Charlie Merrow.* These men were enthusiastic and enlisted other volunteers from Knox Church in Pasadena and gave the project a good, vigorous start.

Dr. Donald A. McGavran, Dean Emeritus of the School of World Mission at Fuller Theological Seminary, early manifested enthusiasm for the Brazil church growth data, even as far back as 1962-1963. In 1965 during the CGRILA (Church Growth in Latin America) research project, he was the motivator that led to initiation of the first computer analysis dealing primarily with church growth data and concepts.

Mr. Roger Schrage, former missionary in Brazil, and now Production Manager at Gospel Light in Glendale, California, was instrumental in coordinating two important meetings that were held in Brazil with Brazilian leaders. Those remarkable meetings eventually led to the formulation of the cooperative program and relationship that now exists between MARC and CASE of the Overseas Crusade Team (SEPAL) in Brazil, seeking to apply findings of the project at the local church. Schrage also coordinated the first test of the conversion profile.

Rev. Harmon Johnson is the organizer and present Director of CASE (Center for Advanced Studies in Evangelism) in São Paulo, Brazil. His enthusiasm and understanding will permit future implementation of the Brazil church growth data in Brazil. Through his center this data bank will be used to generate evangelistic programs and new church planting endeavors.

Mr. Joe R. Wood Jr., deacon of Lake Avenue Congregational Church in Pasadena, California, was an indefatigable and dedicated computer programmer, responsible for the design of the complicated programming procedures and subsequent computer runs connected with the new Brazil 1980 church growth data computer format. When Joe offered his service, it was at a time that he was needed desperately. His persistence, expertise, and long hours at the task produced the extensive computer runs of 1972 and 1973. Many compilations from the Joe Wood computer reports have been used in different chapters of the book to support conclusions and suggestions for future work.

Mr. John Siewert, Director of the Data Processing Department of World Vision, and his staff have given the BRAZIL 1980 project special consideration, support, and assistance. By keeping up with the latest technical advances in the computer field, and always upgrading and increasing the capacity of the computer facility at World Vision, he has helped in the solution of difficult computer problems and procedures involved in the unique applications of the computer to church growth data.

Dr. Tim Smith, a Professor at the California State University at Los Angeles, is one of the new breed of analytic geographers whose skills in statistical analysis and computer science have been assisting and supporting this project since 1971. His innovative approach, his search for new dimensions and ways to use computer technology, and his application of computerized cartography to the BRAZIL 1980 data is in process at the present time.

Dr. Alan R. Tippett, Professor of Anthropology at the School of World Mission, Fuller Theological Seminary has given much time to the organization and revision of many of the different steps involved in the design of the BRAZIL 1980 data bank so that a similar procedure may be used by missionary researchers at Fuller in future church growth studies.

The responsibility for any errors that remain in this text must remain with the authors. However, there have been a faithful cadre of World Vision personnel who have made significant contributions: *Don Aylard* had oversight of most of the artwork. *Mrs. Betty Manchester* had the major responsibility for the typing. *Ann Chilton* and *Ellen Gilbert* somehow managed to get all the component parts assembled for the printer. *Helen Martin* was our indefatigable proofreader. We are in debt to each one.

A great debt of gratitude is felt for all that the MARC staff has done, for all of the different churches who have supported the project by enlisting volunteers and financial help, for individuals and organizations who have stood by us in different ways too numerous to mention. The project, because of its magnitude and scope, has needed much volunteer help, encouragement and funding. This help came when it was needed and is gratefully acknowledged.

Introduction

Brazil is a big country. If we talk about continuous land area, it is the fourth largest country in the world after Russia, Canada, and China. This makes Brazil the largest country in Latin America. Brazil is a fast growing country. In 1950 the population was 50,000,000 people, but by 1970 its population was almost 100,000,000. Every year about 3,000,000 Brazilians are added to the population. Today, more than one-third of all Latin Americans are Brazilian. Brazil is larger in population than any other country in South America. Brazil is a land of big cities, strung out like jewels along the seacoast from Belém to Pôrto Alegre. These cities had a population in 1950 of almost 9,000,000 people. By 1970, close to 24,000,000 Brazilians were crowded into these urban centers. These major cities are rapidly extending their boundaries and are becoming metropolitan areas overflowing with people.

In spite of its tremendous growth, Brazil is still a country with many frontiers. New land stretches out across the horizons. New cities have been built where formerly there was wilderness. Economic and industrial frontiers challenge the Brazilian people. One of Brazil's most challenging frontiers may well be its youth. Fifty-five percent of the population of Brazil was under 20 years of age in 1965.

Brazil is a country with many Protestant Christians. Sixty-five percent of all the Protestants in Latin America are found in this country. Brazil is also a country with almost 3,000 foreign missionaries. There are more North American missionaries in Brazil than in any other country in the world, and the foreign mission investment in Brazil is substantial each year.

The government of Brazil has recently divided the country into 361 important micro-regions, and the BRAZIL 1980 church growth analysis reconstructs the country by previous years to clearly show the development and progress of the Protestant communicants and community in each separate micro-region.

Church growth past, present, and future has been related to the rapid changes taking place in Brazilian society. It shows the relationship of urbanization, industrialization, internal migration, and population growth to the growth of Protestant churches and what the face of the future might be.

The emerging road system that will eventually spread itself like a spider web across the vast Amazon jungle area of Brazil is discussed. This road system will set off one of the greatest land settlement movements of this century and will, by 1980, present the greatest challenge the Protestant church in Brazil has ever had.

Brazilian people are suddenly in motion as never before, moving into the new frontier land areas in west Brazil. This redistribution of Protestant believers throughout the length and breadth of the land is a new opportunity for evangelization and church planting that is described and documented.

High potential response areas for evangelization and church planting in Brazil are carefully described, and it is clear in every chapter that the approach of the authors is that of a cautious, seasoned optimism.

This book has a helpful directory section that lists all church and foreign mission agencies working in Brazil at present, complete with addresses and listing the special functions of each agency in the overall Protestant community. In addition the directory contains the names and addresses of seminaries, Bible institutes, publishers, and a special directory of church and mission areas of opportunity in the 1970's.

Because of its rapid growth, size and location, Brazil is of strategic importance to the countries in Latin America. Because of its dynamic, rapidly growing church, it is of strategic importance to the *churches* in other Latin American countries. Brazilian Protestants are spilling over their borders to influence neighboring countries, through evangelization, establishing churches, and radio broadcasting. Brazilian Protestants need all the encouragement they can receive to complete the great task of evangelization their country faces in the decade of the 1970's, and to dedicate their tremendous resources, natural and in mankind, to God to be used in other parts of the world.

The Missions Advanced Research and Communication Center, a division of World Vision International, undertook a study of Brazil with the confidence that by 1980 great advances will be possible for the Protestant future there. This project is the outgrowth of a two-year study done by the Latin American Church Growth Research team at the School of World Mission at Fuller Theological Seminary, and four years of research of the missionary task by the Missionary Information Bureau.

The BRAZIL 1980 project seeks to answer the question "How can we help and how can we learn from what is going on in Brazil?" If North Americans are to assist the Brazilian Protestant community, and at the same time learn how to take advantage of what God is doing in Brazil, we need to understand more about this giant of the South. We need to do research.

We need to know more about its history, great events and leaders, its people, their opportunities, their hopes, the freedom they have to fulfill their destiny, aspirations, natural talents, and to utilize their resources. Brazil is the world's largest coffee exporter; it has more arable land than all of Europe. Fifteen percent of the world's forests and 35 percent of its iron deposits are found in Brazil. Yet it remains a country where large numbers of its 100,000,000 people are underfed, and sickly. Problems of social justice are always present. While progress has been made in reducing the infant mortality rate, it is still high. Slums and shanty towns grow twice as fast as other parts of the city, and many fight for survival. We must attempt to understand the material needs of Brazil. We cannot overlook the weighty themes of justice - social, civil and religious. Brazil has great spiritual needs as well as great spiritual potential. We must strive for a well balanced understanding of these things and be concerned in it all to see that man's total needs, spiritual as well as material, are met by the redemptive power of Jesus Christ.

BRAZIL 1980: The Protestant Handbook seeks to document some of the things that have been happening in Brazil. Let's look at the churches. In 1950 there were 906,000 Protestant church members. By 1970, this number had grown to nearly 3,000,000 communicant members. In two decades the Church had increased almost four-fold! But in order to really understand what is happening in Brazil, we need to look further into the statistics. This publication is a real look into the statistics and data to show how the Church in Brazil has grown. Churches in different regions have experienced different growth. The greatest growth has occurred in the South and the Southeast where many economic and social changes have taken place. Large numbers of people from other parts of Brazil have poured into those regions. Churches have been growing as many people, both Protestant and others, move into these regions looking for jobs and a chance to get some education for their children.

The number of Protestants has been growing and so has the number of missionaries. Almost two-thirds of the missionaries in Brazil have arrived since 1960. These missionaries face the problems of adapting to a new language and a different culture. They must win the respect of Brazilians before they can communicate the Gospel or even be heard. One of the questions that we have to ask is "Can the missionary task in Brazil be done more effectively?" Many missionaries and missions think that it can. But they need help, practical orientation and information upon which they can base new guidelines for planning their strategy.

God has a strategy for the evangelization of Brazil. Missions research is one key for fulfilling that strategy. At the same time we should remember that the foreign missionary is not the only one attempting to evangelize Brazil. If the unevangelized people of Brazil are to receive the Gospel they will hear it because of the joint efforts of the 3,000 foreign missionaries working side-by-side with 60,000 Protestant church leaders and the 3,000,000 communicant members of their local churches. Essentially, this is the message of *BRAZIL 1980: The Protestant Handbook*.

There are many firsts in this book:

> This is the first time the computer has been used to analyze such a large and significant collection of church growth statistics by an entire country. Fifteen years of church growth data, denomination and county-by-county, is available with projections into 1980.
>
> This is the first time that detailed data has been on hand to study the effects of social transition and modernization on the progress of the Protestant church in a country.
>
> This is the first time that major regions of Brazil have been carefully examined to ascertain the geographical strength and weakness of the Protestant community.
>
> This is the first time the necessary statistics have been available which permit projections of church growth and point to specific areas of potential Protestant penetration for the future.

> <u>This is the first time</u> that the use of <u>indicators</u>, numerical statements of the situation, have been used to discuss church growth.
>
> <u>This is the first time</u> data has been available to permit <u>a basic overall strategy</u> for evangelism, a useful strategy which can be applied at all levels and in many countries of the world.

This then, is the Church at work in the exciting country of Brazil. What is God's strategy for Brazil? He has a strategy! Our job is to understand that strategy and become a part of it. What is it that we need to know in order to do this? First, we need to have a knowledge of how to do research to determine the effectiveness of the various methods of evangelism and resulting church growth. We need a practical way to acquire, share, and use such information and the insights that God gives us. We need a way to evaluate this information to help us understand specific situations. We need plans for the preparation of selected lay leaders for evangelism and in turn for the training of communicant members. We need plans for doing evangelistic work, using every possible opportunity and resource. This whole area of planning is dealt with very ably in this book and shows us the way that these things can be done. And certainly we need an understanding of the economic and social situation in which the local churches must witness.

We have already seen how we can be misled if we do not see the facts under the facts. If someone told us that the Church in Brazil is growing rapidly, we might assume that this means all churches, including ours. The BRAZIL 1980 project was designed to get at the facts under the facts. Research has shown that church growth is sometimes influenced by sociological and economic factors. The Brazilian government is building an important network of new roads that fan out from the new capital of Brasília and out across the Amazon basin from the Northeast. These will have a tremendous impact on the growth of both the population and the church. This frontier road system which is dealt with in this book will penetrate the previously unreached areas of the Amazon Basin. Populous coastal areas will now be linked with the new lands to bring to an end the isolation and backwardness of the rural population. As Brazilians are able to develop and utilize their untapped resources, the Protestant churches in Brazil will have the opportunity to multiply themselves along with the expanding road system. Will they take advantage of this opportunity?

MARC, in cooperation with the Missionary Information Bureau (MIB) put together a team of experts to use research methods to increase their understanding of God's strategy for Brazil. The goal of the BRAZIL 1980 project is to help the Brazilian church and missionaries working in Brazil to become a more effective part of God's strategy. This MARC/MIB team included information specialists, computer scientists, professional managers, as well as trained missionary researchers. Twelve years of data on Protestant church growth have been collected by the Brazilian government. This data has now been stored and analyzed by computer to show in detail how different church groups have progressed in different regions, states and counties of Brazil.

The BRAZIL 1980 project was divided into four major areas: The national Church, missions, data bank, and an information system. The area of working with the national churches has been one of learning from them of their needs and then giving back to them a total picture of what God has been doing in Brazil. The second area of working with missions is an attempt to understand how God is using missionaries in Brazil and how they can be most effective in the work of Christ. The data bank phase includes the storing and making available to the rest of the Church, information about what is happening in Brazil. The information system phase includes the problem of establishing contact with both secular and Christian sources to know what is going on in Brazil today and feeding new data to key leaders. The greatest impact of the MARC/MIB BRAZIL 1980 program will be in the number of persons in Brazil who will have the opportunity to hear the Gospel because of this project. BRAZIL 1980 seeks to document the current situation and define the steps that lie ahead. As we move into the dynamic era of the 1970's, God has again given us the opportunity to communicate His love in a new and meaningful way. The age of missions has not ended. It has barely begun. Dedicated prayer and tough minded decisions, a spirit of gentleness and concern maintained in the arena of the problems we face, hard research that moves us into a new understanding of what God would have us do and have us be - these are the keys to evangelization of Brazil.

1

People of Brazil

SUMMARY

Geography and Population. 8,456,000 square kilometers (3,286,000 square miles). 94,509,000 people in 1970, averaging 11 people per square kilometer.

Ethnic Composition. In the 1960 census Brazilians classified themselves as 70 percent "white," 11 percent black or "negroes," and the remainder as mulatto or "mixed."

Age and Sex. This same 1960 census indicated that 42 percent of the population were under 15 years of age, 27 percent between 15 and 29 years of age, and the remaining 31 percent were 30 years and over. There are a few more females than males in Brazil. However, males in each age class exceed females in rural areas and in the age classes below 10 years in the urban areas.

Literacy. 75 percent of those between 15 and 30 years of age can read and write enough to be classified as "literate." For all ages 15 years and over the proportion was 67 percent in 1970; this contrasts with 35 percent in 1920.

Urban Trend. In 1970, 56 percent of the population lived in urban areas in contrast to 30 percent in 1940. Counties with urban populations of more than 100,000 increased significantly. There were 23 in 1940, 39 in 1950, 65 in 1960, and 75 in 1970. In 1940 these urban counties had 6,500,000 people and in 1970 they had 30,000,000 people.

Economic Status. Although the trend in economic level has been upward, the great majority of the people are economically still below middle class, having a yearly per capita income of less than $360.

Religion. It is estimated that about 85 percent of Brazilians now classify themselves as Roman Catholics, 11 percent as Protestants, and the remainder as spiritists, Jehovah's Witnesses, Latter-day Saints, and other small groups. However, the number of practicing Catholics is apparently much lower and the number of practicing spiritists much higher.

INTRODUCTION

The people of Brazil have a unique historical background. Various ethnic, social, religious, and economic developments have resulted in a cultural mosaic. The complex, technically-oriented society of modern cities contrasts with the remaining small, indigenous Indian tribes which are jealously guarding antiquated customs and with the rapidly mushrooming rural communities springing up along extensive interior highways. In a remarkable way almost all of the different stages of man's social development can be found somewhere in Brazil. Such diversity means that no one approach to communication, no single method of evangelization will begin to touch all the different lives involved. Understanding the diversity and seeing the possibility of adapting to each type of people in their milieu is an important step toward effective evangelism.

Therefore, if the church is to adequately communicate Jesus Christ to the people of Brazil, it needs to understand them in this unusual diversity. Who are they? How do they see themselves? How do we see them? What influences them? What factors have made them what they are? Where are they going? What factors are influencing their national and individual destinies? The Gospel must be communicated and presented within each specific and different culture of the Brazilian people.

GEOGRAPHY AND POPULATION

Until one takes into account the size of the country and the distribution and density of the population, it is impossible to understand the magnitude of the task of evangelization in Brazil. There are many different faces of this country. Brazil has tremendous resources and great potential for growth. These facts need to be adequately understood before we begin to discuss the implications of the growth of the Protestant Churches in Brazil and how they relate to different regions and to the various groups of the population.

FIGURE 1-1

PRINCIPAL REGIONS, STATES, AND TERRITORIES OF BRAZIL

And so we begin.

For the first 400 years following the arrival of Pedro Alvares Cabral from Portugal in 1500, settlement was largely confined to cities which sprang up along the most accessible areas of the 6,000 mile coastline. Brazil's population is still heavily concentrated along the coastline, yet tens of thousands are moving into the expanding industrial centers and sprouting suburban settlements. Here Evangelicals find it possible to form small groups of Protestant believers which soon grow into vigorous new churches. The establishment of the national capital at Brasilia has encouraged migration to that modern city and beyond with consequent development of the sparsely settled Central-West. Brasilia is a hub from which new highways form spokes that reach out into all the country.

Brazil embraces nearly half the continent of South America. Its 8.5 million square kilometers (3,286,000 square miles) make Brazil larger than the continental United States, not including Alaska (Table 1-1). Brazil is irregular in shape (Figure 1-1), but its distance north and south (4,320 kilometers or 2,800 miles) is almost the same as it is east and west (4,328 kilometers or 2,805 miles).

TABLE 1-1

DISTRIBUTION OF AREA AND POPULATION BY REGIONS IN BRAZIL, 1970

Region	Area		Population		Density
	Square Kilometers (1000's)	Percent of Brazil	(1000's)	Percent of Brazil	Persons/ Square Kilometer
North	3,554	42	3,651	4	1
Northeast	1,542	18	28,675	30	19
Southeast	919	11	40,332	43	44
South	562	7	16,684	18	30
Central-West	1,879	22	5,167	5	3
BRAZIL	8,456	100	94,509	100	11

Source: Based on Tables 2 & 4, *Sinopse Preliminar do Censo Demográfico: Brasil-1970*, FUNDAÇÃO IBGE, Instituto Brasileiro de Estatística.

Within the geographical area of Brazil's boundaries can be found the following natural resources:

A variety of climates and vegetation. Brazil extends a little north of the equator to considerably south of the Tropic of Capricorn; plateaus, mountains, and swamplands abound.

Immense river systems, including the great and mighty Amazon, give Brazil one of the world's greatest potential sources for hydro-electric power.

One-fourth of the world's known iron ore reserves and other strategic minerals and metals provide future elements for the atomic age, to say nothing of the unknown reserves of iron, tin, tungsten, oil, and other precious metals waiting to be discovered.

Over 2,000,000 square miles of undeveloped land, including jungle, swamps, and tropical plains exist in Brazil.

Scattered over this extensive area are almost 100 million people who have been among the most responsive in the world to accept the truths of the Gospel. The uneven distribution of Brazil's population in relation to area is shown graphically in Figure 1-2. Note that the North and the Central-West, which embrace most of the Amazon Basin, have together 64 percent of the total area of Brazil but only 9 percent of the population.

FIGURE 1-2

LAND AREA AND POPULATION BY REGIONS, 1970

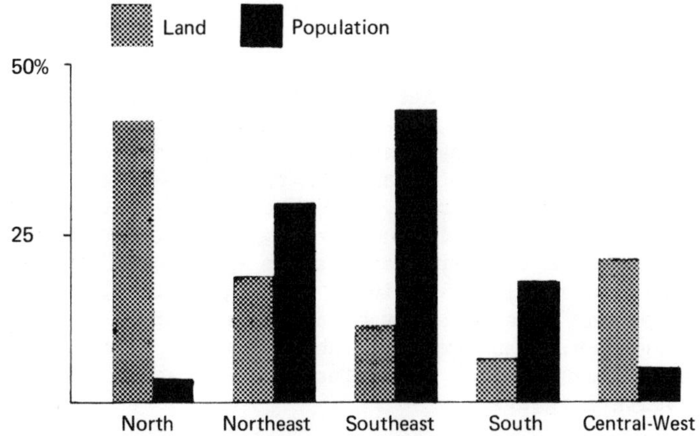

Source: Based on Tables 2 & 4, Sinopse Preliminar do Censo Demográfico: Brasil – 1970, I.B.G.E.

In 1970, Brazil averaged 11 people per square kilometer. Due to the rapidly expanding industrial centers, the density of population in the Southeast was 44 people per square kilometer. The South followed with 30 people per square kilometer, and the Northeast had 19. There were only 3 people per square kilometer in the Central-West and only one in the North, though these are the largest regions.

ETHNIC COMPOSITION

Brazil is one of the outstanding "melting pots" in the world. No other country has had such a blending of red, black, yellow, and white racial stock. Some Brazilian leaders dismiss a study of the effects of this mixture on the basis that race and color are not the big social problem in Brazil that they are in other parts of the world. Others insist that the very same factors that have permitted such a unique racial blend have been instrumental in preparing the stage for Brazil to experience unusual Evangelical growth and have contributed to its development and progress.

In 1960, the last census that took this factor into account, some 70 percent of the people of Brazil classified themselves as "white," 11 percent as "negroes," and the remainder as "mixed," including about 125,000 Indians. This was an increase of 8 percent in the proportion of "whites" over the distribution shown by the census of 1950. The entire shift was from the "mixed" class. This indicates a "whitening by concensus." Those who were at one time classified as "mixed," now prefer to call themselves "white."

Because of a unique heritage from different peoples and tongues of other nations, Brazil has the potential to become a major Protestant missionary-sending country in the world. Here is a nation where the European, African, and Asian stock still maintain large ethnic blocks, even though they have amalgamated to form the nation that is now Brazil. Today, although the predominant language is Portuguese, there are large numbers of Brazilians who still speak fluent German, Italian, Spanish, Dutch, Russian, Yiddish, Slovak, Japanese, Korean, and many other languages. Many would be able to cross national boundaries without serious problems and effectively preach the Gospel in their native language.

AGE AND SEX

The age of a population has a great bearing on the degree of acceptance that might be given the Gospel. The younger the people the greater possibility and potential there are for new ideas to be accepted and new ways to be adopted. Brazil is a young nation, and its young population is rapidly increasing. Men and women in their different age groups differ in their response to various approaches of communication. The Gospel proclamation is no exception.

In 1970, one of the obvious characteristics of the age profile (Figure 1-3) was that Brazil's population was highly concentrated in the young. The same pattern existed in 1940, (Figure 1-3). Nearly 42 percent of the population were less than 15 years old. There were more than 25 million young men and women, or 27 percent, between 15 and 30 years. The proportion of younger age groups was higher in the cities than in the rural areas. A slightly larger proportion of females than males was found in the urban areas reflecting their movement to the cities to serve in industry and as servants in middle and upper class homes.

As Brazilian Evangelicals begin to look at population from the vantage point of age and sex distribution, new opportunities can be pinpointed. Greater emphasis needs to be placed on reaching the youth. The large numbers who move into urban centers appear to respond more favorably as they discard former restraints to accepting the Gospel. This is more difficult for those living in a closed, custom-bound, rural environment. (But it should be noted that in this time of transition they can just as easily become enmeshed in the materialism of urban society.) Young people who move to new rural settlements also appear to come to their new homes and live in an environment that generates a more receptive frame of mind.

FIGURE 1-3

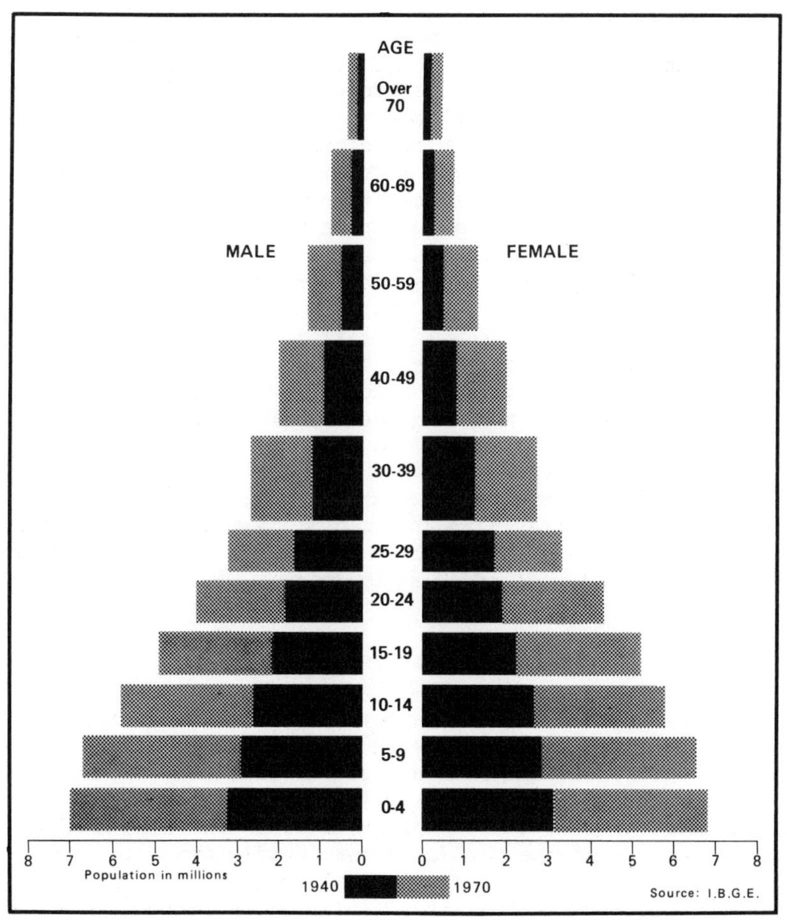

LITERACY

The Gospel is given in written word; therefore, people's ability to read it has a great deal to do with how rapidly they are able to receive it and communicate it to others. Brazil is a country with a growing literacy rate, and it is important to understand how this literacy rate is distributed among the different ethnic groups.

The degree of literacy found in a group of people, a church, or a population is an educational level indicator of the group. The level of literacy varies from place to place and from group to group. It becomes an index for measuring social mobility - the capacity of a group, church, or a segment of a population to advance in society and assume leadership.

The literacy trend is upward for all age groups (Figure 1-4). Whereas in 1920 only 35 percent of those 15 years and over could read and write, the proportion in 1970 was 67 percent. Approximately 74 percent of those between 15 to 30 years of age can now read and write. The proportion is considerably lower in rural than in urban areas, emphasizing the value of radio, primarily shortwave, as a means of communication within the interior. During recent years, the government has made fresh efforts to help adults learn to read and write. Brazilian church leaders generally have been cooperating with this thrust.

The educational system in Brazil is inadequate to meet the needs of the increasing numbers of young people, and is being radically reformed. During the last 10 years Brazil has had over a 100 percent increase in the number of teachers. However, only about two-thirds of the 7 to 11-year-old children are enrolled in school and the number of dropouts is extremely large. Of each 1,000 students enrolled in the first grade in 1966, less than 200 were registered in the fourth grade in 1970. The situation is similarly acute in the higher grades with fewer than 600,000 students enrolled in superior schools.

URBAN TREND

Brazil is changing from a rural to an urban country with a majority of Brazilians now living in the cities. During the past 40 years there has been a steady, relentless expansion of major urban centers in Brazil to a point where these cities now absorb 56 percent of the inhabitants. The 1970 census revealed that 72 percent of the people in the heavily populated Southeast region are now urban dwellers (Figure 1-5). Each of the other regions is experiencing a similar trend though they are still primarily rural.

FIGURE 1-4

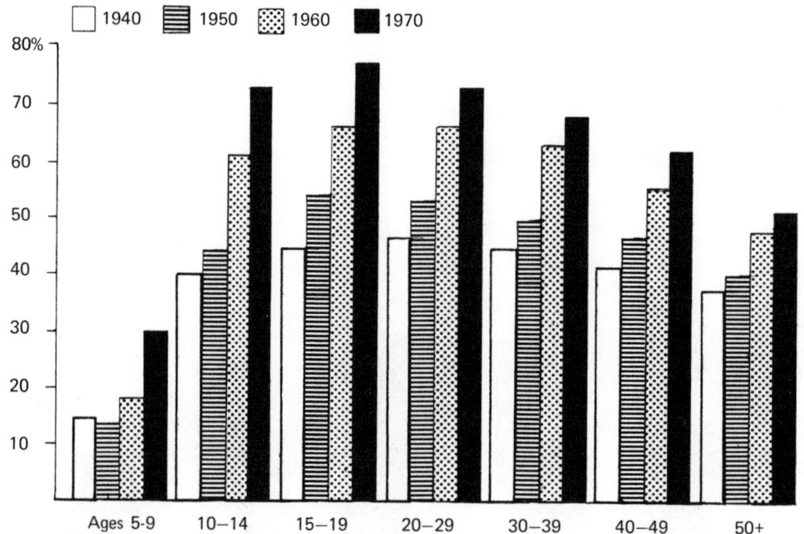

Source: Adapted from I.B.G.E. Atlas do Brasil: 1966, V-2; for 1970 based on Table 3, Tabulações Avancadas do Censo Demográfico: Brasil—1970

People who are in the midst of transition, people who are encountering new experiences and leaving behind old ways and finding new needs, are much more open to new ideas. When homes are uprooted and people migrate to new areas, they leave behind many of their traditions. A great deal of the current transition is the result of the shift toward the cities. This urban trend can aid or detract from our ability to reach people for Christ.

The process of modernization is at work in Brazil. Modernization in Brazil involves the interaction of many factors which cause individuals to move from their traditional way of life to a more complex, technologically advanced, and rapidly changing life-style. Modernization produces dynamic changes among people who are facing the processes of urbanization, industrialization, and secularization in their resettlement pattern from rural to urban living. It means a new style of living, a new openness to religious stimuli, different personal and family aspirations, the facing of problems of illiteracy and education, the challenge of political participation, the entering of a cosmopolitan milieu, and the reception of all the stimulation that comes from the mass media. In many ways, it causes a fragmentation of cultural groups, necessitating a greater understanding of the characteristics of an individual's life-style and behavior in order to determine his position in the complicated spectrum of modernization.

FIGURE 1-5

URBAN POPULATION TREND BY REGIONS

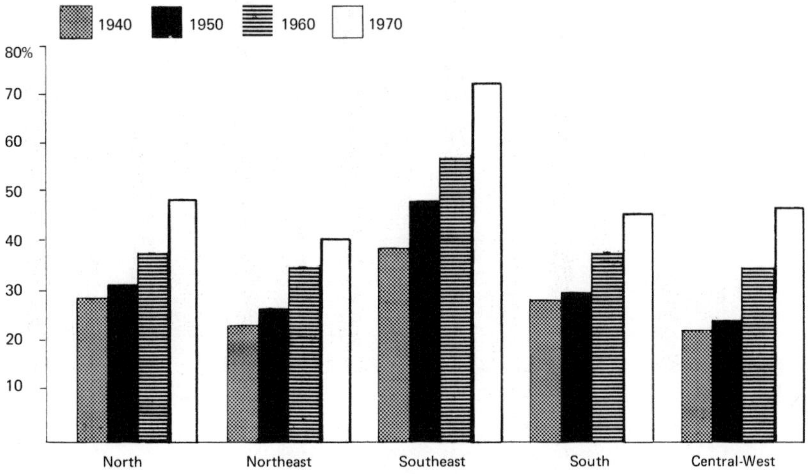

Source: Based on Chart, p.45, Sinopse Preliminar do Censo Demográfico: Brasil—1970, I.B.G.E.

Although it might seem that such a burgeoning urbanization would afford easier access to the masses, this is not always true. The struggle to make a living, with women working and many men holding down two jobs, seriously reduces opportunities to communicate the Gospel to them. With millions of people living in apartments, a new urban culture has begun to surface in Brazilian society. These apartments are organized as condominiums and have a tendency to exclude all outsiders. This places an "off limits" restriction on any religious activity within the apartment houses except by Christian occupants witnessing to their neighbors. Urbanization is causing a whole series of realignments by people in different stations in life. This presents new problems for Evangelicals as to the best, most effective way to evangelize, proclaim the Gospel of Jesus Christ, and to teach disciples.

ECONOMIC AND SOCIAL STATUS

Brazil is a country with large numbers of people in the lower economic classes. There is a very small upper class and close behind a small, elite middle class. The financial and material level of living for the masses is comparatively low, indicating the existence of many inequalities in the present socio-economic system in Brazil. Growth of the Protestant church has been greatest among the masses - those people who suffer economic, social, and educational inequalities and are not participating in a full measure in the money economy. The style of communication for the Gospel that reaches the masses in the lower class generally is not suitable for reaching the middle or upper classes. The variations of the different economic classes require a language which they can understand and which meets their life-style and their present aspirations.

As is true in most societies, the higher the educational, economic, financial, and cultural level of an individual, the less responsive he seems to be to the Gospel message. With agricultural and industrial development, increasing numbers are beginning to make their way up in the social structure, moving into the middle and sometimes upper sectors. As John Wesley pointed out, religious people are generally industrious, and industrious people become wealthy and irreligious!* Race, education, personality, and religious beliefs influence the degree of this movement. One study in the 1950's indicated that only 15 percent of Brazil's population were in the middle and upper sectors (Johnson 1959). Another estimated that a larger proportion was in these classes (Figure 1-6). This latter study showed a higher proportion of "whites" than "mulattos" or "negroes" in the middle and upper classes. Only a small proportion of the latter have been able to attain middle class status. Color is evidently still a significant factor even in this melting pot. Although the trend in economic level has been upward, the great majority of the people are economically still below middle class, having a yearly per capita income of less than $360.

Education plays a significant role in helping Brazilians climb the economic and social ladder. Traditional denominations made a large contribution to education by establishing secular schools. High ethical conduct and solid Christian moral standards stressed among Protestants have slowly resulted in Protestants being sought for responsible positions in industry, commerce, and government.

---

*Max Weber, *The Protestant Ethic and the Spirit of Capitalism* (Scribner, 1930), p. 175.

FIGURE 1-6

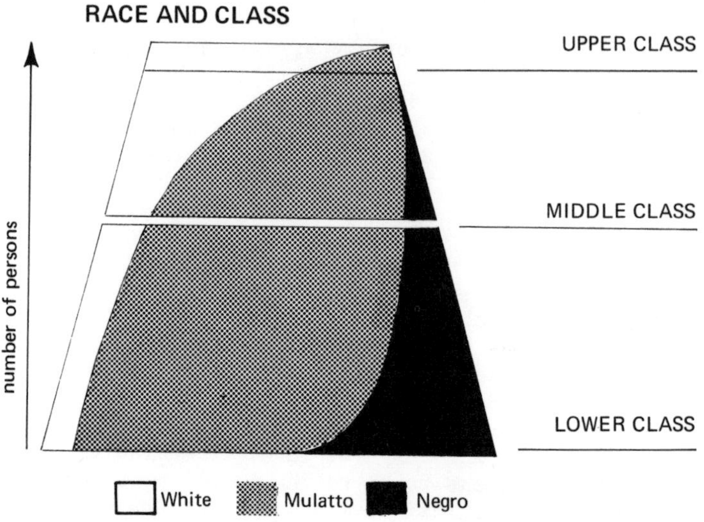

Source: Azevedo, 1959: 114

RELIGIONS

Introduction

Brazil is nominally a Catholic country, but Protestantism has grown very rapidly in recent decades. Jehovah's Witnesses and the Church of Jesus Christ of Latter-day Saints, and spiritism of different types have also made remarkable growth. There are also small groups of Eastern Orthodox Christians, Jews, Buddhists, Shintoists, Positivists, Muslims, and others.

The Roman Catholic Church

Brazil is considered to be the largest Roman Catholic country in the world. Catholic priests from Portugal accompanied the early explorers and remained with the pioneer settlers to conduct worship services and to make converts of the indigenous Indians. Catholic bishops historically participated actively in the various political developments, but their influence has appeared to wane in recent years.

One survey of Latin America by a Roman Catholic authority quoted in *World Christian Handbook*,* reported that although 93 percent of the population claimed to be Catholics, only 10 percent actually practiced the faith. The same survey also reported that the Roman Catholic Church was dying in rural Brazil. Although there has been a resurgence of activity in the Roman Catholic Church in Brazil in recent years, "It is too early to judge the implications of the patterns that are beginning to emerge." (Read, Monterroso, Johnson: 1969).

Since 1955 the Brazilian government has been reported in bulletins entitled *Estatística do Culto Católico*. The items reported for each worship center by ecclesiastical provinces cover number of baptisms, christenings, first communions, marriages, extreme unctions, and burial services.

During 1968, 1,979,602 babies were reported as baptized. For the same year the government reported 1,030,964 live births registered and 44,998 who were born dead. The discrepancy between baptisms and births suggests that up to now the people of Brazil sense more of an urgency to have their children baptized by the Catholic Church than registered by the government. Similarly, the Catholic Church reported 407,113 marriages whereas the government reports only 365,715 as registered for the same year, 1968.

In 1965 the Catholic Church reported that communion was taken 168,111,255 times in their various worship centers. This is an average of only 2 communions per year for each person in Brazil. The practice of reporting all communions was stopped in 1966. Instead, <u>first</u> communions were reported. This number of first communions amounts to approximately 50 percent of the number of children in Brazil reaching an age where they are eligible for first communion.

In 1968, the Catholic Church participated in approximately 18,750 burial services each month. This is approximately 35 percent of the deaths occurring in Brazil during the same period.

The Roman Catholic Church does not report membership figures comparable to those issued for Protestant churches. This makes it somewhat difficult to appraise the pastoral function of the Catholic Church in Brazil. Father Valdeli Carvalho da Costa, a professor at a Catholic university in Brazil said that "90 percent of the 93 million inhabitants of Brazil are Catholic *in*

**World Christian Handbook*, 1962 Edition, ed. by H. Wakelin Coxill and Sir Kenneth Grubb (World Dominion Press, 1962), p. 47.

name but that all *religiosity* in the country is not Catholic." He further noted, according to Latin American Press as reported by Religious News Service January 11, 1972, "that African cults constitute a serious challenge" for the Catholic Church.

On the other hand, the authors of *Latin American Church Growth* (Read, Monterroso, Johnson: 1969) report that there are some signs of renewal within the Roman Catholic Church. There has been an increasing emphasis on the study and use of the Bible. There appears to be a growing recognition of the importance of encouraging the laity to participate in the work of the Church.

In summary it appears that the current strength of the Roman Catholic Church in Brazil is not much greater than that of the Protestant Church, but as this fact is recognized by Roman Catholic leaders, new steps toward renewal are being made. It is estimated that about 85 percent of Brazilians now classify themselves as Roman Catholics, 11 percent as Protestants, and the remainder as spiritists, Jehovah's Witnesses, Latter-day Saints, and other small groups. However, the number of practicing Catholics is apparently much lower and the number of practicing spiritists much higher.

The Protestant Church

The rapidly growing Protestant church now has more than 2,600,000 communicant members. When we take into account other family members who attend Protestant worship services and the large number of others who have been involved through evangelistic activities, it is estimated that the Protestant community today is close to 11 million. If the estimate that only 10 percent of the inhabitants of Brazil are *active* Catholics has validity, the indications are that the number of active Protestants closely approaches that of the Catholics. This fact appears to be borne out by the rapidly increasing strength of the Protestants in business and commerce and in government circles at all levels.

The Brazilian government has conducted an annual census of Protestant churches since 1955. The data has been published in a series known as *Estatística do Culto Protestante*. This data is the primary base of the statistics which are reported in the following pages on the membership of the Protestant church. The government includes within its Protestant classification three sects: Jehovah's Witnesses, the Church of Jesus Christ of the Latter Day Saints, and Christian Science.

Marginal Sects

Jehovah's Witnesses are now found in every region of Brazil. In 1960 the government recorded 6,100 members and in 1970, 18,700. The largest growth has taken place in the Southeast where today more than 12,000 members are located. During this period the South, which has the second largest membership (2,700), doubled in numbers, but the Northeast is rapidly overtaking the South with a 5 times increase during the decade to 2,300 members.

The Church of Jesus Christ of Latter-day Saints has confined its activities to the Southeast and South but has shown a phenomenal growth during the last decade. In 1960 only 1,600 members were recorded by the government as compared to 17,650 in 1970 (this includes less than 500 members associated with Christian Science). The South has had the greatest increase with 12,000 members reported in 1970, with the Southeast reporting the remaining 5,640 members.

Spiritists

Although the Brazilian government reported less than 1,000,000 followers worshiping in organized centers in 1968, estimates run as high as 30 percent of the population being affiliated at one time or another with spiritist activities. This was the opinion of Boaventura Kloppenburg, O.F.M., who reported his observations under the title of *The Prevalence of Spiritism in Brazil* (Considine, ed., 1966). Others estimate that 15 percent of Brazil's population are actively engaged in spiritism, although most of these still classify themselves as Roman Catholics.

There are 2 principal groups of spiritists active in Brazil. The largest of these in terms of followers is undoubtedly the Umbanda. Although the Umbanda reports fewer followers of organized centers of worship than the Kardecistas, "the Umbanda is much more widespread than Kardecism in Brazil." (Read, Monterroso, Johnson: 1969, p. 250) Umbanda groups with local names exist in practically every part of the country. It is primarily an animistic religion, initially introduced into Brazil by African slaves and today most prevalent among the lower classes.

Kardecism, in contrast, appeals largely to the middle and upper classes. This group is named after Allan Kardec, a Frenchman, who introduced this form of spiritism through his writings during the nineteenth century. It is often referred to as *high spiritism* with its emphasis on science, philosophy, and religion. A Brazilian, Chico Xavier, is generally accredited with popularizing Kardecism in Brazil through his writings which adapted this system to the Brazilian culture.

The Brazilian government reported 644,000 followers as Kardecistas and 257,000 as Umbandistas in 1968. For the Kardecistas, this represented a considerable decrease from the 758,000 followers reported in 1966. On the other hand, the Umbandistas worshiping in organized centers increased from 185,000 in the earlier year. In 1966 the Umbandistas, which are more primitive in their worship than the Kardecistas, reported 1,766 organized meeting places. Some 168,649 sessions were held with an average of 65 in attendance. In addition, 13,680 conferences were held and 9,286 parties and social gatherings recorded.

There also were hundreds of meetings held, especially by various small groups associated with the Umbanda movement, in homes and along streams or in wooded areas. Visitors to Brazil are often impressed by the evidence of spiritist activities left in the form of candles or carcasses of chickens that have been sacrificed. However, most observers agree that, "There is no conclusive evidence at the present time that spiritism as such is increasing" (Read, Monterroso, Johnson: 1969, p. 251).

These authors proceed to clearly express the relationship between spiritism and Protestant evangelism pointing out that, "The Pentecostals have been much more effective than other churches in winning spiritists. This is not only because they are willing to allow worship norms that express the cultural dynamics of the people, but also because they grant the spiritists their first premise--that spirits do exist. They preach a positive message of a supreme power that can deliver from evil spirits" (*ibid*, p. 252).

2

Historical Development

SUMMARY

From 1823 to 1909. Lutherans, Congregationalists, Presbyterians, Methodists, Baptists, Episcopalians, and Seventh-Day Adventists made their first contacts and established their first congregations that have become autonomous denominations.

From 1910 to 1970. The two largest Pentecostal denominations, Assemblies of God and Congregação Cristã, arrived in Brazil and began to plant churches before the large number of small denominations and faith missions established themselves in different parts of the country.

In 1970, 2,623,600 Protestant communicant members were reported by the religious census of the Brazilian government. The Assemblies of God led in total membership followed by the Lutherans, Congregação Cristã, Baptists, Presbyterians, and other smaller denominational groups.

Traditional denominations listed by membership in 1970:

Denominational Group	Year Begun	Membership 1970
Lutheran	1823	433,000
Baptist	1881	330,500
Presbyterian	1859	244,050
Seventh-Day Adventist	1900	119,100
Methodist	1880	62,550

Denominational Group	Year Begun	Membership 1970
Congregational	1885	46,100
Episcopalian	1889	20,150
Others	1914	72,650

Pentecostal denominations listed by membership in 1970:

Denominational Group	Year Begun	Membership 1970
Assemblies of God	1910	746,400
Congregação Cristã	1910	357,800
Other Pentecostal	Since 1950	191,300

INTRODUCTION

Brazil was discovered in 1500, and since that time God has been calling unto Himself in diverse manners and places and through different individuals, a people for His Name and preparing laborers for His harvest fields in this large country. For more than 300 years the Roman Catholic Church was the principal missionary organization working in Brazil. Priests accompanied many expeditions into the interior and sought to win converts among the Indians, as well as to minister to the settlers in the towns and plantations that sprang up along the lengthy coastline. During this period, French Huguenots attempted to settle on an island in Guanabara Bay opposite the city of Rio de Janeiro but were driven off. Dutch Huguenots gained a foothold in the north around Recife and remained for almost 20 years, then were expelled by fierce hostility and fighting.

THE PROTESTANT CHURCH TAKES ROOT AND GROWS

The histories which follow are short, concise statements about each of the principal Protestant groups and are designed to provide sufficient background material for general appraisal of the current situation presented in detail in later chapters. These descriptions are not intended to be complete, but to give some idea regarding the type of ministry of each denomination and where each was developed within Brazil.

In 1823 German Lutherans arrived in Brazil, settling first in São Paulo and Rio de Janeiro, where the first Protestant church was organized in 1837. In 1855 Dr. Robert Reid Kalley, a Scottish Presbyterian, organized the first missionary church in Rio de Janeiro. This was the beginning of the Evangelical Congregational Church in Brazil. He was followed by missionaries from the Presbyterian Church in the United States of America in 1859 and by missionaries from the Presbyterian Church in the

FIGURE 2-1

GROWTH OF PROTESTANT DENOMINATIONS IN BRAZIL FROM DATE OF ORIGIN

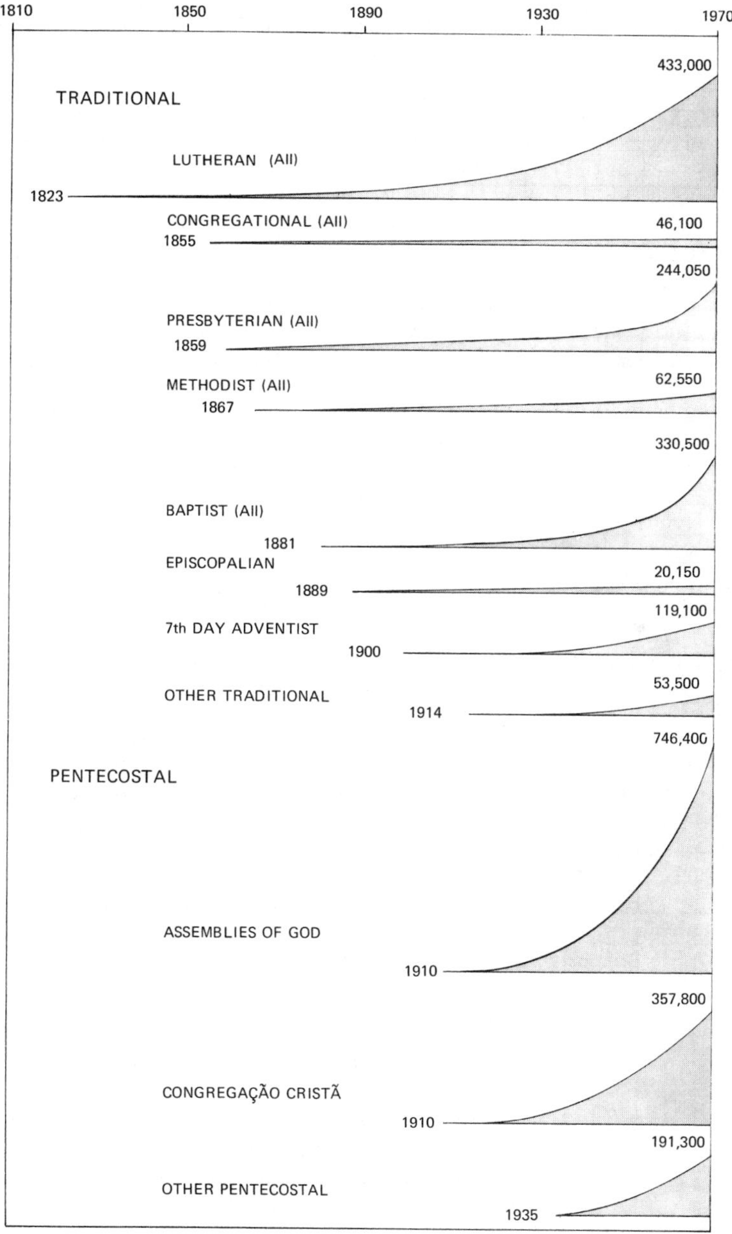

United States (Southern) in 1869. Methodists had visited Brazil before 1850, but their missionaries did not enter Brazil until 1867. The Southern Baptists followed in 1881, the Episcopalians in 1889, and the Seventh-Day Adventists in 1900. The growth and development of the principal Protestant denominations in Brazil is shown in Figure 2-1. Table 2-1 gives an estimate of Protestant membership by denominational groups in 1970.

In 1910, shortly after the beginning of the Pentecostal movement, two North American missionaries of Swedish origin from South Bend, Indiana, founded the Assemblies of God Church in North Brazil. Another North American from the Chicago area began a Pentecostal work in the same year among the Italian-speaking people, first in a small city in the State of Paraná, then in the city of São Paulo. The South American Mission, formerly known as the South American Indian Mission, initiated work among the Indians of Southern Mato Grosso in 1914. The first Japanese missionary arrived in the 1920's. The Unevangelized Fields Mission entered Brazil in 1931, ministering to the Indians and to Brazilians who had settled in the Amazon area. They were soon followed by several small denominational groups and other "faith" missions. The New Tribes Mission began its extensive ministry in 1949 and Wycliffe Bible Translators in 1956.

COMMON ELEMENTS IN DENOMINATIONAL HISTORY

The historical Protestant missionary enterprise, on the whole, has been characterized by the rapid planting, growth, and building of strong national Church denominations in Brazil. A slow but healthy growth began in the early historical periods and set in motion a series of important developmental stages. A step-by-step progression from a basic dependence on foreign mission work to strong maturity, and finally to autonomy and independence can be seen in the listing of some of the common elements that were at work during the history and development of each Protestant-Evangelical denomination in Brazil.

I. Dependency Stage - Pioneer Missionary Participation

1. Foreigners, lay and missionary, were generally responsible for the founding of each major denomination in Brazil.

2. Pioneer missionaries devoted most of their time and effort to direct evangelism and church planting activities, which included wide evangelistic itineration.

3. Pioneer missionaries won many to Christ by faithfully proclaiming the Gospel, and immediately taught and strengthened their converts and sought to prepare leaders in all of the places where they first planted churches.

4. Promising converts were given opportunities to become leaders from the very beginning, which included responsibilities for the ministry of local churches and encouragement to witness and engage in all types of evangelism.

II. Interdependency Stage - Emerging, Growing Church

5. As "mother" or central churches in the major cities extended their influence to outlying preaching points with the aid of trained laymen, these efforts resulted in satellites of the central churches, in time, developing adequate strength as separate churches. They, in turn, soon were able to become "mother" churches.

6. Local churches were officially organized into ecclesiastical groups with varying degrees of missionary and national leadership.

7. The increasing need for trained ministers led to the development of different Bible schools and seminaries with major mission financing, guidance, and control.

8. Developing denominations pioneered in providing improved educational and health facilities with personnel, technical, and financial assistance from foreign missions.

III. Independency Stage - Final Autonomy

9. Many missionaries who arrived during the later periods of church development became involved in administrations of organizations, institutions, and other allied activities that were often separate from the national church denomination.

10. The major administration duty of most of the older traditional church organizations and institutions is now the responsibility of well-prepared Brazilian leaders.

11. Foreign missions generally continue to aid the national churches on the basis of its special needs and at its request. Missionaries frequently are invited to cooperate with national churches as evangelists, church planters, technicians, and specialists of different types.*

BRIEF DENOMINATIONAL HISTORIES**

The 2,623,600 Protestant communicant members reported to the Brazilian government in 1970 are divided into a number of denominational and mission groups (Table 2-1). In Table 2-1 these denominations have been classified as Traditional and Pentecostal denominational groups. Traditional denominations have been working in Brazil a long time. They are the recognized, familiar Protestant denominations which are numerically strong and well-known in the United States and Europe. But Pentecostal denominations have grown in strength in the U.S.A. and have grown rapidly around the world since the early 1900's, and constitute a rapidly growing family of churches who emphasize the person, ministry, and gifts of the Holy Spirit as outlined in the New Testament.

In 1970 the Assemblies of God with nearly 750,000 members, was the largest denomination. The two Lutheran denominations were second with 433,000 members. (These were communicant members, not including children below communicant age.) Another Pentecostal denomination, the Congregação Cristã, was third with 357,800 members. The Baptist Churches held fourth place with 330,500 members and the Presbyterians fifth place with 244,050.

Several traditional denominations entered Brazil with missionary efforts in the latter half of the nineteenth century. In general, the primary responsibility for church growth and development has been shifted to Brazilian leaders. The membership of churches established by small denominations and "faith"

---

*It is important to note that ordinarily, denominations which have developed in this manner have tapered off in their growth. In general, the indigenous churches are much more evangelistic.

**Thumbnail sketches are included on the principal Protestant denominational groups in alphabetical order. Bibliographical suggestions are included in the Bibliography as a guide to those seeking more detail on any denominational group.

missions entering Brazil since 1914 is not large and has been included with the "other" traditional denominations in Table 2-1. The significant growth of the Pentecostal churches in the last 60 years has been tabulated in a separate group.

TABLE 2-1

ESTIMATED DISTRIBUTION OF PROTESTANT COMMUNICANT MEMBERS BY DENOMINATIONAL GROUPS FOR BRAZIL, JANUARY 1, 1970

Denominational Group	Protestant Communicant Members	
	No.	%
TRADITIONAL		
Baptist	330,500	12.6%
Congregational	46,100	1.8
Episcopalian	20,150	0.8
Lutheran	433,000	16.4
Methodist	62,550	2.4
Presbyterian	244,050	9.3
7th Day Adventist	119,100	4.5
Other	72,650	2.8
Sub-total	1,328,100	50.6
PENTECOSTAL		
Assemblies of God	746,400	28.5
Congregação Cristã	357,800	13.6
Other	191,300	7.3
Sub-total	1,295,500	49.4
BRAZIL TOTAL	2,623,600	100.0

During the 1960's a charismatic type renewal was experienced in several hundred Baptist, Congregational, Methodist, and Presbyterian churches. This charismatic renewal incorporated tongues, faith healing, and many other aspects of Pentecostalism which caused the denominational leaders to censure this movement in their respective denominations, resulting in a schism. Most of the censured charismatic groups were expelled from their mother denominations and later organized their own. The large charismatic renewal movement appears to have taken a solid, conservative stand while maintaining an aggressive program of evangelism and emphasis on the use and ministry of spiritual gifts.

TRADITIONAL DENOMINATIONS

Baptists

In 1881 the first Southern Baptist missionaries, Reverend and Mrs. W. B. Bagby, arrived in Brazil. Their evangelistic endeavors and church planting activity began in Rio de Janeiro, later including São Paulo. When missionary reinforcements arrived, Baptist churches were planted in Bahia. By 1970, the Brazilian staff (285) of Southern Baptist missionaries had been able to continue working in cooperation with the rapidly growing autonomous Brazilian Baptist Convention. Regional mission headquarters are maintained in Rio de Janeiro in the Southeast, in Recife in the Northeast, and in Belém in the North.

The Southern Baptist mission has given, and is continuing to give, substantial financial as well as missionary help in the development of secular schools, Bible schools, and seminaries. Since 1940 a publishing house has been functioning which produced more than 200,000 books other than Bibles and over 10 million tracts in 1969. Less than 4 percent of the publishing house budget came from the United States in that year. The Brazilian Baptist Convention also works with other North American Baptist missions and independent Baptist foreign missionaries from other countries of the world.

Large denomination-wide evangelistic meetings have been held from time to time in Brazil. In 1965, simultaneous evangelistic campaigns were sponsored in all parts of Brazil with general success. The latest evangelistic endeavor by the Baptist Convention had a goal of 100,000 new members by 1972. Their church membership goal for their centennial year, 1982, is 1,000,000 members.

Baptist churches are found in every state and territory of Brazil. As of January 1, 1970, all Baptist churches in Brazil were estimated to have had 330,000 members. The principal concentration is in the Southeast where more than 200,000 members are reported and second is the Northeast with a little less than 80,000 members. The Brazilian Baptist Convention claimed 320,000 of the members. The National Baptist Convention, which was founded in 1967 by churches which were separated from the Baptist Convention because of association with the charismatic "renewal" movement, has most of the remaining Baptists in their 95 churches.

There are more than 700 missionaries working in Brazil who come from different types of Baptist churches and missions. The large part of these missionaries arrived in the last two decades and have been primarily involved in evangelism and church planting activity. At least half of them cooperate in some way with the Brazilian Baptist Convention. The work of these other independent Baptist missionaries has resulted in numerous small churches that are scattered throughout Brazil and have a total of approximately 2,000 members.

Congregationalists

This small denomination, that numbered almost 46,100 members in 1970, began in 1855, through the efforts of Dr. Robert Reid Kalley, a Scotch Presbyterian. He arrived in Rio de Janeiro after violent persecution in the Madeira Islands destroyed the churches he had planted there. Dr. Kalley carefully taught his first converts their Christian responsibility and personal ministry as laymen.

Autonomy came early to this church in the Rio de Janeiro area. Churches were established later in Northeast Brazil, in and around Recife, and also in the Central-West sector, centering in Anápolis. Because of the resulting triregional aspect and geographical isolation, it has been difficult for these relatively independent churches to unite for any long periods of time. In recent years, a number of churches have felt the influence of the charismatic "renewal" movement and have left their parent denomination for a Pentecostal-type denominational ministry. Small churches and slow growth have characterized this denomination. Many ministers seek secular employment to supplement their low income from pastoral work, devoting only part time to their ministry.

The different branches of the Evangelical Union of South America have given missionary support to some of the Congregational churches in Brazil, helping them with schools, Bible institutes, and a seminary for the education of young people anticipating pastoral leadership. A pioneer missionary of the EUSA, Fred Glass, was the first to develop an influential Bible colportage ministry in the interior. Small church groups in diverse locations sprang up as a result of this energetic Bible ministry. EUSA, (Evangelical Union of South America) British branch, operates several Evangelical bookstores and has a publishing house for Sunday school materials and other literature for the denomination.

The North American branch of EUSA works with the churches in the Northeast. It has established Bible schools to train Brazilians and cooperates in a ministry among university youth.

Episcopalians

The Protestant Episcopal Church of the U.S.A. sent two American priests to Brazil in 1889. One of the earliest comity agreements ever made in Brazil was negotiated between the Presbyterians, Methodists, and Episcopalians. The agreement left Rio Grande do Sul to the Episcopalians. Reverend Kinsolving, their pioneer church planter, began work in Rio Grande do Sul, and today 80 percent of their estimated membership of 20,150 is located in South Brazil.

The growth of the Episcopal Church has been relatively slow. Their membership is found primarily among the middle and upper classes who have a tendency to appreciate a traditional, high-church type of order and ritual, modified in many ways from that of the Roman Catholic Church. Most of their priests and bishops have come from the Episcopal Seminary which was founded in Porto Alegre in 1900. The Protestant Episcopal Church of the U.S.A. maintains a small staff of foreign missionaries in Brazil and continues to subsidize some of the activities of the Brazilian church which, in turn, sends missionary workers to Mozambique.

Lutherans

In 1823 in Novo Hamburgo, RGS, the Evangelical Church of Lutheran Confession in Brazil, originated as a foreign colony or immigrant church. In certain sections, German immigrants with a Lutheran background, assembled themselves together under lay leadership. German ministers later joined them.

The Lutheran Missouri Synod sent a missionary, J. C. Broders, from the United States in 1899 at the request of a Lutheran pastor who in 1890 had separated from the "mother" church. Broders was succeeded by missionary W. Mahler, who became director of the mission in Brazil. The mission established a seminary in Porto Alegre to provide trained ministers for the churches they established. This denomination adopted the name, Evangelical Lutheran Church of Brazil.

The American Lutheran Church began sending missionaries to Brazil in 1958. These missionaries sought to plant churches in new pioneer areas. Recently, they have been working under a cooperative arrangement made with the large German Evangelical Church of Lutheran Confession in Brazil. These missionaries serve as ministers in the German Church communities and assist in evangelization efforts, stewardship promotion, education, the conducting of Bible study groups, and helping in the training of potential leaders.

The Lutherans have many large churches that serve the German-speaking communities. The membership of these German-Brazilian type communities is usually nominal and inactive in the work of the churches. Responsibility is placed upon the ministers for all of the preaching and pastoral work, for all administration of the sacraments, for any spiritual awakening that might occur, and for family counseling. The Evangelical Church of Lutheran Confession depended upon ministers from Germany until it developed its own seminary in São Leopoldo.

According to estimates based on the government statistics (adjusted as indicated in footnote*), there were approximately 433,000 communicant members in the Lutheran Church as of January 1, 1970. They are primarily located in South Brazil. About one-quarter of the members belong to the Evangelical Lutheran Church of Brazil.

Methodists

Pioneer circuit riding missionaries initiated Methodist church-planting activities in the states of Rio Grande do Sul, Rio de Janeiro, São Paulo, and Minas Gerais after their arrival in 1867. More than two-thirds of the nearly 65,000 communicant members, estimated as of January 1, 1970, are located in South-east Brazil. This denomination early established and gave emphasis to a large, institutional program, specializing in secondary school education. In the 1930's the Methodists had reached a point in their development where most of the leadership was placed in the hands of capable Brazilians. In the 1960's the remaining foreign missionary leaders who were still in administrative positions relinquished their functions to national leaders.

---

*The membership figures reported to the government by the Lutheran denominations have been reduced 40 percent to account for the inclusion of baptized babies and children under "communicant" age.

Methodist Church leadership, both national and foreign missionary, is concerned with the question of what part evangelism has in the matters of social justice, social action, and the role of the Methodist Church in politics and economic development. This denomination has had a regular, but slow church growth, generally below that of population growth. It is largest in the Southeast and secondarily in the South. New churches have been established recently in several large cities such as Brasília, Governador Valadares, Salvador, Recife, and Fortaleza.

About 60 Methodist churches with more than 5,000 members have recently formed a Wesleyan Methodist denomination. These churches have been influenced by the charismatic "renewal" movement. In addition, the Free Methodist Church records some 2,500 members.

Presbyterians

The Reverend Asbel Simonton, a missionary sent out by the Board of Foreign Missions of the Presbyterian Church in the United States of America (the name used before the Civil War), landed in Rio de Janeiro on August 12, 1859. He was soon joined by other Presbyterian missionaries. These missionaries were encouraged by the conversion of a Roman Catholic priest, José Manoel Conceição, who was later ordained as the first national minister of any Protestant church in Brazil. His early evangelistic work was very successful in rural areas that were more receptive to the Gospel at that particular time.

In 1869 the first missionaries of the Presbyterian Church in the United States (Southern) began their work in Campinas in the State of São Paulo. The Presbyterian Church of Brazil continued to grow in the last 3 decades of the nineteenth century through the joint efforts of foreign missionaries, ministerial candidates, and a volunteer lay leadership. In 1888 when the first Synod was organized, two-thirds of the leadership was in the hands of foreign missionaries. In 1903 there was a sharp division in the ranks of this young Presbyterian denomination. It resulted in the establishment of the Independent Presbyterian Church. Certain Presbyterian churches which have been affected in the last decade by the charismatic "renewal" movement are usually incorporated into the Independent Presbyterian Church.

In 1916, a Brazil Plan was adopted by the *Igreja Presbiteriana do Brazil* (IPB), whereby foreign missionaries were given the responsibility to plant churches in rural areas. National leaders were responsible for churches already established in urban centers. By 1950 the IPB had 500 ordained ministers and more than 800 churches that had been organized into 26 Presbyteries. The separation of mission and national church endeavor along the lines of the Brazil Plan permitted the two large foreign mission organizations involved to establish many different types of institutions. These include primary and secondary schools, hospitals and clinics, agricultural school and farm products, Bible institutes, a pre-ministerial training school, and the largest university of its kind in South America. These institutions were helpful in providing a strong educational opportunity for Presbyterians and others, and permitted many to move into professional vocations where they were able to acquire a new social status and perform a new role in Brazilian society, which gave them a high esteem and standing in Brazilian society.

In recent years Bible Presbyterian missionaries have begun evangelistic and church planting work in several of the larger cities. They have organized the Conservative Church in Brazil.

Presbyterian churches are now found in every state of Brazil. More than 65 percent of the 244,050 members in 1970 were located in the Southeast, and less than 15 percent were found in each of the Northeast and South Regions.

Seventh-Day Adventists

The Seventh-Day Adventists initiated work in Brazil in 1900. A well-produced weekly radio program presents their message all over Brazil and offers a correspondence course to all who respond. This ministry was initiated with programs produced in the United States, but is now carried on by a qualified Brazilian team. Programs are prepared in a studio located in Rio de Janeiro. This denomination accounts for 119,100 members in Brazil and is growing rapidly. More than 70 percent of the members are located in the Southeast and in the South.

Other Traditional Groups

A large number of separate organizations exist in Brazil and are found within this classification. Some are denominations which have just begun their missionary work in Brazil and are known as "faith" missions. They engage in direct evangelism and church planting or serve other national church or missionary organizations.

More than 20 denominations and 83 "faith" missions are included under the classification "other traditional" in Table 2-1. They have sent more than 300 missionaries into Brazil to evangelize and plant churches. The Church of the Nazarene and the Christian Reformed Church entered Brazil in 1934. The Churches of Christ and Christian groups have more than 125 missionaries working in Brazil. Three different Mennonite groups with 64 missionaries have made a substantial missionary contribution. Various Brethren missionaries entered Brazil early in this century and carry on their ministry now with the help of more than thirty missionaries, most of whom have adopted Brazil as their homeland. Some progress has been made by other denominational groups, but generally it is too early to draw any conclusions as to the magnitude or significance of their contribution in Brazil.

A recent study of the Missionary Information Bureau disclosed that 83 different "faith" missions were active in Brazil. These missions receive support for their missionaries and projects largely from individuals or churches which are independent of denominational groups. These "faith" missions include several which are working primarily among the Indian tribes. About one-half of them (40) have made notable progress in establishing churches, but as yet the number of communicant members is small when compared with that of the older, traditional denominations. Some 37 missions are primarily engaged in service ministries to national churches or to other missions.

The "faith" missions which are working among the Indian tribes dedicate their efforts to translating the tribal languages into writing and are slowly gaining converts and planting churches.

The South America Mission, formerly known as the South America Indian Mission, was one of the first of these "faith" missions to enter Brazil. It opened work in Southern Mato Grosso among the Terena Indians in 1914. In the mid-1930's headquarters was established in Cuiabá to handle the work of the mission which had expanded among other tribes. In 1970 this mission had 24 missionaries at work.

The Unevangelized Fields Mission (UFM) established a headquarters in Belém, Pará in 1931. They opened work among the Indians of the lower Amazon basin and among the Brazilians found in this area. A network of churches established primarily with Brazilian membership has more than 10,000 communicant members. Later the work of UFM was extended into the territory of Roraima and a separate headquarters was established at Boa Vista. During the late 1960's the English branch of UFM initiated work among Brazilians in northern Minas Gerais and southern Bahia. The UFM in 1970, with 138 missionaries, ranked fifth among missions in Brazil.

The New Tribes Mission entered Brazil in 1949, beginning a vigorous work among the tribes of Southern Brazil with headquarters at Jacutinga, Minas Gerais, where a Bible institute was established. Another headquarters was located in Manaus, Amazonas, for work among the tribes of the Amazon basin. This mission ranks fourth with 141 missionaries in 1970, plus a number of Brazilian missionaries who have been graduated from the Bible institute missionary training course.

Wycliffe Bible Translators entered Brazil in 1956, where they use the name of the Summer Institute of Linguistics. They have a cooperative agreement with the Brazilian government to assist in the development of written languages for many of the tribes, using Bible portions as source material for primary readers. Their headquarters is in Brasília, the capital. This organization had 173 missionaries in Brazil in 1969, ranking second among missions, being exceeded only by the Southern Baptists with 285 missionaries.

One-half of the church planting missions have fewer than five missionaries each. Most of these missions have been working in Brazil less than twenty years. Some train nationals to take responsibility off a few churches but usually their small churches struggle under the administrative direction of missionaries. One-half of the service missions have fewer than five missionaries each and the larger ones less than fifty. These missions have been in Brazil a short time. They are generally assisting the national churches through Bible schools, literature publishing and distribution, radio programming, and the direction of training programs for the development of lay leadership.

PENTECOSTALS

Assemblies of God

The Assemblies of God Church began in Belém, Pará, North Brazil, on November 19, 1910, and has grown rapidly in recent decades. The pioneer labors and ministries of Daniel Berg and Gunnar Vingren from South Bend, Indiana is a remarkable story. Both were born in Sweden. They felt the call to go to Brazil as missionaries during a Pentecostal-type revival that broke out in Chicago.

This church is an outstanding example of evangelistic and church planting work through the activity of an enthusiastic, spiritual lay leadership. Laymen, who receive their training in the "mother" churches, are sent out to plant satellite churches. If they are successful, they are ordained. Congregations are now found in every state and territory. According to the estimates based on the government statistics, this church has more than 745,000 communicant members. Many believe the government census does not include all the membership found in this rapidly growing church.

The Mission Board of the Assemblies of God, Springfield, Missouri, sent their first missionaries, Mr. and Mrs. Frank Stalter, to Brazil in 1934. Today some twenty-two missionaries from the Assemblies' Board cooperate with the denomination through radio programs, Bible schools for the training of lay leaders, city-wide mass meetings for evangelism, and an extensive literature program. Their efforts are a direct contribution to the education and edification of the large number of members who have joined this church from the Brazilian masses.

Congregação Cristã

By early in the twentieth century thousands of Italians had arrived from Europe to settle in and near São Paulo. Luis Francescon, an Italian by birth, arrived from Chicago March 12, 1910, with a call from God to preach the Gospel in Italian to these people. He remained until September 22, 1910. This was the first of ten missionary journeys to Brazil, with his last in 1948. Altogether he spent nearly eleven years in Brazil. As a result of the work of Francescon and lay leaders, vigorous, Pentecostal-type churches were established in two centers - one in the city of São Paulo and the other in rural Paraná, an area where coffee production had attracted large numbers of Italian migrants.

More than two-thirds of its nearly 360,000 members are found in Southeast Brazil and thirty percent in South Brazil. The first twenty-five years passed with most of the worship services conducted in Italian. Between 1930 and 1950, after many of the immigrants and their children had learned to speak Portuguese, members speaking Portuguese began to evangelize Brazilians in the urban masses. By 1932, the song book was partly in Portuguese and partly in Italian. In 1936 the song book was entirely in Portuguese. The church today is essentially Brazilian.

The Congregação has no paid leadership. All worship, evangelistic activity, and other functions depends upon the pastoral gifts of lay leadership. Luis Francescon was the only foreigner to work with this church. It continues to be one of the fastest growing denominations in Brazil with lay evangelism and spiritual enthusiasm carrying it forward. This church is an example of an evangelical "people's movement." It began with one racial group and has succeeded in spilling over into the mainstream of Brazil's urban masses. It is now being carried back into rural areas by migrant converts who were won in the urban centers.

Other Pentecostal Churches

This is the most rapidly growing group of churches in Brazil As of January 1, 1970, they had a communicant membership of almost 200,000, mostly in the Southeast. The membership was less than 40,000 in 1960.

"Brasil Para Cristo" was founded under the leadership of Manoel de Melo, who earlier worked with the Assemblies of God and with the Four Square Gospel Church. Under his charismatic leadership, a large "mother" church evolved in the city of São Paulo. He is now constructing a church building designed to seat 25,000 people. This church claims more than 300 satellite churches in São Paulo alone. The leaders of the satellite churches are under the training and constant surveillance of Manoel de Melo.

The International Church of the Four Square Gospel sent Harold Williams as a missionary to Brazil in the late 1940's. Through mass evangelistic meetings, largely in tents, the denomination known as Cruzada Nacional de Evangelização emerged. Today this church numbers more than 30,000 communicant members.

Numerous other "independent" Pentecostal churches with different types of emphases, exist and continue to grow side by side. Some eighty foreign missionaries work with these churches which have young leaders who are enthusiastic and quite capable as pastors and evangelists. Several of these "independent" Pentecostal Churches are less than ten years old. They achieve notable acceptance among the lower class masses who have come in large numbers to the urban centers from rural areas.

3

Regional Distribution and Growth of Protestants

SUMMARY

Overview by Major and Micro-regions in 1970

	ITEMS OF INFORMATION	PERCENT	
	North Region		
3,552,000	square kilometers	42%	Brazil
3,651,000	people	4%	"
95,000	Protestant members	4%	"
869	lay leaders		
1,000	churches		
510	pastors		
442	foreign missionaries	15%	"
28	micro-regions		
	Northeast Region		
1,540,000	square kilometers	18%	"
28,675,000	people	30%	
354,000	Protestant members	14%	
5,715	lay leaders		
4,270	churches		
2,020	pastors		
453	foreign missionaries	15%	"
128	micro-regions		

SUMMARY (Continued)

Southeast Region

919,000	square kilometers	11%	"
40,332,000	people	43%	"
1,228,000	Protestant members	47%	"
29,235	lay leaders		
11,690	churches		
9,865	pastors		
1,124	foreign missionaries	38%	"
111	micro-regions		

South Region

562,000	square kilometers	7%	"
16,684,000	people	18%	"
826,000	Protestant members	31%	"
8,820	lay leaders		
6,620	churches		
3,475	pastors		
607	foreign missionaries	20%	"
64	micro-regions		

Central West Region

1,879,000	square kilometers	22%	"
5,167,000	people	5%	"
121,000	Protestant members	5%	"
3,210	lay leaders		
1,830	churches		
930	pastors		
365	foreign missionaries	12%	"
830	micro-regions		

When we approach the subject of distribution of the Church geographically, we are faced with the dilemma of wanting to look in detail both denominationally and geographically. Figure 3-1 demonstrates the problem. There are seven geographical levels we could consider and five church levels we could consider. In this chapter we are looking at all Protestants as a group in the depth of their geographical distribution. In Chapter 4 we will look in depth by denominations. In Chapter 5 we will give examples of both. The "X's" in the boxes of Figure 3-1 indicate our coverage here.

FIGURE 3-1

BRAZIL 1980:
CHURCH VS GEOGRAPHICAL DISTRIBUTION

GEOGRAPHICAL DISTRIBUTION							
DENOMINATIONAL DISTRIBUTION	Country	Major Region (5)	State (27)	Urban Region (112)	Micro Region (361)	County (3,997)	District (15,000+)
All Protestants	X	X	X		X	X	
Categories							
Traditions							
Denominations							
Local Church							

INTRODUCTION

In the preceding chapter, *Historical Development of the Protestant Church,* we gave a short history of the principal denominations. It is most helpful now to examine the growth of these churches in the decade of the 1960's and the situation resulting in 1970. The Protestant church must be understood in terms of its communicant membership, the Brazilian leadership, ordained pastors and lay leaders, and the foreign missionary force. Each of these important parts of the Protestant church will be considered separately.

As we begin now to analyze the relationship of Protestantism and the country of Brazil, we are faced with a complex task as Brazil can be divided up geographically by regions, states, micro-regions, and counties, and it can also be divided up by types of Protestants into categories, traditions, and denominations. Table 3-1 will illustrate the complexity of the problem.

In this chapter, we will discuss Brazilian Protestantism as a whole, but we will divide it up geographically by general regions, states, and micro-regions. We will discuss Protestant growth in detail down to the state level. In Chapter 4 we will discuss Brazilian Protestantism by categories, tradition, and denominations, and relate these back to the country. Then in Chapter 5, we will give some specific examples of how this analysis could be applied to the country of Brazil for any one of these levels. The fact that there now exists a data bank of information which would permit the individual researcher to find out the detail at any one of these levels is an important consideration. (See Appendix 2 for description of this data bank and how to go about using it.)

The Brazilian population explosion has produced a wide base upon which population continues to increase annually at the rate of about three percent. Such growth on an enlarged and expanding base is creating a population pressure that is already beginning to affect all phases of economic, social, and religious development. Since 1889, when the Republic of Brazil was proclaimed, and until 1970, the Brazilian population increased more than six times. It grew from 14 million to almost 95 million. During the period between 1960 and 1970, the rate of growth of Protestant membership doubled that of the population growth in all regions except the South.

Brazil is divided into five major regions: North, where the tropical jungles of Amazonia are found; Northeast, where the semi-arid region smitten with recurring droughts sets off migrations into all parts of the country; Southeast, where the large concentrations of population are found clustering around São Paulo, Rio de Janeiro, and Belo Horizonte; South, the region first settled by German and Italian immigrants and containing the rich coffee lands of Northern Paraná, and Central-West, where the new capital, Brasília, was constructed on the highlands of Goiás, and new lands for settlement are found in abundance (Figure 3-2).

There are twenty-seven political divisions which include: twenty-one states, four territories, the Federal District, and the Island of Fernando de Noronha.

The Brazilian Institute of Geography was given the task of dividing Brazil into a series of homogeneous micro-regions that would replace the physiographic zones and become the basic spacial units used for the collection of all information, data, and statistical material in future census compilations. In 1968, Brazil was divided into 361 homogeneous micro-regions and these micro-regions were made the official geographical units for all of the statistical gathering efforts of the Fundação IBGE (Brazilian Census Bureau). There are 28 in the North, 30 in the Central-West, 128 in the Northeast, 111 in the Southeast, and 64 in the South.

FIGURE 3-2

REGIONS OF BRAZIL

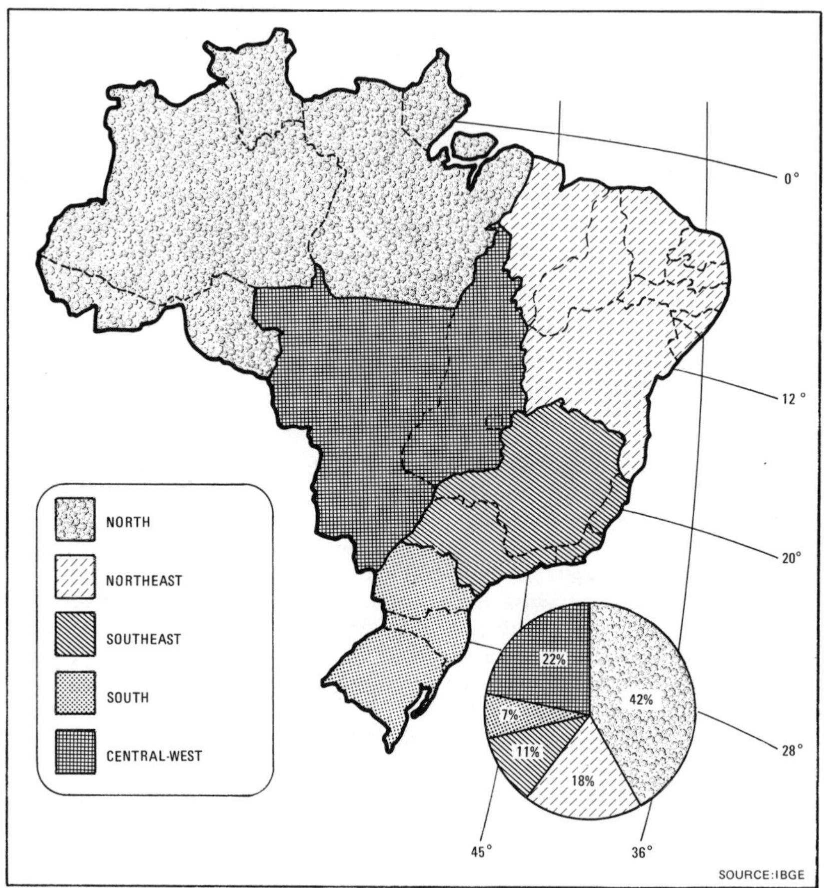

The 27 political divisions in Brazil, along with the 361 micro-regions had 3,952 county units registered within their boundaries in 1970. The number of these county units will be increasing in proportion to the colonization and processes of land settlement and development.

This chapter is a discussion of the regional distribution of the Protestant church of Brazil in two sections. The first section deals with the five major geographical regions while the second section is exclusively taken up with Protestant growth by micro-region. This is the first time that it has been possible to discuss the micro-regional aspect of the increase of Protestantism, and it is only a preliminary statement.

Distribution of Protestant Members by Regions

According to the government census, nearly one-half (46.8 percent) of the Protestant membership in Brazil was located in the Southeast as of January 1, 1970 (Table 3-1). Almost one-third was found in the South. The less populated regions of the North and Central-West had only four and five percent of the membership in Brazil. The remaining thirteen percent was to be found in the Northeast.

Central and Satellite Churches Serve As Worship Centers

These members worship in more than 25,000 organized local churches (Table 3-2). Nearly 9,000 of these are central churches, many of which have established satellite churches in other sections of the same city or county or even in another adjacent county. More than one-half of the central churches are in the Southeast where nearly one-half of the members live. Close to one-quarter of all the churches are in the South where less than one-third of the members are located. In addition, there are thousands of relatively small preaching points where evangelistic meetings are held that produce new converts. Many of these groups will eventually become organized local churches.

CHURCH GROWTH BY REGIONS

North Region

The North Region embraces most of the vast Amazon River Basin. It includes the three large states of Acre, Amazonas, and Pará, and three territories: Amapá, Rondônia, and Roraima. This region with 3,552,000 square kilometers (almost half the size of continental United States) is one of the few remaining unsettled areas of the world. It averages only one person per square kilometer as compared to forty-four in the Southeast.

TABLE 3-1

ESTIMATED DISTRIBUTION OF PROTESTANT COMMUNICANT MEMBERS, BRAZILIAN LEADERS, AND FOREIGN MISSIONARIES BY REGIONS AND STATES IN BRAZIL, JANUARY 1, 1970

REGION State	Protestant Members			Pastors	Lay Leaders	All Leaders			Foreign Missionaries		
	1000's	% of Region	% of Brazil	No.	No.	No.	% of Region	% of Brazil	No.	% of Region	% of Brazil
NORTH REGION											
Rondônia	4	4%	0.2%	10	35	45	3%	0.1%	40	9%	1.3%
Acre	8	8	0.3	25	45	70	5	0.1	2	1	0.1
Amazonas	16	17	0.6	240	240	480	35	0.8	202	45	6.8
Roraima	2	2	0.1	5	10	15	1	-	30	7	1.0
Pará	61	65	2.2	210	390	600	44	0.9	164	37	5.5
Amapá	4	4	0.2	20	140	160	12	0.2	4	1	0.1
NORTH TOTAL	95	100	3.6	510	860	1,370	.100	2.1	442	100	14.8
NORTHEAST REGION											
Maranhão	54	15%	2.1%	160	685	845	11%	1.3%	78	17%	2.6%
Piauí	14	4	0.5	110	210	320	4	0.5	45	10	1.5
Ceará	35	10	1.3	460	570	1,030	13	1.6	94	21	3.1
Rio Grande do Norte	25	7	1.0	70	380	450	6	0.7	22	5	0.7
Paraíba	25	7	1.0	110	650	760	10	1.2	4	1	0.1
Pernambuco	99	29	3.7	420	1,920	2,340	30	3.6	127	28	4.3
Alagoas	18	5	0.7	50	185	235	3	0.4	14	3	0.5
Sergipe	8	2	0.3	45	125	170	2	0.3	15	3	0.5
Bahia	76	21	2.9	595	990	1,585	21	2.4	54	12	1.8
NORTHEAST TOTAL	354	100	13.5	2,020	5,715	7,735	100	12.0	453	100	15.1

TABLE 3-1 (Continued)

SOUTHEAST REGION											
Minas Gerais	189	15%	7.2%	1,240	5,370	6,610	17%	10.1%	240	21%	8.1%
Espírito Santo	102	8	3.9	350	2,075	2,425	6	3.8	30	3	1.0
Rio de Janeiro	191	16	7.3	1,420	6,510	7,930	20	12.3	25	2	0.8
Guanabara	109	9	4.2	1,910	3,760	5,670	15	8.8	146	13	4.9
São Paulo	637	52	24.2	4,945	11,520	16,465	42	25.4	683	61	22.8
SOUTHEAST TOTAL	1,228	100	46.8	9,865	29,235	39,100	100	60.4	1,124	100	37.6
SOUTH											
Paraná	289	35%	11.0%	1,360	3,885	5,245	43%	8.1%	314	51%	10.5%
Santa Catarina	176	21	6.7	995	1,105	2,100	17	3.3	53	9	1.8
Rio Grande do Sul	361	44	13.8	1,120	3,830	4,950	40	7.7	240	40	8.0
SOUTH TOTAL	826	100	31.5	3,475	8,820	12,295	100	19.1	607	100	20.3
CENTRAL-WEST											
Mato Grosso	41	34%	1.6%	440	915	1,355	33%	2.1%	116	32%	3.9%
Goiás	63	52	2.4	345	1,655	2,000	48	3.1	154	42	5.1
Distrito Federal	17	14	0.6	145	640	785	19	1.2	95	26	3.2
CENTRAL-WEST TOTAL	121	100	4.6	930	3,210	4,140	100	6.4	365	100	12.2
BRAZIL TOTAL	2,624	-	100.0%	16,800	47,840	64,640	-	100.0%	2,991	-	100.0%

Source: Protestant communicant members based on *Anuário Estatístico do Brasil, 1971*, Brazilian leaders as of 1970 based on projection of data (see Figure 8); number of foreign missionaries based on Missionary Information Bureau records, 1968.

TABLE 3-2

DISTRIBUTION OF PROTESTANT CHURCHES BY REGIONS AND STATES IN BRAZIL, JANUARY 1, 1970

REGION State	Central Churches	Satellite Churches	All Churches	
	No.	No.	No.	%
NORTH REGION				
Rondônia	10	30	40	0.2%
Acre	20	30	50	0.2
Amazonas	80	130	210	0.8
Roraima	10	10	20	-
Pará	190	440	630	2.5
Amapá	10	40	50	0.2
NORTH TOTAL	320	680	1,000	3.9
NORTHEAST REGION				
Maranhão	160	400	560	2.2%
Piauí	70	130	200	0.8
Ceará	120	370	490	1.9
Rio Grande do Norte	90	180	270	1.1
Paraiba	120	170	290	1.1
Pernambuco	400	700	1,100	4.3
Alagoas	70	120	190	0.7
Sergipe	60	90	150	0.6
Bahia	470	550	1,020	4.1
NORTHEAST TOTAL	1,560	2,710	4,270	16.8
SOUTHEAST REGION				
Minas Gerais	860	1,810	2,670	10.5%
Espírito Santo	370	780	1,150	4.5
Rio de Janeiro	880	1,250	2,130	8.4
Guanabara	370	410	780	3.1
São Paulo	2,210	2,750	4,960	19.5
SOUTHEAST TOTAL	4,690	7,000	11,690	46.0
SOUTH REGION				
Paraná	840	2,150	2,990	11.8%
Santa Catarina	220	880	1,100	4.3
Rio Grande do Sul	500	2,030	2,530	10.0
SOUTH TOTAL	1,560	5,060	6,620	26.1
CENTRAL-WEST REGION				
Mato Grosso	220	380	600	2.5%
Goiás	320	700	1,020	3.9
Distrito Federal	90	120	210	0.8
CENTRAL-WEST TOTAL	630	1,200	1,830	7.2
BRAZIL TOTAL	8,760	16,650	25,410	100.0%

Source: *Anuário Estatístico do Brasil, 1971.*

At one time this region provided most of the world's supply of rubber. The city of Manaus at the confluence of three rivers once thrived on this trade. With the manufacture of synthetic rubber the importance of natural rubber dwindled. The forests were left primarily to the surviving Indian tribes and the few Brazilian settlers scattered throughout the area. Until recently, boat traffic on the Amazon River and its tributaries and air transportation were the only means of access to the interior. The vast forests and a hot, humid climate have discouraged all but the most hardy pioneers. The Brazilian government is now building a series of strategically located highways in an endeavor to encourage the settlement and development of this region. More will be said about this later.

Some interesting comparative proportions and relationships for this region are reflected in Figure 3-3. The North Region has forty-two percent of the total area of Brazil, but less than four percent of its population. It has only four percent of the Protestant members in Brazil, but fifteen percent of the foreign missionaries. Many missionaries are engaged in the linguistic work of putting the language of the Indian tribes into written form and providing translations of portions of the Bible. Others are evangelizing the widely-scattered settlers.

The distribution of the population of Brazil by regions and states is shown in Table 3-3, and of Protestant members by regions and states in Table 3-1. The State of Pará has over two million or 61 percent of the 3.5 million people located in the North region. It has a slightly higher proportion (65 percent) of the Protestant members with a much smaller proportion of both Brazilian leaders (44 percent) and foreign missionaries (37 percent) than of population.

The State of Amazonas with its capital at Manaus has less than half the number of people found in the State of Pará. It has one-fourth as many Protestants. Because of missionary activity among the Indians, more foreign missionaries are found here than in the State of Pará.

The Protestants in the North Region worship in 1,000 organized churches according to the Brazilian government census. This does not include the many thousands of preaching points and other unorganized worship centers that are served by Brazilian ministers, lay leaders, and foreign missionaries in this vast territory. The distribution of the organized worship centers by states may be seen in Table 3-2.

TABLE 3-3

DISTRIBUTION OF AREA AND POPULATION BY REGIONS AND STATES IN BRAZIL, 1970

REGION State	Area			Population			Density
	Square Kilometers 1000's	Percent of Region	Percent of Brazil	1000's	Percent of Region	Percent of Brazil	Persons/ Square Kilometer
NORTH							
Rondônia	243	7%	2.9%	117	3%	0.1%	0.5
Acre	153	4	1.8	218	6	0.2	1.4
Amazonas	1,559	44	18.4	961	26	1.0	0.6
Roraima	230	6	2.7	42	1	-	0.2
Pará	1,228	35	14.5	2,197	61	2.4	1.8
Amapá	139	4	1.6	116	3	0.1	0.8
NORTH TOTAL	3,552	100	41.9	3,651	100	3.8	1.0
NORTHEAST							
Maranhão	325	21%	3.8%	3,037	11%	3.2%	9.4
Piauí	251	16	3.0	1,735	6	1.8	6.9
Ceará	147	10	1.8	4,492	16	4.8	30.6
Rio Grande do Norte	53	3	0.6	1,612	6	1.7	30.4
Paraíba	56	4	0.7	2,445	9	2.6	43.4
Pernambuco	98	6	1.2	5,254	18	5.6	53.7
Alagoas	28	2	0.3	1,606	5	1.7	58.1
Sergipe	22	1	0.3	911	3	1.0	41.4
Bahia	560	37	6.6	7,583	26	8.0	13.5
NORTHEAST TOTAL	1,540	100	18.3	28,675	100	30.4	18.6
SOUTHEAST							
Minas Gerais	583	63%	6.9%	11,645	29%	12.3%	20.0
Espírito Santo	46	5	0.6	1,618	4	1.7	35.5
Rio de Janeiro	42	5	0.5	4,795	12	5.1	113.8
Guanabara	1	-	-	4,316	11	4.6	3,685.5
São Paulo	247	27	2.9	17,958	44	19.0	72.6
SOUTHEAST TOTAL	919	100	10.9	40,332	100	42.7	43.9
SOUTH							
Paraná	199	35%	2.4%	6,999	42%	7.4%	35.2
Santa Catarina	95	17	1.1	2,930	18	3.1	30.7
Rio Grande do Sul	268	48	3.2	6,755	40	7.1	25.2
SOUTH TOTAL	562	100	6.7	16,684	100	17.6	29.7
CENTRAL-WEST							
Mato Grosso	1,231	66%	14.5%	1,624	31%	1.7%	1.3
Goiás	642	34	7.6	2,997	58	3.2	4.7
Distrito Federal	6	-	0.1	546	11	0.6	94.6
CENTRAL-WEST TOTAL	1,879	100	22.2	5,167	100	5.5	2.8
BRAZIL TOTAL	8,452	-	100.0	94,509	-	100.0	11.2

Source: Based on Tables 2 & 4, *Sinopse Preliminar do Censo Demográfico: Brazil-1970*, I.B.G.E.

The rate of growth of Protestant membership in the North Region between 1960 and 1970 more than doubled that of the population (Table 3-4). The Territory of Rondônia was the only area in which the rate of population growth exceeded that of Protestant members. The Territory of Roraima with the smallest population and smallest Protestant membership showed the highest ratio of the latter rate to that of the former (3.6 times). Over this period, up to 1970, the State of Pará had an increase in Protestant membership exceeding the total membership growth of all of the other states and territories in the North.

FIGURE 3-3

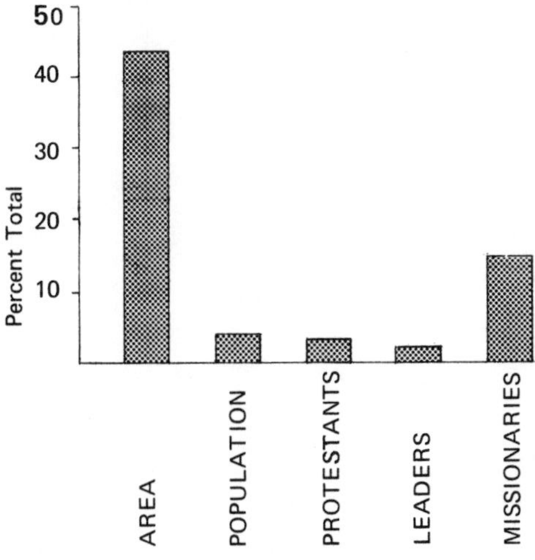

Northeast Region

The Northeast Region embraces the nine states that protrude out into the Atlantic Ocean. It ranges from Maranhão with its capital city of São Luiz to Bahia with the principal city of Salvador. The most important city is Recife, the capital of the State of Pernambuco. This region has been subject to periodic droughts which usually destroy essential crops and leads to the exodus of tens of thousands of people to areas where they can survive. In the process, thousands leave the Northeast to seek

TABLE 3-4

RELATIONSHIP BETWEEN POPULATION AND PROTESTANT COMMUNICANT MEMBERS AVERAGE ANNUAL GROWTH BY REGIONS AND STATES, 1960-1970

REGION State	Growth of Population	Growth of Protestant Members	Ratio of Protestant Member Growth to Population Growth
	%	%	
NORTH REGION			
Rondônia	5.2%	4.5%	0.9%
Acre	3.1	8.4	2.7
Amazonas	2.9	9.1	3.1
Roraima	3.6	12.9	3.6
Pará	3.6	6.5	1.8
Amapá	5.4	11.9	2.2
NORTH AVERAGE	3.4	7.2	2.1
NORTHEAST REGION			
Maranhão	2.0%	6.1%	3.0%
Piauí	3.2	14.0	4.4
Ceará	3.0	3.3	1.1
Rio Grande do Norte	3.4	5.2	1.5
Paraíba	1.9	3.9	2.1
Pernambuco	2.4	4.8	2.0
Alagoas	2.3	5.5	2.4
Sergipe	1.8	6.6	3.7
Bahia	2.4	6.8	2.8
NORTHEAST AVERAGE	2.5	5.5	2.2
SOUTHEAST REGION			
Minas Gerais	1.6%	5.8%	3.6%
Espírito Santo	1.3	3.7	2.8
Rio de Janeiro	3.5	6.3	1.8
Guanabara	2.7	4.9	1.8
São Paulo	3.3	5.7	1.7
SOUTHEAST AVERAGE	2.6	5.5	2.1
SOUTH REGION			
Paraná	5.0%	10.9%	2.2%
Santa Catarina	3.2	2.4	0.8
Rio Grande do Sul	2.2	2.9	1.3
SOUTH AVERAGE	3.5	4.9	1.4
CENTRAL-WEST REGION			
Mato Grosso	6.0%	13.2%	2.2%
Goiás	4.4	8.4	1.9
Distrito Federal	14.5	28.9	2.0
CENTRAL-WEST AVERAGE	5.6	11.4	2.0
BRAZIL AVERAGE	2.9%	5.6%	1.9%

Source: The compound interest rate formula was applied to the Brazilian census of population data and Protestant membership.

better conditions and employment in the Southeast. During the past decade there has been an emphasis on the development of small industries in an effort to improve the economy of the area. A growing attraction is to the newly-developing rural settlements to the west and out along the Trans-Amazonian road.

The totals in area, population, Protestant members, Brazilian church leaders, and foreign missionaries found within the region are shown in Figure 3-4. The Northeast Region has eighteen percent of Brazil's total area with thirty percent of its population. However, it has only thirteen percent of the Protestant members. One might conclude that this has been one of the least responsive sections of Brazil to the Gospel message, but Protestant leaders quickly point out that the percentage of Protestants migrating to other sections is much higher than for the population as a whole.

FIGURE 3-4

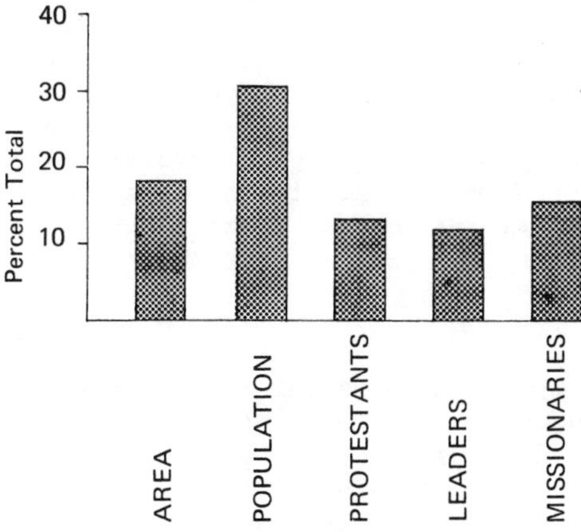

Harmon Johnson documents this trend with:

> "When people become evangelicals they begin to exert greater effort to better their lot in every way.* One church we visited in Rio started with 56 members in 1958. In 1968 it had 558 members. Over 500 of these were transfers from the North and Northeast. Although only 35 percent of the members of the Assembléias de Deus in Brazil are found in the North and Northeast, about 60 percent of the ministers come from these regions." (Johnson 1967:9).

The distribution of Protestant membership and of population by states may be seen by referring to Tables 3-1 and 3-3.

Twenty-nine percent of the Protestants in this region are located in the State of Pernambuco where only 18 percent of the region's population is found. In contrast, Ceará has only 10 percent of the region's Protestants but 16 percent of its total population. The State of Bahia also has a higher proportion of the total regional population (26 percent) than of Protestants (21 percent). Although both Pernambuco and Ceará have experienced considerable economic growth in recent years, Ceará has been the seat of intense Roman Catholicism since its early founding years. This may be one of the reasons for its relatively slow Protestant development.

The Protestants in the Northeast Region worship in more than 4,000 churches (Table 3-2). Nearly two-thirds of these churches are satellites of central churches developed from preaching points that grew until there was sufficient membership to justify formation of an organized church. More than 1,000 of these churches are to be found in each of the states of Bahia and Pernambuco.

---

*See Wesley's comment about the trend to become religious, prosperous, and then irreligious: "John Welsey, the founder of the movement, has summed up this process in what might be called Wesley's Law: '*Wherever riches have increased, the essence of religion has decreased in the same proportion.* Therefore, I do not see how it is possible, in the nature of things, for any revival of religion to continue long. For religion must necessarily produce both industry and frugality, and these cannot but produce riches. But as riches increase, so will pride, anger, and love of the world in all its branches...*Is there no way to prevent this...continual decay of pure religion?*'"
(Kelley 1972:55)

The rate of growth of Protestant membership in the Northeast also was double that of population growth (Table 3-5). Out-migration explains why this region showed the lowest percent of population growth.

Southeast Region

This region includes six states, two of which are the most populous in Brazil, São Paulo and Minas Gerais. This is the most progressive region of all Brazil. Brazil's three largest cities - São Paulo, Rio de Janeiro, and Belo Horizonte form a remarkable triangle of economic and industrial development. Here are found extensive mineral resources. It has the strongest economy, employment, and financial growth of any region. This region continues to attract hundreds of thousands of Brazilians who seek better social, economic, and educational opportunities.

The proportion of the region's totals in area, population, Protestant members, Brazilian church leaders, and foreign missionaries are shown in Figure 3-5. Although this region has only eleven percent of Brazil's area, it has nearly forty-three percent of the population and forty-seven percent of the Protestants. Seminaries and Bible schools in this region have produced many Brazilian leaders. In 1970 we find this region with sixty percent of Brazil's church leaders and thirty-eight percent of the foreign missionaries.

The relative importance of population and Protestant membership varies by states within the region as shown in Tables 3-3 and 3-1. The State of São Paulo, with 44 percent of the region's population, has 52 percent of its protestants and 61 percent of its foreign missionaries. The State of Minas Gerais, with 29 percent of the region's population, has only 15 percent of its Protestants. Roman Catholicism has been relatively strong in this state where 275 cities or nearly 40 percent of the total do not have organized Protestant worship centers recorded in the government census. The State of Rio de Janeiro, with a similar proportion of Protestant members, has only 12 percent of the region's population.

The Southeast Region has nearly 12,000 organized churches (Table 3-2) besides many thousands of unrecorded preaching points and small meeting places. Almost 5,000 of these churches are found in the State of São Paulo and an additional 5,000 distributed throughout the States of Minas Gerais and Rio de Janeiro. The city of Rio de Janeiro (the State of Guanabara) alone has some 800 churches.

The rate of growth of the Protestant membership in this region is double that of the population during the ten year period, 1960-1970 (Table 3-5). The State of Minas Gerais showed the highest ratio of Protestant member growth to that of population - namely, 3.6 times - followed by Espírito Santo with 2.8 times. Numerically, the State of São Paulo with a total membership growth of 269,000, accounted for more than half of the total membership growth for the region.

FIGURE 3-5

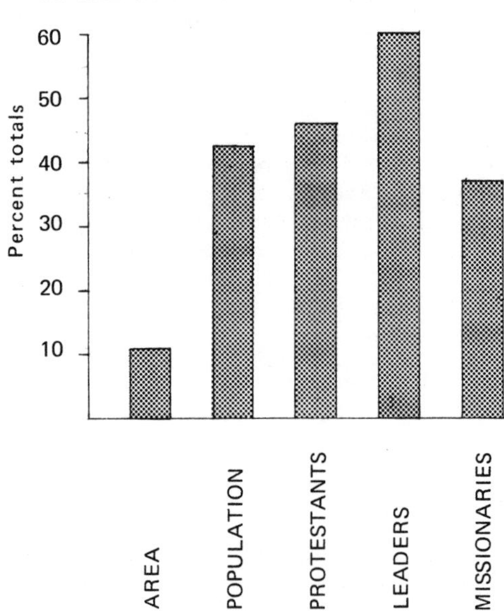

South Region

The South Region is made up of the three states: Paraná, Santa Catarina, and Rio Grande do Sul, and comprises the southern tip of Brazil. The northern-most state, Paraná, has been the site of the latest expansion of coffee-growing although many owners are turning to more diversified crops and to cattle raising. Pôrto Alegre, the capital city of Rio Grande do Sul, is rapidly approaching a population of one million people.

The proportions of Brazil's totals of area, population, Protestant members, Brazilian church leaders, and foreign missionaries in this region are shown in Figure 3-6. Although this region has less than seven percent of Brazil's area, it has eighteen percent of the population and thirty-two percent of the Protestant members. The proportion of the Brazilian church leaders and foreign missionaries found in this region is similar to the proportion of the population; namely, nineteen and twenty percent, respectively.

The distribution of population and Protestant membership by states within the region is shown in Tables 3-3 and 3-1. Protestant growth prior to 1960 failed to keep pace with the rapid expansion of population in the State of Paraná. This state has forty-two percent of the region's population but only thirty-five percent of the Protestants. The proportion of Protestants in the other two states of this region - Santa Catarina and Rio Grande do Sul - exceeds that of population.

The Protestants of the South Region have organized more than 6,600 churches. The State of Paraná has the largest number of these churches - nearly 3,000 - followed by Rio Grande do Sul with more than 2,500. The State of Santa Catarina has 1,100 churches. Although there are fewer preaching points and unorganized meeting places in the South in comparison to other regions, there are still estimated to be several thousand of these small worship centers.

This region experienced the smallest ratio of Protestant membership growth percent to that for population growth of any region - only 1.4 times. It is a difficult region for the work of church planting and aggressive evangelism because of the strong social institutions and the traditional conservative mentality of European ethnic stock. The State of Santa Catarina had a membership growth percent lower than that for population, and Rio Grande do Sul only slightly exceeded that for population. The numerical growth in members during the 1960's for the State of Paraná (185,000) far exceeded the total growth of the other two states.

FIGURE 3-6

PROPORTION OF BRAZIL'S TOTALS IN THE SOUTH REGION

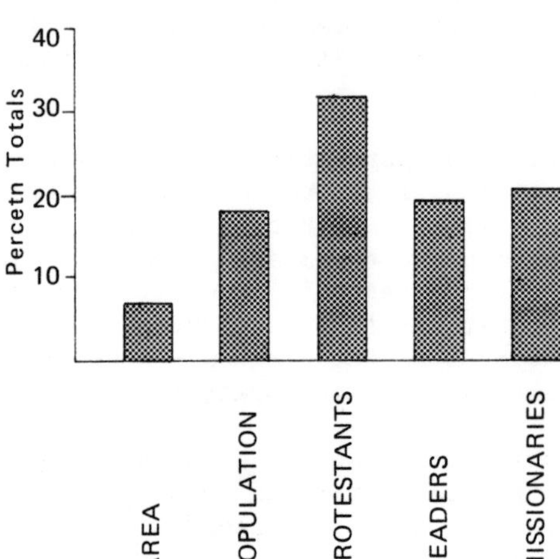

Central-West Region

This region has two of the larger states in Brazil in area Mato Grosso and Goiás, and the currently well-established capital of the country, Brasília, which is a part of the Federal District. These states like the north region also embrace a part of the Amazon River Basin. They are sparsely settled, having an average of less than three people per square kilometer. The establishment of the capital of Brazil in this region has led to an influx of settlers from other regions as well as the movement of the seat of government from the former capital, Rio de Janeiro.

The proportion of Brazil's totals of area, population, Protestant members, Brazilian church leaders, and foreign missionaries in the region is shown in Figure 3-7. This region embraces twenty-two percent of the land area but less than six percent of the population. Although only five percent of the Protestant members are found in this region, some six percent of Brazilian church leaders are located here, and twelve percent of the foreign missionaries. These latter proportions may indicate that missionaries and leaders have been attracted to the region by prospects of a rapidly growing population.

FIGURE 3-7

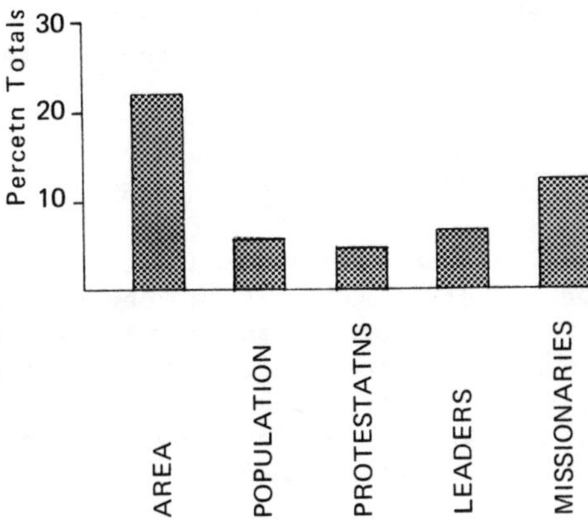

The distribution of population and Protestant members by states within the region is shown in Tables 3-3 and 3-1. Mato Grosso has 31 percent of the region's population and 34 percent of its Protestants. Goiás, with 58 percent of the regional total population (nearly twice the population of Mato Grosso), has 52 percent of the region's Protestants. The Federal District with the new capital Brasília, has only eleven percent of the region's population but 26 percent of its missionaries. The Federal District, with 14 percent of the Protestants, reflects an unusually high proportional influx of Protestants into this rapidly growing center.

The Protestants of the Central-West Region have established more than 1,800 churches (Table 3-2). Slightly over 1,000 of these are located in the State of Goiás. Already more than 200 churches have been organized in the Federal District, most of which are located in the capital city of Brasília. In addition, Brazilian evangelists and foreign missionaries conduct services in several thousand preaching points and small meeting places.

The average annual percent growth rate of Protestant membership for this region during the 1960's was double the rate of population growth (Table 3-4). This region experienced the highest rate of population growth of any during the 1960's and this immigration may account for the high rate of membership growth if the theory that Protestants move into new areas more readily than others is valid. The Federal District had the highest rate of both population and membership growth, followed by Mato Grosso. The State of Goiás had the largest numerical increase with 29,000 new members net.

CHURCH GROWTH BY MICRO-REGION

In 1968 the Brazilian Census Bureau published a micro-region division plan for all of Brazil. It had been officially approved as the way in which all future census surveys would be taken, employing the new micro-region distribution of land areas within the States and Territories of the entire land mass of Brazil. Three hundred and sixty micro-regions suddenly became an important consideration. The decision was made in the BRAZIL 1980 computer analysis to incorporate all of the church growth data and adapt it to this new division of land areas. After nine months of careful map work and tracing through the different county relationships and recording the new counties, all church growth data was redistributed and placed into its proper geographic micro-region units.

In Table 3-5 will be found the total membership for all Protestant denominations for each micro-region in Brazil where Protestant membership was recorded in the religious census for 1966. This is the first listing of church membership by micro-regions ever to be published. It becomes the basis for a new field of research into the relationships that exist between socio-economic factors, demography, migration, urbanization, settlement, transportation networks, industrialization, and the growth of Protestantism.

Micro-Regions With The Largest Protestant Membership

Micro-regions with the largest Protestant membership have been separated for 1955, 1960, 1965, and 1970. Table 3-6 displays the top ten percent (36) of all the micro-regions (361) in these different years.

TABLE 3-5

MEMBERSHIP TOTALS OF ALL PROTESTANT DENOMINATIONS FOUND WITHIN MICRO-REGIONS OF BRAZIL IN 1966

NORTH

Rondônia	
Micro-Region 1	3,996
Acre	
Micro-Region 2	1,689
Micro-Region 3	4,080
Amazonas	
Micro-Region 4	2,513
Micro-Region 5	158
Micro-Region 6	1,369
Micro-Region 7	176
Micro-Region 8	312
Micro-Region 9	220
Micro-Region 10	10,444
Roraima	
Micro-Region 11	1,526
Pará	
Micro-Region 12	3,888
Micro-Region 13	121
Micro-Region 14	322
Micro-Region 15	856
Micro-Region 16	3,473
Micro-Region 17	1,046
Micro-Region 18	3,962
Micro-Region 19	885
Micro-Region 20	209
Micro-Region 21	1,169
Micro-Region 22	4,435
Micro-Region 23	4,424
Micro-Region 24	8,834
Micro-Region 25	13,185
Micro-Region 26	699
Amapá	
Micro-Region 27	4,091
Micro-Region 28	-

NORTHEAST

Maranhão	
Micro-Region 29	1,122
Micro-Region 30	3,811
Micro-Region 31	4,975
Micro-Region 32	828
Micro-Region 33	1,205
Micro-Region 34	6,456
Micro-Region 35	6,872
Micro-Region 36	6,446
Micro-Region 37	1,463
Micro-Region 38	3,830
Micro-Region 39	1,614
Micro-Region 40	2,347
Micro-Region 41	264
Micro-Region 42	507
Micro-Region 43	212
Micro-Region 44	88
Piauí	
Micro-Region 45	1,639
Micro-Region 46	1,317
Micro-Region 47	4,042
Micro-Region 48	563
Micro-Region 49	391
Micro-Region 50	763
Micro-Region 51	1,156
Micro-Region 52	108
Micro-Region 53	-
Micro-Region 54	126
Micro-Region 55	822
Ceará	
Micro-Region 56	1,157
Micro-Region 57	28
Micro-Region 58	3,756
Micro-Region 59	14,933
Micro-Region 60	595
Micro-Region 61	1,417
Micro-Region 62	268
Micro-Region 63	237
Micro-Region 64	54
Micro-Region 65	688
Micro-Region 66	57
Micro-Region 67	221
Micro-Region 68	1,792
Micro-Region 69	60
Micro-Region 70	189
Micro-Region 71	-
Micro-Region 72	541
Micro-Region 73	957
Micro-Region 74	675
Micro-Region 75	50
Micro-Region 76	-
Micro-Region 77	177
Micro-Region 78	721
Rio Grande do Norte	
Micro-Region 79	2,277
Micro-Region 80	-
Micro-Region 81	1,406
Micro-Region 82	329
Micro-Region 83	748
Micro-Region 84	13,263
Micro-Region 85	1,300
Micro-Region 86	1,508
Micro-Region 87	536
Micro-Region 88	599
Paraíba	
Micro-Region 89	1,001
Micro-Region 90	454
Micro-Region 91	360
Micro-Region 92	1,632
Micro-Region 93	8,119
Micro-Region 94	511
Micro-Region 95	2,391
Micro-Region 96	229
Micro-Region 97	4,959
Micro-Region 98	193
Micro-Region 99	2,154
Micro-Region 100	262
Pernambuco	
Micro-Region 101	242
Micro-Region 102	114
Micro-Region 103	521
Micro-Region 104	552
Micro-Region 105	265
Micro-Region 106	916
Micro-Region 107	1,371
Micro-Region 108	5,140
Micro-Region 109	4,971
Micro-Region 110	15,537
Micro-Region 111	42,457
Micro-Region 112	16,910
Alagoas	
Micro-Region 113	64
Micro-Region 114	656
Micro-Region 115	884
Micro-Region 116	2,844
Micro-Region 117	1,294
Micro-Region 118	864
Micro-Region 119	126
Micro-Region 120	8,538
Micro-Region 121	276

TABLE 3-5 (CONTINUED)

Fernando de Noronha	
Micro-Region 122	-

Sergipe	
Micro-Region 123	-
Micro-Region 124	119
Micro-Region 125	42
Micro-Region 126	258
Micro-Region 127	163
Micro-Region 128	527
Micro-Region 129	5,132
Micro-Region 130	13

Bahia	
Micro-Region 131	259
Micro-Region 132	528
Micro-Region 133	223
Micro-Region 134	468
Micro-Region 135	1,185
Micro-Region 136	559
Micro-Region 137	1,372
Micro-Region 138	1,455
Micro-Region 139	3,237
Micro-Region 140	839
Micro-Region 141	888
Micro-Region 142	980
Micro-Region 143	3,556
Micro-Region 144	3,220
Micro-Region 145	3,622
Micro-Region 146	1,935
Micro-Region 147	474
Micro-Region 148	1,356
Micro-Region 149	109
Micro-Region 150	14,525
Micro-Region 151	3,236
Micro-Region 152	937
Micro-Region 153	1,833
Micro-Region 154	10,816
Micro-Region 155	1,852
Micro-Region 156	1,943

SOUTHEAST

Minas Gerais	
Micro-Region 157	596
Micro-Region 158	1,458
Micro-Region 159	971
Micro-Region 160	2,043
Micro-Region 161	694
Micro-Region 162	1,623
Micro-Region 163	-
Micro-Region 164	190
Micro-Region 165	293
Micro-Region 166	856
Micro-Region 167	-
Micro-Region 168	2,580
Micro-Region 169	2,773
Micro-Region 170	7,013
Micro-Region 171	2,645
Micro-Region 172	1,865
Micro-Region 173	282
Micro-Region 174	327
Micro-Region 175	6,850
Micro-Region 176	8,177
Micro-Region 177	1,689
Micro-Region 178	2,763
Micro-Region 179	633
Micro-Region 180	1,196
Micro-Region 181	1,802
Micro-Region 182	23,938
Micro-Region 183	6,835
Micro-Region 184	10,821
Micro-Region 185	18,520
Micro-Region 186	1,433
Micro-Region 187	902
Micro-Region 188	1,261
Micro-Region 189	8,984
Micro-Region 190	4,445
Micro-Region 191	943
Micro-Region 192	222
Micro-Region 193	3,051
Micro-Region 194	2,732
Micro-Region 195	1,037
Micro-Region 196	1,317
Micro-Region 197	4,530
Micro-Region 198	5,773
Micro-Region 199	1,720
Micro-Region 200	10,983
Micro-Region 201	3,875
Micro-Region 202	3,845

Espirito Santo	
Micro-Region 203	3,852
Micro-Region 204	31,157
Micro-Region 205	6,230
Micro-Region 206	35,266
Micro-Region 207	13,024
Micro-Region 208	4,682
Micro-Region 209	12,120
Micro-Region 210	3,756

Rio de Janeiro	
Micro-Region 211	6,496
Micro-Region 212	2,902
Micro-Region 213	21,752
Micro-Region 214	2,973
Micro-Region 215	2,795
Micro-Region 216	1,759
Micro-Region 217	9,808
Micro-Region 218	15,509
Micro-Region 219	2,882
Micro-Region 220	5,088
Micro-Region 221	96,299
Micro-Region 222	7,914
Micro-Region 223	2,667

Guanabara	
Micro-Region 224	104,627

São Paulo	
Micro-Region 225	12,485
Micro-Region 226	3,336
Micro-Region 227	843
Micro-Region 228	4,066
Micro-Region 229	4,651
Micro-Region 230	1,057
Micro-Region 231	12,826
Micro-Region 232	1,829
Micro-Region 233	2,492
Micro-Region 234	6,658
Micro-Region 235	7,087
Micro-Region 236	3,030
Micro-Region 237	6,104
Micro-Region 238	851
Micro-Region 239	9,030
Micro-Region 240	4,178
Micro-Region 241	12,306
Micro-Region 242	12,183
Micro-Region 243	4,484
Micro-Region 244	4,083
Micro-Region 245	11,218
Micro-Region 246	2,613
Micro-Region 247	5,848
Micro-Region 248	23,652
Micro-Region 249	1,407
Micro-Region 250	10,611
Micro-Region 251	8,036
Micro-Region 252	8,065
Micro-Region 253	6,925
Micro-Region 254	2,065
Micro-Region 255	4,888
Micro-Region 256	25,738
Micro-Region 257	9,065
Micro-Region 258	8,149
Micro-Region 259	6,704
Micro-Region 260	8,856
Micro-Region 261	5,930
Micro-Region 262	261,018
Micro-Region 263	622
Micro-Region 264	1,642
Micro-Region 265	8,275
Micro-Region 266	15,218
Micro-Region 267	1,690

SOUTH

Paraná	
Micro-Region 268	21,572
Micro-Region 269	5,369
Micro-Region 270	469
Micro-Region 271	233
Micro-Region 272	3,727
Micro-Region 273	11,239
Micro-Region 274	1,337
Micro-Region 275	260
Micro-Region 276	3,011
Micro-Region 277	1,585
Micro-Region 278	5,931
Micro-Region 279	12,510
Micro-Region 280	4,192
Micro-Region 281	41,661
Micro-Region 282	17,086

TABLE 3-5 (CONTINUED)

Micro-Region 283	14,377
Micro-Region 284	15,657
Micro-Region 285	18,564
Micro-Region 286	12,866
Micro-Region 287	72
Micro-Region 288	25,934
Micro-Region 289	8,199
Micro-Region 290	3,266
Micro-Region 291	2,040
Santa Catarina	
Micro-Region 292	55,448
Micro-Region 293	6,041
Micro-Region 294	64,732
Micro-Region 295	12,302
Micro-Region 296	20,666
Micro-Region 297	5,151
Micro-Region 298	7,681
Micro-Region 299	609
Micro-Region 300	7,098
Micro-Region 301	1,036
Micro-Region 302	121
Micro-Region 303	1,875
Micro-Region 304	740
Micro-Region 305	25,507
Micro-Region 306	22,578
Micro-Region 307	10,858
Rio Grande do Sul	
Micro-Region 308	95,685
Micro-Region 309	63,057
Micro-Region 310	6,359
Micro-Region 311	2,650
Micro-Region 312	-
Micro-Region 313	38,949
Micro-Region 314	58,288
Micro-Region 315	16,509
Micro-Region 316	11,037
Micro-Region 317	30,995
Micro-Region 318	2,629
Micro-Region 319	673
Micro-Region 320	1,124
Micro-Region 321	14,552
Micro-Region 322	14,337
Micro-Region 323	11,664
Micro-Region 324	59,882
Micro-Region 325	7,058
Micro-Region 326	11,095
Micro-Region 327	26,654
Micro-Region 328	22,806
Micro-Region 329	7,788
Micro-Region 330	1,761
Micro-Region 331	343

CENTRAL-WEST

Mato Grosso	
Micro-Region 332	77
Micro-Region 333	858
Micro-Region 334	523
Micro-Region 335	2,291
Micro-Region 336	2,243
Micro-Region 337	1,290
Micro-Region 338	4,341
Micro-Region 339	849
Micro-Region 340	661
Micro-Region 341	491
Micro-Region 342	5,656
Micro-Region 343	1,285
Micro-Region 344	9,585
Goiás	
Micro-Region 345	1,095
Micro-Region 346	234
Micro-Region 347	350
Micro-Region 348	1,004
Micro-Region 349	199
Micro-Region 350	1,336
Micro-Region 351	119
Micro-Region 352	264
Micro-Region 353	604
Micro-Region 354	21,771
Micro-Region 355	6,400
Micro-Region 356	1,381
Micro-Region 357	2,728
Micro-Region 358	1,440
Micro-Region 359	1,404
Micro-Region 360	3,653
Distrito Federal	
Micro-Region 361	12,134

Brazil Total 2,554,222

Micro-Regions With No Protestants Registered

In all of Brazil there were only nine micro-regions that had no record of Protestant membership in 1966 (Table 3-7). This does not mean that there may not be Protestants in these micro-regions but only that there were no organized churches recorded.

TABLE 3-7

MICRO-REGIONS WITHOUT ORGANIZED PROTESTANT CHURCHES RECORDED, 1966

	M/R	STATE
1.	28	Amapá
2.	53	Piauí
3.	71	Piauí
4.	76	Piauí
5.	122	Fernando de Noronha
6.	123	Sergipe
7.	163	Minas Gerais
8.	167	Minas Gerais
9.	312	Rio Grande do Sul

Micro-Regions With Highest Percentage of Growth

Between 1955-1966. Those micro-regions that registered the largest rate of growth in this eleven-year period are listed below. Table 3-8 shows the membership in 1955 and in 1966 and the percentage of growth that was recorded for the period.

TABLE 3-6

THIRTY-SIX MICRO-REGIONS HAVING LARGEST PROTESTANT MEMBERSHIP
1955, 1960, 1965, AND 1970

1955			
NO.	M/R	STATE	MEMB.
1	262	SP	106,212
2	308	RGS	60,587
3	224	GB	54,235
4	294	SC	53,023
5	309	RGS	48,796
6	292	SC	45,137
7	324	RGS	41,501
8	314	RGS	40,457
9	313	RGS	34,449
10	212	RJ	31,007
11	206	ES	24,304
12	315	RGS	23,091
13	204	ES	20,960
14	305	SC	19,783
15	317	RGS	19,728
16	327	RGS	19,341
17	111	PE	18,504
18	185	MG	18,104
19	296	SC	17,307
20	281	PR	17,051
21	328	RGS	14,981
22	213	RJ	13,234
23	59	CE	12,226
24	322	RGS	12,207
25	354	GO	11,431
26	295	SC	11,350
27	218	RJ	11,168
28	306	SC	10,920
29	326	RGS	10,783
30	209	ES	10,457
31	323	RGS	10,364
32	245	SP	10,120
33	112	PE	9,786
34	248	SP	9,506
35	256	SP	8,889
36	25	PA	8,387
		TOTAL	889,385

1960			
NO.	M/R	STATE	MEMB.
1	262	SP	165,969
2	308	RGS	76,532
3	224	GB	73,238
4	294	SC	56,755
5	309	RGS	55,284
6	314	RGS	52,014
7	221	RJ	49,727
8	292	SC	49,721
9	324	RGS	48,587
10	313	RGS	38,886
11	111	PER	31,913
12	204	ES	31,012
13	206	ES	30,572
14	281	PR	25,430
15	305	SC	23,226
16	317	RGS	22,299
17	185	MG	21,891
18	296	SC	21,449
19	256	SP	21,018
20	327	RGS	20,593
21	175	MG	19,037
22	306	SC	18,273
23	354	GO	17,894
24	213	RJ	17,495
25	59	CE	17,373
26	315	RGS	15,439
27	248	SP	14,667
28	322	RGS	14,226
29	328	RGS	14,064
30	323	RGS	13,693
31	112	PE	13,506
32	266	SP	13,233
33	268	PR	12,512
34	25	PA	12,131
35	110	PE	11,823
36	218	RJ	11,320
		TOTAL	1,091,233

1965			
NO.	M/R	STATE	MEMB.
1	262	SP	244,664
2	224	GB	100,542
3	308	RGS	93,451
4	221	RJ	85,677
5	294	SC	64,996
6	309	RGS	61,713
7	314	RGS	57,807
8	324	RGS	57,632
9	292	SC	54,201
10	111	PER	40,088
11	313	RGS	38,171
12	281	PR	38,158
13	206	ES	35,248
14	204	ES	31,255
15	317	RGS	30,379
16	327	RGS	26,039
17	305	SC	24,882
18	256	SP	24,675
19	354	GO	21,785
20	213	RJ	21,572
21	248	SP	21,513
22	306	SC	21,508
23	288	PR	21,246
24	328	RGS	21,217
25	268	PR	20,813
26	297	SC	20,257
27	182	MG	19,050
28	185	MG	17,999
29	285	PR	17,421
30	282	PR	17,195
31	112	PE	16,514
31	315	RGS	15,883
33	218	RJ	14,771
34	150	BA	14,463
35	209	ES	14,383
36	322	RGS	14,304
		TOTAL	1,419,637

1970			
NO.	M/R	STATE	MEMB.
1	262	SP	360,402
2	224	GB	131,541
3	221	RJ	153,158
4	308	RGS	108,113
5	294	SC	76,019
6	111	PER	73,486
7	324	RGS	71,137
8	309	RGS	68,792
9	292	SC	68,171
10	288	PR	65,091
11	314	RGS	65,096
12	281	PR	59,024
13	182	MG	46,097
14	285	PR	44,031
15	206	ES	41,415
16	313	RGS	40,000
17	317	RGS	38,543
18	286	PR	35,629
19	204	ES	35,000
20	268	PR	33,823
21	248	SP	31,941
22	284	PR	31,503
23	327	RGS	30,468
24	282	PR	30,197
25	305	SC	30,000
26	256	SP	29,421
27	328	RGS	28,360
28	361	DF	28,045
29	306	SC	25,809
30	213	RJ	25,545
31	296	SC	25,000
32	354	GO	24,886
33	185	MG	23,000
34	321	RGS	22,572
35	344	MT	21,726
36	112	PE	20,790
		TOTAL	2,018,786

TABLE 3-8

MICRO-REGIONS REGISTERING LARGEST PERCENTAGE OF PROTESTANT GROWTH BETWEEN 1955 AND 1966

COMMUNICANTS

No.	M/R	STATE	1955	1966	% INCREASE
1	155	BA	19	1,852	9,647.4%
2	158	MG	36	1,458	3,950.0%
3	343	MT	41	1,285	3,034.1%
4	51	PI	38	1,156	2,942.1%
5	346	GO	8	234	2,825.0%
6	288	PR	902	25,934	2,775.2%
7	289	PR	323	8,199	2,438.4%
8	285	PR	751	18,564	2,371.9%
9	63	CE	10	237	2,270.0%
10	181	MG	81	1,802	2,124.7%
11	336	MT	101	2,243	2,120.8%
12	87	RGN	26	536	1,961.5%
13	157	MG	29	596	1,955.2%
14	304	SC	47	740	1,475.5%
15	298	SC	495	7,681	1,451.7%
16	183	MG	488	6,835	1,300.6%
17	333	MT	63	858	1,261.9%
18	200	MG	938	10,893	1,070.9%
19	165	MG	26	293	1,026.8%
20	164	MG	18	190	995.6%
21	4	AM	251	2,513	901.2%
22	300	SC	764	7,098	829.1%
23	361	DF	0	12,134	802.8%
24	101	PE	27	242	796.3%
25	203	ES	438	3,852	779.5%
26	353	GO	69	604	775.4%
27	62	CE	0	268	764.5%
28	169	MG	324	2,773	755.9%
29	258	SP	1,012	8,149	705.2%
30	232	SP	235	1,829	678.3%
31	20	PA	27	209	674.1%
32	357	GO	378	2,728	621.7%
33	199	MG	241	1,720	613.7%
34	96	PB	33	229	593.9%
35	38	MA	556	3,830	588.8%
36	319	RGS	98	673	586.7%
		TOTALS	8,893	140,437	

PROTESTANT LEADERSHIP IN BRAZIL

From the initiation of missionary efforts and during the various stages of development of the Protestant church in Brazil, God has been calling and prospering gifted Brazilians to lead His Church. These men early assumed the major responsibility for the growth and development of the churches and/or denominations in Brazil. Such leaders, tried in the fires of hardship, privation, and prepared by God in unique ways to accept their responsibilities, make decisions that affect the spiritual welfare of thousands of Evangelicals.

Although the government statistics enable us to report on the number of ministers, deacons, and elders, we do not have much information about them. A general survey covering the characteristics of Brazilian ministers and lay leaders has not as yet been made. Such questions as the following would provide information useful to an appraisal of this leadership: How old are they? What is their marital status? How many children do they have? What region of Brazil did they come from? What is their educational background? To what denomination do they belong? When were they ordained? What do they do: preach, counsel, administrate, evangelize, etc? Do they engage in secular employment? What relation does the above personal data have to the growth of their church?

The Number of Brazilian Leaders Increased Rapidly During the 1960's

The increase of Brazilian Evangelical leadership exceeded 100 percent between 1960 and 1970 (Figure 3-8). In the same period, the membership rolls increased less than 50 percent. Table 3-1 gives the number of ministers and lay leaders (deacons and elders) by regions and states in 1970. The number of ministers increased from a little over 7,000 to nearly 17,000 during this period. Correspondingly, the number of elders and deacons grew from about 22,000 to 48,000. In addition, there are thousands of laymen in leadership positions who are not included in the classification as elders or deacons.

Where Are They Located

Some sixty percent of the Brazilian pastors and lay leaders are found in the Southeast where forty-seven percent of the church members and thirty-eight percent of the foreign missionaries are located. In contrast, in the South only nineteen percent of the leaders and twenty percent of the foreign missionaries are working where more than thirty-one percent of the membership is recorded.

FIGURE 3-8

BRAZILIAN PROTESTANT LEADERSHIP GROWTH, 1960–1970

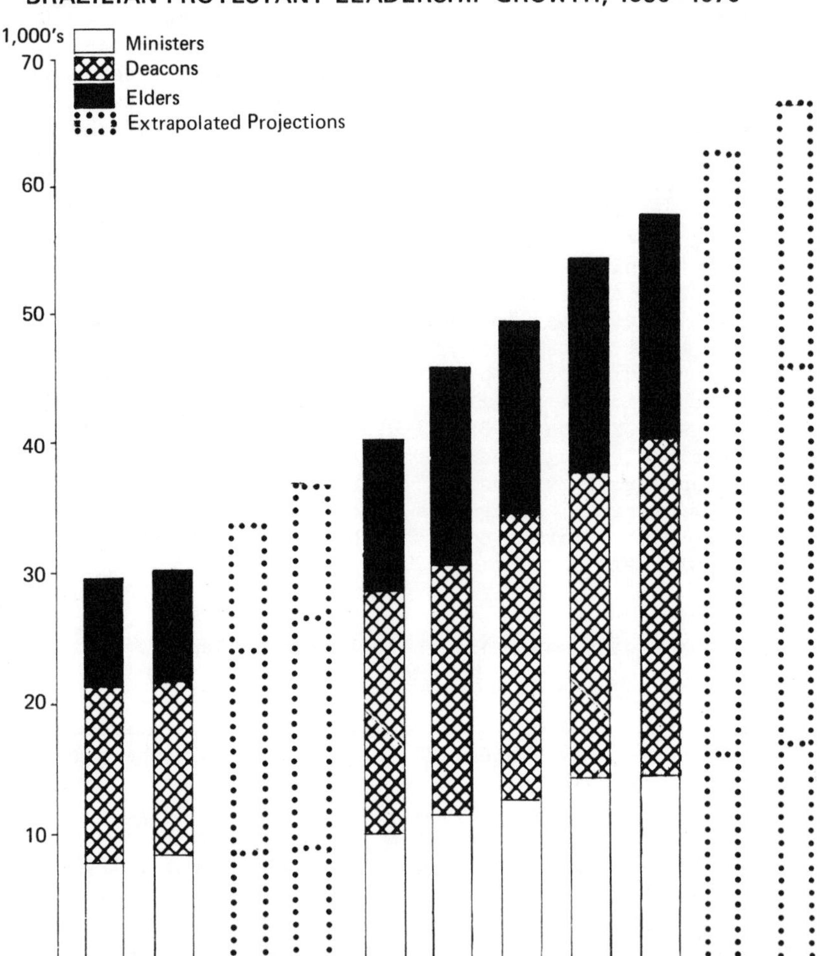

Source: Anuário Estatística do Brasil. IBGE/Conselho Nacional De Estatística.

What Responsibilities Do They Have?

Ministers have been ordained to proclaim the Gospel, to train other potential leaders, to teach the membership, and to minister to the many material and spiritual needs of their members and of their communities. Some are working as evangelists and others as administrators. It is estimated that less than fifty percent of this group have had an opportunity for training in a theological seminary. Less than thirty percent of the ordained ministers in Protestant churches in Brazil devote their full time to the pastorate. The remainder give the time that is needed to secular employment in order to meet their living expenses. However, in the Pentecostal churches there are several thousand elders and other laymen who give full time to the ministry.

4

Denominational Analysis: Its Composition and Growth

SUMMARY

Protestant Churches*	1960	1970	Increase
All Communicant members	1,527,200	2,623,550	1,096,350
Traditional Denominations	938,650	1,328,050	399,400
Pentecostal Denominations	588,550	1,295,500	708,850

As we noted at the beginning of Chapter 3, we have chosen to examine the Protestant church in Brazil in depth geographically in Chapter 3 and in depth denominationally in this chapter. The "X's" in Figure 4-1 show the areas covered in this chapter.

---

*Note: These membership figures are taken from the Religious Census publications *Culto Protestante* for the years indicated. It is the only source available for this church growth information. A reduction has been made for the non-communicant membership reported by the Lutheran churches in 1960 and 1970.

FIGURE 4-1

BRAZIL 1980: CHURCH VS GEOGRAPHICAL DISTRIBUTION

GEOGRAPHICAL DISTRIBUTION							
DENOMINATIONAL DISTRIBUTION	**Country**	**Major Region (5)**	**State (27)**	**Urban Region (112)**	**Micro Region (361)**	**County (3,997)**	**District (15,000+)**
All Protestants	X	X	X				
Categories	X	X	X				
Traditions	X	X	X				
Denominations	X						
Local Church							

INTRODUCTION

With the completion of the latest MARC/MIB 1980 computer church growth analysis, it has been possible to take a different kind of an overall look at Protestant growth by denominations in Brazil. Only a small part of this new look at the growth of the Protestant church will be presented in this chapter. This is the first comprehensive computer analysis of the church growth data found in the large collection of *Culto Protestante* books published by the Brazilian Religious Census that have been completed each year since 1955 for every county of Brazil. The long effort to utilize this remarkable church growth data for evangelism and church planting began more than ten years ago. Only now has the first substantial application of computer technology to a dynamic Protestant church growth situation in any part of the world been possible. Brazil happened to be that country in which these new data processing applications could be applied, and this large task was undertaken before 1969 by the MARC/MIB team. With the experience gained from this effort in Brazil, other countries in the world may be able to utilize some of these new techniques that will in turn enhance their efforts in evangelism and church planting.

This chapter will present several representative statistical profiles of denominational growth displayed in five-year periods beginning in 1955. A denominational listing of all churches who reported their membership will be given which will indicate growth in five-year periods. A study of different aspects of growth for the decade of the 60's has been made. This third section captures the growth patterns that occurred in this unusual decade. Different ways in which Protestant denominations have been growing, classified by categories and families of churches such as the "traditional," "Pentecostal," and "others," have been brought together.

The statistical data upon which the greater part of this chapter is based have been produced in its present form on the World Vision IBM 360 computer located in Monrovia, California. These data constitute a valuable bank of church growth material needing more definite interpretative study beyond the scope of the Brazil 1980 effort. This data bank consists of a series of different types of computer printouts of the Brazil 1980 analysis of church growth. They were produced between 1970 and the end of March, 1973. The computerized analysis, in order to be available for extensive use by leaders of the Brazilian Protestant churches, has been turned over to the Center for Advanced Studies in Evangelism (CASE), in São Paulo, Brazil.* Appendix 4 describes the purpose and function of CASE in Brazil.

In this chapter we list the comparative data for every denomination in Brazil. Then an analysis is made by categories: Traditional and Pentecostal. These are presented by regions.

Protestant Growth: A Denominational Listing for Brazil

Table 4-1 is the first complete listing ever published of the growth of Protestant membership in Brazil by denominations. It charts this growth in six different periods: 1) 1955-56; 2) 1957-58; 3) 1959-60; 4) 1961-62; 5) 1963-64; 6) 1965-66. In Table 4-1, Growth of Protestant Membership by Denominations in Periods, 1955 to 1966, the data for each denomination listed in the Brazilian Religious Census *Culto Protestante* is reproduced

---

*CASE, The Reverend Harmon Johnson, Director, Caixa Postal 30, 548, São Paulo, Brazil, S.A.

by six one-year periods. Each box has six important items of data about each denomination whose name is found in the left-hand column under different headings on the list such as Baptist, Methodist, Adventist, etc. An example of this would be the first box of six items of data for the *Igreja Batista Brasileira* under "Baptists." The first line presents the membership of this denomination in 1955 which was 152,649. The second line reports its membership in 1956 which had grown to 169,709. The third line has the abbreviation "EXCL," and indicates the number of members whose names were taken off the rolls of the different churches in this denomination for any reason, during the year. This year the *Igreja Batista Brasileira* lost 12,132 members. Line four carries the heading "% GR" which gives the computer calculated percent of growth from 1955 to 1956, 11.2 percent. Line five, "CC", displays the total number of central churches. These came to a total of 1,261 in this period. Last, line six carries the abbreviation "SC" which indicates satellite churches and newly formed congregations. In the first period of 1955 to 1956, the accurate reporting of satellite churches had not been provided for on the Religious Census Bureau questionnaire that went to each Protestant church through the census representatives in each county. However, by 1957 and 1958, when the importance of this vast network of satellite churches was recognized, the questionnaire was revised to include them and the congregations connected in any way with the central churches. The last five periods listed on Table 4-1 give a clear cut-picture of the data on satellite churches, an important factor in producing a significant denominational profile of growth for particular denominations for the entire period of 1955 to 1966.

The magnitude of the Brazil 1980 church growth analysis required the labor of 70 or more volunteers who were enlisted to help in the tremendous job of working over this mass of church growth data. The data behind this denominational listing represents 39,000 church records that have been handled from 1955 to 1966. Each of these individual church records, punched onto IBM cards, required ten separate items of information. A total of 390,000 units of information was transferred onto the coding cards used by the computers to give us this listing.

Protestant Denominations by Categories Within Micro-Regions

The list of denominations in Brazil that are found in Table 4-1 was reduced into thirteen denominational families or groupings of churches that could be used to bring together, in an arbitrary way, all Protestant church groups in Brazil, thus making a hierarchy of denominations for special studies.

TABLE 4-1

GROWTH OF PROTESTANT MEMBERSHIP BY DENOMINATIONS IN PERIODS, 1955 to 1966

NAME OF DENOMINATION \ GROWTH PERIODS		1955 / 1956	1957 / 1958	1959 / 1960	1961 / 1962	1963 / 1964	1965 / 1966
BAPTISTS 33 Igreja Batista Brasileira	1955 1	152,649	177,291	185,021	197,985	222,135	249,635
	1956 2	169,709	180,478	193,702	204,357	234,694	264,137
	EXCL 3	12,132	25,219	21,639	21,875	25,364	30,233
	% GR 4	11.2	1.8	4.7	3.2	5.7	5.8
	CC 5	1,261	1,316	1,397	1,467	1,625	1,825
	SC 6	30	1,970	2,325	2,536	2,825	4,305
34 Igreja Batista Regular	1	417	428	742	843	954	1,435
	2	436	465	828	839	1,213	1,552
	3	58	54	66	100	40	144
	4	4.6	8.6	11.6	6.5	27.1	8.2
	5	8	7	9	9	12	14
	6	4	11	21	15	21	24
35 Igreja Batista Restrita	1	189	278	246	304	448	909
	2	235	297	214	306	693	937
	3	22	24	1	74	37	67
	4	24.3	6.8	-13.0	.7	54.7	2.5
	5	4	8	5	7	7	9
	6	0	10	7	8	12	7
36 Missão Batista Da Fé	1	518	330	399	432	487	0
	2	633	341	408	442	498	0
	3	15	4	6	4	4	0
	4	22.2	3.3	2.3	2.3	2.3	.0
	5	3	2	2	2	2	0
	6	0	3	8	8	9	0
37 Igreja Cristã Batista Biblica	1	625	118	0	0	15	151
	2	648	88	0	0	21	147
	3	0	41	0	0	0	10
	4	3.7	-25.4	.0	.0	40.0	-2.6
	5	1	1	0	0	1	2
	6	0	1	0	0	1	2
64 Igreja Batista Revelação	1	0	0	0	0	59	547
	2	0	11	0	23	57	800
	3	0	2	0	2	5	21
	4	.0	.0	.0	.0	-3.4	46.3
	5	0	1	0	1	7	8
	6	0	1	0	1	7	9
CONGREGATIONAL 52 Igreja Evangélica Congregacional Cristã Do Brasil	1	27,895	25,586	26,168	27,939	33,507	50,737
	2	30,496	26,107	27,705	28,980	36,648	56,386
	3	2,223	3,004	2,516	1,842	2,767	3,457
	4	9.3	2.0	5.9	3.7	9.4	11.1
	5	247	217	230	247	273	367
	6	8	377	438	490	530	748
EPISCOPALIAN 56 Igreja Episcopal Brasileira	1	8,414	11,699	14,207	15,334	15,225	16,377
	2	9,640	12,713	15,522	15,820	15,809	16,724
	3	350	634	595	1,813	716	776
	4	14.6	8.7	9.3	3.2	3.8	2.1
	5	63	70	78	85	83	83
	6	1	92	128	135	130	152
LUTHERANS [7] 31 Igreja Evangélica De Confissão Luterana	1	285,784	440,780	507,323	480,060	537,089	618,107
	2	294,685	445,957	520,773	489,355	538,110	625,576
	3	7,332	13,028	12,799	11,748	14,915	5,978
	4	3.1	1.2	2.7	1.9	.2	1.2
	5	1,435	194	238	221	238	273
	6	0	921	1,108	1,124	1,213	1,673
32 Igreja Evangélica Luterana Do Brasil 8	1	273,301	122,338	113,895	163,970	152,775	76,581
	2	283,850	128,079	117,389	169,507	154,065	77,728
	3	5,885	5,224	6,479	5,709	8,156	3,708
	4	3.9	4.7	3.1	3.4	.8	1.5
	5	577	140	134	156	152	91
	6	0	526	561	713	743	388
METHODISTS 48 Igreja Metodista	1	46,711	51,463	53,007	54,633	56,785	57,273
	2	50,261	51,603	54,379	55,627	57,630	58,118
	3	4,709	7,872	6,363	5,701	5,797	6,846
	4	7.6	.3	2.6	7.8	1.5	1.5
	5	314	269	298	307	324	343
	6	0	516	587	639	644	665

TABLE 4-1 Continued

GROWTH OF PROTESTANT MEMBERSHIP BY DENOMINATIONS IN PERIODS, 1955 to 1966

NAME OF DENOMINATION / GROWTH PERIODS	1955	1957	1959	1961	1963	1965
	1956	1958	1960	1962	1964	1966
	EXCL	EXCL	EXCL	EXCL	EXCL	EXCL
	% GR	% GR	% GR	% GR	% GR	% GR
	CC	CC	CC	CC	CC	CC
	SC	SC	SC	SC	SC	SC
49 Igreja Metodista Livre	198	212	720	444	445	307
	255	265	818	397	471	350
	1	11	53	97	48	2
	28.8	25.0	13.6	-10.6	5.8	14.0
	6	5	9	4	8	5
	0	5	9	9	10	13
50 Igreja Evangélica Holiness Do Brasil	133	193	378	614	841	367
	162	270	483	615	876	468
	0	13	23	60	62	82
	21.8	39.9	27.8	.2	4.2	31.1
	4	8	8	10	9	8
	0	9	11	16	24	16
51 Irmandade Metodista Ortodoxo	422	666	1,248	283	421	202
	442	675	1,430	291	448	236
	18	49	90	108	51	14
	4.7	1.4	14.6	2.8	6.4	16.8
	5	6	5	3	4	3
	0	6	11	3	4	3
PRESBYTERIANS 38 Igreja Presbiteriana Do Brasil	135,902	156,524	163,999	167,709	176,444	179,142
	146,042	163,451	168,709	171,405	177,391	183,808
	7,880	11,939	12,977	13,411	16,397	14,960
	7.5	4.4	2.9	2.2	.5	2.6
	786	681	758	769	837	896
	20	1,345	1,495	1,663	1,755	2,174
39 Igreja Presbiteriana Independente	36,435	37,531	39,445	42,444	44,096	40,494
	39,352	38,629	39,558	43,089	44,777	40,692
	1,220	2,559	3,223	2,223	2,715	3,500
	8.0	2.9	.3	1.5	1.5	.5
	207	186	197	201	221	225
	3	333	331	365	403	387
40 Igreja Presbiteriana Conservadora Do Brasil	1,989	2,227	1,406	1,787	852	449
	2,173	2,372	1,011	1,424	812	594
	78	100	505	453	92	45
	9.3	6.5	-28.1	-20.3	-4.7	32.3
	19	20	16	17	13	11
	0	33	23	26	18	22
41 Igreja Presbiteriana Fundamentalista	339	521	233	634	775	752
	372	652	277	556	812	776
	27	37	0	96	48	8
	9.7	25.1	18.9	-12.3	4.8	3.2
	4	6	4	6	9	7
	0	12	6	8	9	10
42 Igreja Reformada	7,409	7,930	5,037	8,255	8,263	8,395
	7,496	7,964	8,046	8,288	8,412	8,429
	4	96	86	82	46	32
	1.2	.4	59.7	.4	1.8	.4
	3	4	3	5	4	4
	0	11	4	9	5	9
7th DAY ADVENTISTS 43 Adventista Do Sétimo Dia	31,294	35,501	40,647	52,194	63,836	64,817
	33,561	37,746	43,625	57,526	70,544	73,583
	2,809	3,466	3,751	4,227	4,781	4,214
	7.2	6.3	7.3	10.2	10.5	13.5
	489	373	396	379	409	438
	4	559	636	806	876	997
44 Adventista Da Promessa	226	393	789	1,872	3,403	5,657
	264	523	1,037	2,385	3,619	6,006
	12	20	43	42	142	424
	16.8	33.1	30.8	27.4	6.3	6.3
	5	7	11	15	22	35
	0	7	26	39	65	111
45 Adventista Da Reforma	386	230	145	72	108	62
	360	215	102	78	69	123
	40	26	71	0	46	25
	-6.7	-32.8	-29.7	8.3	-36.1	98.4
	4	4	4	2	3	4
	0	4	8	3	4	5

TABLE 4-1 Continued

GROWTH OF PROTESTANT MEMBERSHIP BY DENOMINATIONS IN PERIODS, 1955 to 1966

NAME OF DENOMINATION \ GROWTH PERIODS	1955 1956 EXCL % GR CC SC	1957 1958 EXCL % GR CC SC	1959 1960 EXCL % GR CC SC	1961 1962 EXCL % GR CC SC	1963 1964 EXCL % GR CC SC	1965 1966 EXCL % GR CC SC
46 Adventista Da Reforma Completa	21	114	133	231	0	278
	20	209	194	235	0	278
	3	7	3	14	0	0
	-4.8	83.3	45.9	107	.0	.0
	1	3	2	2	0	1
	0	3	2	4	0	1
47 Adventista Apostolica	61	0	0	0	210	166
	61	0	0	0	210	66
	1	0	0	0	0	100
	.0	.0	.0	.0	.0	-60.2
	1	0	0	0	1	1
	0	0	0	0	6	5
OTHERS (TRADITIONAL) 54 Igreja Evangélica Menonita	441	486	686	580	809	1,078
	495	472	769	572	844	1,530
	6	58	37	60	160	122
	12.2	-2.9	12.1	-1.4	4.3	41.9
	3	5	10	9	12	12
	0	7	17	16	20	28
55 Igreja Dos Irmãos	135	148	349	410	697	699
	117	199	369	420	799	674
	33	11	33	8	53	106
	-13.3	34.5	5.7	2.4	14.6	-3.6
	4	7	7	7	14	12
	0	9	12	11	25	23
58 Exercito De Salvação	3,402	3,035	1,451	2,156	2,970	2,520
	3,310	5,851	1,854	2,568	2,701	2,827
	765	207	178	228	430	205
	-2.7	92.8	27.8	19.1	-9.1	12.2
	20	18	22	22	19	18
	0	28	72	27	24	21
59 Igreja De Cristo	1,165	2,002	1,459	2,231	1,691	2,671
	1,190	1,916	1,849	2,578	1,866	3,167
	77	212	10	137	258	292
	2.1	-4.3	26.7	15.6	10.3	18.6
	10	14	18	20	20	27
	3	20	24	30	35	48
60 Igreja Cristianismo Decidido	137	127	133	229	293	172
	163	140	136	228	239	183
	0	1	7	3	66	20
	19.0	10.2	2.3	-.4	-18.4	6.4
	2	2	2	3	4	4
	0	4	5	6	7	6
61 Igreja De Nosso Senhor Jesus Cristo	0	0	0	194	0	644
	0	0	0	240	25	631
	0	0	0	1	1	203
	.0	.0	.0	23.7	.0	-2.0
	0	0	0	2	1	8
	0	0	0	2	1	14
62 Igreja Nazareno	378	675	773	8,716	705	844
	475	772	790	8,692	721	1,210
	8	22	0	110	120	96
	25.7	14.4	7.8	-.3	2.3	43.4
	2	2	4	6	9	15
	0	5	13	16	18	46
63 Igreja Evangélica Neo-Testementario	322	392	424	393	514	299
	335	431	542	423	544	389
	16	20	8	4	62	24
	4.0	9.9	27.8	7.6	5.8	30.1
	4	4	6	5	7	5
	0	4	8	5	11	8
65 Missão Amazonas	0	0	0	199	204	0
	0	0	0	204	239	0
	0	0	0	10	3	0
	.0	.0	.0	2.5	17.2	.0
	0	0	0	1	1	0
	0	1	0	4	4	0

TABLE 4-1 Continued

GROWTH OF PROTESTANT MEMBERSHIP BY DENOMINATIONS IN PERIODS, 1955 to 1966

GROWTH PERIODS / NAME OF DENOMINATION	1955	1957	1959	1961	1963	1965
	1956	1958	1960	1962	1964	1966
	EXCL	EXCL	EXCL	EXCL	EXCL	EXCL
	% GR	% GR	% GR	% GR	% GR	% GR
	CC	CC	CC	CC	CC	CC
	SC	SC	SC	SC	SC	SC
66 Casa De Oração	473	404	323	745	1,564	1,576
	472	439	346	693	1,383	2,117
	19	16	6	91	166	95
	-.2	8.7	7.1	-7.0	-8.1	34.3
	6	5	5	7	10	19
	0	5	5	8	10	215
67 Irmandade Dos Vearadores Cristãos	10	17	37	11	13	20
	10	24	58	14	11	17
	0	1	4	1	2	3
	.0	41.2	56.8	27.3	-15.4	-15.0
	1	1	1	1	1	1
	0	1	2	1	1	1
68 Darbista	0	35	26	20	396	21
	0	35	22	20	409	22
	0	0	8	0	5	2
	.0	.0	-15.4	.0	3.3	4.8
	0	1	1	1	3	1
	0	1	1	1	3	1
69 Igreja União Evangélica	11,349	16,983	24,762	20,251	33,271	25,402
	12,203	17,345	26,683	20,746	33,292	28,029
	344	868	759	654	757	1,230
	7.5	2.1	7.8	2.4	.1	10.3
	65	65	63	63	74	90
	0	99	123	150	202	352
71 Igreja Cristã Apostólica	71	63	202	447	635	59
	62	59	375	553	725	63
	33	25	18	11	48	7
	-12.7	-6.3	65.6	23.7	14.2	40.7
	1	2	2	3	2	2
	0	2	8	11	10	2
72 Igreja Missionária Do Brasil	9	12	8	66	371	290
	9	4	12	66	490	338
	0	8	3	8	36	54
	.0	-66.7	50.0	.0	32.1	16.6
	1	1	1	2	7	6
	0	1	1	2	10	10
75 Igreja Biblica Do Paraguai	0	0	0	49	71	112
	0	0	28	60	58	114
	0	0	0	1	15	6
	.0	.0	.0	22.4	-18.3	1.8
	0	0	1	1	1	1
	0	0	1	1	1	2
76 Culto Da Missão Evangelizadora	0	0	5	0	8	71
	0	0	56	0	51	40
	0	0	0	0	11	1
	.0	.0	20.0	.0	537.5	90.5
	0	0	2	0	1	1
	0	0	6	0	1	1
77 Igreja Bíblica	53	66	0	152	1,023	4,575
	70	67	0	108	1,288	5,443
	0	5	0	69	112	568
	32.1	1.5	0	-28.9	25.9	19.0
	1	1	0	3	15	30
	0	1	0	3	29	79
78 Campanha Nacional De Evangelização	0	0	0	0	0	0
	0	0	97	0	0	0
	0	0	0	0	0	0
	.0	.0	.0	.0	.0	.0
	0	0	1	0	0	0
	0	0		0	0	0
80 Igreja Evangélica Interdenominacional	193	165	205	282	267	206
	213	250	317	240	266	257
	0	1	0	1	31	5
	10.4	51.5	54.6	-14.9	1.5	24.8
	3	2	3	4	5	4
	0	3	6	5	6	5

GROWTH OF PROTESTANT MEMBERSHIP BY DENOMINATIONS IN PERIODS, 1955 to 1966

GROWTH PERIODS / NAME OF DENOMINATION	1955 1956 EXCL % GR CC SC	1957 1958 EXCL % GR CC SC	1959 1960 EXCL % GR CC SC	1961 1962 EXCL % GR CC SC	1963 1964 EXCL % GR CC SC	1965 1966 EXCL % GR CC SC
84 Igreja Cristã Primitiva	766	922	766	1,169	1,098	941
	865	955	791	1,281	1,041	960
	0	13	14	23	111	15
	12.9	3.6	3.3	7.9	-5.2	2.0
	4	4	5	6	6	7
	0	6	7	16	14	12
93 Igreja Nova Apostólica	0	0	0	0	10	572
	0	0	0	0	9	577
	0	0	0	0	1	4
	.0	.0	.0	.0	-10.0	.9
	0	0	0	0	1	2
	0	0	0	0	1	3
94 Igreja Apostólica Brasileira	0	0	0	0	300	0
	0	0	0	0	400	0
	0	0	0	0	0	0
	.0	.0	.0	.0	33.3	.0
	0	0	0	0	1	0
	0	0	0	0	1	0
97 Associação Cristã Interdenominacional	48	0	0	0	0	0
	51	0	0	0	0	0
	0	0	0	0	0	0
	6.3	.0	.0	.0	.0	.0
	1	1	1	0	0	0
	0	1	1	0	0	0
98 Igreja Monte Das Oliveiras	258	0	0	0	0	0
	263	0	0	0	0	0
	22	0	0	0	0	0
	1.9	.0	.0	.0	.0	.0
	1	0	0	0	0	0
	0	0	0	0	0	0
99 Instituição Evangélica Do Brasil	42	62	63	63	48	68
	46	66	68	50	58	66
	0	4	1	14	1	10
	9.8	6.5	7.9	-20.9	20.8	-2.9
	1	1	1	1	1	1
	0	1	1	2	2	2
ASSEMBLY OF GOD 1 Assembléia De Deus	255,954	323,042	386,879	426,197	511,812	579,653
	290,902	356,572	426,974	452,850	553,358	636,370
	13,074	22,168	24,526	23,416	29,666	35,382
	13.7	10.4	10.4	6.3	8.1	8.7
	1,100	1,003	1,083	1,168	1,246	1,291
	26	2,620	3,687	4,336	5,332	9,399
CONGREGAÇÃO CRISTÃ 2 Congregação Cristã No Brasil	41,515	154,517	173,712	191,558	236,063	266,484
	123,195	172,073	186,547	205,415	255,827	282,233
	2,607	8,188	7,556	7,769	12,136	13,030
	34.6	11.4	7.4	7.2	8.4	5.9
	450	506	612	686	796	826
	0	750	844	1,005	1,348	1,546
OTHERS (PENTECOSTAL) 4 Igreja Evangélho Quadrangular	1,577	2,605	6,187	11,956	14,528	20,869
	2,080	3,310	10,209	12,842	16,341	25,071
	48	488	291	423	1,183	769
	31.9	27.1	65.0	7.4	12.5	20.1
	7	9	20	29	39	57
	0	21	41	66	72	127
5 Cruzada Nacional De Evangelização	0	1,576	2,081	2,418	2,633	3,624
	0	1,793	2,053	2,540	2,982	4,912
	0	50	249	220	125	372
	.0	13.6	-1.1	5.0	13.3	35.5
	0	7	11	15	19	24
	0	0	12	17	24	44
6 Igreja Evangélica Do Avivamento Bíblico	82	1,244	2,515	3,273	2,129	52
	111	1,454	3.162	1,672	2,298	58
	7	57	78	801	240	2
	35.4	16.9	25.7	-48.9	7.9	11.5
	4	10	13	8	12	1
	0	36	57	25	34	4

GROWTH OF PROTESTANT MEMBERSHIP BY DENOMINATIONS IN PERIODS, 1955 to 1966

NAME OF DENOMINATION / GROWTH PERIODS	1955	1957	1959	1961	1963	1965
	1956	1958	1960	1962	1964	1966
	EXCL	EXCL	EXCL	EXCL	EXCL	EXCL
	% GR	% GR	% GR	% GR	% GR	% GR
	CC	CC	CC	CC	CC	CC
	SC	SC	SC	SC	SC	SC
7 Cruzada Bíblica Sagrada	0	40	80	164	305	416
	0	50	106	181	344	309
	0	0	2	8	11	113
	.0	25.0	32.5	10.4	12.8	-25.7
	0	2	1	4	6	3
	0	3	1	4	7	3
8 Igreja Pentecostal Independente	1,735	289	703	68	500	0
	1,939	303	795	80	503	0
	75	50	50	2	26	0
	11.8	4.8	13.1	17.6	.6	.0
	13	5	7	4	4	1
	0	8	14	4	6	1
9 Igreja Pentecostal De Oracão	2,492	163	123	585	189	0
	2,631	204	135	619	217	0
	165	19	5	18	8	0
	5.6	25.2	9.8	5.8	14.8	.0
	16	3	2	8	2	0
	0	4	2	19	2	0
10 Igreja Apostólica Evangélica	168	0	7	0	17	175
	198	0	11	15	14	337
	0	0	0	0	5	3
	17.9	.0	57.1	.0	-17.5	89.7
	1	0	1	1	1	2
	0	0	1	1	1	19
11 Assembléia De Deus Missão Batista	400	0	0	0	439	0
	199	0	0	0	490	0
	220	0	0	0	51	0
	-50.3	.0	.0	.0	11.6	.0
	1	0	0	0	3	0
	0	0	0	0	12	0
12 Igreja Cristã Pentecostal Do Brasil	1,224	2,163	1,661	2,134	3,284	774
	1,296	2,169	1,799	2,406	3,593	1,329
	34	255	50	114	174	39
	5.9	.3	8.3	12.7	9.4	71.7
	7	10	6	8	12	10
	0	25	12	23	27	16
13 Igreja Cristã Pentecostal De Evangelização	0	117	0	0	159	0
	0	281	0	0	195	0
	0	5	0	0	12	0
	.0	140.2	.0	.0	22.6	.0
	0	1	1	1	1	1
	0	8	2	1	3	1
14 Cruzada Evangélica De Salvação	0	0	0	0	0	70
	0	0	0	0	0	108
	0	0	0	0	0	2
	.0	.0	.0	.0	.0	54.3
	0	2	2	1	0	2
	0	2	2	1	0	2
15 Igreja De Cristo Pentecostal	230	104	591	804	1,875	2,549
	238	131	692	882	1,839	2,528
	18	9	43	86	272	576
	3.5	26.0	17.1	9.7	-1.9	-.8
	2	2	6	5	14	19
	0	3	26	22	35	56
16 Igreja De Deus Pentecostal Do Brasil	133	227	745	1,238	1,409	3,655
	141	237	839	1,242	1,578	3,927
	0	8	104	123	220	404
	6.0	2.2	12.6	.3	12.0	7.3
	2	4	13	18	20	27
	0	5	13	21	34	151
17 Igreja Evangélica Apostólica	211	0	0	146	656	26
	220	0	0	153	749	23
	0	0	0	3	15	5
	4.3	.0	.0	4.8	14.2	-11.5
	2	0	1	2	5	1
	0	0	1	4	6	2

GROWTH OF PROTESTANT MEMBERSHIP BY DENOMINATIONS IN PERIODS, 1955 to 1966

NAME OF DENOMINATION / GROWTH PERIODS	1955	1957	1959	1961	1963	1965
	1956	1958	1960	1962	1964	1966
	EXCL	EXCL	EXCL	EXCL	EXCL	EXCL
	% GR	% GR	% GR	% GR	% GR	% GR
	CC	CC	CC	CC	CC	CC
	SC	SC	SC	SC	SC	SC
18 Igreja O Brasil Para Cristo	3,118	4,397	11,534	13,028	18,214	79,361
	3,381	4,849	14,101	14,569	23,046	93,096
	592	210	777	724	968	2,405
	8.4	10.6	22.5	12.0	26.1	14.3
	31	35	51	58	92	108
	0	75	120	152	251	359
19 Igreja Evangélica Pentecostal Livre	209	341	36	106	297	50
	190	342	40	196	197	57
	28	19	12	6	145	0
	-9.1	.3	11.1	84.9	-33.7	14.0
	2	3	1	1	1	2
	0	3	1	5	3	2
20 Missão Evangélica Pentecostal	157	253	220	372	312	416
	220	275	241	401	366	732
	4	11	17	24	7	21
	40.1	8.7	9.5	7.8	17.3	76.0
	3	4	4	6	3	5
	2	4	4	6	3	238
21 Igreja Messiánico Mundial Do Brasil	0	0	0	0	756	0
	0	0	0	0	944	117
	0	0	0	0	125	1
	.0	.0	.0	.0	24.9	.0
	0	0	0	0	1	1
	0	0	0	0	1	2
22 Assembleía De Deus Presbiteriana	475	406	270	351	374	0
	556	406	291	316	419	0
	1	0	5	41	78	0
	16.8	.0	7.8	-10.0	12.0	.0
	4	4	7	5	5	0
	0	4	7	5	5	0
23 Igreja Pentecostal	615	2,298	1,642	2,236	2,072	5,472
	924	2,370	1,703	2,301	2,843	7,402
	55	221	258	137	170	341
	50.2	3.1	3.7	2.9	37.2	35.3
	8	17	11	13	20	21
	1	24	25	34	57	26
JEHOVAH'S WITNESSES 53 Testemunhas de Jeova	2,578	4,007	5,586	6,019	9,560	12,061
	2,919	4,306	6,292	6,861	10,198	13,539
	237	491	709	490	1,208	1,243
	13.2	7.5	12.6	14.0	6.7	12.3
	41	73	100	108	155	200
	0	95	132	120	166	235
MORMONS 57 Igreja De Jesus Cristo Dos Santos Dos Últimos Dias	484	995	1,100	2,335	4,989	10,188
	609	1,166	1,517	2,994	6,061	12,606
	2	33	43	88	517	616
	25.8	17.2	37.9	28.2	21.5	23.7
	11	19	24	26	29	30
	0	19	27	30	33	41
CHRISTIAN SCIENCE 70 Congregação Da Ciencia Cristá	61	63	68	135	76	74
	66	67	67	174	76	74
	12	2	1	4	9	1
	8.2	6.3	-1.5	28.9	.0	.0
	2	2	2	4	2	2
	0	2	2	4	2	2

NOTES TO TABLE 4-1

1. Membership as of December 31st of this year.

2. Membership as of December 31st of this year.

3. EXCL Denote exclusions that occurred for any reason during the period.

4. % GR The percentage growth rate in the particular period.

5. CC Means the number of central churches of a particular denomination in the specific period being considered.

6. SC This abbreviation indicates the number of satellite churches and congregations that are connected in different ways to the central churches.

7. A reduction has been made for the non-communicant membership reported by the Lutheran churches.

8. Examination of membership totals year by year for the Igreja Evangélica Luterana do Brasil indicates that some volunteer transcribers confused this church with the Igreja Evangélica de Confissão Luterana.

9. Data for 1961 and 1962 was transcribed by error resulting in a computer report in thousands rather than hundreds of members.

10. Incomplete reporting may account for the wide margin between membership reported for 1965 and 1966 in comparison with that for other years.

The thirteen denominational family groups were divided into three categories. Category I is called the "traditional" denominations. These are churches mentioned previously that have been established in Brazil for decades and are considered to be the old-line historical churches of Protestantism. Lutherans, Presbyterians, Baptists, and "others" are included in the first category. Category II is the Pentecostal family of churches. This category includes the different denominations that emphasize the doctrine of the Holy Spirit and follow the experience of the Apostolic church in the New Testament. Three Pentecostal groups are brought together in this category, the Congregação Cristã no Brasil, the Assemblies of God, and all the Independent Pentecostal churches that comprise group number ten. Category III is given the name "sects" and includes the Seventh-Day Adventists, Latter-day Saints (Mormons), and Jehovah's Witnesses. Several Adventist denominations are brought together to form the Sabbath observance type of denomination.

The designation of "others" includes many smaller denominations whose size could not permit them to be classified easily with other groupings. The term "sects" was chosen for lack of a more descriptive word that was suitable. This group includes these religious groups regarded by the majority of Protestants to be outside of the traditional Protestant denominational pattern.

The government religious census recorded 1,527,200* communicant members in all Protestant churches in Brazil as of January 1, 1960, (Table 4-2). At that time, all of the traditional Protestant denominations made up 62 percent of this membership and the Pentecostal groups 38 percent. By 1970, the total membership had increased by one million members. The Pentecostal churches had increased to almost the same membership found in the traditional Protestant denominations (Table 4-3). In 1960 the Assemblies of God, with a membership of 376,800, held a margin of 10,000 over the Lutheran Church. This margin had increased to 313,000 by 1970.

During this same period, the Assemblies of God grew to 746,000 members, while the Lutheran adult communicant membership increased to 433,000. The Congregação Cristã, though limited primarily to the Southeast and South Regions, grew from 178,000 members in 1960 to 358,000 in 1970. The "other" Pentecostal groups exhibited a remarkable growth from 33,500 to 191,000 members.

---

*This includes only adult communicant membership.

TABLE 4-2

ESTIMATED DISTRIBUTION OF PROTESTANT COMMUNICANT MEMBERS
OF DENOMINATIONAL GROUPS AND REGIONS FOR BRAZIL, JANUARY 1, 1960

Denominational Group	Protestant Communicant Members					Brazil	
	North	North-east	South-east	South	Central-West		
	No.	No.	No.	No.	No.	No.	%
TRADITIONAL							
Baptist	3,500	42,950	121,900	13,450	5,100	186,900	12.2%
Congregational	0	5,300	13,500	3,850	3,550	26,200	1.7
Episcopalian	50	300	4,150	9,700	0	14,200	0.9
Lutheran	0	200	35,950	329,950	50	366,150	24.0
Methodist	0	100	42,750	11,750	1,250	55,850	3.7
Presbyterian	1,800	31,300	143,550	23,250	11,000	210,900	13.8
7th Day Adventist	3,300	4,500	21,300	11,500	1,950	42,550	2.8
Other	1,600	3,700	10,550	19,000	1,050	35,900	2.4
Sub-total	10,250	88,350	393,650	422,450	23,950	938,650	61.5
PENTECOSTAL							
Assemblies of God	36,850	113,700	154,450	55,950	15,850	376,800	24.6%
Congregaçao Crista	0	400	145,600	31,150	1,100	178,250	11.7
Other	300	4,400	23,900	4,550	350	33,500	2.2
Sub-total	37,150	118,500	323,950	91,650	17,300	588,550	38.5
GRAND TOTAL	47,400	206,850	717,600	514,100	41,250	1,527,200	100.0%

Source: Based on membership statistics, *Estatística do Culto Protestante do Brasil*, 1959-60, I.B.G.E.

TABLE 4-3

ESTIMATED DISTRIBUTION OF PROTESTANT COMMUNICANT MEMBERS
OF DENOMINATIONAL GROUPS AND REGIONS FOR BRAZIL, JANUARY 1, 1970

Denominational Group	Protestant Communicant Members					Brazil	
	North	North-east	South-east	South	Central-West		
	No.	No.	No.	No.	No.	No.	%
TRADITIONAL							
Baptist	9,400	76,700	201,850	29,950	12,600	330,500	12.6%
Congregational	0	11,400	19,350	10,450	4,900	46,100	1.8
Episcopalian	150	200	3,650	16,100	50	20,150	0.8
Lutheran	0	150	43,700	388,550	600	433,000	16.4
Methodist	0	400	45,800	14,500	1,800	62,500	2.4
Presbyterian	2,300	35,100	159,200	28,600	18,850	244,050	9.3
7th Day Adventist	8,150	19,100	47,750	36,500	7,600	119,100	4.5
Other	3,950	7,500	17,600	39,100	4,500	72,650	2.8
Sub-total	23,950	150,550	538,900	563,750	50,900	1,328,050	50.6
PENTECOSTAL							
Assemblies of God	70,100	191,050	297,300	136,350	51,600	746,400	28.5%
Congregação Cristã	0	1,050	241,450	105,000	10,300	357,800	13.6
Other	850	10,800	150,350	21,300	8,000	191,300	7.3
Sub-total	70,950	202,900	689,100	262,650	69,900	1,295,500	49.4
GRAND TOTAL	94,900	353,450	1,228,000	826,400	120,800	2,623,550	100.0%

Among the traditional denominations, the Baptists moved ahead of the Presbyterians into second place behind the Lutherans with a growth from 187,000 in 1960 to 330,000 in 1970. The Seventh-Day Adventists almost tripled in this period, ending 1970 with 119,000 members. The growth of the Congregationalists, Episcopalians, and Methodists was comparatively small.

Comparative Growth Rates of the Protestant Churches by Groups

The average annual growth rates by denominational groups for the period 1960-1970 show considerable variation from one region to another (Table 4-4). This fluctuation is generally due to the relative size of membership. If comparisons are made between the 1960 and 1970 membership in Tables 4-2 and 4-3, the higher growth rates will usually be found where the membership base in 1960 was relatively small. For instance, the Lutheran Church in the Central-West grew from 50 members in 1960 to 600 in 1970, thus showing a 28.2 percent rate. Similarly, the "other" Pentecostal groups grew from 350 members in 1960 to 8,000 in 1970.

The Lutherans, Presbyterians, and Methodists each had average annual rates of growth of less than two percent during the decade of the 1960's. This was considerably below the reported population rate of 2.9 percent.* The Seventh-Day Adventists with 10.9 percent led the traditional denominations. The Congregational, Baptist, and "other" traditional groups also had average rates in excess of five percent.

The Pentecostal churches with an average annual rate of 8.2 percent were by far the fastest growing group. The independent Pentecostal churches were growing at the fastest average rate, 19.1 percent, followed by the Congregação Cristã with 7.2 percent, and the Assemblies of God with 7.1 percent.

ANALYSIS BY REGIONS

North Region

The membership of the principal denominations in the North by states as of January 1, 1960 and January 1, 1970 is shown in Tables 4-5a and Table 4-5b.

---

*IBGE: 1970 Census of Brazil related to 1960 Census.

TABLE 4-4

AVERAGE ANNUAL GROWTH OF PROTESTANT COMMUNICANT MEMBERS BY DENOMINATIONAL GROUPS AND REGIONS IN BRAZIL FOR 1960 - 1970

Denominational Groups	Regions					Brazil
	North	North-east	South-east	South	Central-West	
	%	%	%	%	%	%
TRADITIONAL						
Baptist	10.4	5.8	5.2	8.4	9.5	5.9
Congregational	-	8.0	3.7	10.5	3.3	5.8
Episcopalian	11.7	4.2	Neg.	5.2	*	3.6
Lutheran	-	Neg.	1.9	1.7	*	1.7
Methodist	-	14.9	0.7	2.1	3.7	1.1
Presbyterian	2.5	1.1	1.0	2.1	5.5	1.5
7th-Day Adventist	9.5	15.6	8.4	12.3	14.6	10.9
Other	9.5	7.4	5.3	7.5	15.7	7.3
Sub-total	8.9	5.5	3.2	2.9	7.9	3.5
PENTECOSTAL						
Assemblies of God	6.7	5.3	6.8	9.4	12.6	7.1
Congregação Cristã	-	10.2	5.2	13.0	25.2	7.2
Other	11.0	9.4	20.2	16.8	*	19.1
Sub-total	6.7	5.6	7.9	11.3	15.0	8.2
GRAND TOTAL	7.2	5.5	5.5	4.9	11.4	5.6

Neg. - Negative

* Unusually high rate of growth

Source: The compound interest rate formula was applied to the data in Tables 4-2 and 4-3 to determine the average annual growth rate from January 1, 1960 to January 1, 1970.

TABLE 4-5a

ESTIMATED DISTRIBUTION OF PROTESTANT COMMUNICANT MEMBERS
BY DENOMINATIONAL GROUPS AND STATES FOR THE NORTH REGION, JANUARY 1, 1960

Denominational Groups	States						Region	
	Rondônia	Acre	Amazonas	Roraima	Pará	Amapá		
	Number	Number	Number	Number	Number	Number	Number	Percent
TRADITIONAL								
Baptist	150	600	1,100	100	1,450	100	3,500	7.3
Congregational	0	0	0	0	0	0	0	0.0
Episcopalian	0	0	0	0	50	0	50	0.1
Lutheran	0	0	0	0	0	0	0	0.0
Methodist	0	0	0	0	0	0	0	0.0
Presbyterian	0	0	150	50	1,450	150	1,800	3.8
7th-Day Adventist	0	0	1,550	0	1,650	100	3,300	7.0
Other	0	450	550	0	500	100	1,600	3.4
Sub-total	150	1,050	3,350	150	5,100	450	10,250	21.6
PENTECOSTAL								
Assemblies of God	2,500	2,450	3,250	450	27,250	950	36,850	77.8
Congregação Cristã	0	0	0	0	0	0	0	0.0
Other	0	0	100	0	200	0	300	0.6
Sub-total	2,500	2,450	3,350	450	27,450	950	37,150	78.4
GRAND TOTAL	2,650	3,500	6,700	600	32,550	1,400	47,400	100.0

Source: Based on membership statistics, Estatística do Culto Protestante do Brasil, 1959-60, I.B.G.E., adjusted to state totals as of December 31, 1959.

TABLE 4-5b

ESTIMATED DISTRIBUTION OF PROTESTANT COMMUNICANT MEMBERS
BY DENOMINATIONAL GROUPS AND STATES FOR THE NORTH REGION, JANUARY 1, 1970

Denominational Groups	States						Region	
	Rondônia	Acre	Amazonas	Roraima	Pará	Amapá		
	Number	Number	Number	Number	Number	Number	Number	Percent
TRADITIONAL								
Baptist	300	1,200	4,050	100	3,650	100	9,400	9.9
Congregational	0	0	0	0	0	0	·0	0.0
Episcopalian	0	0	0	0	150	0	150	0.2
Lutheran	0	0	0	0	0	0	0	0.0
Methodist	0	0	0	0	0	0	0	0.0
Presbyterian	100	0	400	50	1,550	200	2,300	2.4
7th-Day Adventist	150	50	3,700	50	4,000	200	8,150	8.6
Other	0	0	1,100	0	2,650	200	3,950	4.2
Sub-total	550	1,250	9,250	200	12,000	700	23,950	25.3
PENTECOSTAL								
Assemblies of God	3,550	6,600	6,200	1,800	48,350	3,600	70,100	73.8
Congregação Cristã	0	0	0	0	0	0	0	0.0
Other	0	0	500	0	350	0	850	0.9
Sub-total	3,550	6,600	6,700	1,800	48,700	3,600	70,950	74.7
GRAND TOTAL	4,100	7,850	15,950	2,000	60,700	4,300	94,900	100.0

Source: Based on projection of membership statistics, Estatística do Culto Protestante do Brasil, I.B.G.E., for 1955-66, adjusted to state totals as of December 31, 1969.

TABLE 4-6a

ESTIMATED DISTRIBUTION OF PROTESTANT COMMUNICANT MEMBERS
BY DENOMINATIONAL GROUPS AND STATES FOR THE NORTHEAST REGION, JANUARY 1, 1960

Denominational Groups	Protestant Communicant Members										
	Maranhão	Piaui	Ceará	Rio Grande do Norte	Paraiba	Pernambuco	Alagoas	Sergipe	Bahia	Northeast Region Total	
	Number	Number	Number	Number	Number	Number	Number	Number	Number	Number	Percent
TRADITIONAL											
Baptist	2,600	1,850	1,050	1,600	2,000	14,600	2,100	750	16,400	42,950	20.8
Congregational	0	0	450	50	2,150	2,000	50	150	450	5,300	2.6
Episcopalian	0	0	0	0	0	150	0	0	150	300	0.1
Lutheran	0	0	0	0	0	100	0	0	100	200	0.1
Methodist	0	0	0	0	0	0	0	0	100	100	-
Presbyterian	1,750	100	3,950	2,100	3,350	9,100	700	1,550	8,700	31,300	15.1
7th-Day Adventist	750	200	300	100	250	900	100	300	1,600	4,500	2.2
Other	1,850	50	250	1,000	0	400	0	0	150	3,700	1.8
Sub-total	6,950	2,200	6,000	4,850	7,750	27,250	2,950	2,750	27,650	88,350	42.7
PENTECOSTAL											
Assemblies of God	22,500	1,200	19,200	8,800	8,700	34,100	7,300	1,200	10,700	113,700	55.0
Congregação Cristã	0	0	0	0	0	50	150	100	100	400	0.2
Other	500	250	0	1,400	350	850	50	0	1,000	4,400	2.1
Sub-total	23,000	1,450	19,200	10,200	9,050	35,000	7,500	1,300	11,800	118,500	57.3
Total	29,950	3,650	25,200	15,050	16,800	62,250	10,450	4,050	39,450	206,850	100.0

Source: Based on membership statistics, *Estatística do Culto Protestante do Brasil*, 1959-60, I.B.G.E., adjusted to state totals as of December 31, 1959.

TABLE 4-6b

ESTIMATED DISTRIBUTION OF PROTESTANT COMMUNICANT MEMBERS
BY DENOMINATIONAL GROUPS AND STATES FOR THE NORTHEAST REGION, JANUARY 1, 1970

Denominational Groups	Protestant Communicant Members										
	Maranhão	Piaui	Ceará	Rio Grande do Norte	Paraiba	Pernambuco	Alagoas	Sergipe	Bahia	Northeast Region Total	
	Number	Number	Number	Number	Number	Number	Number	Number	Number	Number	Percent
TRADITIONAL											
Baptist	10,500	3,000	3,950	2,350	3,600	22,050	3,850	1,550	25,850	76,700	21.7
Congregational	0	0	550	50	3,000	4,000	300	900	2,600	11,400	3.2
Episcopalian	0	0	0	0	0	50	0	0	150	200	0.1
Lutheran	0	0	0	0	0	100	0	0	50	150	0.1
Methodist	0	0	0	0	0	100	0	0	300	400	0.1
Presbyterian	2,200	350	3,500	2,200	3,800	12,000	550	2,000	8,500	35,100	9.9
7th-Day Adventist	6,000	900	300	450	750	4,400	500	700	5,100	19,100	5.4
Other	3,300	250	1,800	900	0	650	50	50	500	7,500	2.1
Sub-total	22,000	4,500	10,100	5,950	11,150	43,350	5,250	5,200	43,050	150,550	42.6
PENTECOSTAL											
Assemblies of God	31,000	8,000	24,650	17,500	11,900	53,450	12,000	2,250	30,300	191,050	54.0
Congregação Cristã	300	0	0	0	150	150	0	150	300	1,050	0.3
Other	1,000	1,000	200	1,400	1,500	2,500	500	100	2,600	10,800	3.1
Sub-total	32,300	9,000	24,850	18,900	13,550	56,100	12,500	2,500	33,200	202,900	57.4
Total	54,300	13,500	34,950	24,850	24,700	99,450	17,750	7,700	76,250	353,450	100.0

Source: Based on projection of membership statistics, *Estatística do Culto Protestante do Brasil,* I.B.G.E., for 1955-66, adjusted to state totals as of December 31, 1969.

TABLE 4-7a

ESTIMATED DISTRIBUTION OF PROTESTANT COMMUNICANT MEMBERS
BY DENOMINATIONAL GROUPS AND STATES FOR THE SOUTHEAST REGION, JANUARY 1, 1960

Denominational Groups	States					Region	
	Minas Gerais	Espírito Santo	Rio de Janeiro	Guana-bara	São Paulo		
	Number	Number	Number	Number	Number	Number	Percent
TRADITIONAL							
Baptist	14,700	16,350	40,550	22,600	27,700	121,900	17.0
Congregational	1,350	2,000	5,000	3,050	2,100	13,500	1.9
Episcopalian	0	0	300	1,500	2,350	4,150	0.6
Lutheran	3,050	23,650	2,400	350	6,500	35,950	5.0
Methodist	8,450	2,700	5,900	4,500	21,200	42,750	6.0
Presbyterian	44,700	17,100	9,300	10,300	62,150	143,550	19.9
7th-Day Adventist	2,850	2,650	1,000	1,600	13,200	21,300	3.0
Other	2,800	100	700	2,650	4,300	10,550	1.5
Sub-total	77,900	64,550	65,150	46,550	139,500	393,650	54.9
PENTECOSTAL							
Assemblies of God	20,500	6,350	36,950	17,950	72,700	154,450	21.5
Congregação Cristã	5,200	0	750	650	139,000	145,600	20.3
Other	3,600	350	300	2,650	17,000	23,900	3.3
Sub-total	29,300	6,700	38,000	21,250	228,700	323,950	45.1
GRAND TOTAL	107,200	71,250	103,150	67,800	368,200	717,600	100.0

Source: Based on membership statistics, Estatística do Culto Protestante do Brasil, 1959-60, I.B.G.E., adjusted to state totals as of December 31, 1959.

TABLE 4-7b

ESTIMATED DISTRIBUTION OF PROTESTANT COMMUNICANT MEMBERS
BY DENOMINATIONAL GROUPS AND STATES FOR THE SOUTHEAST REGION, JANUARY 1, 1970

Denominational Groups	States					Region	
	Minas Gerais	Espírito Santo	Rio de Janeiro	Guana-bara	São Paulo		
	Number	Number	Number	Number	Number	Number	Percent
TRADITIONAL							
Baptist	27,000	25,000	71,850	37,000	41,000	201,850	16.4
Congregational	3,800	2,800	4,800	4,850	3,100	19,350	1.6
Episcopalian	50	0	300	1,400	1,900	3,650	0.3
Lutheran	2,750	30,400	2,800	1,150	6,600	43,700	3.6
Methodist	9,800	2,500	8,000	5,500	20,000	45,800	3.7
Presbyterian	52,700	15,000	14,000	10,500	67,000	159,200	13.0
7th-Day Adventist	8,500	5,250	3,200	2,800	28,000	47,750	3.9
Other	3,400	100	1,800	1,850	10,450	17,600	1.4
Sub-total	108,000	81,050	106,750	65,050	178,050	538,900	43.9
PENTECOSTAL							
Assemblies of God	57,000	14,000	80,800	36,500	109,000	297,300	24.2
Congregação Cristã	15,400	0	1,650	2,400	222,000	241,450	19.7
Other	8,600	7,000	1,300	5,450	128,000	150,350	12.2
Sub-total	81,000	21,000	83,750	44,350	459,000	689,100	56.1
GRAND TOTAL	189,000	102,050	190,500	109,400	637,050	1,228,000	100.0

Source: Based on projection of membership statistics, Estatística do Culto Protestante do Brasil, I.B.G.E., for 1955-66, adjusted to state totals as of December 31, 1969.

The Assemblies of God, with membership in every state and territory, had about three-fourths of the Protestants in the North on both of these dates. The proportion was a little lower in 1970 than in 1960, reflecting the increasing strength of the traditional denominations. The Assemblies of God membership grew from 37,000 to 70,000 during this ten-year period. Around 50,000 of these may be found today in the State of Pará where the response to the proclamation of the Gospel is still outstanding.

Northeast Region

The distribution of Protestant members by denominations and states in the Northeast as of January 1, 1960 and January 1, 1970 is shown in Tables 4-6a and 4-6b. The Assemblies of God, with 191,000 members in 1970, had more than the combined membership of all of the other denominational groups at the beginning and end of this period. They were strongest numerically in the State of Pernambuco but growing substantially in the other states of the region. The Baptists were in second place with 77,000 members in 1970, which represents more than one-half of the membership found in traditional churches. The Presbyterians hold third place, followed by the rapidly growing Seventh Day Adventists.

Southeast Region

The distribution of Protestant members by denominations and states in the Southeast as of January 1, 1960 and January 1, 1970 is shown in Tables 4-7a and 4-7b. At the beginning of this period, the membership of the traditional denominations was larger than that of the Pentecostals. By the end of the period the situation was reversed. The Assemblies of God with nearly 300,000 members are followed closely by the Congregação Cristã with more than 240,000. Both of these denominations are most numerous in the State of São Paulo. The Baptists have slightly over 200,000 members in this region, with more than one-half of these in the States of Rio de Janeiro and Guanabara (the city of Rio de Janeiro). The Presbyterians, with 159,000, have their largest membership in the State of São Paulo.

South Region

The distribution of Protestant members by denominations and states in the South as of January 1, 1960, and January 1, 1970, is shown in Tables 4-8a and 4-8b. The Lutherans alone had more than three times the communicant membership of all of the

TABLE 4-8a

ESTIMATED DISTRIBUTION OF PROTESTANT COMMUNICANT MEMBERS BY DENOMINATIONAL GROUPS AND STATES FOR THE SOUTH REGION, JANUARY 1, 1960

Denominational Groups	States Paraná	Santa Catarina	Rio Grande do Sul	Region	
	Number	Number	Number	Number	Percent
TRADITIONAL					
Baptist	7,200	700	5,550	13,450	2.6
Congregational	1,050	800	2,000	3,850	0.7
Episcopalian	200	950	8,550	9,700	1.9
Lutheran	13,300	99,500	217,150	329,950	64.3
Methodist	3,450	300	8,000	11,750	2.3
Presbyterian	20,500	2,750	0	23,250	4.5
7th-Day Adventist	5,050	1,550	4,900	11,500	2.2
Other	1,250	16,450	1,300	19,000	3.7
Sub-total	52,000	123,000	247,450	422,450	82.2
PENTECOSTAL					
Assemblies of God	16,900	15,550	23,500	55,950	10.8
Congregação Cristã	31,150	0	0	31,150	6.1
Other	3,100	350	1,100	4,550	0.9
Sub-total	51,150	15,900	24,600	91,650	17.8
GRAND TOTAL	103,150	138,900	272,050	514,100	100.0

Source: Based on membership statistics, Estatística do Culto Protestante do Brasil, 1959-60, I.B.G.E., adjusted to state totals as of December 31, 1959.

TABLE 4-8b

ESTIMATED DISTRIBUTION OF PROTESTANT COMMUNICANT MEMBERS BY DENOMINATIONAL GROUPS AND STATES FOR THE SOUTH REGION, JANUARY 1, 1970

Denominational Groups	States			Region	
	Paraná	Santa Catarina	Rio Grande do Sul		
	Number	Number	Number	Number	Percent
TRADITIONAL					
Baptist	18,000	1,650	10,300	29,950	3.6
Congregational	5,000	1,650	3,800	10,450	1.3
Episcopalian	950	1,150	14,000	16,100	1.9
Lutheran	27,200	119,350	242,000	388,550	47.0
Methodist	4,200	500	9,800	14,500	1.8
Presbyterian	24,000	3,600	1,000	28,600	3.5
7th-Day Adventist	20,000	2,500	14,000	36,500	4.4
Other	15,000	20,000	4,100	39,100	4.7
Sub-total	114,350	150,400	299,000	563,750	68.2
PENTECOSTAL					
Assemblies of God	57,000	22,150	57,200	136,350	16.5
Congregação Cristã	104,900	100	0	105,000	12.7
Other	13,000	3,500	4,800	21,300	2.6
Sub-total	174,900	25,750	62,000	262,650	31.8
GRAND TOTAL	289,250	176,150	361,000	826,400	100.0

Source: Based on projection of membership statistics, Estatística do Culto Protestante do Brasil, I.B.G.E., for 1955-66, adjusted to state totals as of Dec. 31, 1969.

Pentecostal churches in this region in 1960, but by 1970 the latter groups were within two-thirds of the Lutheran membership. This reflected a 171,000 member increase of Pentecostals but only 58,000 increase in Lutherans. The other traditional denominations grew by 83,000 during the same period. The Lutherans predominate in Santa Catarina and Rio Grande do Sul where German colonists settled in large numbers, but the Pentecostals lead in the State of Paraná. In 1970 the majority of the region's 29,000 Presbyterians were found in the State of Paraná together with more than one-half of the region's Baptists.

General-West Region

The distribution of Protestant members by denominations and states in the Central-West as of January 1, 1960 and January 1, 1970 is shown in Tables 4-9a and 4-9b. The membership of the Pentecostal churches, which was somewhat behind that of the traditional denominations in 1960, had outstripped the latter considerably by 1970. The Assemblies of God Church alone now has as many members as all of the traditional denomination churches together. The Presbyterian churches have the second largest membership of any denominational group with nearly 20,000 enrolled. The Baptists more than doubled their membership during this period and continue to grow in each of the states and in the Federal District.

TABLE 4-9a

ESTIMATED DISTRIBUTION OF PROTESTANT COMMUNICANT MEMBERS BY DENOMINATIONAL GROUPS AND STATES FOR THE CENTRAL-WEST REGION, JANUARY 1, 1960

Denominational Groups	States			Region	
	Mato Grosso	Goias	Distrito Federal		
	Number	Number	Number	Number	Percent
TRADITIONAL					
Baptist	2,300	2,600	200	5,100	12.4
Congregational	0	3,500	50	3,550	8.6
Episcopalian	0	0	0	0	0.0
Lutheran	0	50	0	50	0.1
Methodist	550	650	50	1,250	3.0
Presbyterian	3,150	7,700	150	11,000	26.8
7th-Day Adventist	1,100	850	0	1,950	4.7
Other	850	200	0	1,050	2.5
Sub-total	7,950	15,550	450	23,950	58.1
PENTECOSTAL					
Assemblies of God	3,500	11,500	850	15,850	38.4
Congregação Cristã	500	600	0	1,100	2.7
Other	0	300	50	350	0.8
Sub-total	4,000	12,400	900	17,300	41.9
GRAND TOTAL	11,950	27,950	1,350	41,250	100.0

Source: Based on membership statistics, Estatística do Culto Protestante do Brasil, 1959-60, I.B.G.E., adjusted to state totals as of December 31, 1959.

TABLE 4-9b

ESTIMATED DISTRIBUTION OF PROTESTANT COMMUNICANT MEMBERS BY DENOMINATIONAL GROUPS AND STATES FOR THE CENTRAL-WEST REGION, JANUARY 1, 1970

Denominational Groups	States			Region	
	Mato Grosso	Goias	Distrito Federal		
	Number	Number	Number	Number	Percent
TRADITIONAL					
Baptist	5,350	4,400	2,850	12,600	10.4
Congregational	400	4,000	500	4,900	4.1
Episcopalian	0	0	50	50	0.0
Lutheran	50	500	50	600	0.5
Methodist	400	700	700	1,800	1.5
Presbyterian	4,650	11,600	2,600	18,850	15.6
7th-Day Adventist	4,050	2,150	1,400	7,600	6.3
Other	2,600	1,500	400	4,500	3.7
Sub-total	17,500	24,850	8,550	50,900	42.1
PENTECOSTAL					
Assemblies of God	14,400	31,900	5,300	51,600	42.8
Congregação Cristã	5,700	3,600	1,000	10,300	8.5
Other	3,400	2,300	2,300	8,000	6.6
Sub-total	23,500	37,800	8,600	69,900	57.9
GRAND TOTAL	41,000	62,650	17,150	120,800	100.0

Source: Based on projection of membership statistics, Estatística do Culto Protestante do Brasil, I.B.G.E., for 1955-66, adjusted to state totals as of Dec. 31, 1969.

5

Profiles of Church Growth

SUMMARY

Below are statistical profiles summarized for different denominations, showing the communicant membership for five-year periods from 1955 to 1970.

Name	1955	1960	1965	1970
For a Country				
Baptists	151,300	186,900	250,650	330,500
Assemblies of God	255,850	376,800	588,300	746,400
Adventists	30,250	42,550	78,800	119,100
For a State				
Presbyterians in Minas Gerais	35,650	43,550	45,350	51,400
Congregação Cristã in São Paulo	70,200	141,550	189,250	250,250
For a County				
County of Santo André, São Paulo	5,150	5,850	13,100	20,500

In Chapters 3 and 4 we examined the Protestant church in Brazil first in depth geographically and second in depth denominationally. In both cases we were unable to cover the entire spectrum that would eventually examine every local church in every local district. However, with the data available this can be done. In this chapter we have selected examples of what can be done. The "X's" in Figure 5-1 show what combinations we have used in those examples.

FIGURE 5-1

BRAZIL 1980: CHURCH VS GEOGRAPHICAL DISTRIBUTION

DENOMINATIONAL DISTRIBUTION	GEOGRAPHICAL DISTRIBUTION: Country	Major Region (5)	State (27)	Urban Region (112)	Micro Region (361)	County (3,997)	District (15,000+)
All Protestants							
Categories					X		
Traditions	X				X	X	
Denominations	X		X				
Local Church							

INTRODUCTION

In the previous chapters we have attempted an introductory look at the growth of Protestantism in Brazil, first by geographical distribution (Chapter 3), and then by denominational distribution (Chapter 4). In this chapter we would like to give examples of how such data can be used in much more detail. Consequently, we will give a profile for selected denominations at the country level, at the state level, at the micro-region level, and at the county level.

TABLE 5-1

GROWTH OF BAPTISTS IN BRAZIL
BY STATES - FROM 1955, 1960, 1965, AND 1970

	1955	1960	1965	1970
NORTH				
1 Rondônia	100	150	200	300
2 Acre	200	600	900	1,200
3 Amazonas	1,000	1,100	1,300	4,050
4 Roraima	100	100	100	100
5 Pará	950	1,450	2,400	3,650
6 Amapá	50	100	100	100
TOTALS	2,400	3,500	5,000	9,400
NORTHEAST				
7 Maranhão	1,800	2,600	5,750	10,500
8 Piauí	1,400	1,850	2,450	3,000
9 Ceara	800	1,050	2,350	3,950
10 RGN	850	1,600	2,000	2,350
11 Paraíba	1,200	2,000	3,050	3,600
12 Pernambuco	13,950	14,600	17,750	22,050
13 Alagoas	1,050	2,100	2,650	3,850
14 Sergipe	650	750	1,100	1,550
15 Bahia	15,500	16,400	20,350	25,850
TOTALS	37,200	42,950	57,450	76,700
SOUTHEAST				
16 Minas Gerais	11,000	14,700	20,300	27,000
17 Espirito Santo	13,600	16,350	21,250	25,000
18 Rio de Janeiro	31,400	40,550	55,500	71,850
27 Guanabara	19,750	27,700	31,700	41,000
19 São Paulo	21,400	22,600	30,850	37,000
TOTALS	97,150	121,900	159,600	201,850
SOUTH				
20 Paraná	6,300	7,200	10,800	18,000
21 Santa Catarina	550	700	900	1,650
23 RGS	3,750	5,550	8,000	10,300
TOTALS	10,600	13,450	19,700	29,950
CENTRAL-WEST				
24 Mato Grosso	1,850	2,300	3,600	5,350
25 Goiás	2,100	2,600	3,450	4,400
26 Brasília	-	200	1,850	2,850
TOTALS	3,950	5,100	8,900	12,600
ALL BRAZIL				
NORTH	2,400	3,500	5,000	9,400
NORTHEAST	37,200	42,950	57,450	76,700
SOUTHEAST	97,150	121,900	159,600	201,850
SOUTH	10,600	13,450	19,700	29,950
CENTRAL-WEST	3,950	5,100	8,900	12,600
TOTALS	151,300	186,900	250,650	330,500

The reader should remember that specific information is available in the MARC/CASE data bank* for an analysis of any denomination at any one of these levels. (See Appendix 2)

FOR A COUNTRY

Baptists

The Baptists in Brazil have been working very hard to plant churches, conduct extensive and coordinated evangelistic campaigns in all of Brazil through state-wide campaigns and in city-wide evangelistic efforts, and simultaneous evangelistic efforts in the local churches.

The principal Baptist denomination which includes more than ninety percent of all Baptists in Brazil maintains a well-equipped department of statistics and has published yearly statistical tables of membership in the minutes of the proceedings of each general conference. What is recorded in Table 5-1, is the growth in membership of all Baptists in Brazil by region and states for five-year periods beginning in 1955 and concluding with curved projections made for 1970 based on the growth pattern achieved between 1955 and 1966.

The Religious Census of Brazil is as accurate as the statistics that each Baptist church has turned in to the Census representative found in each county of Brazil. This Baptist profile for their evangelistic and church planting efforts in Brazil should compare favorably with their denominational statistics, and in some instances could even include some membership data that did not get to the Baptist Director of Statistics, in Rio de Janeiro.

Assemblies of God

In Chapter 2 a little was said about the arrival of the first Assemblies of God missionaries. They began their work in

---

*Any question, inquiry, or special request for information about this collection of church growth data should be addressed to the Reverend Harmon Johnson, Director of CASE, Caixa Postal 30,548, São Paulo, Brazil, S. A. or in the U. S. to MARC Department, 919 West Huntington Drive, Monrovia, California, 91016.

TABLE 5-2

GROWTH OF ASSEMBLIES OF GOD IN BRAZIL
BY STATES - FROM 1955, 1960, 1965, AND 1970

		1955	1960	1965	1970
NORTH					
1	Rondônia	1,650	2,500	3,400	3,550
2	Acre	1,800	2,450	4,250	6.600
3	Amazonas	1,550	3,250	3,550	6,200
4	Roraima	250	450	1,300	1,800
5	Pará	21,850	27,250	33,500	48,350
6	Amapá	600	950	3,350	3,600
	TOTALS	27,700	36,850	49,350	70,100
NORTHEAST					
7	Maranhão	12,950	22,500	25,500	31,000
8	Piauí	1,100	1,200	5,200	8,000
9	Ceará	13,500	19,200	21,000	24,650
10	RGN	6,100	8,800	14,300	17,500
11	Paraiba	6,800	8,700	10,650	11,900
12	Pernambuco	19,500	34,100	46,450	53,450
13	Alagoas	6,200	7,300	11,200	12,000
14	Sergipe	1,100	1,200	2,000	2,250
15	Bahia	5,200	10,700	21,000	30,300
	TOTALS	77,450	113,700	157,300	191,050
SOUTHEAST					
16	Minas Gerais	16,500	20,500	39,550	57,000
17	Espirito Santo	3,900	6,350	12,250	14,000
18	Rio de Janeiro	31,350	36,950	73,750	80,800
27	Guanabara	17,200	17,950	33,150	36,500
19	São Paulo	46,350	72,700	89,350	109,000
	TOTALS	115,300	154,450	248,050	297,300
SOUTH					
20	Paraná	9,200	16,900	38,450	57,000
21	Santa Catarina	5,750	15,550	17,750	22,150
23	RGS	18,400	23,500	44,800	57,200
	TOTALS	33,350	55,950	101,000	136,350
CENTRAL-WEST					
24	Mato Grosso	1,400	3,500	9,600	14,400
25	Goiás	5,650	11,500	18,900	31,900
26	Brasília	-	850	4,100	5,300
	TOTALS	7,050	15,850	32,600	51,600
ALL BRAZIL					
	NORTH	27,700	36,850	49,350	70,100
	NORTHEAST	72,450	113,700	157,300	191,050
	SOUTHEAST	115,300	154,450	248,050	297,300
	SOUTH	33,350	55,950	101,000	136,350
	CENTRAL-WEST	7,050	15,850	32,600	51,600
	TOTALS	255,850	376,800	588,300	746,400

Belém in the State of Pará and from this center spread to all parts of Brazil. The individual churches found in this denomination have different ways in which they keep membership records, but they have been so preoccupied with the evangelistic and pastoral aspect of their denominational activity that the time has not been available for them to establish their own department of statistics until only recently. What we have in Table 5-2 is the most definitive statistical record that has ever been published for the growth of the Assemblies of God Church in Brazil. The Religious Census Bureau publishes their statistical findings each year, but the churches are recorded by county and never presented by denomination. This is a historical statistical profile of growth for the Assemblies in Brazil and can become a definitive statistical report upon which the director of the Department of Statistics in Rio de Janeiro can reconstruct part of the historical growth pattern of that denomination as they plan the best way to resume annual statistical reports for every one of their churches in Brazil.

To illustrate what can be done with these profiles of denominational growth, a series of bar graphs were drawn to display graphically the growth of this denomination in Brazil. More was said about the regional distribution of growth in Chapter 3. Each region is represented, and the five-year growth achieved in each region can be seen (Figure 5-2).

If we want to know a little more about the membership growth pattern that is beginning to be of interest to us from our study of Table 5-2, we can select the states in each region that appear to be achieving the outstanding increase. Graphically, these states can be compared in relation to each other and more insight received about actually locating those areas in Brazil where accelerated growth is happening, according to the Religious Census figures. According to the graph in Figure 5-3, the areas of accelerated growth are found in the States of Pernambuco, Rio de Janeiro, and Paraná. As these are entire states, some examination is needed to ascertain the specific areas in which this accelerated growth occurred, and this can be accomplished by a careful "in-depth" study of the Brazil 1980 computer analysis by micro-regions or counties that is available at CASE offices in São Paulo.

Adventists

This denomination has an unusual pattern of growth and relatively little is known by other Protestant denominations about the distribution and extension of the Seventh-Day Adventist churches in Brazil. The profile of growth in Table 5-3 points out a heavy concentration of this denomination in São Paulo, Paraná, Rio Grande do Sul, and Minas Gerais. It should also be pointed out that this denomination historically has been part of the Protestant community, but has remained aloof, and in turn, is shunned by other Protestants in Brazil. This church has more than doubled its membership between 1955 and 1965, and again between 1960 and 1970. The Adventists carry on a vigorous evangelistic program and require new converts to go through a lengthy process of indoctrination. Despite this long process, they have achieved a notable, consistent index of increase.

FIGURE 5-2

GROWTH OF ASSEMBLIES OF GOD DENOMINATION
WITHIN REGIONS FOR 1955, 1960, 1965, and 1970

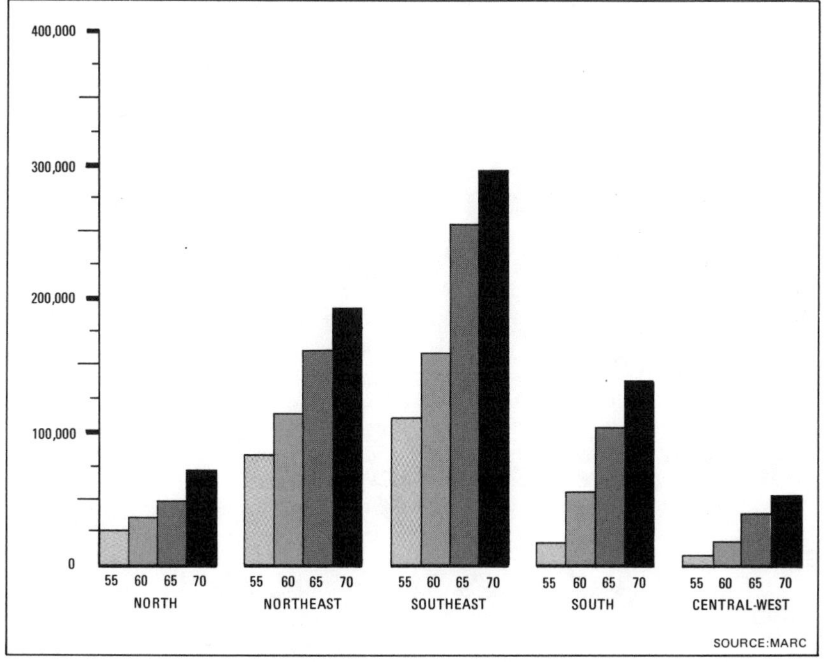

Much can be learned from a careful study of any Protestant denomination, and certain studies of a comparative nature would be helpful, for there is a specific reason why one church grows when other Protestant churches in the same area do not achieve such growth.

TABLE 5-3

GROWTH OF ADVENTISTS IN BRAZIL
BY STATES - FROM 1955, 1960, 1965, AND 1970

	1955	1960	1965	1970
NORTH				
1 Rondônia	0	0	100	150
2 Acre	0	0	50	50
3 Amazonas	800	1,550	3,350	3,700
4 Roraima	0	0	50	50
5 Pará	400	1,650	2,600	4,000
6 Amapá	50	100	100	200
TOTALS	1,250	3,300	6,250	8,150
NORTHEAST				
7 Maranhão	750	750	1,600	6,000
8 Piauí	100	200	700	900
9 Ceará	250	300	300	300
10 RGN	50	100	250	450
11 Paraíba	100	250	600	750
12 Pernambuco	900	900	2,700	4,400
13 Alagoas	100	100	200	500
14 Sergipe	150	300	500	700
15 Bahia	1,200	1,600	3,250	5,100
TOTALS	3,600	4,500	10,100	19,100
SOUTHEAST				
16 Minas Gerais	2,250	2,850	5,550	8,500
17 Espirito Santo	1,600	2,650	4,150	5,250
18 Rio de Janeiro	700	1,000	2,550	3,200
27 Guanabara	1,150	1,600	2,300	2,800
19 São Paulo	8,950	13,200	19,350	28,000
TOTALS	14,650	21,300	33,900	47,750
SOUTH				
20 Paraná	4,000	5,050	11,650	20,000
21 Santa Catarina	1,150	1,550	2,200	2,500
23 RGS	4,500	4,900	10,300	14,000
TOTALS	9,650	11,500	24,150	36,500
CENTRAL-WEST				
24 Mato Grosso	600	1,100	2,050	4,050
25 Goiás	500	850	1,450	2,150
26 Brasília	-	0	900	1,400
TOTALS	1,100	1,950	4,400	7,600
ALL BRAZIL				
NORTH	1,250	3,300	6,250	8,150
NORTHEAST	3,600	4,500	10,100	19,100
SOUTHEAST	14,650	21,300	33,900	47,750
SOUTH	9,650	11,500	24,150	36,500
CENTRAL-WEST	1,100	1,950	4,400	7,600
TOTALS	30,250	42,550	78,800	119,100

FIGURE 5-3

GROWTH OF ASSEMBLIES OF GOD IN STATES HAVING LARGEST AMOUNT OF COMMUNICANTS IN EACH REGION IN 1955, 1960, 1965, and 1970

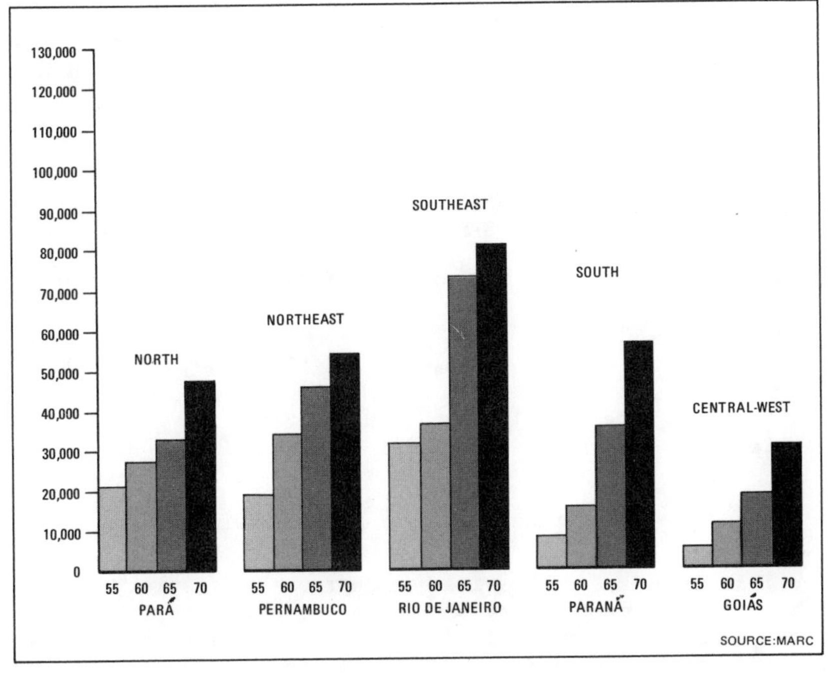

FOR A STATE

Presbyterian Denomination in the State of Minas Gerais

A knowledge of what has happened to a single denomination in a certain state begins with an examination of the totals of membership growth during a fifteen year period. Comparison of the membership for 1955 with that of 1965 reveals growth. Similarly, if 1960 and 1970 are compared, again growth is indicated (Table 5-4).

The large communicant membership of the Igreja Presbiteriana do Brasil in the State of Minas Gerais had a steady rate of growth in the fifteen year period. More "in-depth" study made by Presbyterian leaders would be helpful in order to ascertain areas in which special growth and development took place. This Table indicates a 33.7 percent rate of growth in the twelve year period from 1955 to 1966, and when it was computed from 1961-1966, the yearly rate of growth was 1.9 percent. This is much less than the yearly rate of natural increase of the population in the State of Minas Gerais. The Presbyterian leadership wants to establish new churches in Brazil, and their paper, *Brasil Presbiteriano,* usually highlights any new Presbyterian church that is organized. But in this state a study made to determine the reasons for the slow growth of these churches would be most helpful.

TABLE 5-4

GROWTH OF PRESBYTERIAN DENOMINATION
IN STATE OF MINAS GERAIS, 1955, 1960, 1965, 1970

DENOMINATION	1955	1960	1965	1970
Igreja Presbiteriana do Brasil	35,650	43,550	45,350	51,400

% Growth rate from 1955 to 1966 - 33.7%
Yearly % growth rate from 1961 to 1966 - 1.9%

Congregação Cristã in São Paulo State

This denomination has its headquarters in its largest church, located in the city of São Paulo, Brás district. At Easter time each year the leaders from practically every church in the denomination arrive in São Paulo for the annual three-day conference. Each church in this denomination submits its statistical forms and reports on everything that happened during the year. The Religious Census office in Rio de Janeiro receives these statistics that are routed back through their county offices throughout Brazil. The annual report published by the Congregação then becomes one of the most unique statistical resumés of any Protestant denomination in Brazil. If the statistics are not reported, it is the fault of the Census representative in the county where the local Congregação is located. The yearly handbook of all their churches published soon after the Easter meeting has never been carefully compared with the Religious Census statistics for the Protestant Churches in Brazil. When this is done, it will reveal the exact number of churches of this denomination that were not reported in any year of the *Culto Protestante* and give a good idea of the "additional" membership that should be recorded for this unusual Pentecostal denomination.

In Table 5-5 the growth of this church in the State of São Paulo is recorded in the five year periods, 1955 to 1970. This church doubled in the five year period between 1955-1960.

TABLE 5-5

GROWTH OF CONGREGAÇÃO CRISTÃ DENOMINATION
IN STATE OF SÃO PAULO, 1955, 1960, 1965, 1970

DENOMINATION	1955	1960	1965	1970
Congregação Cristã no Brasil	70,200	141,550	189,250	250,250

% growth rate from 1955 to 1966 - 179.2
Yearly % growth rate from 1961 to 1966 - 6.3

FIGURE 5-4

MICRO-REGION #221 IN STATE OF RIO DE JANEIRO

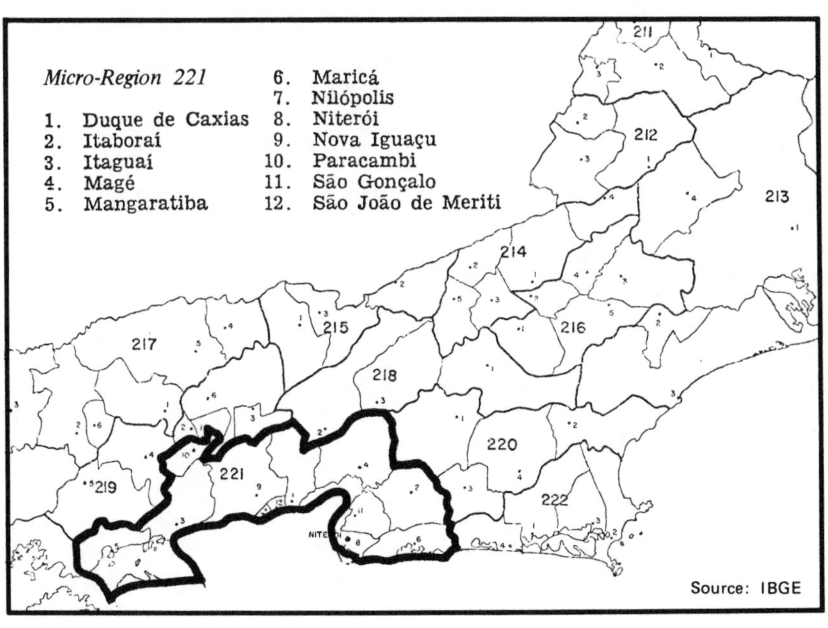

The rate of increase from 1955 to 1966 - the latter being the last year of *Culto Protestante* statistics available from the Religious Census Bureau (IBGE) - was 179.2 percent. Only the five-year statistical report was used for this table, but the growth of this denomination in the State of São Paulo between 1955 and 1965 indicates this high rate of increase. When the calculation was made by the computer, its growth rate between 1961 and 1966 was found to be 6.3 percent each year and this is the percentage rate used by the computer to project growth for 1970.

The size of any Protestant denomination in Brazil in any state can be found by consulting the Brazil 1980 statistical analysis of church growth at the CASE Center.

FOR A MICRO-REGION

The fourteen denominational family groups which were listed in Table 5-8 have been divided into three categories. Category I is called the "traditional" denominations. These are churches mentioned previously that have been established in Brazil for decades and are considered to be the old-line historical churches of Protestantism. Lutherans, Presbyterians, Baptists, and "others" are included in the first category. Category II is the Pentecostal family of churches. This category includes the different denominations that emphasize the doctrine of the Holy Spirit and follow the experience of the Apostolic church in the New Testament. Three Pentecostal groups are brought together in this category, the Congregação Cristã no Brasil, the Assemblies of God, and the Independent Pentecostal churches that comprise group number eleven (11). Category III is given the name "other sects" and includes the Seventh-Day Adventists, Christian Science, the Latter-day Saints (Mormons), and Jehovah's Witnesses. The term "other sects" was selected for lack of a more descriptive word. This group includes those religious groups regarded by the majority of Protestants to be outside the traditional Protestant denominational pattern.

Two micro-regions are examined using the denominational categories described above. Such an examination will provide a little evidence, using only these two micro-regions, to show some of the dynamics of growth that are at work in these different denominational categories.

Micro-region #221. This micro-region, shown in Figure 5-4, is made up of twelve counties and is adjacent to the city of Rio de Janeiro and the State of Guanabara. This area is receiving many migrants from the surrounding rural areas. They move into the suburbs and seek employment and education for their children. These are the suburbs around Rio de Janeiro that are served by the network of inter-urban trains of the "Brasil Central" rail system and settlement is clustered along these tracks. More and more buses are being used because of the crowded suburban trains.

Charles W. Gates discusses this micro-region in his book, *Industrialization: Brazil's Catalyst for Church Growth.* After his examination of the sixteen counties in the State of Rio de Janeiro that have the largest Protestant communicant membership, Gates makes a comparison of these counties with sixteen counties in the state that have the highest recorded industrial production, and says:

> Micro-region 221 had 43.8 percent of the state's Protestant population. However, 84.1 percent of the Protestants of the micro-region reside in the six counties of the region... having a production value of Cr$1,000,000. These six are the counties of Duque de Caxias, Magé, Nova Iguaçu, Nilópolis, Niterói, and São Gonçalo (Gates 1972:24).

After a further discussion of the role of industrialization as a catalyst for Protestant church growth in Brazil, Gates uses this profile of church growth in Micro-region 221 to point out the accelerated growth of the Protestant family of churches (Category II) in Table 5-6, and then concludes that:

> Industrialization in Brazil has helped provide the climate and stage for socio-cultural change which reaches to the masses of nearly 90,000,000 Brazilians (Gates 1972:30).

The unusual percentage of increase in Micro-region 221 between 1955 and 1966, a twelve-year period, is 210.6 percent. The Brazil 1980 data bank records this rate of growth and when such increase is recorded, it should receive special attention from those who are interested in the dynamics and some of the answers of "how the Church grows" in different locations in such a spectacular way. Much more study is needed on the growth of the different categories of Protestant churches, and when such research is completed, many important factors - now little understood - will come to light. To take advantage of the opportunities presented in Micro-region 221 and others of similar nature, Protestant leaders and their people will require a great deal of wisdom, understanding, and willingness to quickly move and adapt to remarkable social transitions that have been set in motion in Brazil in the past decade.

TABLE 5-6

PROTESTANT GROWTH BY DENOMINATIONAL CATEGORIES
IN MICRO-REGION #221: 1955, 1960, 1965, 1970

CATEGORY	1955	1960	1965	1970	% INCREASE 1955 - 1966
I Traditional	18,327	24,900	34,808	58,345	122.3%
II Pentecostal	12,450	24,128	49,344	93,339	331.6%
III Other Sects	230	699	1,525	3,615	694.3%
TOTALS	31,007	49,727	85,677	155,299	210.6%

Micro-region #262. This micro-region, the metropolitan area of São Paulo, is discussed in greater detail in Chapter 8 (Figure 8-8 and Table 8-3). However, the classification of the membership in this micro-region by denominational category has not been presented before (Table 5-7).

The "traditional" category of churches increased slowly in comparison to the Pentecostal category. In the 1961-1966 period, the traditional churches were plotted by the computer at a 1.3 percent increase per year while the Pentecostal churches increased at the rate of 12.5 percent annually.

The different ways of looking at denominational growth of Protestant churches in Brazil offers a rich variety of statistical analysis and information that can help denominational leaders understand different trends that are beginning to appear with regularity in the complex mosaic of Protestant church growth in Brazil.

TABLE 5-7

PROTESTANT GROWTH BY DENOMINATIONAL CATEGORIES
IN MICRO-REGION #262: 1955, 1960, 1965, 1970

CATEGORY	1955	1960	1965	1970	% INCREASE 1955 - 1966
I Traditional	46,987	51,714	54,852	59,973	21.2%
II Pentecostal	54,564	105,720	184,438	315,352	260.8%
III Other Sects	4,661	8,535	5,374	---	54.3%
TOTALS	106,212	165,969	244,664	375,325	145.8%

FOR A COUNTY

The Brazil 1980 computer analysis gives more detail beyond the micro-region for each micro-region has from four to fifty counties in it. To show what happens in a county, Table 5-8 has been designed for Santo André, São Paulo. This is one of the counties found in micro-region #262 which is part of the metropolitan area of larger São Paulo - a highly urbanized county unit. In this table the denominations have been grouped in three different categories: the traditional churches, the Pentecostal churches, and "others" which include the Mormons, Jehovah's Witnesses, and other denominations sometimes classified as sects by many of the Protestants in Brazil.

A careful look at the totals will reveal a rather slow period from 1955 to 1960 for all of the churches that is rapidly changed in 1965 and 1970. This is probably due to the influx of people, new industrial growth, and increased urbanization that assisted the development and growth of these different denominations within this county.

The Brazil 1980 data bank material, mentioned throughout *The Protestant Handbook*, has been used in a special way in this chapter to look at a few selected situations. It is not the purpose here to go into any "in-depth" interpretation of these different case studies. This must be done by Protestant leaders themselves. The material in Chapter 5 is presented as an illustration of the ways in which the Brazil 1980 church growth analysis covers such a wide spectrum of applications.

It is now possible for Protestant decision makers to examine their individual growth patterns using the "Church vs. Geographical Distribution" grid, Figure 5-1, in at least thirty-five different ways. Only six of these possibilities have been suggested here and briefly presented as mere illustrations, and this capability is further enhanced by the use of "indicators" which are dealt with in the chapter which follows.

TABLE 5-8

GROWTH OF PROTESTANT DENOMINATIONS FOUND
IN COUNTY OF SANTO ANDRÉ, SÃO PAULO

DENOMINATION	1955	1960	1965	1970
Baptist	324	319	981	1,464
Presbyterian	305	677	875	1,583
Independent Presbyterian	722	920	719	800
Methodist	318	325	309	325
Congregational	143	125	158	173
Episcopal	38	43	42	50
Nazarene		86		109
Evangelical Union				609
TOTALS	1,850	2,495	3,084	5,113
Assemblies of God	1,471	1,085	3,200	4,309
Congregação Cristã	1,601	1,288	3,670	5,643
Evangélico Bíblico				
De Cristo Pentecostal		461	935	1,155
Pentecostal			1,435	3,200
TOTALS	3,072	2,834	9,240	14,307
Adventist	248	535	771	1,082

PROTESTANT DENOMINATIONS IN COUNTY BY CATEGORIES

	1955	1960	1965	1970
TRADITIONAL	1,850	2,495	3,084	5,113
PENTECOSTALS	3,072	2,834	9,240	14,307
OTHER	248	535	771	1,082
TOTALS	5,170	5,864	13,095	20,502

6

Indicators and Their Use

SUMMARY

This chapter deals with "indicators" as tools for the examination of church growth. These indicators compare population with the number of Protestant members, the number of Brazilian Protestant leaders, and the number of foreign missionaries. An examination is made of non-Protestant family units, comparing them with the number of Brazilian Protestant leaders and the number of such families per meeting place.

In this comparative study some of these indicators become helpful in thinking about the mobilization of Protestants in Brazil. Population growth is compared to Protestant growth, and areas without Protestants reported are discussed.

INTRODUCTION

A Way To Implement Church Growth Information

Other chapters have presented information, data, and statistical detail on the growth and status of the Protestant church in Brazil. The beginnings and background of the Protestant churches have been mentioned, and some of the historical events were considered, beginning with the years of pioneer evangelism by foreign missionaries. As the churches grew numerically and matured in the faith there was a gradual transfer of pastoral responsibility and ecclesiastical leadership to Brazilians. The rapid growth of the Protestant churches in Brazil during the past decade was portrayed. A picture of this growth and the strength of Protestantism is presented as of January 1, 1970. We must now deal with the way in which we can utilize and implement this array of information effectively to assist the Protestant leaders and responsible decision makers in planning strategy for Brazil during the 1970's.

Each genuine member found in the Body of Christ in the country of Brazil has been given unique spiritual gifts for service and ministry and needs to find the place where these gifts can be effective in the task of evangelization. Most true believers feel a responsibility which grows out of gratitude to God. This responsibility needs to be reinforced by some courageous planning that will augment and multiply the total evangelistic endeavor, effectiveness, and ultimate fruit bearing ministry.

A Way of Understanding Complex Situations

The use of indicators to provide information and insight for complex social systems - such as churches, large groups of people, or other institutional factors - is neither new nor unusual (Brewer 1973:79). National economies are studied by means of indicators. A limited number or a sample of tested variables are analyzed to give a picture of the entire economy. In the study of nations, indicators such as population, government activity, economic growth, and mass media availability have been carefully described and outlined by social relationships. Projections can be calculated by the activity of a few major variables.

There are different categories as well as different levels of indicators. For example, indicators that are applicable to a local organization or small groups of people would not necessarily be useful at the national level or in larger groupings of people. Indicators selected to monitor the work of a local church will differ from those applied to denominations in a national or an international association.

Indicators are usually expressed in mathematical terms such as ratios, percentages, and fractions. One such mathematical indicator might be the ratio of the total number of people (population) per church member in a given area. Such an indicator gives a rough, but comprehensive idea of the magnitude of the evangelistic task.

To be useful, indicator data must be available, valid, and measurable. These are some of the basic rules for the use of indicators. Applied to the task of evangelism, church indicators need to be developed that relate to the force for evangelism, the methods used for evangelism, and the receptivity and felt needs of the people to be evangelized. Familiarity with indicators of this nature will help Protestant decision makers in Brazil at all levels to be more effective in their efforts to proclaim Christ to the Brazilian people.

INDICATORS - HELPFUL TOOLS FOR APPRAISING THE TASK

Tools which can be used to identify and assess certain key elements of the situation we face are called "indicators." Indicators are helpful to the Church in analyzing and appraising the magnitude of the evangelistic task that is ever before each individual believer. An indicator is also a way of partially describing a larger system. In concept, one or more indicators will provide clues to the activity at work throughout the entire system. In other words, these indicators will change in a similar manner as changes take place in the entire system (such as a denomination). If we can understand what these indicators are doing, we will have a better idea of the condition of the entire system itself.

Indicators are helpful tools because:

1. They permit us to compare what is happening in one region or area with the same thing that happens in another.

2. They permit us to observe change, discover trends, and measure growth.

3. They give us simple terms and a common vocabulary that can be used in the communication process involved in the consideration of very complex situations and changes.

MUCH WORK TO BE DONE WITH INDICATORS

The specific indicators that we will discuss in this chapter need to be tested in local and regional situations by church planters. The comments which follow are partial and tentative and are presented as a way of thinking about the different aspects of the expansion and ministry of the Church in a broad scope. The indicators that will be discussed relate generally to the entire population and to elements of the Christian population.

Indicators of this type were chosen because they have been found to be related to the Brazil data bank. Research needs to be encouraged on indicators of effectiveness that measure the organic and qualitative aspects of church growth as well as the quantitative side (Tippett 1967:30-31). The conversion survey described in Appendix 1 may uncover many such useful indicators.

FACTORS FOR IMPLEMENTATION OF CHURCH GROWTH INFORMATION

The indicators that follow are described in terms of the total country of Brazil. They are drawn from the country, region, and state statistics. They will further explain the meaning of "indicators." At the same time, they will give us a broader indication of the task that is faced by Protestants in evangelizing the total country of Brazil. These indicators have been calculated from the basic data given in earlier chapters and are displayed and tabulated in Tables 6-1 and 6-2. The following selected indicators will be discussed:

Population Per Protestant
Population Per Brazilian Leader
Population Per Foreign Missionary
Non-Protestant Family Units Per Protestant Member
Non-Protestant Family Units Per Brazilian Leader
Non-Protestant Family Units Per Meeting Place
Protestant Members Per Brazilian Leader
Protestant Members Per Foreign Missionary
Population Growth Versus Growth of Protestant Members
Proportion Counties Without Protestant Worship Centers Reported.

Population per Protestant Members

The number of people (population) in a given area per Protestant member is a useful indicator. It can be calculated for the area that is served by a local church or for a larger area that receives the ministry of different churches in a denomination. This indicator shows the number of people each member would need to contact on the average to maximize the work of personal evangelism. The smaller the number to be contacted, the less difficult the task.*

---

*Notice that since the population includes the Christians in the area the ratio of non-Christians to Christians is lower.

FIGURE 6-1

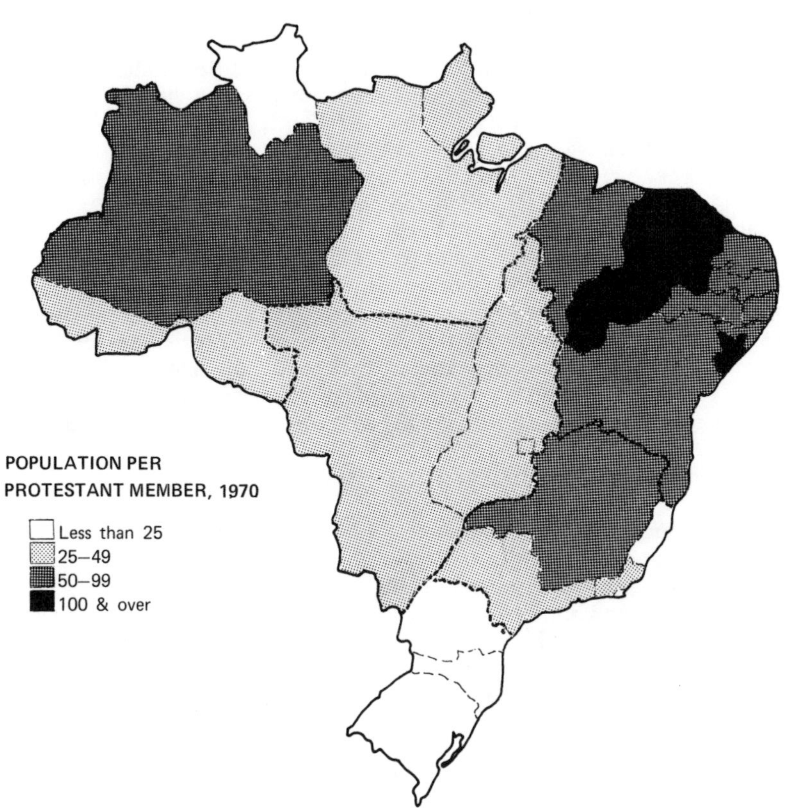

A variation of this indicator could be found by adapting and basing it on a particular segment of the population in a region, a prescribed area, a socio-economic class, or an ethnic group. Another use of this indicator would be to change the designation of "member" to "active member," making the assumption that only a certain proportion of the members in any church will participate in actual personal evangelism.

The indicators for population per Protestant member have been calculated for the different states and regions of Brazil. These indicators are based on the data given in the third column of Table 4-4a and 4-4b, and have been displayed on the map of Brazil found in Figure 6-1. There is only one state, Ceará, which in 1970 had more than 100 people per Protestant member; and the almost solid Northeast, including the states of Minas Gerais and Goiás, had 50 to 99 people per Protestant member. These states have the least number of Protestant members in relation to the total population.

In 1970 nine states or territories had less than twenty-five people per Protestant member. Four of these are in the sparsely settled section of the North and the Central-West. The others are found in the heavily settled coastal states of the Southeast and South. The task of evangelism in these states will be a lighter load per individual believer if the Protestant members and believers accept their responsibility for witness and evangelistic endeavor.

The population per Protestant member figures were quite different in 1960 as compared to the same figures in 1970. Similar indicators were calculated for 1960 and are shown in Figure 6-2. When this map is compared with that for 1970, twelve states show an improvement in classification. The map also indicates that church membership in these states has grown much faster than the population.

One question that needs to be answered when planning a strategy for the evangelism of the people within a given area is: How many members can we count on to participate in evangelism? If we can depend upon 50 percent of the believers, the indicator would be doubled. If the plan is to evangelize only a segment, making up 25 percent of the population in a given area, the original indicator would be reduced to one-fourth, and so forth.

Population of Brazilian Protestant Leaders

The prevalent general idea is that evangelism is the sole task of the pastor or foreign missionary. Others place the evangelism responsibility upon deacons and elders as well as the pastors. Few recognize that evangelism is a task that should include the whole church, involving everyone in one way or another. This section, and the one that follows, may be helpful in demonstrating the fact that it is always impractical to expect the pastors, lay leaders, and foreign missionaries to assume the ultimate responsibility for this task.

The number of people needing to be evangelized per Brazilian Protestant leader was 1,470 for all of Brazil in 1970 according to Table 6-1. This indicator exceeds by 50 times the number each Protestant member would have responsibility for if each were able to participate actively and effectively in the evangelistic endeavor. This fact demonstrates one of the reasons pastors must rely on periodic, regular evangelistic services in their local churches and enlist the help of the church members in bringing non-Protestants into the meetings. In this case, the average number of people for which each Brazilian pastor (not including the deacons and elders) would be responsible is nearly 6,000. This number is too many. Participation by the entire church body needs to be enlisted if evangelization is to be effective. These indicators focus on the need for each believer to be motivated in the evangelistic task.

FIGURE 6-2

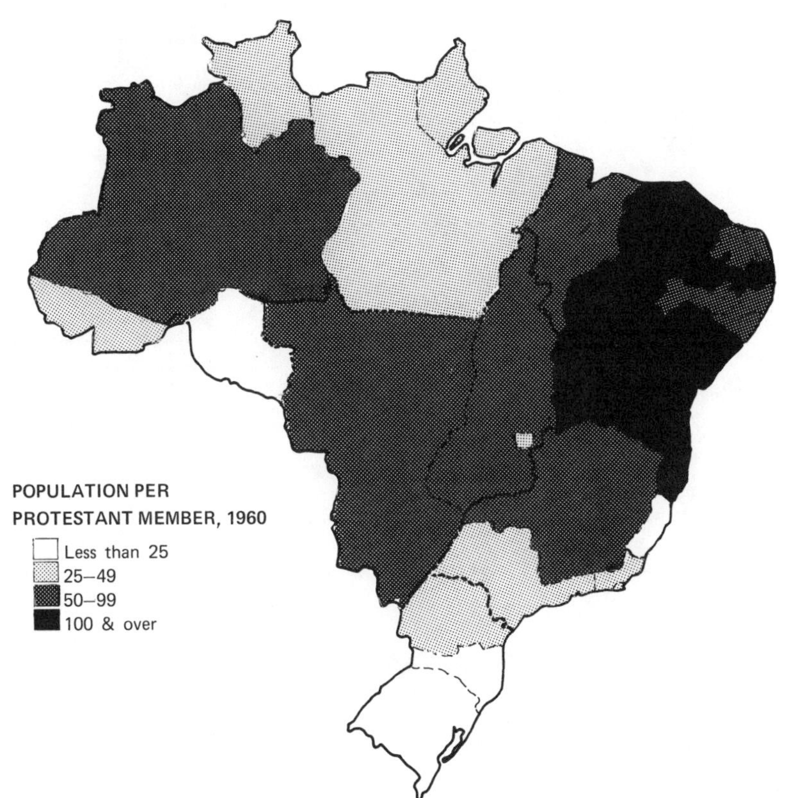

The number of people for whom each Brazilian leader would be responsible varies greatly from state to state. This can be seen in Figure 6-3. In personal evangelism each leader would have to contact more than 5,000 people in Alagoas and Sergipe, whereas those in Amapá, Rio de Janeiro, Guanabara, and the Federal District would have to contact fewer than 800 (still a relatively large number). Table 6-1 shows that thousands would have to be touched evangelistically in other states.

TABLE 6-1

RELATIVE FACTORS INVOLVED IN MOBILIZATION OF THE EVANGELISTIC FORCE BY STATES AND REGIONS IN BRAZIL, 1970

States and Regions	Population per Protestant	Population per Brazilian Leader	Population per Foreign Missionary	Protestants per Meeting Place	Protestants per Brazilian Leader	Protestants per Foreign Missionary	Brazilian Leaders per Missionary	Meeting Places per Missionary
North								
RO	26	2,870	3,200	160	110	120	1	1
AC	27	3,070	107,500	153	116	4,050	35	26
AM	40	2,000	47,500	89	49	120	2	1
RR	23	3,070	1,500	83	160	80	1	1
PA	35	3,420	12,500	92	98	360	4	4
AP	15	740	29,800	82	49	1,960	40	24
Region	33	2,570	8,000	95	77	240	3	3
Northeast								
MA	73	4,470	43,400	95	62	670	11	7
PI	70	4,570	32,500	61	66	470	7	8
CE	138	3,880	42,500	56	28	300	11	5
RGN	58	2,960	60,600	88	51	1,030	20	12
PB	93	3,060	580,000	70	32	6,170	190	88
PE	38	2,100	38,700	99	56	1,040	18	10
AL	65	6,130	103,000	118	94	1,570	17	13
SE	97	5,160	58,500	34	51	570	11	17
BA	95	4,540	133,000	67	48	1,410	29	21
Region	70	3,530	44,400	79	50	860	17	11
Southeast								
MG	51	1,810	50,000	65	36	980	28	15
ES	22	1,020	82,200	97	46	3,690	81	38
RJ	21	610	194,000	81	29	9,160	317	114
GB	32	770	30,100	131	24	950	39	7
SP	22	1,080	26,000	156	50	1,200	24	8
Region	27	1,060	36,900	110	39	1,360	35	12
South								
PR	31	1,580	26,300	78	51	860	17	11
SC	11	1,370	54,200	200	124	4,890	40	24
RGS	13	1,400	28,800	232	107	2,200	21	10
Region	17	1,470	29,700	150	86	1,740	20	12
Central-West								
MT	23	1,120	13,100	97	50	580	12	6
GO	61	1,500	19,600	50	24	320	13	6
DF	18	560	4,600	91	30	250	8	3
Region	36	1,200	13,600	73	34	380	11	5
Brazil	30	1,470	31,900	112	50	1,080	22	10

Based on data from preceding tables

Population per Foreign Missionary

When the magnitude of the evangelistic task in Brazil is considered, the 3,000 foreign missionaries now in Brazil are small in number. More than one-half of these missionaries from outside of Brazil are still engaging in evangelism as one of their activities. An increasing proportion devote most of their time to serving the national church in a variety of ways. For every foreign missionary there are more than twenty Brazilian Protestant leaders and more than 1,000 Protestant members.

Our indicators show that the number of people per foreign missionary in all of Brazil averages 32,000 (Table 6-1). When we consider this situation by different states, we find that our indicator moves from less than 15,000 per missionary in five states or territories to more than 60,000 in seven states. This situation is graphically displayed in Figure 6-4. This indicator reaches its lowest point in the North where missionaries work with sparsely populated Indian tribes and with widely scattered Brazilian settlements in the vast Amazon Basin. In the Northeast and the Southeast this indicator shows that there are about 30,000 people per foreign missionary in these regions. The indicator for the populous State of São Paulo is less than this, however, showing 26,000 per foreign missionary.

FIGURE 6-3

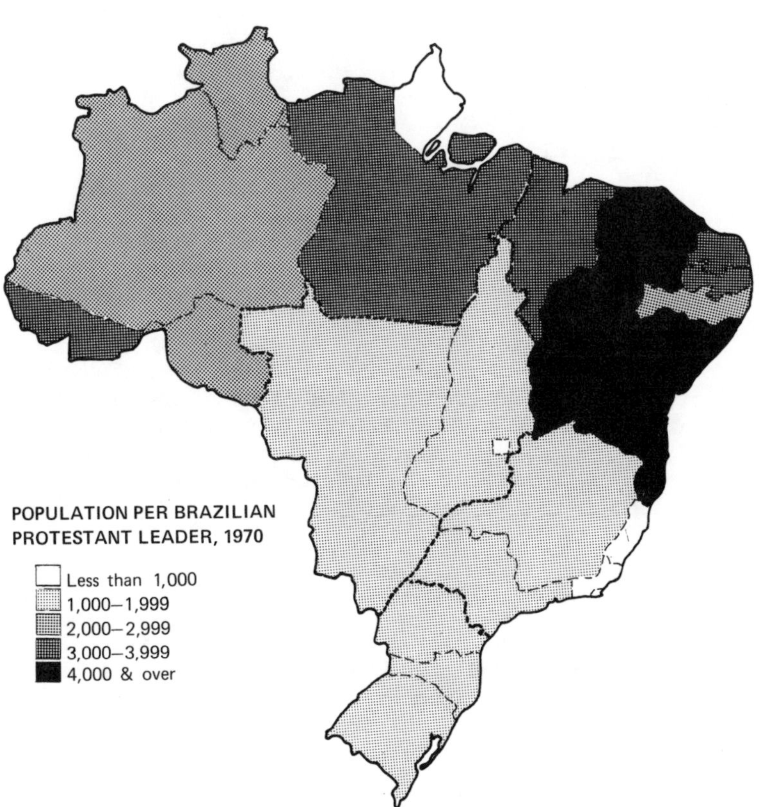

FIGURE 6-4

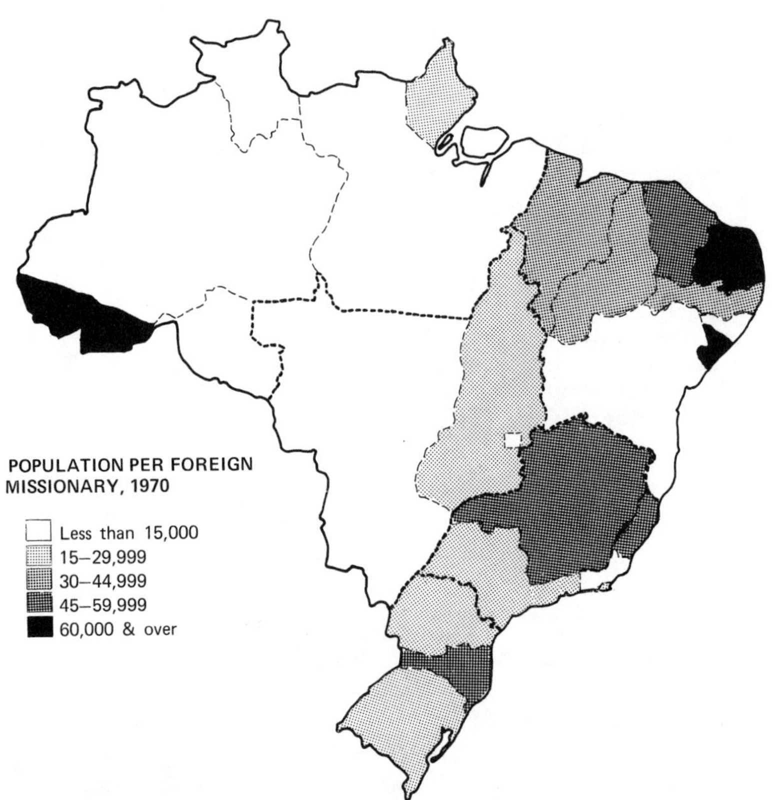

The population per missionary indicator is useful for comparing distribution and concentration of missionaries. Since Christianity was introduced into Brazil by missionaries, the impact of the missionary can not be taken lightly. The important thing is that the missionary be located in the right place, in the right job, at the right time.

Non-Protestant Family Units

In Brazil where the Protestant members comprise only three percent of the total population, an indicator that is based on population per Protestant member is a very useful tool. When a sizable proportion of the population is already Protestant, this type of indicator would not be as helpful unless it could be based on the non-Protestant population per Protestant member. We have, therefore, estimated the non-Protestant population of Brazil for each state and territory. This data has been converted into non-Protestant family units and is shown in Table 6-2.

Non-Protestant Families Per Protestant Member

When planning strategy for evangelism of the people within their area of responsibility, denominations, missions and local churches would like to know the number of non-Protestant family units or homes and their location. Many plans involve church members working in teams to contact each home within the area with a personal witness, Gospel tracts, or invitations to attend evangelistic services. The information gleaned from these contacts makes it possible to plan evangelistic campaigns carefully and effectively.

Table 6-2 indicates that the average number of Brazilian non-Protestant family units per Protestant member is less than five. In 1970 it was estimated that there existed over fifteen million non-Protestant families for the three million Protestants. Each believer should visit an average of five families. This same indicator shows that for the Northeast, thirteen families must be visited, which is a considerably larger task than the average for Brazil as a whole. Figure 6-5 provides graphic comparisons using this indicator.

Non-Protestant Families Per Brazilian Protestant Leader

To get an idea of how many non-Protestant families for whom each Protestant leader would have a responsibility, subtract an estimate of the Protestant community (the number of members, their families, and others attending services) from the total population. Then divide the remainder (the non-Protestant community) by the average number of people per dwelling unit based on the decennial census. Dividing this number by the number of Brazilian leaders, we obtain an idea of the number of non-Protestant families for which each Protestant leader might feel responsible.

For each local community, it is possible to estimate the average number of people in each family unit and then divide this into the non-Protestant population. The heavily populated cities generally average five or less people per family and in the rural areas the average is around six.

TABLE 6-2

ESTIMATED DISTRIBUTION OF FAMILY UNITS IN BRAZIL BY REGIONS, JAN. 1, 1970, AND FACTORS RELATED TO THE EVANGELISTIC FORCE

Region	Family Units			Non-Protestant Family Units			
	Total	Protestant	Non-protestant				
	Thousands	Thousands	Thousands	Per protestant	Per leader	Per meeting place	Per missionary
North	560	50	510	4.8	370	450	1,200
Northeast	5,250	220	5,030	13.0	650	1,100	11,100
Southeast	7,700	950	6,750	4.4	170	460	6,000
South	3,150	560	2,590	2.5	210	390	4,300
Central-West	840	80	760	5.4	180	400	2,100
Brazil	17,500	1,860	15,640	4.8	240	540	5,200

Source: Estimates of the number of family units, Jan. 1, 1970, were based on factors of the number of people per domicile in each State determined from projection of the averages for 1940, 1950, and 1960. Recenseamento Geral do Brasil, I.B.G.E.

The picture that our family unit indicator gives of the responsibility for non-Protestant family units by Brazilian leaders, varies from 170 families in the Southeast to 650 in the Northeast. The North shows 370 non-Protestant families per Brazilian leader. These two regions, as the indicator spells out, appear to need additional Brazilian leaders when compared with the other regions. The large pastoral responsibility that Brazilian leaders have for teaching (edifying) and caring for their members, is pointed up graphically in Figure 6-5.

Non-Protestant Families Per Meeting Place

Another indicator would show that each local meeting place, including the central church, has a sphere of responsibility for an average of 540 non-Protestant families in Brazil according to Table 6-2 and Figure 6-5. This particular indicator is less for all regions except the Northeast where it rises substantially to 1,100 or double the average for Brazil. Again, such an indicator shows that the Northeast stands out as a remarkable region of need in the country.

FIGURE 6-5

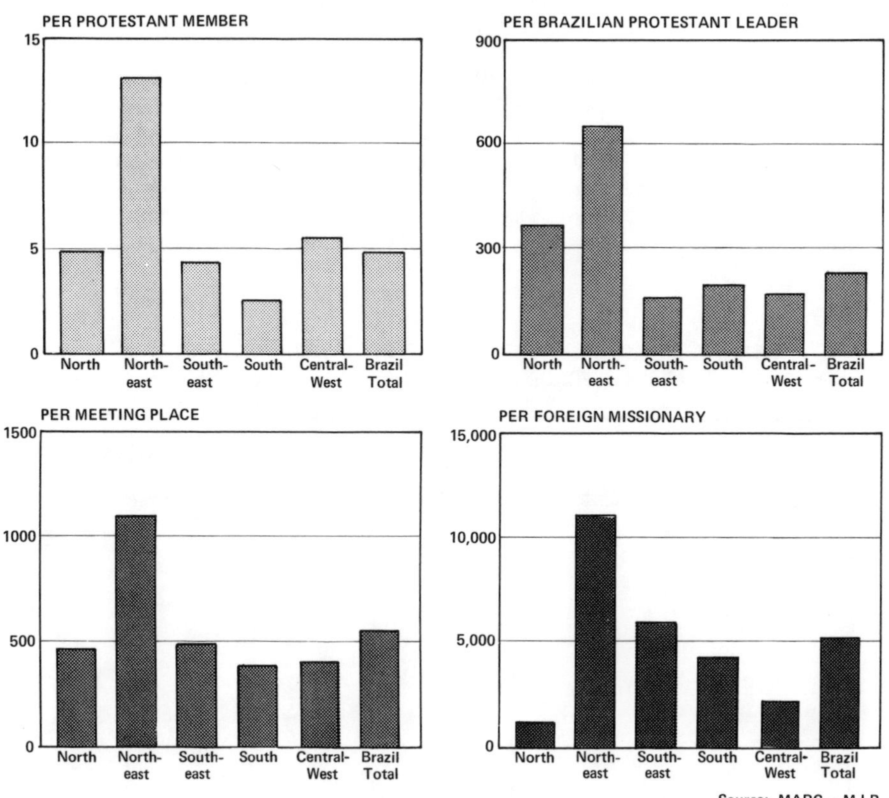

Source: MARC — M.I.B.

Non-Protestant Families Per Foreign Missionary

Another indicator would give every missionary in Brazil the responsibility for evangelizing the non-Protestant families of Brazil. Each missionary would have to communicate the Gospel to 5,200 families. By using the information in Table 6-2 and Figure 6-5 the number of non-Protestant families per missionary rises as high as 11,000 in the Northeast and in the Southeast is above the average where more than 1,000 of the missionaries are located.

Protestant Members Related to Meeting Places

Every meeting place, whether a large central church or a small preaching point, is a potential center for evangelistic activity. Planning strategy for evangelism, therefore, requires information regarding the number of members who can be counted on to assist in the evangelistic effort as well as the population of the area and the number of homes or families embraced.

The average number of Protestant members per meeting place in Brazil is 112 according to the indicators in Table 6-3. These averages varied from 73 in the Central-West, where new churches are springing up, to 160 in the South, where the Lutheran Church has long been entrenched. The North and the Northeast also have relatively small memberships, on the average. Averages per meeting place will vary even more widely between states.

TABLE 6-3

RELATIVE FACTORS INVOLVED IN MOBILIZATION OF THE EVANGELISTIC FORCE BY REGIONS IN BRAZIL, 1970

Region	Number of Protestant Members			Brazilian Leaders	Meeting Places
	Per meet-place	Per leader	Per missionary	Per missionary	Per missionary
North	95	77	240	3	3
Northeast	85	50	860	17	11
Southeast	104	39	1,360	35	12
South	160	86	1,740	20	12
Central-West	73	34	380	11	5
Brazil	112	50	1,080	22	10

Protestant Members Related to Brazilian Leaders

These members are the primary responsibility of the Brazilian Protestant leaders, "for the perfecting of the saints for the work of the ministry, for the edifying of the body of Christ" (Ephesians 4:12). They need to be taught their responsibilities for active participation in witness and evangelism and in building and maturing one another in the faith.

The number of Protestant members per leader averages 50 for Brazil as a whole. This average varies from only 34 in the Central-West to 86 in the South. Such an average indicates that there are a relatively large number of leaders in the areas where new rural settlements are growing rapidly and, except for the South, smaller numbers in the areas where churches have long been established. If all of the Brazilian Protestant leaders - pastors, elders, and deacons - cooperate in the task of training members for participation in the evangelistic task, the size of the job does not seem unreasonable for any region. For pastors alone, the job would be about four times that for all leaders.

The average number of members per leader varies from state to state as shown in Figure 6-6. Nine of the states, two in the South and seven in the North or Northeast, average sixty or more members per Brazilian Protestant leader, including pastors, elders, and deacons. The detail by states is given in Table 6-1. This shows a range of indicators from twenty-four members per leader in Guanabara and Goiás to 160 in Roraima.

FIGURE 6-6

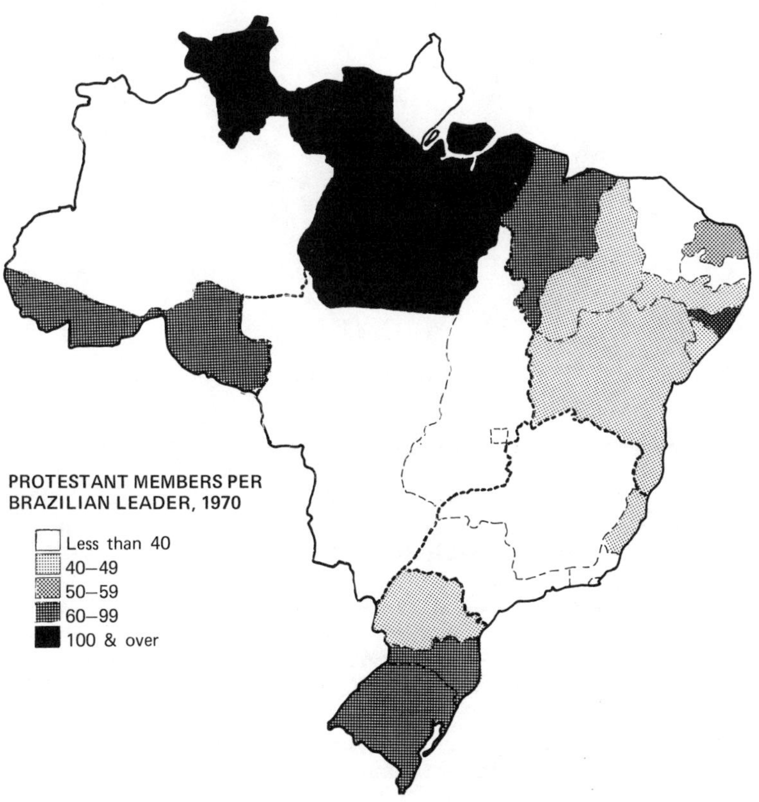

FIGURE 6-7

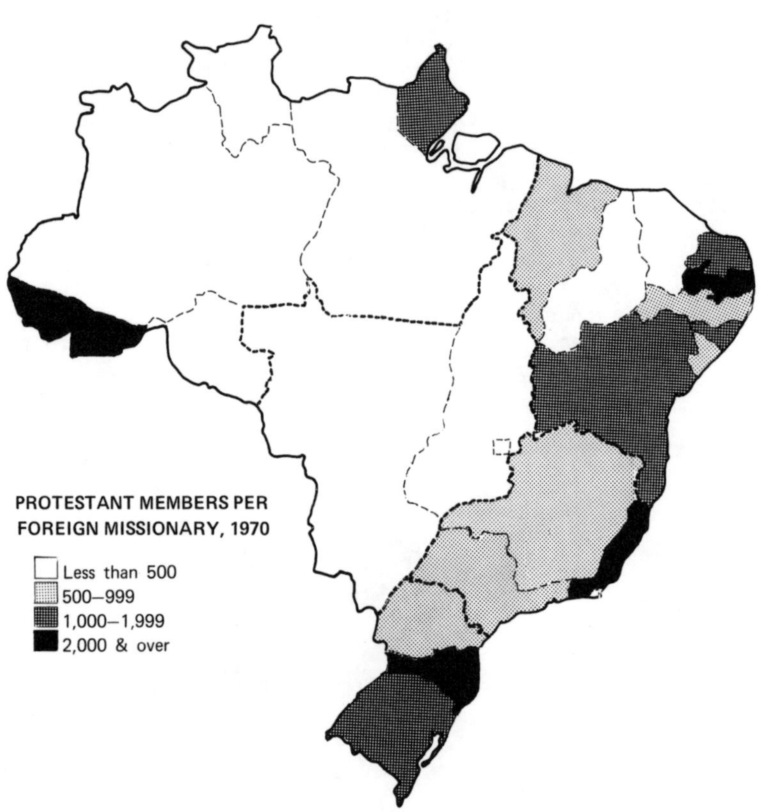

Protestant Members Related to Foreign Missionaries

Today many foreign missionaries in Brazil assist pastors and lay leaders with the edification, training, and other ecclesiastical and pastoral administrative functions that relate to churches and their membership. Some foreign missionaries conduct evangelistic campaigns of different types in cities of different sizes and minister in remote interior points. As national church groups grow and mature, many missionaries work closely with them, and upon special requests perform certain special types of ministries - usually under the jurisdiction of the national church. Some missionaries are still engaged in planting churches and usually turn their strongest churches over to the national church leadership for ecclesiastical control as soon as they become relatively self-sufficient. Relationships between foreign missions and national churches that are positive and productive need a great deal of negotiation, understanding, and increasing mutual respect. If we consider the number of Protestant members that exist in every state in Brazil and then relate them to the foreign missionary, we have a very interesting ratio of Protestant church members to foreign missionaries. In 1970 it would have been seen as shown in Figure 6-7.

Population Growth Versus The Growth of Protestant Members

The first results of the 1970 Brazilian census report the average annual rate of population growth between 1960 and 1970 to be 2.74 percent. The analysis which follows has been based on the Brazilian Bureau of the Census (I.B.G.E.) estimates for the period before taking the latest census. These pre-1970 census estimates show an average annual rate of 3.0 percent for Brazil. The detailed estimates and the wide varieties found in each state are given in Table 6-4.

The estimated average annual population growth rate for the Northeast region was only two percent. This was the lowest population growth of the five regions. This reflects the movement of people out of the section of the country due to pressures such as periodic droughts, depletion of soil nutrients in rural areas, education for their children, and a search for higher standards of living in other parts of Brazil. The Central-West had an average population growth of 5.2 percent, the highest in the nation. This region experienced rapid growth as new settlers from all parts of Brazil were attracted to frontier areas opened up by the expanding frontier highway network. The growth of population in the State of Paraná, with the expansion of new coffee plantations, often resulting in a boom economy situation, carries an average annual population growth rate of 6.8 percent.

The rate of growth of Protestant members usually exceeds that of the general population. This was not true, however, for the Territory of Rondônia or the States of Maranhão, Ceará, Espirito Santo, Santa Catarina, and Rio Grande do Sul. These states had a lower average annual rate of Protestant members than of population. The relationship that exists between the rates of growth for population and the rates of growth for Protestant members is shown in Table 6-4 in the last column. The rate of Protestant membership growth in all of Brazil was 1.8 times that of the population growth rate, but the South region has a lower rate of growth for Protestant members than for population. These regional factors and relationships are important and need to be pondered and studied in depth by all Protestant leaders.

TABLE 6-4

RELATIONSHIP BETWEEN AVERAGE ANNUAL GROWTH PERCENTS FOR PROTESTANT MEMBERS AND POPULATION, 1960 - 1970

States and Regions	Average Annual Population Growth	Growth, 1960-1970 Protestant Members	1970 / 1960
North	Percent	Percent	Ratio
Rondônia	6.2	4.4	0.7
Ácre	3.0	8.8	2.9
Amazonas	2.9	11.5	4.0
Roraima (Rio Branco)	4.8	14.6	3.0
Pará	2.8	4.2	1.5
Amapá	5.6	8.7	1.6
Subtotal	3.1	6.2	2.0
Northeast			
Maranhão	4.2	3.8	0.9
Piaui	1.5	13.0	8.7
Ceará	1.8	0.8	0.4
Rio Grande do Norte	1.4	2.9	2.1
Paraiba	1.4	3.1	2.2
Pernambuco	1.7	7.0	4.1
Alagoas	1.2	5.3	4.4
Sergipe	1.5	7.7	5.1
Bahia	1.7	6.0	3.3
Subtotal	2.0	5.4	2.7
Southeast			
Minas Gerais	2.0	6.0	3.0
Espirito Santo	4.6	1.4	0.3
Rio de Janeiro	3.7	7.7	2.1
Guanabara	2.9	6.7	2.3
São Paulo	3.2	7.5	2.3
Subtotal	2.9	6.6	2.4
South			
Paraná	6.8	6.9	1.0
Santa Catarina	3.0	2.1	0.7
Rio Grande do Sul	2.4	2.1	0.9
Subtotal	4.2	3.1	0.7
Central-West			
Mato Grosso	5.3	18.8	3.5
Goiás	4.4	4.8	1.1
Distrito Federal (Brasília)	12.0	22.4	1.9
Subtotal	5.2	11.9	2.3
Totals	3.0	5.3	1.8

The average annual overall rate of growth of Protestant members for Brazil was 5.3 percent. This average varies from 11.9 percent in the Central-West, where Brasília is located and which experienced a large amount of immigration, to 3.1 percent for the South. Among the States, the Federal District stood out with a high of 22.4 percent and Ceará the lowest with 0.8 percent. A series of studies should be initiated to determine the basic factors which have influenced these different rates of growth in Brazil, state by state. Migration appears to be one of the principal factors responsible for some of the high and low rates of growth. The different socio-economic variables will be confirmed through research that has already been initiated in Brazil through the CASE (Center for Advanced Studies in Evangelism) in São Paulo.

Counties Without Organized Protestant Worship Centers Reported

The government census of Protestant churches in 1967 does not contain reports for 1,909 counties as noted in Table 6-5, indicating there are still large areas of Brazil which do not have a sufficient number of believers to develop organized Protestant worship centers. However, every area of this type should be investigated thoroughly before any decision is made to initiate evangelistic efforts. The CASE Center in São Paulo has a detailed list from which each of these counties may be carefully studied within their micro-regions. They should be contacted for initial information on these underdeveloped Protestant areas. The reports on the Protestant churches obtained Templo Sede or "central churches." These pastors and leaders report the central church membership at the beginning and end of the year, but also include any satellite churches or preaching points in their reports for which the central church is responsible. These satellite churches may be found in other sections of the same city or located where the central church is situated or may be found in other cities or countries.

Where are these counties that do not report any Protestant membership located? The largest number, 805, is located in the Northeast. These comprise 59 percent of all the counties found in this region. The large State of Bahia has 170 of these counties; Rio Grande do Norte has 118, and Paraíba, 116. Surprising as it may seem, 596 of these counties who report no Protestant worship centers are located in the populous Southeast, principally in the States of Minas Gerais and São Paulo. Studies of certain church directories indicate that some of these counties have a few satellite churches or meeting places sponsored by large central churches in other counties.

Additional Indicators Needed

Brazil is passing through a very accelerated process of cultural, social, and economic change in the decade of the 1970's.

TABLE 6-5

NUMBERS OF COUNTIES WITHOUT REPORTED PROTESTANT WORSHIP CENTERS BY STATES AND REGIONS FOR BRAZIL, 1967

States and Regions	All Counties	Counties without Reported Protestant Worship Centers	
North	Number	Number	Percent
Rondônia	2	0	0
Ácre	7	0	0
Amazonas	44	23	52
Roraima (Rio Branco)	2	1	50
Pará	83	20	24
Amapá	5	4	80
Region	143	48	34
Northeast			
Maranhão	129	52	40
Piaui	114	82	72
Ceará	142	93	66
Rio Grande do Norte	150	118	78
Paraiba	170	116	68
Pernambuco	164	68	41
Alagoas	94	58	62
Sergipe	74	48	65
Bahia	335	170	51
Region	1,374	805	59
Southeast			
Minas Gerais	722	467	65
Espirito Santo	53	4	8
Rio de Janeiro	63	1	2
Guanabara	1	0	0
São Paulo	572	124	22
Region	1,411	596	42
South			
Paraná	277	86	31
Santa Catarina	195	118	60
Rio Grande do Sul	232	106	46
Region	704	310	44
Central-West			
Mato Grosso	84	26	31
Goiás	222	124	56
Distrito Federal (Brasilia)	1	0	0
Region	307	150	49
Brazil totals	3,939	1,909	48

Source: Based on I. B. G. E., Estatistica dos Cultos Protestantes, 1966.

In order that Protestant leaders can better understand these rapid social transformations and the implications that such rapid transitions have for the establishment, growth, and ministry of their churches, more work needs to be done in this field of designing indicators to accurately measure the progress and prospects of the Protestant church. Additional indicators are needed to develop an effective way of measuring these important elements.

The rapid growth of urbanization in Brazil will continue throughout this decade. A special set of indicators is needed that will be able to measure the effectiveness of the Protestant effort in the 112 urban regions that were made official in 1968 by the Brazilian Census Bureau as the definitive urban regional divisions for Brazil (Fundacao IBGE, 1968:207). Since 1968, all data and information on urban growth in Brazil has been reported and published within the general framework of this new urban classification system and using these new urban regions for reference.

The BRAZIL 1980 church growth computer analysis, available at the CASE Center in São Paulo (Appendix 2), is an information resource that Brazilian leaders can use as a tool to design and develop such special church indicators that will apply to the rapidly developing sector of urbanization that has now been broken down into 112 different geographical units by the Brazilian government.

In the same way other sets of church indicators could be developed to monitor the inter-related changes taking place between the church and its environment in important sectors such as: the different areas of economic growth, the industrial areas, the age and sex differentiations found within the population, the changing rates of literacy for all ages, the upward mobility trends of people of all ages in the social structure, and other areas that contribute to and produce the various "islands of modernization" in Brazil. For a more complete discussion of modernization and what effect it is having on the growth of the Protestant church, see Chapter 8.

Each of the many different denominations found within the Protestant community in Brazil could derive great benefit in the decade of the 1970's from the results of efforts or work done to develop such a set of church indicators. Specialized church indicators of this nature could be unique catalytic agents drawn from basic sources of information that will serve to point out important trends of Protestant advance, decline, or retreat in the different sectors of Brazilian society under observation. Such indicators have been effectively used by industry, government, and certain disciplines within the academic world. The Protestant community in Brazil could be one of the first religious entities in the world to effectively utilize and apply these tools of social science to the responsive network of growth that is found among the Brazilian Protestant churches. If this could be done effectively in Brazil, it can be done in other parts of the world.

7

The Foreign Mission Force

SUMMARY

NUMBER OF MISSIONARIES IN BRAZIL

In 1960........1,000
In 1970........2,990

MISSIONARY LOCATIONS BY REGION

Southeast........40%
South............18%
North............15%
Northeast........15%
Central-West.....12%

IDENTIFICATION OF MISSIONARIES BY ASSOCIATIONS

Older traditional denominations....1,256
Newer denominations..................317
Associated with IFMA or EFMA.......1,053
Independent Missions, et al..........264

MISSIONARY ARRIVALS AND TIME ON THE FIELD

Before 1949...............15%
Between 1949-1958.........25%
Between 1959-1968.........68%

MISSIONARY AREAS OF ORIGIN

From U.S.A..........80%
Europe, Asia,
and Canada..........20%

CLASSIFICATION OF MISSIONARIES BY AGE

Under 28 years..........5%
28 to 37 years.........42%
38 to 47 years.........32%
48 to 57 years.........12%
Over 58 years...........9%

INTRODUCTION

The Missionary Information Bureau (MIB) in São Paulo has for several years obtained detailed information regarding foreign missionaries working in Brazil. This information covers such questions as: How many are there? When did they arrive? Where did they come from? How old are they? What is their marital status? What are the ages of their children? What are the men missionaries doing? What are the women missionaries doing?

The first known foreign missionary to Brazil was a Scotch Presbyterian, Dr. Robert Kalley. He arrived in Rio de Janeiro in 1855 and began planting churches which developed into the Evangelical Congregational Church. He was the first of many other missionaries to arrive in Brazil to carry on the task of evangelism and establishing churches. As the number of these churches grew, denominations were formed which for many years remained largely under the direction of the missionaries. However, since World War II the older traditional denominations have completed the transfer of administrative responsibility to Brazilians.

Missionaries continue to function at the invitation and under the direction of Brazilian leaders of the larger traditional denominations. Since the 1960's, a fresh influx of foreign missionaries of "faith missions" have endeavored to establish new churches and to help the already established churches in different ways such as with literature, radio and television programs, and in Bible schools and seminaries.

How Many Are There?

The total number of missionaries by decades since 1900 is graphically recorded in Figure 7-1. This indicates an increase from about 250 to nearly 3,000 by 1970, with a decrease during World War II. Although there has been an influx of missionaries of many new denominations and "faith missions" during the last two decades, the large increase for 1970 in comparison to that for 1960 may reflect the results of new research rather than a real increase in numbers. During the last five years the Missionary Information Bureau has made a special effort to locate every foreign missionary in Brazil.

Where Are They Located?

Substantial missionary activity among the Indian tribes of the North and Central-West Regions, fifteen and twelve percent respectively, engage missionaries in these areas where only four and five percent of the Protestant membership are located (Table 3-3). Nearly 40 percent of the missionaries work in the Southeast where 47 percent of the members are located and eighteen percent are found in the South. Another 15 percent are to be found in the Northeast.

Foreign Mission Affiliation?

The approximately 3,000 foreign missionaries (including wives) in Brazil work in more than 150 different mission organizations. About 1,256 missionaries are associated with older traditional denominations. Three hundred seventeen work with various denominations, having relatively new work. One thousand fifty-three are associated with "faith missions." Of these, the majority (480) are engaged in translating the Bible into Indian languages and evangelizing these groups, 344 are seeking to plant churches, and 229 are primarily engaged in serving established national churches. Only 104 missionaries are associated with Pentecostal churches.

---

*Fred E. Edwards has written about the "faith missions" in Brazil in his book, *The Role of the Faith Mission: A Brazilian Case Study*, see Bibliography.

FIGURE 7-1

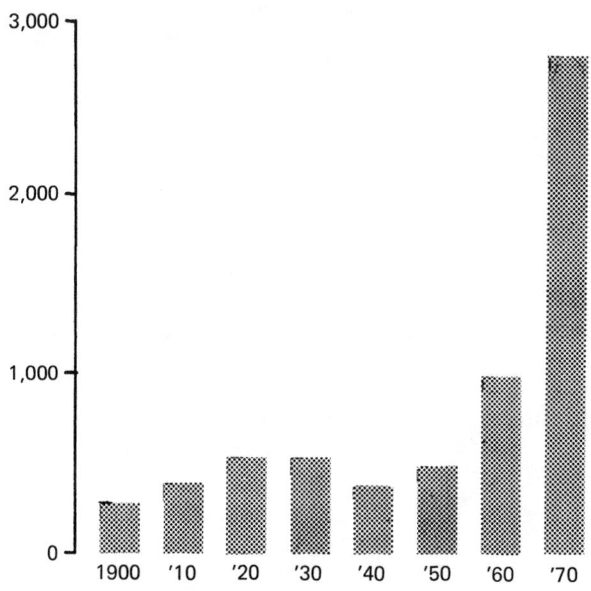

Note: Large recorded increase in last decade may be the result of better data collection.

Source: Data for 1900 to 1960 based on various sources; for 1970, MARC–MIB, 1969.

When Did They Arrive?

Figure 7-2 shows that almost 60 percent of these missionaries arrived between 1959 and 1968. More than 25 percent of them arrived between 1949 and 1958. Nearly 15 percent arrived before 1949.

Many experienced missionary statesmen and knowledgeable observers say that it takes at least two terms of service on a mission field for a missionary to pass through the necessary adaptive stages, changes, and language-learning processes in order that he may perform effectively in a national church situation. On this basis, only 40 percent of these missionaries have reached a stage of usefulness and can be fairly well adapted to the life-style, customs, and language of the Brazilian people. These seasoned missionaries generally have earned a right to be heard by Brazilians and serve effectively in the cultural situation in which they live.

FIGURE 7-2

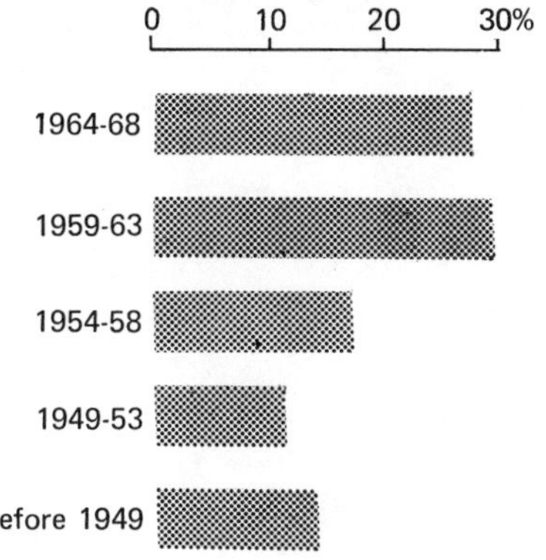

Source: MARC – MIB, 1969

The United States has been the principal sending country, and relatively few Brazilians, even today, speak and understand English. Furthermore, as one mission leader points out, "The missionaries keep pretty much to themselves in their daily affairs and social relationships." It means that the Brazilian is looked upon as "the work." The result is that too often the missionary has only a professional attitude toward the people to whom he seeks to minister.

The missionaries from Europe and from Japan are ministering primarily to Brazilians who either speak and understand their language or have a similar cultural background. This is especially true for German missionaries working among communities with German background in the South Region.*

FIGURE 7-3

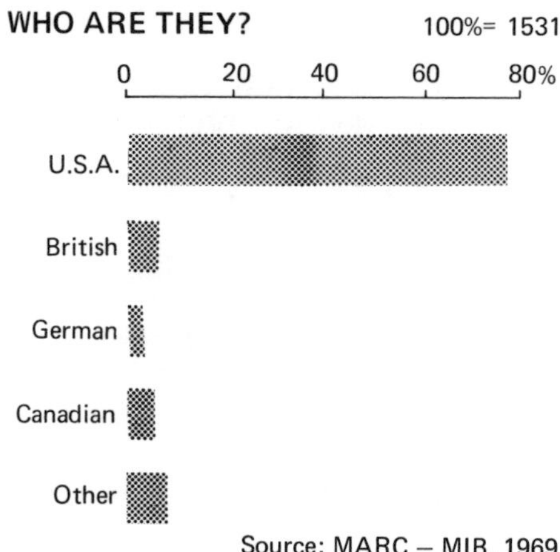

Who Are They? Where Did They Come From?

According to Figure 7-3, slightly less than 80 percent of these missionaries were from the United States and the remainder were principally from Canada, the British Isles, and European countries. (Because the questionnaire was in English, these proportions do not accurately reflect the countries-of-origin of the entire foreign missionary family. There is a higher proportion of Germans than indicated by Figure 7-3 and probably of other nationalities that do not use English.)

---

*This is a case of M^2 missions using Dr. Ralph D. Winter's three-fold classification of missions. (M^1, the agents of mission and evangelization originate in the same culture and minister and evangelize in the same geographical area. M^2, the agents of mission and evangelization originate in a similar cultural group and minister or evangelize in similar culture groups found in a different geographical area. M^3, the agents of mission and evangelization originate in a different culture and evangelize in a different culture in an adjacent or distant geographical area.)

In 1968 MARC and MIB collaborated in the publication of a directory of *Protestant Missions in Brazil** listing foreign missionary agencies with missionaries assigned to work in that country. The 162 organizations listed were from the following countries:

U.S.A.	122	Sweden	2
England	14	Switzerland	2
Germany	7	Ireland	1
Japan	6	South Africa	1
Canada	3	Finland	1
Holland	3	TOTAL	162

How Old Are They?

The largest number of foreign missionaries found in Brazil, according to Figure 7-4 are between 28 and 37 years of age. Seventy-five percent of the foreign missionaries are between 28 and 47 years of age. Nearly 20 percent are 48 years of age or older. There are very few missionaries in Brazil under 28 years of age. This reflects a tendency of missions to select older men and women to send to Brazil, some to serve the national church in various ways, and others to seek to establish new churches. In 1973, MIB published a *Directory of Missionaries in Brazil* (see Bibliography).

What is Their Marital Status?

As is generally true in other countries, there are more women than men missionaries working in Brazil. One-third of the women reporting were single and five percent of the men reporting stated that they were single. This would indicate that there are eight single women missionaries for each single male missionary in Brazil.

What Are The Ages of Their Children?

More than 90 percent of the married missionaries reported having children. About 17 percent of the children are under six years of age, according to Figure 7-5. The largest proportion (31 percent) is in the six-to-ten age group and 26 percent,

---

*See the 1973 Directory of Mission agencies working in Brazil in the Directory section of this book. In 1973 there were more than 250 agencies working in the country.

and 26 percent, 11-to-15-year olds. One mission leader points out that "this factor makes adaptation harder and longer - especially when the missionary wants his children to get American schooling." Another 26 percent of the children are 16 years of age or older, and many of these are attending high schools and colleges in their country of origin.

FIGURE 7-4

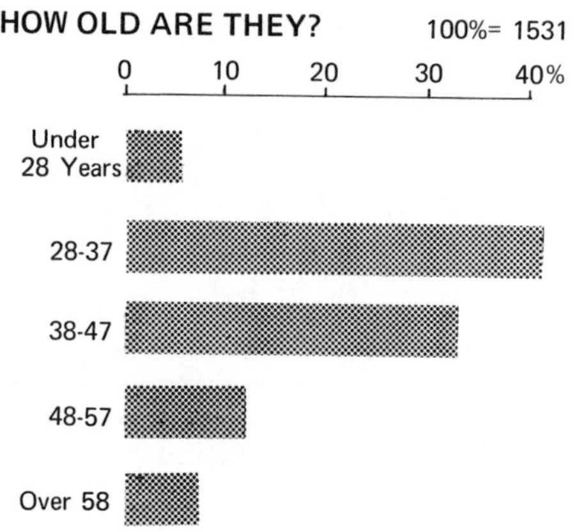

Seventy-five percent of the children of missionaries are attending school. The majority of these are attending schools where English is the principal language. These schools are eigher run by foreign missions or by the American community in the larger cities. Most missionary children do not attend Brazilian schools regularly. The result is that missionary homes are usually culturally oriented toward the homeland.

What Are The Men Missionaries Doing?

Approximately 75 percent of the 639 men missionaries reporting stated that they had more than one responsibility. Although one may note from Figure 7-6 that 65 percent stated that they were engaged fully or part-time in evangelism and preaching the Gospel, many were spending considerable time in service activities. A little more than 30 percent are engaged in educational activities: Bible schools, seminaries, and secular schools. Almost one-fourth of them have administrative responsibilities. The mass media, literature, and radio/television claimed the attention of more than 20 percent.

FIGURE 7-5

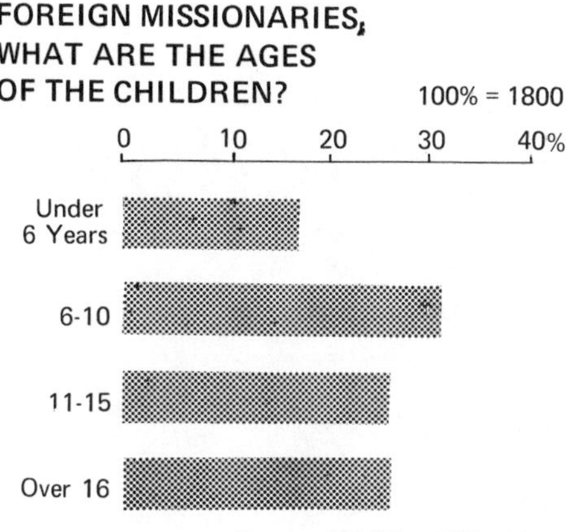

What Are The Women Missionaries Doing?

More than 80 percent of the 892 women missionaries reporting stated that they were engaged in some form of missionary activity. Less than 20 percent indicated they spent their full time caring for their children and homemaking. About 30 percent are engaged part-time in more than one missionary activity. Figure 7-7 shows that some 44 percent are engaged in some way in evangelistic activities. Educational activities, such as in Bible and secular schools and teaching the missionaries' children, requires the time of 35 percent of the women. More than ten percent are engaged in literature or radio or television activities. Only seven percent have responsibilities associated with administration, eight percent in medical activities and linguistics claim the attention of another seven percent of the women.

FIGURE 7-6

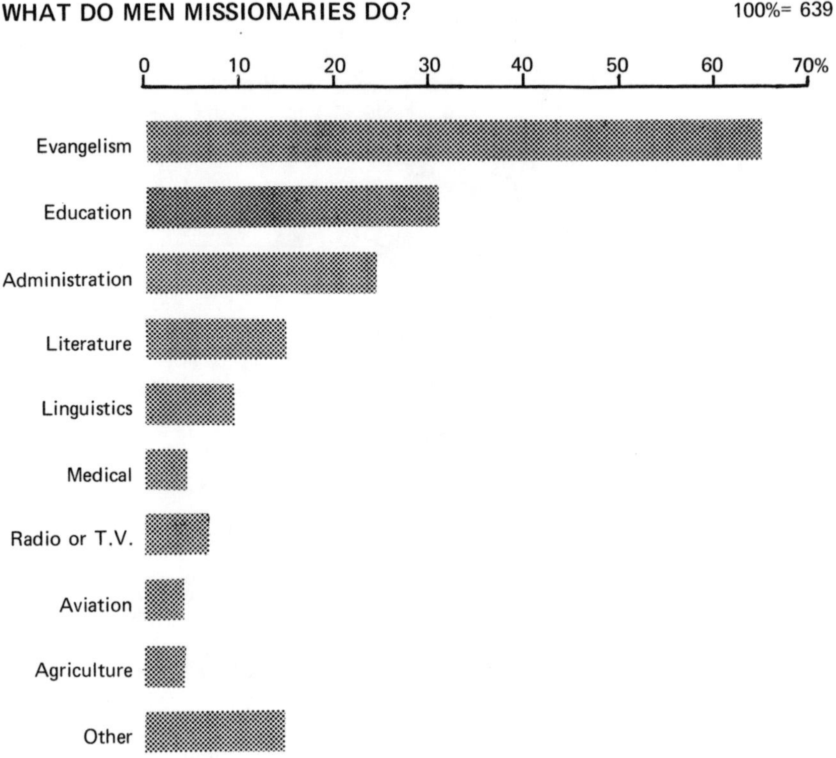
WHAT DO MEN MISSIONARIES DO?
100%= 639
0
10
20
30
40
50
60
70%
Evangelism
Education
Administration
Literature
Linguistics
Medical
Radio or T.V.
Aviation
Agriculture
Other
Source: MARC– MIB, 1969

FIGURE 7-7

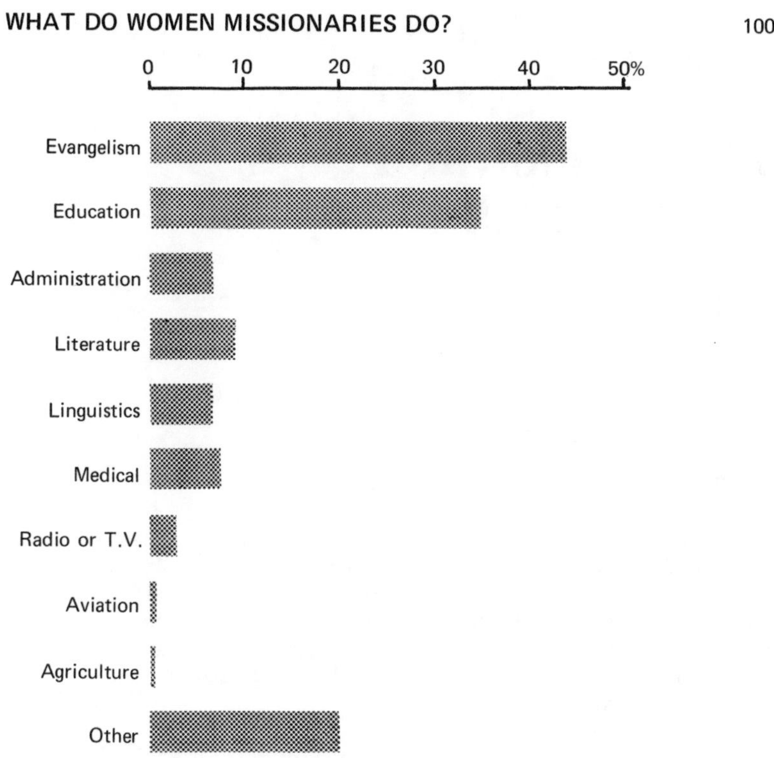
WHAT DO WOMEN MISSIONARIES DO?
100%= 892
0
10
20
30
40
50%
Evangelism
Education
Administration
Literature
Linguistics
Medical
Radio or T.V.
Aviation
Agriculture
Other
Source: MARC— MIB, 1969

Modernization and Church Growth

SUMMARY

The term <u>modernization</u> is introduced and defined in this chapter as the change that is now taking place in Brazilian society as it moves from a traditional, rural to a modern, urban nation. Church growth is happening within the context of this modernization process and needs to be understood in terms of urbanization, industrialization and the westward expansion to settle new land areas.

Historical factors such as the cycle of coffee production have been used to introduce innovations and social change. When these things happen in a society a new climate settles over the land for the acceptance and receptiveness of the gospel proclamation. Protestant growth in this climate of change and modernization is discussed and some future projections of growth are considered along with some timely precautions.

INTRODUCTION

This chapter is an introduction to modernization. It will first define this term and second attempt to relate the implications of the modernization process going on in Brazil to the growth of Protestant churches. A third objective of this chapter will be to project Protestant church growth up to the year 1980 in these areas of innovation and modernization in order to anticipate at the beginning of this momentous decade what is ahead for the Protestant community.

The conclusions are in the form of a hypothesis. The information that has been used was collected from many sources, and the unique church growth analysis data that is the primary basis of these projections is found in the MARC/MIB Data Bank produced in the Brazil 1980 project under the auspices of MARC.* Brazil is now in a stage of national development and integration comparable to the "take-off stage" suggested by Rostow in his writing on the process of economic development. (Rostow 1967:36). In the next three decades the "take-off" will happen in Brazil. The rapidly expanding road network and increasing tempo of the process of industrialization will continue to move together in the years ahead to penetrate all Brazilian society and to integrate Brazil both physically and economically.

Definition of Modernization

Modernization is defined as the process of social change and transformation that affects an entire society. It can be change that comes from within or without, a country changing its traditional rural way of life so that it becomes a modern, urban society caught up into increasing levels of productivity brought about by innovations in technology. This produces long-term gains to increasing numbers of people which share increasingly, certain basic characteristics with people who live in the developed nations of the world.

Modernization deals with the whole gamut of social change during which new ideas are introduced into a social system in the hope of generating a higher per capita income and higher levels of living through more modern production methods and the redesign of social organization. Modernization is also the process by which individuals change from a traditional way of life to a more complex, technologically advanced, and rapidly changing life-style. Modernization is not to be identified with Europeanization or Westernization, nor does it necessarily result in the greatest benefit for members of less developed countries.

The centralization process and development of the economic, educational, and political institutions that accompany modernization affect other major social institutions such as family and religion. These changes, in turn, cause social differentiation and cultural integrations to accelerate, producing a more complex society.

---

*See Appendix 3 for description of this project.

Guidelines for Studies

Why is the study of modernization of interest to the church? Four reasons are suggested:

1. Modernization is a valuable and helpful term to identify what is now going on in the country.

2. The study of modernization permits comparisons to be made in quantifiable terms and this can give knowledge of what is happening in specific areas of Brazil.

3. Modernization helps us visualize the many innovative factors at work in society and see them working together in the large process of social change.

4. The study of modernization can be used as a practical tool whose applications have far-reaching results for those who want to know how to think about a changing Brazil - those who are given the responsibility to make decisions and formulate plans for advance in the Protestant community.

If the rush toward modernization in Brazil is not understood now by Protestant leaders, it may be impossible to prepare for the many changes that lie ahead. Corrective steps and action will be a matter of too little too late.

We recognize that different aspects of change in a society are necessary. Life is not static and unless certain changes do occur, societies will languish and die. A dynamic is found within the life processes of a culture. The change we hope for in modernization is a change from within that preserves essential elements of the past, develops and borrows from the present, and incorporates the best of past and present into the future.

Modernization then, is a many-sided transformation that goes on within a country. Our discussion in this chapter can only be introductory and will open up the topic for us in three major areas: urbanization, industrialization, and westward expansion in Brazil. These three areas will be used to illustrate the process of modernization at work in Brazil and how the Protestant churches have grown in these areas, and projections of church growth up to 1980.

Urbanization

In 1930 the worldwide economic depression paralyzed exportation of agricultural production, but it stimulated the

FIGURE 8-1

NINE MAJOR METROPOLITAN CENTERS IN BRAZIL IN 1970

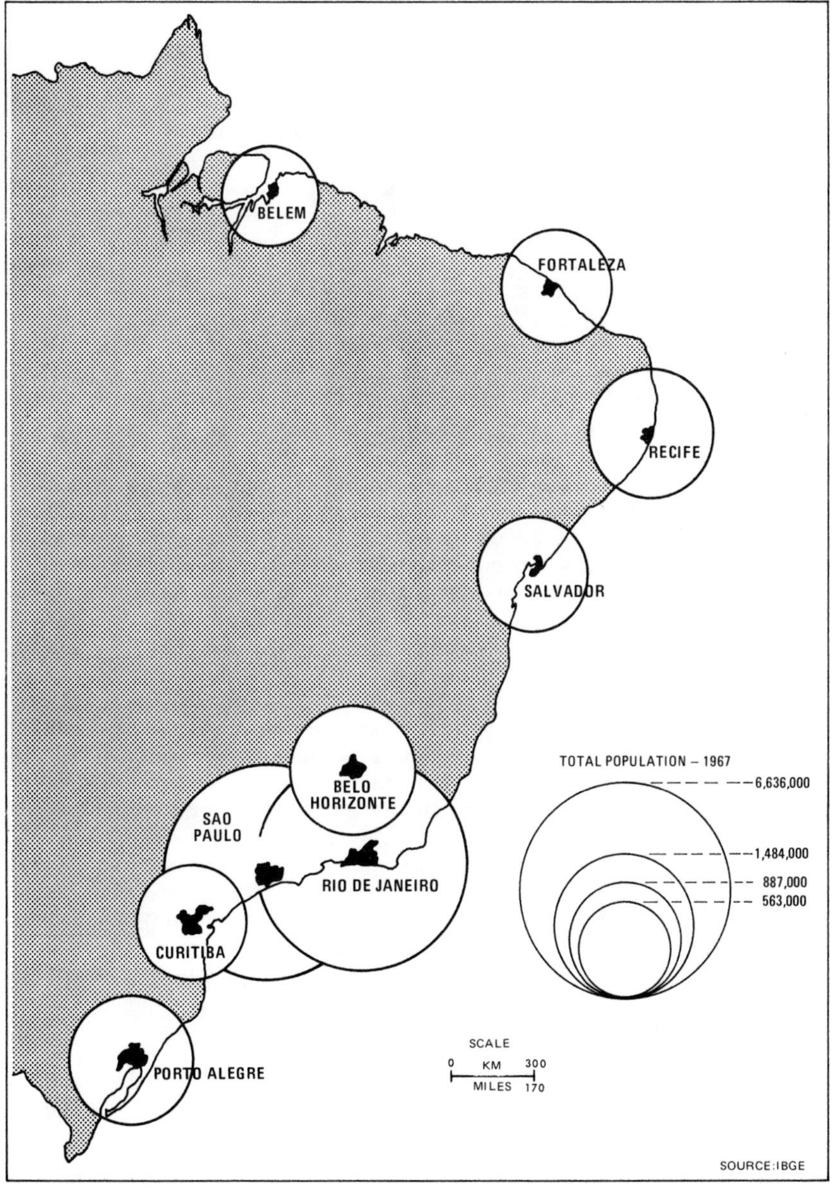

establishment of an infant industrial sector. By 1940 the growth of industry in São Paulo and Rio de Janeiro was beginning to attract people from different parts of Brazil and causing an imbalance in the socio-economic panorama of the country. By 1950 the urban-industrial sector had begun to create great disparities between the urban and agricultural sectors, with major concentrations in the Southeast. At the same time, the rate of natural increase in the Brazilian population began to soar in the regions with less economic opportunities.

This regional discrepancy between the increase of the population and the increase in the money economy became the fundamental push-pull factor increasing the level of internal migrations. The increasing mobility of the population was made possible by the expansion of the existing road system.

The diffusion of urban culture began to accelerate through the means of modern mass communication media such as movies, magazines, transistor radios, television, and other things that stimulated the ambition of people for a higher position in the social structure and has often been spoken of as the movement toward "higher expectations" among the masses in the population.

High pressure density areas of urban population began to develop which, in turn, served as strong centers of attraction for people in nine large urban centers. By 1970 the general increased instability of the Brazilian population had been heightened by this process of urbanization and a definite pattern of urban growth had developed around these metropolitan centers. (See Figure 8-1). By 1950 almost nine million people were living in these cities. By 1960 the figure had increased to almost 15 million, but ten years later close to 24 million inhabitants could be found in these areas - almost 25 percent of the total population in Brazil by 1970. In 1950 strong currents of internal migration had developed and were moving into these centers. An example of this can be seen in Figure 8-2.

In 1960 this same pattern of internal migration had increased and its magnitude is shown in Figure 8-3. The large circles indicate the millions of people living in 1960 that were born in that region. The percentage figures indicated the portion of people who had migrated to another region from the region of their birth. The numbers with arrows, in thousands, represents the people who relocated in different regions of Brazil.

An example of the internal migration within the State of Minas Gerais in 1966 can be seen in Figure 8-4. The thickness of lines is a clue to the amount of people who came into Belo Horizonte from these different areas in the state.

FIGURE 8-2

INTERNAL MIGRATION IN BRAZIL IN 1950
THREE PATTERNS

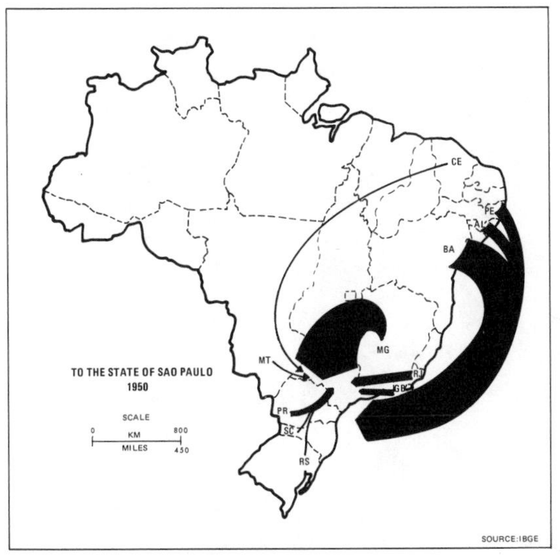

FIGURE 8-2

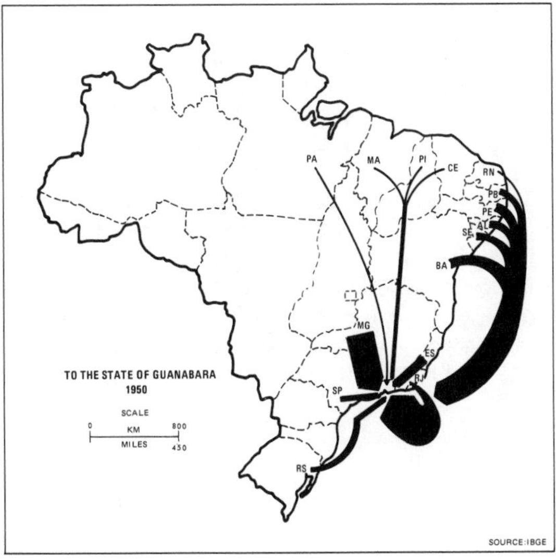

FIGURE 8-2, CONTINUED

The density pattern of the population in 1940 and 1960 can be seen in Figure 8-5. By 1970 the density of the population presented a pattern that looked like Figure 8-6.

FLIGHT TO THE CITIES

Growth of Cities in Brazil 1940-1970

In the past twenty years the number of inhabitants in Brazil has doubled. In the same period of time the population has quadrupled in the large urban centers like Rio de Janeiro, São Paulo, Belo Horizonte, Recife, and Pôrto Alegre.

In 1940 less than a third of the Brazilians lived in the cities. Ten years later this was about the same with a little more than a third being city-dwellers. Between 1950 and 1960 something began to take place that changed the urban-rural population pattern. In this decade, with the accelerated growth of industry, the process of urbanization took a great jump. By 1960 almost half of the Brazilian population was to be found in cities.

FIGURE 8-3

INTERNAL MIGRATIONS

Origin of Brazilians according to the region of their birth and where they were in 1960.

numbers in circles = millions of people born in each region
percentages = proportion of people that left their region of birth
numbers with arrows = thousands of people re-located

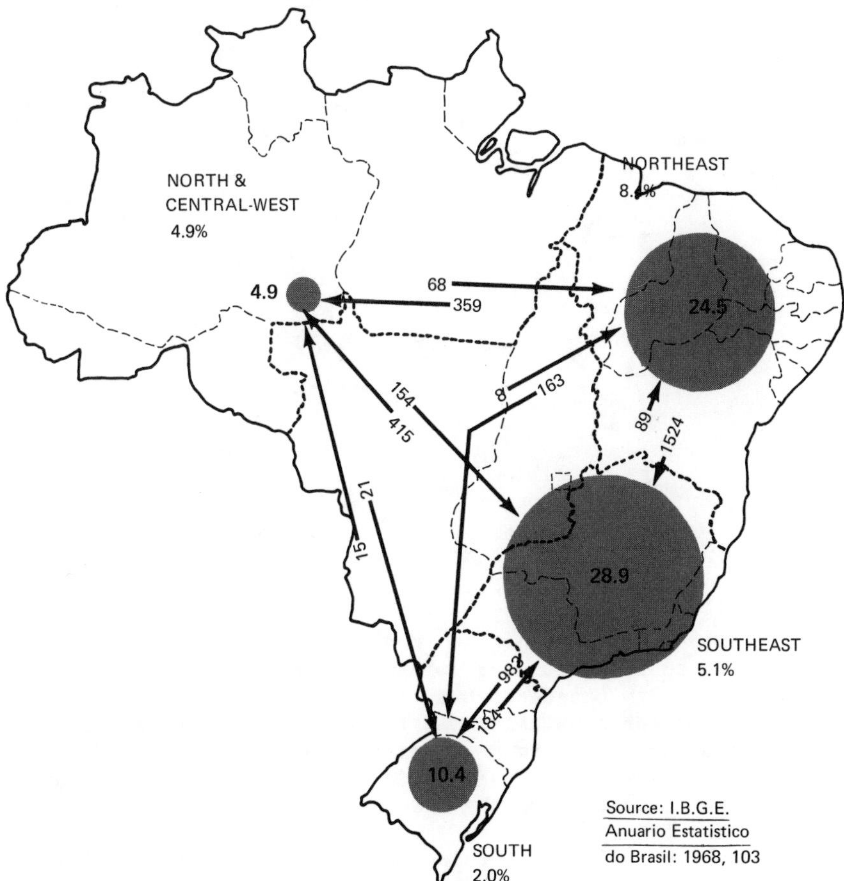

FIGURE 8-4

PATTERN OF INTERNAL MIGRATION IN STATE OF MINAS GERAIS IN 1960

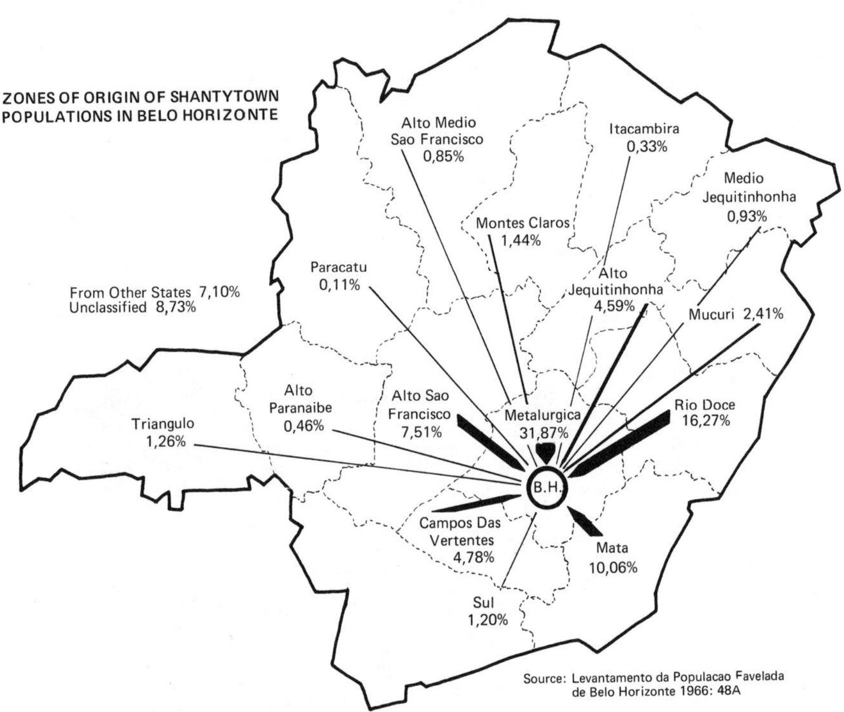

In 1969 two-thirds of the people living in the state of São Paulo lived in urban centers. In the States of Paraná, Santa Catarina, and Rio Grande do Sul, as well as the Northeast region, 40 percent of the population was found in the cities and 60 percent in the rural sectors. In Minas Gerais, the state of Rio de Janeiro, Guanabara, and Espírito Santo, the urban populations, on the average, came to more than 50 percent.

Today, in 1973, the population found in all of the cities in Brazil comprises close to 60 percent of all inhabitants.

Growth of Large, Populous Counties 1940-1970

The number of counties having more than 160,000 people has increased significantly. In 1940 there were 23 counties that had more than 100,000 people. In 1950 there were 39, in 1960 there were 65, and by 1970 this number had grown to 75 counties.

FIGURE 8-5

POPULATION DENSITY PATTERNS IN BRAZIL; 1940 AND 1960

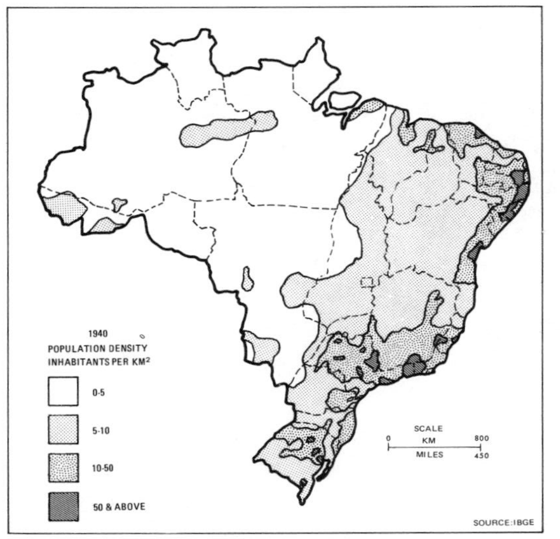

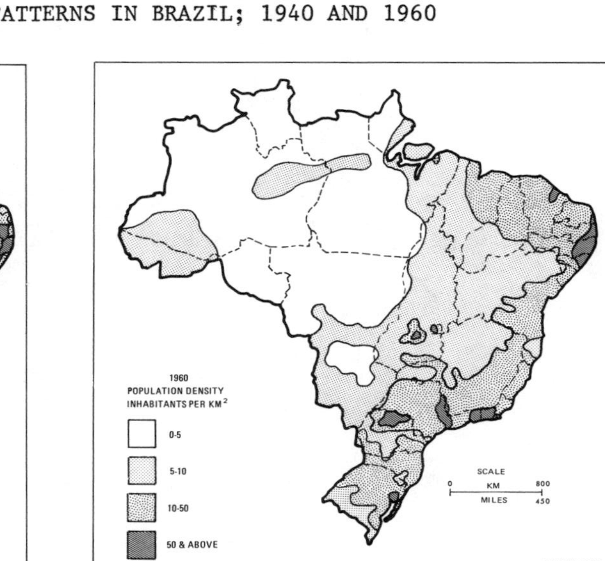

FIGURE 8-6

POPULATION DENSITY FOR BRAZIL IN 1970

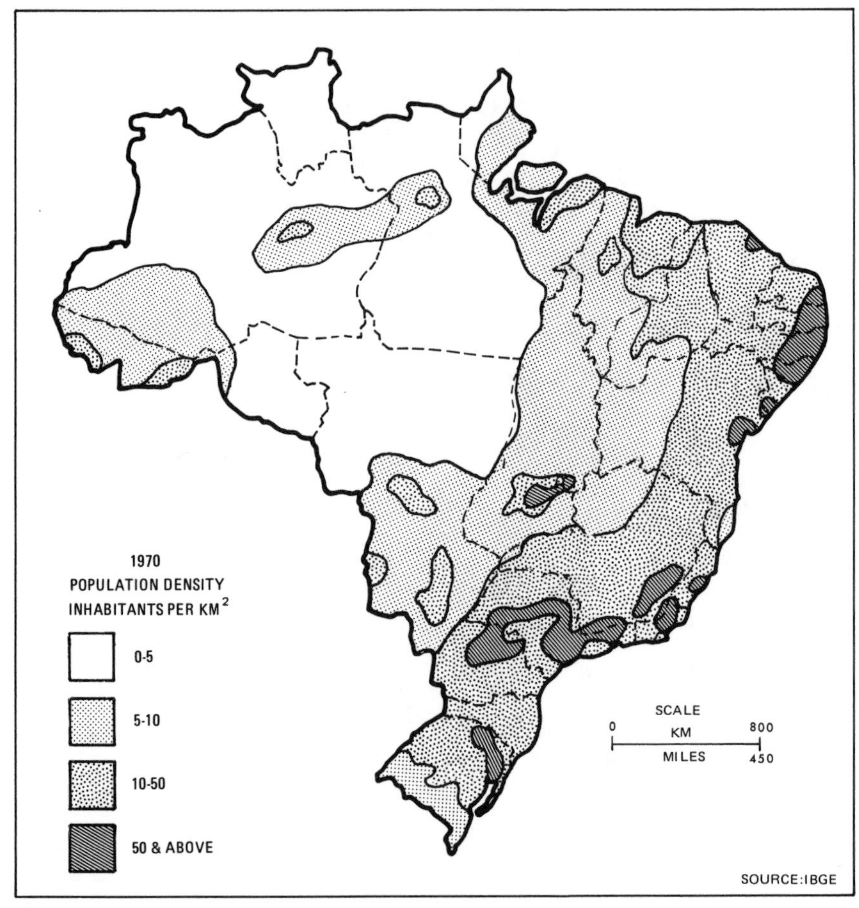

TABLE 8-1

COUNTIES HAVING MORE THAN
200,000 POPULATION IN 1970

No. DE ORDEM	MUNICÍPIO	UNIDADE DA FEDERAÇÃO	POPULAÇÃO RECENSEADA
1	São Paulo	São Paulo	5 978 977
2	Guanabara	Guanabara	4 315 746
3	Belo Horizonte	Minas Gerais	1 255 415
4	Recife	Pernambuco	1 084 459
5	Salvador	Bahia	1 027 142
6	Pôrto Alegre	Rio Grande do Sul	903 175
7	Fortaleza	Ceará	872 702
8	Nova Iguaçu	Rio de Janeiro	731 814
9	Belém	Pará	624 362
10	Curitiba	Paraná	642 362
11	Brasília	Distrito Federal	546 015
12	Duque de Caxias	Rio de Janeiro	434 654
13	São Gonçalo	Rio de Janeiro	433 985
14	Santo André	São Paulo	420 828
15	Goiânia	Goiás	389 784
16	Campinas	São Paulo	382 097
17	Santos	São Paulo	350 293
18	Niterói	Rio de Janeiro	330 396
19	Campos	Rio de Janeiro	321 370
20	Manaus	Amazonas	314 197
21	São João de Meriti	Rio de Janeiro	304 817
22	Osasco	São Paulo	285 160
23	São Luís	Maranhão	270 651
24	Natal	Rio Grande do Norte	270 127
25	Maceió	Alagoas	269 415
26	Juiz de Fora	Minas Gerais	244 002
27	Guarulhos	São Paulo	237 900
28	Londrina	Paraná	231 688
29	Teresina	Piauí	230 168
30	João Pessoa	Paraíba	228 418
31	Ribeirão Prêto	São Paulo	218 584
32	Pelotas	Rio Grande do Sul	213 152
33	Jaboatão	Pernambuco	202 715
34	São Bernardo do Campo	São Paulo	202 505
		TOTAL	24,769,074

The population of these counties grew from 6,500,000 in 1940 to 11,000,000 in 1950 to 20,000,000 in 1960, and had reached almost 30,000,000 in 1970. In 30 years this represents an increase of four to five times the number of people living in such counties.

Thirty-four counties, each having a population of over 200,000 in 1970 accounted for one-four of the national population, 24,769,074 (Table 8-1).

Growth of the Cities in São Paulo State

Throughout the State of São Paulo the economic opportunity has been so pronounced that there has been a strong interweaving of various economic activities in the same areas. Cattle raising, agriculture, and industrial activity have grown together in such a way that the state of São Paulo is a model of the intense diversity of occupations among its people, giving it the largest population (18,000,000) of any state in Brazil in 1970. There are some areas in the state that are less populated, but the soils of these regions are poor when compared to the rich purple loam found in the western part.

Coffee was responsible for the influx of population into many of the different regions of the *Paulista* state (São Paulo). Coffee production began in the valley of the Paraíba River and slowly moved west and into the north until it reached the region around Campinas where conditions of soil and climate were extremely favorable. In later years it spread throughout the lands of western São Paulo where the large areas of purple loam and the fertile sandy lands of Baurú gave the plantations their greatest expansion.

Coffee fields occupy the higher elevations of land between the rivers that flow west into the Paraná River, which is the boundary between the States of São Paulo and Mato Grosso. The railroads and the principal roads pushed behind this coffee boom frontier, and cities sprang up in a regular pattern along these "fingers" into southwest São Paulo.

The phenomena of the "hollow frontier" that swarmed with people, then suddenly dissipated, followed the sweep of population westward across the state in search of new coffee lands. In many instances the lands became exhausted and were abandoned after the soils had ceased to produce suitable yields of coffee. As this happened, the land was given over to other crops: cotton, sugarcane, or citrus fruit culture. At the same time great areas were given over to pasture lands and cattle and milk production became important. The large number of people who had been employed in coffee production moved on to new coffee lands or returned to the large urban centers like São Paulo or its neighboring cities to seek employment in the industries that had begun. The march of coffee in Brazil is very important and moved through its different stages in rapid succession (Figure 8-7).

FIGURE 8-7

ADVANCE OF THE COFFEE FRONTIER IN SÃO PAULO

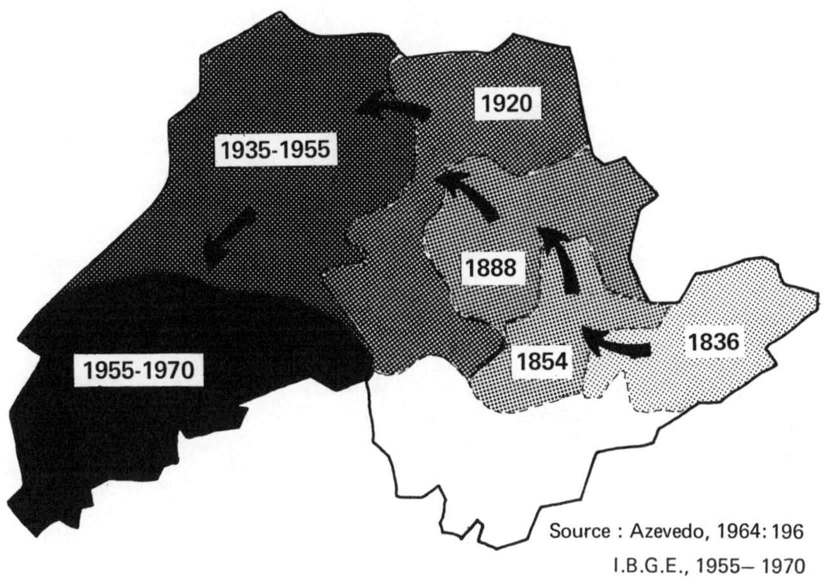

Source : Azevedo, 1964: 196
I.B.G.E., 1955– 1970

It was one of the important historical factors that generated the capital necessary to begin the huge industrial sector found in São Paulo today.

This historical sweep of coffee through the state and the whiplash of the "hollow frontier" distributed people into all parts of the state. The urban growth in the state of São Paulo was fed by the large numbers of immigrants that were attracted by the coffee boom and later became the settlers in the embryonic urban centers in the state. The growth of cities since 1940 in São Paulo State has been remarkable. Reflecting the 1970 census, Table 8-2 shows the growth of cities in the state in each decade since 1940.

TABLE 8-2

GROWTH OF CITIES IN STATE OF SÃO PAULO IN
1940, 1950, 1960, 1970 BY NUMBER OF INHABITANTS

INHABITANTS	NUMBER				POPULATION			
	1940	1950	1960	1970	1940	1950	1960	1970
TOTAL	270	369	503	571	2 930 937	4 552 092	7 805 394	13 468 481
0 to 500	5	5	14	12	1 959	1 859	5 716	4 534
500 to 1000	28	44	72	55	21 473	33 322	55 329	41 750
1,001 to 2,000 ...	66	102	115	125	94 937	145 313	165 821	176 510
2,001 to 5,000 ...	86	103	131	141	265 233	313 501	418 506	466 812
5,001 to 10,000.	45	59	68	89	301 262	415 212	474 560	635 628
10,001 to 20,000	24	28	56	61	330 197	394 431	767 877	884 532
over 20,000	16	28	47	88	1 915 876	3 248 454	5 917 585	11 258 715

These cities have grown from 270 in 1940 to 571 in 1970, and from a population of 2,930,937 in 1940 to 13,468,481 in 1970. More than thirteen million people in the state live in these 571 cities, but eleven million are found in the 88 cities that have a population that exceeds 20,000.

Growth of São Paulo 1940-1970

In 1967 a law established the limits of the São Paulo metropolitan area to 2,300 square miles which was 2.43 percent of the state area with about 7,200,000 people or 40 percent of the state population. This metropolitan area was formed out of 38 counties that surrounded the city of São Paulo itself. The five largest counties, Guarulhous, Osasco, Santo André, São Bernardo, and São Caetano form, with São Paulo, a continuous urban concentration whose streets converge in the downtown section.

This metropolitan area is the converging point of the state's communication system, three railroads, five main highways, and the airport connecting with all local travel within the state. Within it are found 800,000 buildings; 8,500 buildings with five or more stories; 320,000 telephones; 600,000 automobiles; 25,000 industrial establishments; 650,000 industrial workers; 19 radio stations; 6 TV transmitters; 21 daily papers; 6,000 intercity buses; 846 banking agencies; 194 movie theaters; 8,500 hotel rooms; 200 hospitals; 6,000 doctors; 2,200 elementary schools; 380 secondary schools; 40 university level schools.

It is true that São Paulo is not as well-known outside of South America as cities like Rio de Janeiro or Buenos Aires in Argentina, yet greater São Paulo with a population in 1973 that exceeds eight million is now the seventh largest city in the world and the largest in Latin America. By 1990, it is expected to have a metropolitan area population of 20,000,000. Paulistas say that there are at least seven new multi-story buildings under construction on any given day and that a building is completed every eight minutes.

The yearly growth rate of the population in greater São Paulo is between 6.3 percent - 5.7 percent in the center and 9.8 percent in the fast growing suburbs. About 60 percent of this growth is due to a relentless migration from the interior of the state and other areas of Brazil. The growth of population for the state is 580,000 per year and for the city 280,000, which is almost twice the growth rate of the three Scandanavian countries.

São Paulo's population has kept pace with its industrial expansion. The population has doubled since 1964. Besides the Brazilians who pour in from every part of Brazil, São Paulo has been the destination of immigrants from at least thirty-five different countries since World War I. All were attracted by the hope of good jobs in the offices and factories of larger São Paulo. At the turn of the century it looked like an Italian city. The style of its buildings and the tremendous influx of Italian immigrants had turned it into a little Italy. Now, more than eighty nationalities are represented and a well-known historian, Arnold Toynbee, after a recent visit, declared São Paulo to be the largest racial melting pot in the world.

São Paulo is the megalopolis in the tropics where the greatest surge of modernization in all of Latin America is now in process. Greater São Paulo is now responsible for more than 50 percent of the value of the country's industrial production and accounts for half of the manufactured products exported by Brazil. It contains 44 percent of the industrial establishments in the state - about 25,000 out of 56,000; but employs 54 percent of the industrial workers - 650,000 out of 1,210,000.

FIGURE 8-8

MICRO-REGION #262 IN STATE OF SÃO PAULO IN 1967

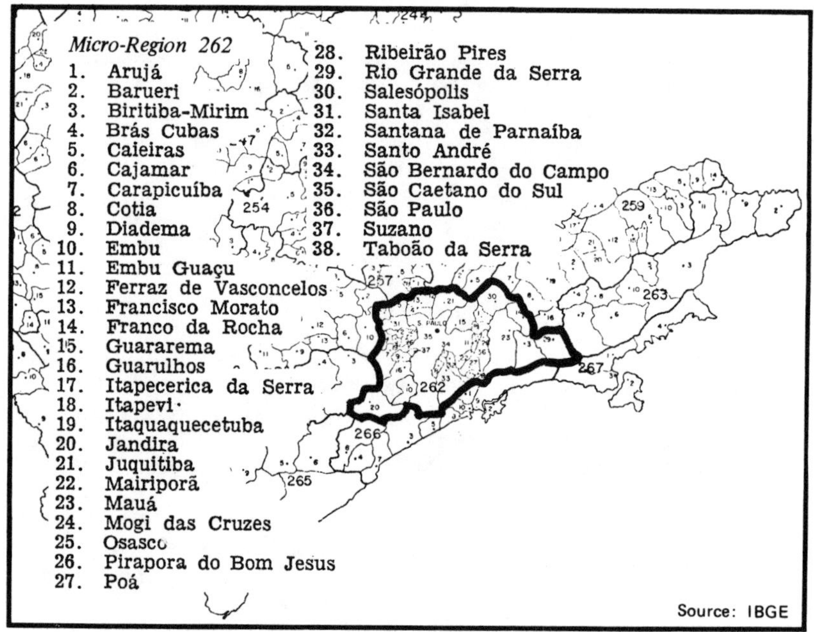

How the Church Grows in Micro-region 262

In 1967 greater São Paulo was officially made into a metropolitan region and placed within the boundaries of a new homogenous micro-region #262 (Figure 8-8).

This micro-region has 38 counties that are grouped around the urban core of São Paulo. The MARC Church Growth Data Bank gives the totals for the growth of the Protestant churches in this micro-region since 1955 in Table 8-3.

This increase of Protestant communicant membership from 1955-1966 represents a 145.8 percent gain for the 12-year period. The projection of the growth of Protestants in micro-region #262 based on the yearly average of percentile increase of 8.4 percent, gave micro-region #262, 360,402 estimated communicants in 1970. By 1972 this estimate had grown to 423,493 and the projection for 1974 is 497,628.

TABLE 8-3

GROWTH OF PROTESTANT MEMBERSHIP IN M/R #262 1955-1966

YEAR	MEMBERSHIP
1955	106,212
1956	130,544
1957	143,215
1958	158,792
1959	151,651
1960	165,969
1961	173,052
1962	182,427
1963	203,134
1964	213,783
1965	244,664
1966	261,018

In 1966 there were 261,018 communicants in greater São Paulo and 294,392 communicants for the rest of the state - a total of 555,410 communicants for the entire state. In 1966 more than 46 percent of the communicants in the State of São Paulo were found in micro-region #262. It is important to attempt to understand how the Protestant churches have grown in this micro-region since 1955 to the present for this growth is likely to continue, and prediction that São Paulo could be the world's largest metropolis before the year 2000 is not mere speculation.

Comparative studies of church growth in this micro-region are needed to discover those churches that have grown the fastest in urban centers. This requires more church growth research in depth for this unique micro-region to become one of the most fruitful church growth research areas in any urban area in Latin America. How does a denomination plan for church growth in such an area of modernization for 1975, 1980 and beyond? This is a critical area that immediately requires this type of church growth research and it cannot be done by one organization: each denomination needs to begin such a study as soon as possible.

INDUSTRIALIZATION

Mention has already been made of the important role that coffee played in the establishment of the industrial sector in São Paulo. The coffee plantations or *fazendas* on the rich soil in the state of São Paulo became the source of the nation's first surge of economic progress in the 1850's. A combination of factors help to explain the formation of what has now become the largest industrial park in all of Latin America.

First was the expansion of coffee after 1870-80 into Paulista lands (Figure 8-7). Coffee became the uncontested money crop of Brazil in the lands that the Brazilians call *areas cristalenas* and in the *arenito-basaltico* highlands of the hinterland of the city of São Paulo. But it was the city of São Paulo that became the great benefactor of the riches and capital that was accumulated from the unparalleled production of coffee in the period up to 1930.

Second has been the multiplication of railways into the Paulista highlands, fanning out from São Paulo and Santos. This system of transportation carried the heavy load of migrants to the pioneer frontiers, laid down the pattern of settlement along the railroad lines, and in the last two decades of the nineteenth century carried the tremendous load for this unabated coffee boom that reached into each new frontier settlement and provided a prosperity hitherto unknown.

Third, the immigration of foreigners, especially Italians, to Brazil was substantial between 1880 and 1920. The news of the coffee boom and its opportunities acted like a magnet that brought Europeans in wave after wave to seek their fortune in the expansion of coffee. In one ten-year period 900,000 immigrants made their way into these interior areas of coffee production and then returned to the city of São Paulo where they settled with their large families. Eventually they found employment that utilized their professional skills obtained in the "old country".

Fourth, the influx of foreign capital at the turn of the century - especially the British, Canadian, and North American capital - made it possible to develop the hydroelectric potential of the Paulista highlands. Soon electricity was available for the streetcar transportation, and the power needed to establish the industrial sector.

Fifth, the demand for consumer goods after 1920 increased substantially. Capital from the exportation of coffee was available and was employed in the creation of the Paulista industrial park which is considered today to be the most powerful in all of South America, and which came to demand, in ever increasing numbers, workers who were technically oriented and specialized in the setting up of new industrial establishments.

Sixth, large numbers of people from adjacent rural populations came in streams from the interior and other parts of Brazil, attracted by supposed and real advantages of a dynamic metropolitan area or wanting steady work and educational opportunities for their children. The influx of people from all parts of the world fed the need for workers in São Paulo to build factories, houses, and skyscrapers, and the tempo of these activities has not diminished since World War II.

Seventh, the large properties that were once expansive *fazendas* (farms) around the city of São Paulo were cut up into lots and new districts. Villas and sections of greater São Paulo were filled with residences of many different types, providing room for the economically active population. Today, one who arrives in São Paulo by plane is surprised at the limitless skyline of gleaming white and beige houses, buildings, and skyscrapers, all topped with the characteristic red tile roofs. What you see in a glance at one moment is only half of this big unknown city. The other half lies just beyond the next set of hills.

These seven factors and many more came together simultaneously to form this enormous industrial complex. It was coffee-rails-immigration, or immigration-capital-industry, or still industry-workers-urban development. However you want to say it, it is the most unusual area of modernization to be found in all of Latin America and must be understood in this way. São Paulo is an arena of constant innovation, change, and flux; everchanging, churning, and in different states of evolution. This industrial sector began in and around São Paulo and has spread in many different directions.

The Industrial Sectors of Brazil in 1970

The Southeastern region is the most highly industrialized in the country. In 1960, 73 percent of the total manpower, 84 percent of the capital, 85 percent of the electric consumption and 79 percent of the industrial output of the country were concentrated in this industrial sector. Within this region industrial activity is extremely concentrated, and the two huge centers correspond to the metropolitan areas of São Paulo and Rio de Janeiro together with the so-called metallurgy zone around Belo Horizonte and beyond São Paulo in an industrial belt that reaches Campinas.

The concentration of industrial activity in Rio de Janeiro, São Paulo, and the Paulista region (Jundiaí and Americana) has made the utilization of this area something special and unique. The strong concentration of factories and its resultant industrial diversification pattern is something that has happened since 1940. The contrast in the way industry is distributed in the interior of the State reflects another evolution in the industrial patte: Stretches of country where earlier forms of industrialization made themselves felt, but which were not intensely involved in the recent stage since 1940, are marked by small centers of industry which are decaying or only holding their own. These are characterized by the predominance of textiles.

All of these factors and conditions are typical of a new ar underdeveloped country. They help to explain the concentration of industry in the Southeast of Brazil. Rio de Janeiro was the main industrial center in the first decades of the twentieth century, but began to give way to the surge of industrializatior in São Paulo after 1930.

But there are other areas of economic activity which deserv our attention. A description of these major regions of industrial activity follows:

1. A region spreading out from the city of São Paulo and divided into the metropolitan area, the *Paulista* area, and a strip of the Paraíba River Valley. The <u>metropolitan area</u> is the major industrial complex where basic industry is located complete in blocks of factories and sections of worker's housing alongside. The nucleus of the city border large plants and other smaller commercial concerns. Big industry is found in the satellite towns and suburbs along the larger arteries of transportation. The *Paulista* area i where new industrial establishments are located, having modern textile mills, mechanical, chemical, and metallurgic engineering plants that are concentrated in neighboring cities that move away from São Paulo such as Jundiaí, Campinas, Americana, and Piracicaba. The <u>strip of the Paraíba River Valley</u> contains former textile centers that have been rejuvenated acquiring new industrial functions and importance because of the influence of São Paulo, but have not developed any substantial industrial center.

2. The Sorocaba area is a traditional textile, single industry center that has benefited because of the influence of neighboring São Paulo, but development of new products has been less than in the Paraíba strip.

3. This region of mechanized industry in the west changes from the highly industrialized areas mentioned above and concentrates on mechanical activity connected with farm implements and food processing industries that serve areas given over primarily to farming in the regional centers of Bauru and Ribeirão Prêto.

4. No great factories are located in the area of western São Paulo highlands and the Minas Triangle, but the industry here is concerned with the processing of farm produce in a rural and predominately agricultural sector.

5. The region of Rio de Janeiro is the second region of importance industrially in the country and takes in the metropolitan area of greater Rio de Janeiro where the port has an important role. When compared with São Paulo the difference of industrial activity is not only in the quantity but the significance of the goods produced and the degree of industrial diversification. In the Guanabara area no industrial suburbs have emerged and only Nova Iguaçu, Duque de Caxias, and São Gonçalo come close.

6. The industrialized area in the Paraíba Valley extends from Barra do Piraí to Cruzeiro and on to Volta Redonda, including the metallurgical center where the expansion of chemical plants is taking place.

7. In the mountain area along the border between the States of Rio de Janeiro and Minas Gerais, the familiar textile factories are found. No industrial surge is recorded in this area except in Juiz de Fora.

8. In the central areas of Minas Gerais which are the fringe areas of Belo Horizonte metallurgy is giving economic life to new centers and the process of revitalization is at work in the older centers. The industry in this area is beginning to develop into an important industrial nucleus.

9. The greater parts of the states of Rio de Janeiro, Minas Gerais, and Espírito Santo are agricultural but some industrial activity exists to transform agricultural and timber production into consumer products. Sugar refining centers like Campos, those in the Recôncavo area of Salvador, and Recife stand out. The small textile efforts in northeast Brazil are generally home industries and should be mentioned here.

The process of modernization is strongest in these areas of outstanding economic development (Figure 8-9). The concentration of industrial activity in these areas make them the prime areas of economic development in Brazil and centers of the processes of modernization. A constant schedule of rapid social change is to be expected as social institutions adopt new ways and experiment with the innovations of a society embarking on a new lifestyle - a society in the full sway of modernization.

The process of industrialization triggers this increasing cycle of modernization. It controls large movements of population, trade, construction, means of transportation, and eventually the flow of agricultural products and the agricultural activities required to produce such raw materials and maintain the technical progress required for farming by the use of fertilizers and farm machinery.

FIGURE 8-9

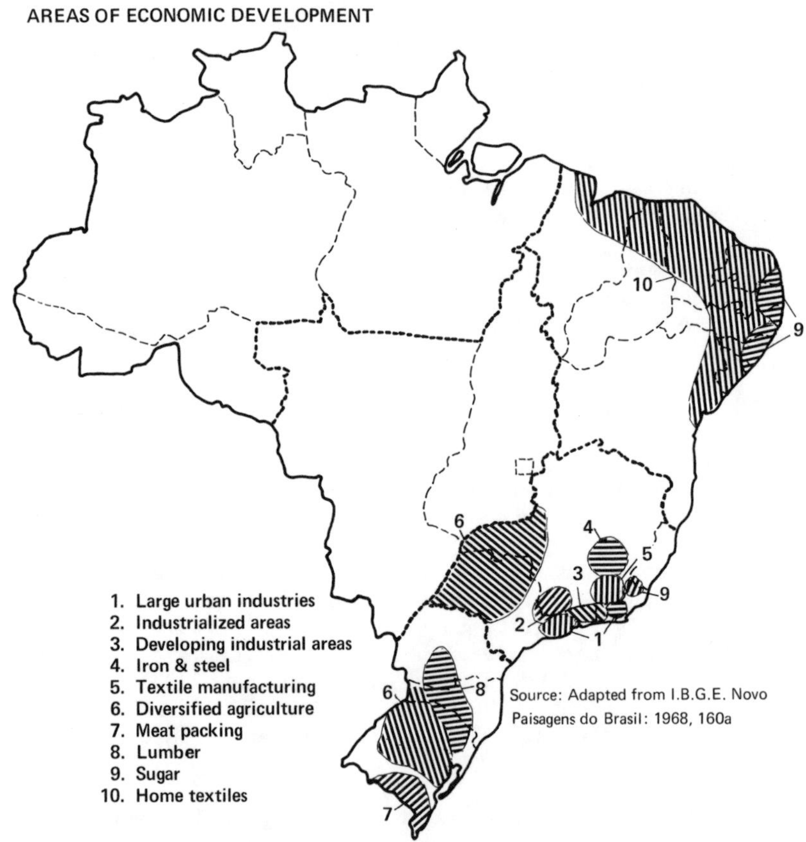

The entire structure of cities is radically altered by this rapid growth of industry in such a short period and in such magnitude. It has produced a hungry economic apparatus that modifies and reshapes the focus and center of all human activity and affects the growth of the Protestant churches in a radical way. It provides a new environment for modern man.

The dynamic movement of all this change might be termed the "M" factor. This "M" factor is at work in these areas of economic development. It creates a receptivity on the part of the hearer of the gospel proclamation. When the ties of a traditional past are broken by the "M" factor by substantial movement, migration, and mobility, then we can expect a new climate of acceptance to the Protestant message by large numbers who are caught up in this "M" factor. Motion by people on this magnitude means change. Old institutions are left behind, and dramatically so, by migrants who are not average people, but courageous pioneers who have paid a price to put themselves in motion. Those caught up in the "M" factor are exposed to these new circumstances and a new way of life develops as they move from the traditional to the modern style of life. Accidents, hardships, and new encounters occur.

There is an exposure to new places, new people, and a new, strange society in formation. The "M" factor - movement - means exposure, and successive exposures lead to unexpected transformations and, for many, spiritual conversion from an old life to a new life in Christ.

No movement of people of such magnitude can take place without great alterations. The unique phenomena of the rural to urban migration selects special types for this move and at the same time subjects them to exceptional strains on the journey. It compels them to rebuild, and they have a liberty to do so that they never had before. Many use this newfound liberty to choose Jesus Christ.

As we have seen, the "M" factor serves to change the physical population, institutions, group structures, social habits, and traditions, and can alter the personal character and attitude of the migrants. This is the dynamic new thing that has shaken and is in the process of reshaping the Brazilian, his family, and ultimately his nation.

In this whole process, the "M" factor has not only been opening up minds to accept the Gospel but has also been recirculating Protestant believers from all parts of Brazil. In the process there has been a ministry of evangelization whereby new Protestant believers are won by aggressive evangelism and personal appeals by these Protestant immigrants.

It is significant to note that the twenty-three micro-regions in Brazil with the highest concentrations of Protestant communicants - the largest numbers in each micro-region - are all located within the areas of highest economic development (Figure 8-10). Each dot on the map indicates the location of one of these

FIGURE 8-10

MICRO-REGIONS HAVING LARGEST CONCENTRATION OF PROTESTANT COMMUNICANT MEMBERS IN 1966

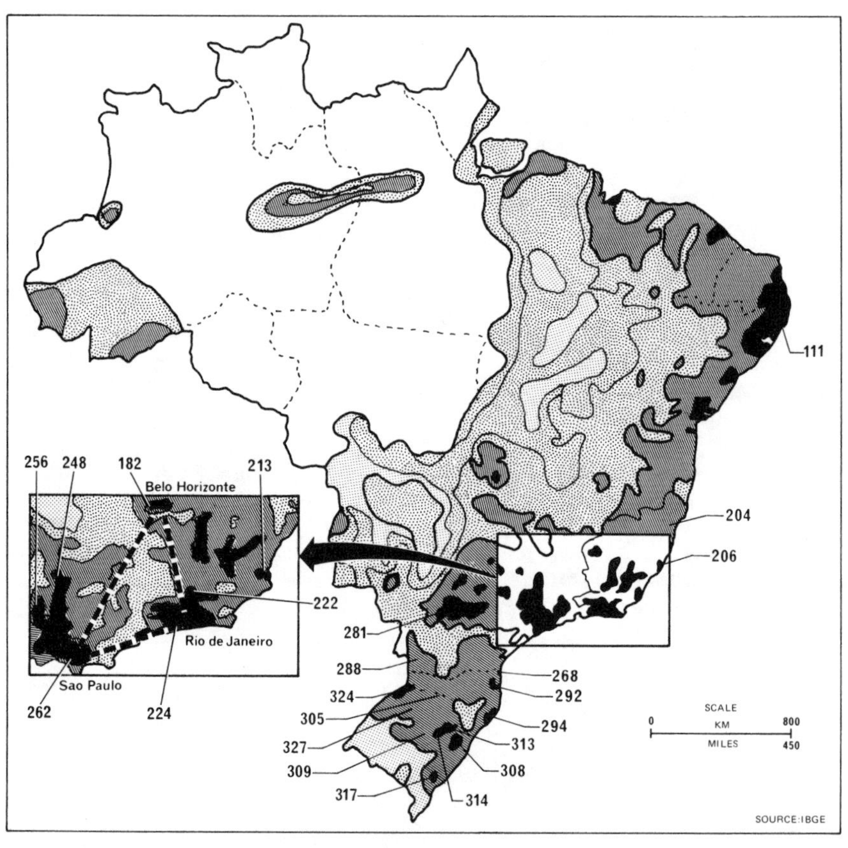

high density Protestant micro-regions. Only ten states are represented in this list of micro-regions (Table 8-4).

The number of Protestants found in these twenty-three micro-regions in 1966 represented 49 percent of the communicant membership in Brazil. It is significant that such a large number of Protestant believers are located in the exact areas where the major economic areas in Brazil are found. These areas also happen to be the major areas of modernization in Brazil! In the rectangular box in Figure 8-10 which represents the São Paulo, Rio de Janeiro, and Belo Horizonte industrial triangle, seven of these micro-regions are found (Table 8-5).

TABLE 8-4

MICRO-REGIONS IN BRAZIL AND THEIR STATES HAVING
THE LARGEST PROTESTANT MEMBERSHIPS IN 1966

No.	State	Micro-Region	Protestant Membership
1	Pernambuco	#111	42,457
2	Espirito Santo	#204	31,157
3	Espirito Santo	#206	35,266
4	Paraná	#268	21,572
5	Paraná	#281	41,661
6	Paraná	#288	25,934
7	Santa Catarina	#292	55,448
8	Santa Catarina	#294	64,732
9	Santa Catarina	#305	25,507
10	Minas Gerais	#182	23,938
11	Rio de Janeiro	#213	21,752
12	Rio de Janeiro	#222	96,290
13	Guanabara	#224	104,627
14	São Paulo	#248	23,652
15	São Paulo	#256	25,730
16	São Paulo	#262	261,018
17	RGS	#308	95,685
18	RGS	#309	63,057
19	RGS	#313	38,949
20	RGS	#314	58,288
21	RGS	#317	30,995
22	RGS	#324	59,882
23	Goiás	#354	21,771
		TOTAL	1,269,376

More than one half million Protestant believers are located in this area alone. Later we will examine the potential for growth in these micro-regions for the years ahead. The "M" factor is at work here as is modernization, and the churches have grown substantially. To understand what has happened to cause such an increase of believers much more research needs to be expended in these areas of high potential for Protestant growth.

The islands of modernization grow larger every year in the areas of economic development and in the areas where there is a high concentration of urban population. In 1969 nine of these major urban areas were studied, and each was found to have all the characteristics necessary to be officialized by the Brazilian government as metropolitan regions (Figure 8-1). Each metropolitan area was given jurisdiction by law over all of the affairs governing the growth and further urbanization of their respective areas.

TABLE 8-5

SEVEN MAJOR MICRO-REGIONS IN THE SP/BELO/RIO TRIANGLE IN 1966

No.	State	Micro-Region	Protestant Membership
1	Minas Gerais	#182	23,938
2	Rio de Janeiro	#213	21,752
3	Rio de Janeiro	#222	96,290
4	Guanabara	#224	104,627
5	São Paulo	#248	23,652
6	São Paulo	#256	25,730
7	São Paulo	#262	261,018
		TOTAL	557,015

These are the primary areas of modernization in Brazil today. The great extension reached in the last decade by these, and many other Brazilian cities, and the increasingly intense rhythm of urban growth has made it clear that this growth must be directed to provide the adequate solution to the problems that a disordered urbanization brings.

Studies need to be made in each of these metropolitan regions to determine how and why Protestant churches grow. Such a study should seek to define the areas where church growth has been accelerated, and why certain micro-regions within these islands of modernization exceed other micro-regions in similar situations by their extreme density of believers and by the various characteristics of growth being experienced by each denominational family within such micro-regions.

Data for these studies is available; the CASE (Center for Advanced Studies in Evangelism) offices of Overseas Crusades whose headquarters are in São Paulo can be requested to direct such church growth surveys for each metropolitan area, including Brasília, the new Federal Capitol. Ten distinct studies of this nature are needed using the MARC Brazil Data Bank that was transferred to CASE in February of 1973. In 18 months, qualified researchers from each large denomination in Brazil could provide excellent studies of these ten areas of modernization. Insights from such a series of church growth studies, using the surveys, studies, and MARC Data Bank for Brazil as tools, could be some of the instruments from which guidelines for planning evangelistic advance up to 1980 could be made by every major Protestant denomination in Brazil.

WESTWARD EXPANSION AND SETTLEMENT

The construction of roads in Brazil is a complex undertaking. At present there are plans being made for roads by each different level of government: federal, state, and county. Only recently has this planning been moving toward one integrated and coordinated plan. A strategy is being hammered out whose goal will be the integration of every geographical part of the vast Brazilian landmass. The importance of roads in a country like Brazil cannot be overestimated, for their excellence in engineering fades into insignificance when their role as agents of economic and social change are clearly understood.

FIGURE 8-11

FUTURE ROAD SYSTEM FOR BRAZIL - 1965

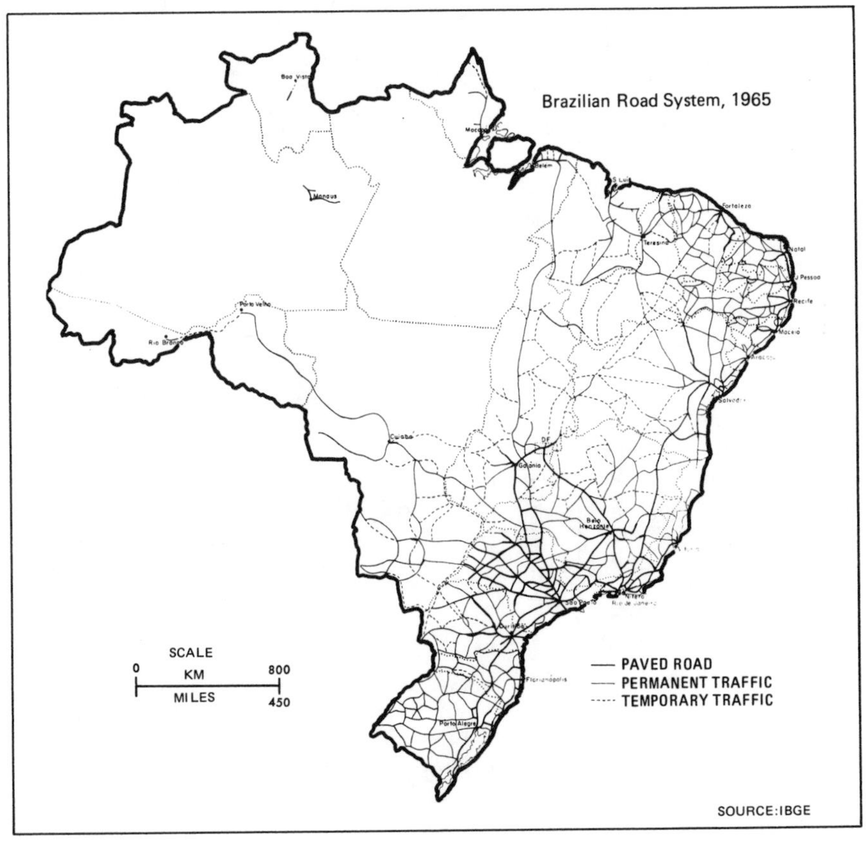

TABLE 8-6

ROAD NETWORK BY STATE, COUNTY, AND FEDERAL IN KILOMETERS

1961-70

	State and County			Federal			Total Road System		
Year	Paved	Unpaved	Total	Paved	Unpaved	Total	Paved	Unpaved	Total
1961	4,453	71,915	463,274	9,422	26,176	35,598	-	-	498,872
1962	5,553	74,305	487,045	10,725	25,377	36,102	-	-	523,147
1963	5,529	75,639	500,639	11,425	24,962	36,387	-	-	537,026
1964	5,613	77,533	507,571	12,157	25,719	37,876	-	-	545,447
1965	13,835	81,003*	716,335	12,589	22,003	34,592	-	-	750,927
1966	16,618	771,137	787,755	13,803	23,184	36,987	30,421	794,321	824,742
1967	23,026	869,737	892,763	14,944	23,715	38,659	37,970	893,452	931,422
1968	24,527	971,001	995,258	19,353	27,499	46,852	43,610	998,499	1,042,110
1969	26,473	1,082,530	1,109,003	22,015	28,087	50,102	48,488	1,110,617	1,159,105
1970	28,754	1,207,515	1,236,269	23,674	29,493	53,167	52,428	1,237,008	1,289,436

*"Unpaved" jumps from 81,003 in 1965 to 771,137 in 1966. This is probably due to better reporting and mapping procedures of existing roads rather than the number of kilometers added in 1966. For this reason 5 years of "totals" are omitted.

In 1965, the official plan of the federal government for highway development was published. This document could well be the single most important document to point out where Brazil is moving and what this country will become in the years between 1980 and 2000.

Highways are the economic and social arteries for the development of the country. Railroads were important, but were somewhat limited in the last half of the nineteenth century. They cannot fulfill the role of a well-planned road system. The road plan that was published in 1965 by the Department of Planning and the Division of National Roads is reproduced in Figure 8-11.

This map indicates the major categories of roads and those that were definitely planned for construction. Notice the absence of any roads in the Amazonia region. This plan was formulated before action was taken in 1969 to inaugurate the Trans-Amazonian road through the heart of the Amazon jungle. The master road plan of 1965 gives an incomplete idea of what the road map of Brazil will be like in 1980. Those who have lived in Brazil for two decades and know the limitations of travel in the 1950's and 1960's due to inadequate roads, may easily be surprised by what evidently lies ahead.

The present pattern of all-weather roads is found primarily in the densely populated zone that extends along a 200-mile belt inland from the Atlantic ocean from north to south. In the 1950's, under the government of Juscelino Kubitschek, highways were constructed at a rate never known before in Brazilian history. This aggressive policy of road building has continued with every government since. Table 8-6 indicates this accelerated road building in terms of kilometers (5/9th of a mile) completed by county, state, and federal authorities from 1961-1970.

As we look at Figure 8-11 and Table 8-6 the following observations can be made:

1. More roads can be expected by 1980.

2. Many more places and areas are scheduled to be served by highways.

3. More crossroad intersections will serve as market centers, storage depots, and warehouse facilities, and centers for new towns and cities will be established.

4. More alternate routes will be available instead of trunk lines, reducing the possibility of isolation and neglect of certain areas for lack of transporation linkages.

5. More roads will be paved and receive all weather maintenance.

6. More pioneer roads will be constructed in unsettled lands.

The present aim of the *Departamento Nacional de Estradas de Rodagem* (DNER) "National Department of Roads," is to consolidate and improve the existing road network, extend the main roads from the farthest points in the national territory to link them with the new national capital, to construct connecting roads which utilize existing towns as the crossroads, and to recognize the Amazon Basin to be an important part of the national territory that must be adequately served by a road system.

The result of this effort will lift the present value of land and give a new value to agricultural and industrial production as greater access to local, national, and in some instances, world markets is acquired. This expanding road system will enhance the process and distribution of the modernization phenomenon to these new areas, whether they be older, traditional settled areas or the new pioneer areas. These are the type of areas where the "M" factor operates most effectively and a new development mentality prevails. Here is a landscape to be settled in a modern way. Traditional status and prestige patterns of the historical oligarchies will perhaps hinder this development effort, but in most cases it will prevail. Conservative thinking will now be replaced by a more progressive approach to settlement and the working out of a new life. The frontier for modernization will appear in the ribbon of settlements that are now forming along the new principal trunk highways that radiate in every direction from Brasília. Every new road becomes the axis of transportation and a foundation upon which modernization can develop.

At the time of the publication of the Brazilian government plan for highway development in 1965, not more than one-third of the total national territory was reachable. By 1980 one-half of the national territory should be developed and by the year 2000, two-thirds of the total national territory.

Such a highway system in the year 2000 could mean that the benefits and the penalties of economic development and the resultant islands of modernization will be carried to the farthest corners of the nation and the disparities in economic level from one region to another will diminish. A hierarchy of hinterlands will emerge that will be part of the system of large regional urban centers in the same way that São Paulo and Rio de Janeiro have their supportive economic regions. The future growth of a productive population can take place in a natural process of economic development in such regional areas.

New Land Settlements

Little has been said about the "new land" areas of the 50's and 60's that are still receiving people. Many such land areas are yet to be opened by the type of spontaneous colonization that has become the way of life for many humble Brazilians. Figure 8-12 indicates some of these major regions.

1. Zone of the Mata in the State of Espírito Santo, southern Bahia, and eastern Minas Gerais, sometimes included in the area of "dispute," claimed by Minas Gerais.

2. Western part of the states of São Paulo, Santa Catarina, and Rio Grande do Sul where four distinct patterns of frontier activities exist.

3. The different areas in Goiás: (a) adjacent to Porangatu (b) area around Xavantina close to the Xingu River (c) a section in the Valley of the Sonhos that almost extends to the Garças River (d) the long strip on the eastern edge of the Island of Bananal formed by the Tocantins River (e) the region south of Imperatriz on another tributary of the Tocantins River along the BR-14 highway.

4. In Maranhão, the section between the Gurupi River and the Turiaçu River has been settled by many people from the Northeast.

5. In Pará, the area on the Capim River is active with a spontaneous colonization settlement and extends to the Tomé Açu region.

6. In addition to these six locations on the map, other areas can be found where spontaneous settlement has been heavy. The State of Mato Grosso is receiving a large influx of settlers. This is happening in southern Mato Grosso in the region between Varzea Grande, Terenos, and Ponta Porã. In central Mato Grosso a steady stream of people arrived since 1965 to setttle in the area beyond Cuiabá.

FIGURE 8-12

NEW LAND SETTLEMENTS IN THE 1950'S – 1960'S

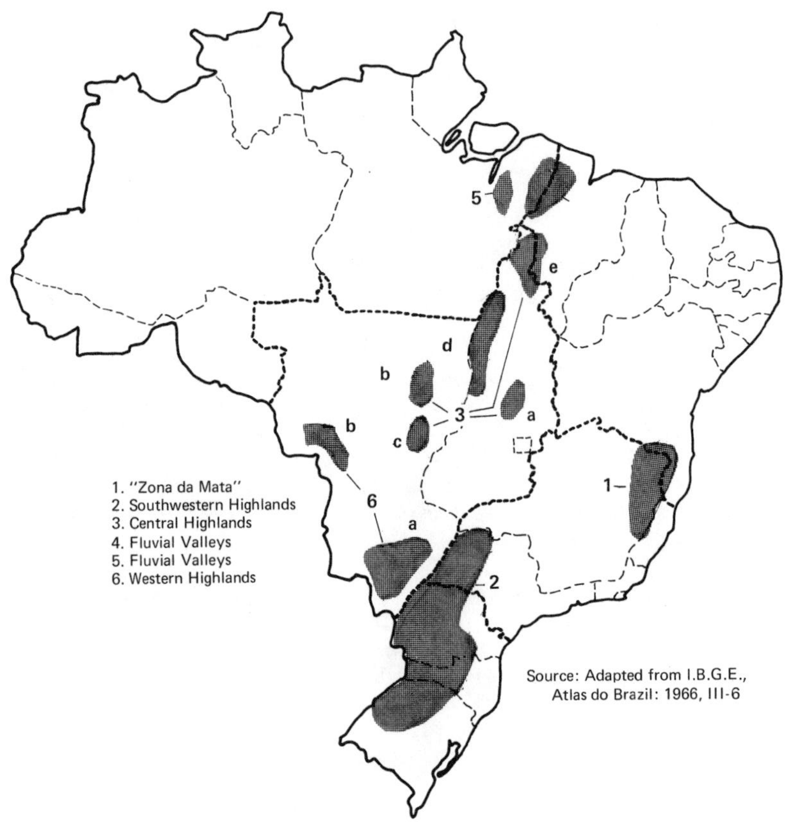

Other places could increase this list of new land settlements in the 1950's and 1960's to indicate the scope of this type of Brazilian "M" factor which continues unabated, often happening in spurts and dribbles, but at times in huge waves.

Westward Movement in Brazil

Brazil is not only an underdeveloped country, it is one of the largest unopened countries in the world. Perhaps the anticipation that this country would one day open to the west is one of the reasons why Brazil has more foreign missionaries from North

America than any other country in the world. A large land mass and a rapidly increasing population have already provided the pressure that has triggered one of the most dramatic land settlements in our generation.

In 1970, Mario Andreazza, the Minister of Transporation, announced publically that the major thrust of the National Plan of Integration had been decided upon (Andreazza 1970:1). There was to be a national effort to assist the Northeast and develop Amazonia simultaneously by putting large numbers of people to work in a program of settlement along the developing pioneer road system that would penetrate deep into the Amazon Basin from centers in the States of Piauí, Goiás, and Mato Grosso (Figure 8-13).

FIGURE 8-13

NEW LAND SETTLEMENT AREAS IN THE 1970's

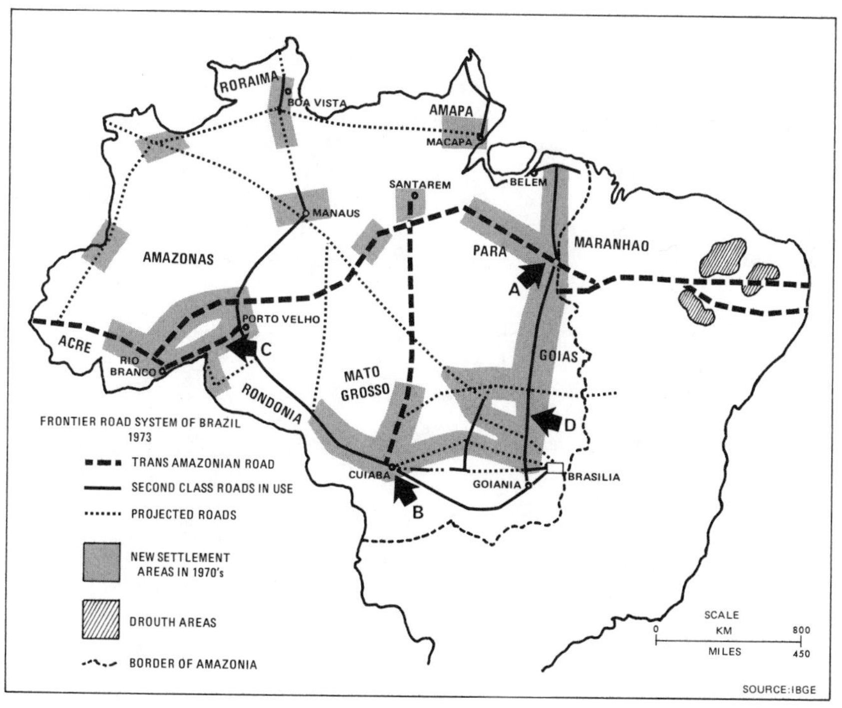

For the Northeast, this plan would mean the relocation of many rural workers from distressed regions in Brazil's famous "calamity areas" into the untouched stretches of land along the

Tapajós River in the State of Pará, and in other pockets of tropical land found in the heavily forested areas of western Maranhão and Pará (See A in Figure 8-13).

In the east central region of Amazonia, this would mean that a new road would be cut from Cuiabá, Mato Grosso, to Santarém, one of the centers of the vast Amazon basin (See B in Figure 8-13). At the same time, a road would be opened from Porto Velho, in the Territory of Rondônia to Manaus, the geographical center of Amazonia (See C in Figure 8-13).

This extension of the westward movement of settlement into Amazonia began when Brasília was constructed in the highlands of Goiás in the late 1950's. The success of Highway BR-14 between Brasília and Belém (see Chapter 9), is an example of what will happen along these new roads planned for Amazonia. These projected roads will give new life and continuity to the westward movement that began in the 1950's. This westward movement in the 70's will open many new lands for settlement (see "D" in Figure 8-13), and provide opportunity for the Evangelical church in Brazil to evangelize and plant churches in these pioneer frontier settlements.

An illustration of what can happen is a pioneer land settlement frontier in Northwestern Paraná. For the past fifteen years there has been an accelerated influx of migrants from all parts of Brazil into this settlement frontier. Micro-region #288 is located in the State of Paraná and is made up of nineteen counties and had a population in 1970 of more than 250,000 (Figure 8-14).

The primary economic activities are lumber, cattle, and agricultural production. The area is subject to frost, and for this reason coffee production on a large scale is a great risk. Toledo, one of the county seat towns, is the center of pork production for the whole area. Cascavel is the principal urban center and all of the major roads of the area run into this regional trade center.

Guaira, on the Paraná River, is a fresh water port that ships agricultural products into São Paulo. Foz do Iguaçu is another riverport town for shipping commercial products of the region to Paraguay and Argentina.

The major paved road, BR-277, connecting Foz do Iguaçu with the port city of Paranaguá on the Atlantic, passes through this micro-region and opens it up to an accelerated rate of economic advance for the decade ahead.

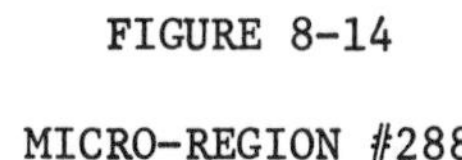

FIGURE 8-14

MICRO-REGION #288

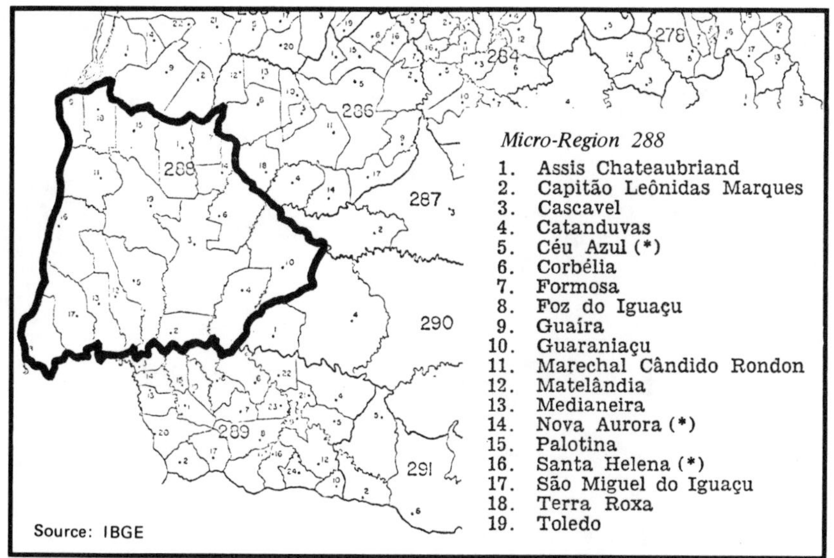

The population density is low - 10.4 people per square kilometer - but it has a strong yearly current of demographic increase, receiving migrants from two strong currents: in the southern section, bringing settlers from Rio Grande do Sul and Santa Catarina, and the northern section, bringing settlers in from Northern Paraná, São Paulo, and other parts of Brazil.

In 1966 there were more than 25,000 Protestant communicant members registered in micro-region #288. They represented 12 percent of the population. By 1970 the projections of Protestant church growth, based on the rate of increase from 1961-1966 which was 26.3 percent each year, would give this micro-region more than 50,000 communicant members in all Evangelical churches and increase the percent of Protestants in the total population of the micro-region to almost 20 percent.

Ten of the nineteen counties found in micro-region #288 record Protestant membership statistics. Three out of the nine counties had a complete record of church membership between 1955 and 1966. Another county began recording the presence of evangelical believers in 1957, two counties in 1961, two in 1963, one in 1965, and another in 1966. The three centers - Toledo,

Foz do Iguaçu and Cascavel - were the first towns in this new region and the first settlers probably got their bearings in these different centers and received orientation to settle close enough to these embryonic commercial and trade centers to make these regional county seat towns their base for contact with the world. Settlement of other areas proceeded in the decade between 1955-1965 and the recording of membership statistics in various years for the remaining seven counties is evidence of the people and their families in the pioneer migration frontier pushing into new lands to begin a new life.

The dynamic of this wave of migration, and the redistribution of Protestants from other areas is seen in the record of the total church membership in micro-region #288 in the State of Paraná from 1955-1966 (Table 8-7).

TABLE 8-7

TOTAL PROTESTANT MEMBERSHIP IN MICRO-REGION #288, 1955-1966

1955 -	902	1961 -	8,106
1956 -	1,132	1962 -	8,762
1957 -	3,864	1963 -	15,328
1958 -	4,716	1964 -	19,963
1959 -	6,336	1965 -	21,246
1960 -	7,674	1966 -	25,934

An increase from 902 communicant members in 1955 to 25,934 communicants in 1966 is a remarkable record of growth.* Lutherans, who usually report non-communicant membership, were in abundance in this micro-region, and probably indicate the strong wave of migration from Rio Grande do Sul and Santa Catarina where the Lutheran Church membership, communicant and non-communicant totals exceed all other churches. Communicant membership only would give the Lutherans a growth of 418 to 8,450 in the same period. Lutherans grew from 697 to 14,083 in the period under consideration. Presbyterians grew from 0 to 532, Episcopalians from 9 to 570, Baptists from 94 to 1,345, Assembly of God from 53 to 2,198, and Adventists from 25 to 1,087.

---

*Communicant membership only would chart this increase on the basis of 623 in 1955 to 20,301 communicants in 1966.

When the different Protestant churches in the micro-region are grouped into three categories, we find that there were 19,718 members of traditional type Protestant churches, 5,104 members were registered in Pentecostal churches and 1,112 members were found in the small sects somewhat removed from the standard Protestant doctrinal standards.

This same rapid increase in Protestant membership characterizes such frontier zones, and the amount of evangelization and enlistment of new members that goes on is not currently available. All we have is a series of interviews with pastors and church leaders who have ministered in such periods of influx and settlement activity. The information they have given indicates that new members who are recorded on the roles of these newly established churches are 50 percent from transfers and 50 percent new members who make their profession of faith and are baptized after vigorous evangelistic efforts and incorporated into these newly established churches fresh "out of the world," as the majority of Brazilian Protestants express it.

This first stage of pioneer settlement can last as long as two decades. After the initial excitement is over, the momentum subsides and the process of consolidation in the churches begins. In micro-region #288 nine counties do not record any Protestant membership. These are opportunity areas for the next two decades and can be expected to produce a fair share of Protestant churches with their respective growth pattern adding to year by year increase in the micro-region. The rapid rate of increase from 1955 to 1966 can be expected to diminish a little, but it should last for another decade. The overall percentage index of increase from 1955-1966 was 3,478 percent. The very low membership figure in 1955 compared with the large membership in 1966 does not make this unreasonable. However, growth in the decade ahead will be much slower, for it has a larger base to build upon. If an increase of 25 percent per year for the next decade is reasonable, we can expect the membership in 1974 to be close to 100,000 members. If the population in 1974 has grown to 50,000, it is not unreasonable to predict that Evangelicals could constitute 20 percent of the population in this micro-region. This is a high rate of Protestant density for a frontier land area, but in this case the large influx of Lutherans from the south makes this a viable possibility. Whenever Protestants constitute more than 10 percent of the population in a frontier land settlement region, the future possibilities for growth and expansion are exceptional.

TABLE 8-8

PROJECTION OF PROTESTANT GROWTH IN 23 MICRO-REGIONS, 1970-1980

State and Micro-region	Percent of Growth* 1961-1966	1966	1970	1972	1974	1976	1978	1980
Pernambuco								
M/R 111	14.7	42,457	73,486	96,679	127,192	167,335	220,147	289,627
Minas Gerais								
M/R 182	17.8	23,938	46,097	63,968	88,767	123,181	170,936	237,205
Espírito Santo								
M/R 204	1.6	31,157	40,000	45,000	47,000	50,000	54,000	55,000
M/R 206	4.1	35,268	41,415	44,888	48,637	52,707	57,118	61,898
Rio de Janeiro								
M/R 213	4.1	21,752	25,545	27,683	30,000	32,510	35,230	38,178
M/R 222	12.3	96,290	153,158	193,152	243,590	307,198	387,416	488,582
Guanabara								
M/R 224	4.1	104,627	122,870	133,152	144,294	156,369	169,454	183,634
São Paulo								
M/R 248	7.8	23,652	31,941	37,118	43,134	50,125	58,249	67,690
M/R 256	3.5	25,730	29,421	31,456	33,631	35,957	38,444	41,103
M/R 262	8.4	261,018	360,402	423,493	497,628	587,741	687,103	807,385
Paraná								
M/R 268	11.9	21,572	33,823	42,352	53,032	66,405	83,150	104,117
M/R 281	9.1	41,661	59,024	70,255	83,623	99,535	118,475	141,019
M/R 288	26.3	25,934	65,991	105,267	167,919	267,859	427,280	681,584
Santa Catarina								
M/R 292	5.3	55,448	68,171	75,589	83,814	92,934	103,046	114,258
M/R 294	4.1	64,732	76,019	82,380	89,274	96,745	104,841	113,614
M/R 305	2.3	25,507	27,000	29,000	30,000	33,000	35,000	37,000
Rio Grande do Sul**								
M/R 308	3.1	95,685	108,113	114,920	122,155	129,846	138,021	146,711
M/R 309	2.2	63,057	68,792	71,852	75,048	78,386	81,873	85,515
M/R 313	1.1	38,949	39,500	40,500	42,000	43,500	45,000	47,000
M/R 314	2.8	58,288	65,096	68,792	72,698	76,826	81,188	85,798
M/R 317	5.6	30,995	38,543	42,981	47,930	53,448	59,602	66,464
M/R 324	4.4	59,882	71,137	77,535	84,508	92,108	100,392	109,421
Goiás								
M/R 354	3.4	21,771	24,886	26,607	28,447	30,414	32,517	34,766
TOTALS		1,269,376	1,670,430	1,944,619	2,284,321	2,721,129	3,288,482	4,099,467

*Percent of growth 1961-1966 represents the average annual percentage of growth

**Lutheran membership in the micro-regions of South Brazil includes both communicant and non-communicant membership.

Projections of Protestant Church Growth to 1980

A simple mathematical projection of Protestant growth in areas of modernization based on the percentage of increase of Evangelicals in each micro-region from the years 1961 to 1966 produce some startling projections. Table 8-8 shows projections to serve as a stimulant to our thinking about the opportunities for Protestant church growth in areas of innovation and modernization in the decade ahead and the implications of such projections for Evangelical church leadership (Table 8-8).

The micro-regions in this table are also found in Figure 8-8, Table 8-4, and Table 8-5. They are located in the areas where the greatest amount of social change is occurring and coincide with the same areas of modernization, whether it be in the strong sectors of urbanization (micro-regions #182, 213, 222, 224, 248, 256, 262) or in the strong sectors of frontier land settlement (micro-regions #268, 281, 288, and 354).

Notice the totals for these projections found in Table 8-8 for 1970, 72, 74, 76, 78, and 80. These 23 micro-regions could very well carry 50 percent of all growth that will take place in Protestant churches in the next decade. These areas of modernization incorporate all of the dynamic that is found in the "M" factor that has been discussed briefly in this chapter.

These projections cannot be considered as a *fait acompli*, but must be taken as a vehicle of a strong trend that is at work in Brazil today among Protestant churches. It cannot be ignored but must be studied in more detail, documented, and used as a valuable insight and tool that God is giving to his people to make the necessary preparations for the harvest that is ahead. There is much more to be said about the opportunities for church growth in frontier land areas, and the chapter on the Trans-Amazonian road touches on this. For Protestants, Brazil in 1980 is a nation of remarkable promise and opportunity, and what happens in the regions of modernization will determine the size, ministry, and impact of the Protestant message on the nation of Brazil.

A WORD OF CAUTION

Modernization Produces a Special Set of Problems

Problems of modernization are the problems that arise when there is a concentration of the key functions of a society and its populations in a few key areas. These areas of concentration become the "islands of modernization" which soon are the centers of finance, culture, and government that subjugate the large, adjacent areas and populations under a system of domination and control.

The degree of urban stability provides a basis for measuring the potential for urbanization that a country has. Brazil has been classified by Hardoy as a country that is "urbanistically unstable" (Hardoy 1971:20). He makes use of certain social and economic indicators to compare and correlate the factors of urban stability, the potential for urbanization, and the different levels of development. Stable countries usually had the highest income per capita, the largest literate population, the most students registered in their universities, a large amount of their population working in the secondary sector of the economy, and were highly urbanized in 1970. Countries with the highest potential for urbanization usually have a small total population. Brazil, with its large population is considered to be "urbanistically unstable," and will have to face the problems of absorbing 3,300,000 new urban dwellers each year into the urban sector. By 1985 a total of 49,500,000 new people will have been incorporated and absorbed into the urban populations in Brazil that form these major "islands of modernization." Large problems face the Brazilian nation in the days ahead.

The Sinister Shadow of Unemployment

Unemployment is already one of the biggest problems that exists in these sectors of modernization in Brazil. Rural migrants moving to the cities bring all of their problems with them into the urban situation as they seek employment in the factories and opportunities for education. Industrial management is learning how to produce more goods, more commodities, always increasing their productive capacity without necessarily employing more workers. It is being done by the use of new machines, new mechanical procedures and routines, the new technology, and industrial production techniques that are "capital intensive." Industry that is "capital intensive" requires the expenditure of large amounts of capital in order to increase production. "Labor intensive" was the pattern of the past when industry required many new laborers and factory workers to increase production. All of this is different now. As presently forecast, increase of industrial production will be achieved by using the new technology that is "capital intensive." A modern synthetic rubber factory in northeast Brazil is so mechanized that only fifty workers are required. Each day these complicated machines attack and transform mountains of raw materials into stacks of new synthetic tires. It is a "capital intensive" operation, the new type of factory that is very carefully planned by management to be "cost effective." Such cost effectiveness will cast a long shadow of unemployment over these islands of modernization that are growing so rapidly in the 1970's.

Lack of Urban Services Is the Order of the Day

Attempts to provide adequate housing in urban centers produce the problems of furnishing the urban services so desperately needed. Paved streets with curbs and sidewalks are needed. Fresh water systems, sewage disposal, adequate electricity, telephone services, garbage disposal, urban transporation lines, health and hospital facilities, new schools, are all required by the new urban arrivals, and still the list grows. How is it possible for local governments in the public sector to handle the urbanization needs of the large influx of new dwellers expected in the cities in the 1970's? The next fifteen years will compound these problems. What will it be like in 1985?

Newspaper articles coming from São Paulo indicate that the mayor and his administrators lament the large backlog of problems connected with providing urban facilities for the incessant flow of people into greater São Paulo. An estimate for the cost of providing a moderate, yet adequate housing unit in Brazil for one person which has the necessary urbanization facilities mentioned above comes to about US $1,500. If this per capita estimate (Hardoy 1971:22) to settle a person in the urban situation is applied to the 3,300,000 new urban dwellers expected each year for all of Brazil, the many different levels of government will have to account for almost five billion dollars each year.

Apex of the Process of Modernization

By the year 2000, regardless of any lack of foresight, inadequate urban planning, inept urban policies, or the inability of political leaders to solve the urban problems, a large island of modernization will exist that will engulf Rio de Janeiro and São Paulo, moving up the Paraíba River Valley. This "island of modernization" - an urban megalopolis - will have a population of forty million people. If Brazilians have not learned how to build, to live, and to solve the problems of cities having more than one million inhabitants, how will it be possible to build, to live, and to solve the problems presented by this urban giant, this "island of modernization" where forty million people must live?

If Protestant leaders in Brazil find it difficult now to evangelize, plant churches, and shepherd and pastor their flocks in cities having more than one million inhabitants, what will it be like in a large urban center with forty million people? The process of modernization going on in Brazil in the 1970's offers great opportunities for Protestants, but modernization also produces its own special set of problems and obstacles.

Challenge of Brazil's Frontier Road System

SUMMARY

Latin America is a hollow continent, but a road is now being cut through the Amazon basin that will link the continent from coast to coast and hasten the settlement of the land of Amazonia. An idea of what might happen along this new road system can be obtained from reading a little about the road from Brasília to Belém that is now ten years old. This chapter indicates what church growth has been along this highway and looks at Imperatriz as a model for understanding future possibilities. By 1980 this road will have changed the landscape of the hollow continent and will demand a new strategy for future evangelization and church growth endeavor.

A Hollow Continent

Geographers call Latin America a "hollow" continent. Highlands and mountains along the coastline present geographic barriers that protect the inland plains. In relief, the South American continent is generally high on the outside and low on the inside. The inland basin has a hot, inhospitable climate and a lush tropical jungle that covers its great core. Because of the difficult environment of this "hollow" area most of the population is found along the coastline. This hollow core of Latin America sometimes called the Green Inferno, much of which includes Brazil, is in the process of radical change in the decade of the 1970's. Brazil now has a population of 100 million people. This country, that occupies 47 percent of the entire land area of South America made a big decision in 1970. As a result, a road is now being cut through the center of the vast Amazonian jungle. The third class road that is now being built through the jungle will soon develop into a road system that will provide access to every part of the hollow portion of the continent.

Road Cut Through the Jungle

Before the highway is completely finished, another great continental land rush to settle this area will have begun. Equal in size to all of the land in the United States west of the Mississippi River, its magnitude is difficult to grasp. Compare the Amazon basin watershed with the total land area of the United States (Figure 9-1). When the complete river system of the Amazon River is superimposed over a surface map of the United States, the tributaries in the north reach Canadian territory, those in the south reach into the Gulf of Mexico, and the mouth of the Amazon reaches beyond the Great Lakes into the Valley of the St. Lawrence River in Canada!

FIGURE 9-1

AMAZON RIVER SYSTEM
SUPERIMPOSED OVER MAP OF U. S. A.

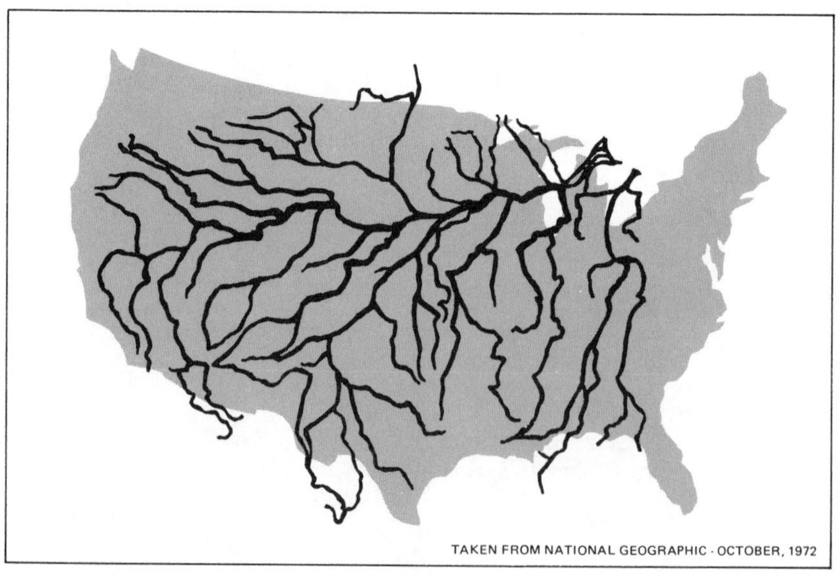

Pan American Airways has a flight once a week from Brasília to Panama. This is a 2,800 mile flight over one of the largest unsettled land frontier areas found in the world. It passes directly over the Xingu National Park, an 8,500 square mile refuge for Brazilian Indians. Seven years ago, a passenger taking this flight would see no roads cut across the Green Inferno. An occasional landing strip might be seen beside some isolated ranch houses; rich enterprising cattlemen are always first to purchase vast tracts of land to develop into pasture for their herds of Indu-Brazil hybrid cattle that are adapted to and thrive in the humid tropical climate. But in 1973 the same flight passes over something new being carved upon the floor of the Green Inferno. Flying at 37,000 feet in altitude, gaping scars appear on this jungle floor as a series of roads emerged through the dense carpet of trees and jungle. These are the first cuts of the frontier road system that will eventually crisscross all of Amazonia. It staggers the imagination to ponder what the same flight over Amazonia will reveal by 1980.

What is happening in 1973 in Amazonia captivates the Brazilian mind. Magazines and newspapers appear with pictures and articles about this dramatic, strategic road. Such issues sell out quickly at all the newsstands. Anything about Amazonia becomes a lead item in Brazilian newspapers.

Continent to be Linked Coast to Coast

What does it really mean? It is the road of the century for Brazilians that will connect the Atlantic to the Pacific. It is being cut through the largest, thickest jungle in the world. This long arching cut through the heart of the Brazilian jungles will connect with the proposed Trans-Andean road in Peru. When this happens, the continent will be united along its widest expanse of land from east to west. The Brazilian part of the Trans-Amazonian road will be 2,250 miles in length beginning at Estreito in the State of Maranhão, and will make its way to the last jungle village in Brazil called Boqueirão da Esperança (Valley of Hope) on the border between Brazil (Acre) and Peru (Figure 9-2). By 1976 it is hoped that the Trans-Amazonia road will make a connection with the Peruvian road that begins in Lima and crosses the tortuous Andes mountains. Already 1,180 miles of the Brazilian part of this road is laid open in the fierce jungle. The work continues uninterrupted in spite of the rainy season. Modern machinery now available faces the primeval enemies of mankind in this formidable jungle vastness, regardless of the rain that falls almost daily from November to May.

FIGURE 9-2

PROJECTED ROUTE OF BRAZIL'S
TRANS-AMAZON HIGHWAY AND PERUVIAN ROAD TO LIMA

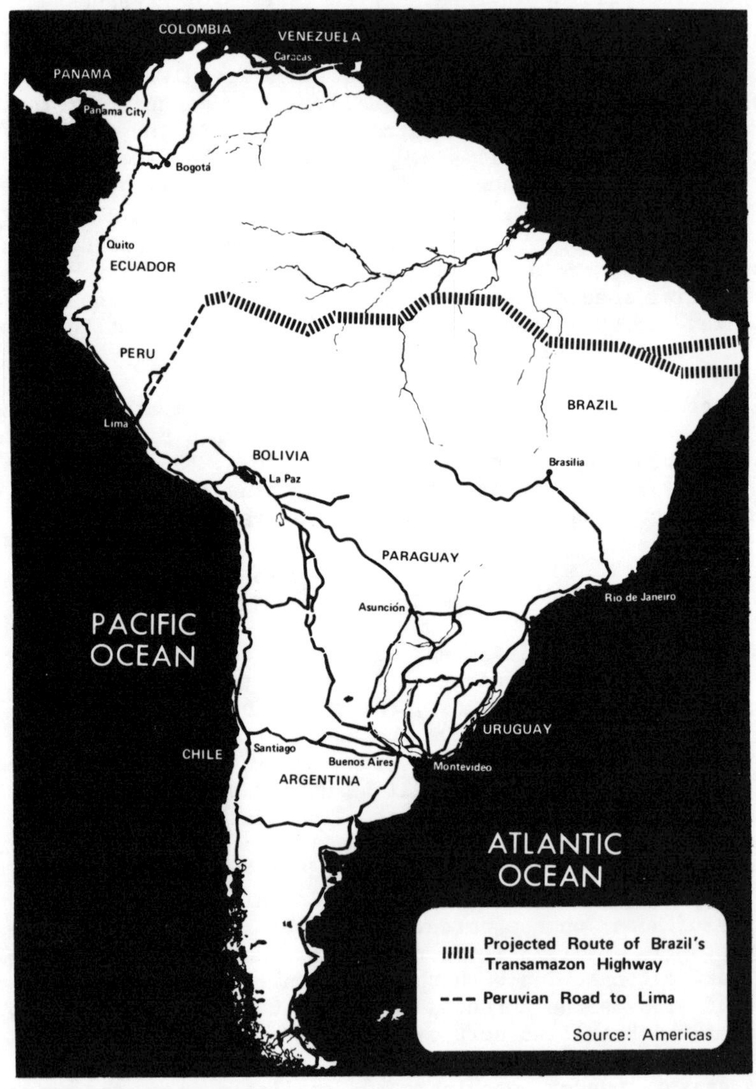

On some parts of this road, the soil has little consistency. It does not hold together, and the ground is like mercury shifting with no firm base. In such areas, the earth literally dissolves in the rain and defies construction work in the squishy mud. In this quagmire, powerful tractors bog down, but the work continues with no slackening. As of 1973, two rainy seasons have passed, and the roadbed has survived the torrential downpour. With this, the road builders press on to cross the jungle lands.

A series of landing strips has been provided along the road which is the only means of maintaining supply lines from civilization. Food, gasoline, oil, and repair parts needed for the different types of earthmoving machines and tractors arrive by air for the advance parties cutting through the forests. In the dense jungle areas trees must be cut that are more than 220 feet high and 75 feet thick at the base. These mighty bastions, triangular in shape, would look peculiar placed beside the giant sequoias of California, yet each would contain the same amount of wood in square feet and volume.

Settlement Along the Trans-Amazonian Road

The internal migration that we see here is a restless rural-to-rural "colonization." It is a movement of country people that leave their old lands in obedience to push-pull factors. They travel from place to place and eventually settle these new lands they have heard so much about. Many will stay four to six years, and if they can find their bonanza, they remain, but if not, they are ready to move on.

This has been the pattern from 1940 to 1960 in such locations as western São Paulo, north Paraná, west Santa Catarina, southwest Paraná, south Mato Grosso, central-south Goiás, north Espirito Santo, and northeast Minas Gerais. As a result of the construction of Brasília in the decade of the 1960's, important new roads now radiate from the new capital and from other points in the southeast into these newly accessible regions. Included in a gigantic crescent running through the heartland of Brazil (Figure 9-3), are a rich reservoir of forest, pastoral, and agricultural lands. Between 1960 and 1970 these diverse lands attracted close to 3,000,000 new people. What will this settlement in the 1970's in the crescent region and along the new frontier road system mean for the rapidly growing Protestant churches in Brazil? This question is being asked by different missionary leaders and frankly discussed by leaders of some of the larger, independent denominations.

FIGURE 9-3

AREAS OF FRONTIER LAND
SETTLEMENT IN THE 1970'S

The Belém-Brasília Highway

Part of the answer is to be found in what has happened along the road that was built from Brasília to Belém - the famous BR-14. What happened along BR-14 is reason for Evangelical Protestant leaders to be highly motivated and alerted to this new opportunity for evangelization and church planting.

In 1962, the Brasília-Belém highway was finished (Figure 9-4). In a decade this new highway has attracted large numbers of people who have come from all parts of Brazil. In 1962 this road had only

FIGURE 9-4

BELÉM-BRASÍLIA HIGHWAY

ten inhabited towns. In 1972 there were more than 120. New centers began to emerge day-to-day as new people arrived, and as conditions became favorable for settlement, another center would be in formation.

The population along this road now exceeds two million people. By the end of 1973 this road will be a first-class, hard surfaced road with asphalt - a primary, all season road. People are coming from every part of Brazil. They come by bus, car, motorcycle, and truck from the overcrowded, depressed areas. New arrivals will be settling along the feeder roads that are now pushing out from the main road to the connector roads that will move into the new lands that are adjacent. Such roads will begin to provide rapid access to markets, trade, and commerce.

Church Planting Along the BR-14 (Belém-Brasília Highway)

In ten years, the Protestant church membership along this highway has grown to about 35,000 communicant members. This is only a start. The next decade could triple this number of believers who are now members in the different Evangelical churches that are here because of this new highway and its growing tributaries.

No recent statistical records are available to chart the growth of Evangelical denominations along this road. This study is now being made by CASE (Center for Advanced Studies in Evangelism). When this study is published, it will be of great value to missionary and national church leaders who are contemplating different ministries along this road system. What has happened in this ten-year period on the BR-14 will give valuable insight and information about possibilities along other new roads.

However, we do have the record now of what the Brazil Mission of the Presbyterian Church in the U.S. (Southern) did during this period. They gave very high priority to church planting along this road. Now they have more than fifteen churches established in key centers from Brasília to Belém. Each major church the Presbyterians established is developing its own network of congregations and preaching points in the surrounding region and training its leadership, but this is only the beginning.

The moderator of the Presbyterian Church in the U.S. (Southern) visited Southern Presbyterian evangelistic work along the Brasília-Belém highway in 1972, and spent time in the Porangatu field. This is one of the important centers on this highway (Figure 9-4). Having observed first hand the frontier church planting opportunities that exist for Presbyterian churches growing along the highway, he returned from Brazil, anxious to recommend that his church in the U.S.A. amplify and expand this exciting church planting activity along all of the newest roads that will be added in the next decade to this growing road system. In a meeting in Brasília he spoke to a number of Brazilian Presbyterian Church leaders. He emphasized with vigor and enthusiasm the desire that his church had to provide additional resources for the important pioneer evangelistic task of planting churches along this developing road system, and expressed a conviction that this was one of the essential ways a North American church can make a vital contribution to the evangelization of Brazil at this most important time in Brazilian history. He was concerned that the field mission organization of his church be given the freedom needed to work out a suitable plan by which they could work harmoniously with the Igreja Presbiteriana do Brazil in a satisfactory partnership arrangement.

Protestant Leaders Study the New Opportunity

The proper timing, the magnitude of the church planting task among the new settlers, and the problems that any effort along this road will face in the next two decades is great. Many of the foreign missions presently in Brazil are pursuing the policy of watchful waiting, taking time to get more information and carefully examining this highly fluid opportunity. At the same time, many mission leaders have made exploratory survey trips into the Amazon Basin areas. Their surveys, their impressions, and their contacts will become the means by which these missions will be able to bring together all of the information they need that will permit them to formulate a strategy for their church planting effort in this vast hinterland. National church leaders are also traveling in the area. They receive with interest the latest reports that come back from this advancing road system. Some of these leaders are trying to determine what resources should be set aside for an effective evangelistic endeavor that their churches can initiate in some of the more strategic locations. To make these important decisions, a continuing familiarity with the population growth along the entire road system in all of its diversity and vastness is a necessity.

Initiative Taken by Pentecostal Leaders

Some leaders of Pentecostal churches in Brazil feel that it is too early for them to think about any highly concentrated work in this Amazon region. When the cities along the road are larger, teaming with people, they intend to make their move into these frontier areas and consolidate their people into churches. Other Pentecostal leaders remember that it was difficult to acquire suitable property for their growing churches in urban centers. These leaders are apprehensive about waiting too long before moving into these new lands and already are sending evangelists in to begin the first work of church planting.

In general, Pentecostal success has come in areas of large populations that have a substantial money economy where they can acquire the momentum and large number of members they need to build their churches. Pentecostal plans and strategy for the present include the enlargement and strengthening of mother churches in the large centers of Brasília, Anápolis, and Bélem. From such centers will come the pastors and evangelists needed to do the evangelistic work along the road, plant new churches, and provide pastoral ministries for new believers in the church. Enterprising Pentecostal pastors travel up and down the Brasília-Belém highway several times a year to visit the small Pentecostal congregations that have sprung up with the arrival of Pentecostals in the first waves of this remarkable internal migration. Although Pentecostal leaders may seem separated and divided, they are together in keeping abreast of new developments along the highways. The Assemblies of God has decided to send evangelists to minister in each *agrovila*.* More will follow. A Pentecostal communication system based on news brought by travelers and visitors along the route operates up and down these roads to keep the leaders informed and provides a good feel for what is happening in their churches and where new groups are beginning to form through the coming and going of their people. Several maintain contact with the people through radio programs from the major cities.

Pentecostals have been active in Imperatriz, a town closer to Belém than it is to Brasília. In 1953 the first automobile was taken in by boat. In 1958, when the road arrived, the county of Imperatriz had a population of 6,000 people. Two years later the population had doubled. In 1970, this same county had a population of 100,000, and 36,000 of these inhabitants were classified as urban and lived in the city itself.

---

*The name of the "planned" villages of settlement along the Trans-Amazonian highway.

Protestant Church Growth at Imperatriz

The following table shows a decade of growth for six protestant churches in Imperatriz. Note what happened in 1958 and 1959 (Table 9-1), the year the road opened. This information was taken from the religious census which the census bureau takes every year for the Protestant churches (IBGE 1955-1965). Evangelical membership for the period doubled every three years. This represents a total Evangelical communicant membership growth that is close to 800 percent for the decade. If the Assemblies of God Church had been able to grow without the schism that was registered between 1961 and 1962, the overall percentage index of growth could have been much higher.

If this rate of growth continues, there will be close to 5,000 evangelical believers in Imperatriz by 1980. This does not include communicant membership in the embryonic, yet-to-be established congregations, and churches that are already established but connected with the larger churches in the city (and reported in their statistics). A total membership in the county of Imperatriz could soar to 10,000 by 1980. This is only one of the 120 centers on this particular road! A series of church growth studies is now in process that will show the growth of all evangelical churches that have been planted along this road since 1962. When CASE makes this study available, it will provide many helpful insights, lessons, and suggestions for growth patterns that mission and national church leaders could use at this particular time.

Future Possibilities of Development

Many factors encourage the people of Imperatriz to believe that this is one of the cities that will continue to accelerate in its growth and development. Much inexpensive land is still available for the new arrivals and rich reserves of lumber are close by. It is a good agricultural and cattle-growing region. It is the largest city near the intersection of the Brasília-Belém highway and the Trans-Amazonia highway. These two roads come together at Estreito. Imperatriz will serve as the major trading center that will be close to the new iron discoveries at Marabá. A road is now under construction to this region, 112 miles away. Those who come from the Northeast of Brazil call Imperatriz their "Canaan," for they can get a new start here. Good land can be purchased for about one-fifth the price of the land they left behind. Instituto Nacional de Reforma Agrária (INCRA) provides loans and other helpful services for qualified, serious people who will work hard on the land that they desperately want to call their own. This is the "promised land" that is continuing to attract thousands.

TABLE 9-1

GROWTH OF PROTESTESTANT CHURCHES IN IMPERATRIZ 1955 - 1956

Denomination	1955	1956	1957	1958	1959	1960	1961	1962	1963	1964	1965	1966
Adventist												
Assemblies of God	200	201	228	573	1220	1941	2193	641	765	879	1114	1233
Congregacão Cristã								22	145	157		
Baptist				28	45	62	69	51	65	111	155	182
Presbyterian									318	333	351	371
Evan. Christian	17	16	31	44	69	92	110	124			80	88
TOTALS	217	217	259	645	1334	2095	2372	838	1291	1480	1700	1876

An Expanding Road System

Multiply the story of Imperatriz twenty or more times in the next decade. This is only the beginning of the story of a road system that is yet to stretch across the length and breadth of this vast area that was recently described in these words:

> "Having defied occupation for hundreds of years, the Amazon has its own special mystique. Its description runs all in superlatives - the area is a massive five million square km., equal to half the surface of the moon. Alone it would be the eighth largest country in the world. It has 1/20 of the world's area, one fifth of its fresh water, one third of its forests and probably one half of its oxygen supply. The Amazon River is the longest navigable river in the world - 6,447 km. Its potential wealth includes the barely scratched but already fantastic mineral deposits, huge lumber reserves, and probably the world's largest oil bed." (Thayer 1972:8).

This system includes much more than the main artery of the Belém-Brasília and the Trans-Amazonia roads (Figure 9-5). It is an extended series of connector roads, bringing together all the roads that will crisscross this huge unsettled land area. This map includes the projected Northern Perimeter Highway and the Northeast Radial Highway (Henriques 1972:9). These roads will eventually push into the Guianas, Venezuela, and Colombia (McIntyre 1972:473). These roads could be in their first stage of operation by the end of the 70's. The different stretches of road, even though built in a fast, apparently disorganized way, with only a few plans for a full utilization of the lands adjacent, will produce a tremendous stimulous for their respective regions. These roads act as magnets that attract new settlers. In a short time villages, towns, and major cities will be planted, and still more urban centers will spring up in the better locations that will be found along the roadway. Herds of cattle will graze on adjoining lands. Eventually the normal subsistence farming of these new regions will give way to a more intensive cultivation of corn, beans, rice, and cotton.

This has already happened on the Belém-Brasília highway. A comprehensive study of what has happened along the Belém-Brasília highway, already ten years old, is a preview of what could happen on a larger frontier road system that will expand and be at least ten times larger by 1980.

FIGURE 9-5

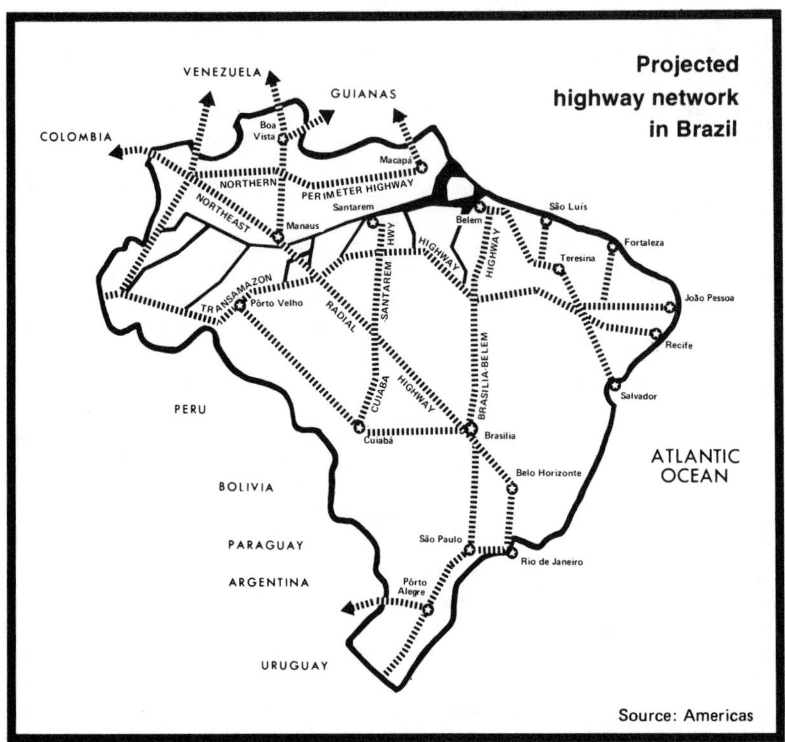

Some highways have been in use for years, while others are to be finished within a decade. When completed, the network will connect remote regions with ports and commercial centers, facilitating colonization and development. Map by Susana Villagrán

Plans and Strategy Needed

At this important time in the history of the Evangelical church in Brazil, a solid study of frontier missionary work among the new settlers and the Indians would be a substantial contribution to all mission and national church groups. The CASE center in São Paulo has begun to collect this information that is so greatly needed for evangelical leaders who must make important decisions in these areas. Soon this information will be published to help the Protestant church leadership decide what ministry is needed along this rapidly expanding frontier road system. This is a logical time for missionary and national church leaders to initiate a regular series of survey trips throughout the entire area that is being turned upside down. All of the significant literature in English and Portuguese should be made available, read, digested, and carefully considered. All of this firsthand information and data must be on hand and available for use in preparing courageous plans, both long and short term, for planting churches among these areas of opportunity in this largest of all remaining tropical frontier land areas of the world.

10

Planning for Church Growth Advance

Edward R. Dayton*

In 1792 William Carey, an English shoemaker, wrote a landmark book entitled: *An Enquiry Into the Obligation of Christians to Use Means for the Conversion of the Heathen.* In many ways Carey's book was much like this *Protestant Handbook.* It, too, was filled with page after page of statistics (Figure 10-1). Only instead of giving statistics for one country, Carey attempted to give statistics for the whole world as it was understood at that time. His book lists each country for which information was available, giving the estimated population, the number of Protestants, the number of Roman Catholics and, the number of "pagans" (Carey 1792:38).

William Carey was the "father" of the modern mission movement. At the time Carey wrote his *Enquiry* only one-third of the nations of the world had a gospel witness. Today, 180 years later, Christians have visited and given a witness in every nation of the world, and to thousands of different tribes, kindreds, and peoples.

---

*Edward R. Dayton is Director of the MARC (Missions Advanced Research and Communications Center) division of World Vision International.

FIGURE 10-1

AN ENQUIRY INTO THE OBLIGATION OF CHRISTIANS
TO USE MEANS FOR THE CONVERSION OF THE HEATHEN

SECT. III.

Containing a Survey of the preſent State of the World.

IN this ſurvey I ſhall conſider the world as divided, according to its uſual diviſion, into four parts, *EUROPE*, *ASIA*, *AFRICA*, and *AMERICA*, and take notice of the extent of the ſeveral countries, their population, civilization, and religion. The article of religion I ſhall divide into Chriſtian, Jewiſh, Mahometan, and Pagan; and ſhall now and then hint at the particular ſect of them that prevails in the places which I ſhall deſcribe. The following Tables will exhibit a more comprehenſive view of what I propoſe, than any thing I can offer on the ſubject.

--William Carey

Carey's book laid before the Church the challenge of reaching an entire world with the Gospel. This *Protestant Handbook* attempts to lay before the Church the opportunity of reaching an entire country for Christ.

Carey's *Enquiry* attempted to deal with all the current objections to missions task. It was a document that motivated thousands of men and women to move out beyond the shores of their native lands to bring the good news of salvation in Jesus Christ to those who had never heard or, in many cases, had lost the message in an environment of pseudo-Christianity. It was the example and inspiration of men like William Carey that brought early Protestant missionaries to the country of Brazil. These men came to this great new dynamic nation because they were constrained by Christian love to give the millions of people in

Brazil an opportunity to accept Jesus Christ. Here too there were those who had either never heard or had forgotten the true meaning of the radical nature of Christian conversion and the life change that it brings about in those who accept Christ.

As Carey's statistics of the unfinished task challenged the Western world to carry the Gospel to all men, so we hope that the challenge of the evangelistic task that is presented in *The Protestant Handbook* will motivate mission and Church leaders in Brazil and the Church around the world to get on with the task of bringing glory to God through the most effective evangelization and church planting ministry within this country.

But statistics and motivation are not enough. They may excite us to the potential, but leave us frustrated as to how to move forward. How do we move out to get on with the task? How does each part of the Body of Christ in Brazil and around the world play its role in the great drama which God is unfolding? While it is clear on the one hand that God holds us accountable to act in the task of carrying His Good News to all men, such action requires that we use our wills and our minds, as well as our spirit and body. At the same time, the Bible is just as clear in stating that it is God who does the work, we are only co-laborers with Him. The Bible makes no attempt to reconcile these two seemingly opposite views, nor is it necessary for us to do so. The Bible instructs us to act as though both of these apparently paradoxical statements were true. Experience shows that when we act on both of these assumptions, we find that they are practical and consistent with one another.

Perhaps a working theology can be summed up in the phrase that "It is the task of the Church to attempt to understand God's strategy and to become a part of it."

But how can we do that? Is there one grand method that God would have us to use? Is there one approach that is applicable, regardless of the situation? Brazil has been described as having the characteristics of as many as ten different countries. Is there one great procedure that will be useful in all of these ten different "countries"? The answer is obvious. God has used many different methods and many different men and women at different times in history to carry out His purposes.

How, then, do we discover where we fit? How do we make plans for the future? How do we understand God's strategy and become a part of it? What God wants us to do in any situation may eventually be to use a "method" - a way of evangelization

FIGURE 10-2

AMERICA.

Countries.	EXTENT. Length. Miles.	Breadth Miles.	Number of Inhabitants.	Religion.
Brazil	2900	900	14,000,000	Pagans and Papifts.
Paraguay	1140	460	10,000,000	Pagans.
Chili	1200	500	2,000,000	Pagans and Papifts.
Peru	1800	600	10,000,000	Pagans and Papifts.
Country of the Amazons	1200	900	8,000,000	Pagans.
Terra Firma . . .	1400	700	10,000,000	Pagans and Papifts.
Guiana	780	480	2,000,000	Ditto.
Terra Magellanica . .	1400	460	9,000,000	Pagans.
Old Mexico . . .	2220	600	13,500,000	Ditto, and Papifts.
New Mexico . . .	2000	1000	14,000,000	Ditto.
The States of America	1000	600	3,700,000	Chriftians, of various denominations.
Terra de Labrador, Nova-Scotia, Louifiana, Canada, and all the country inland from Mexico to Hudfon's-Bay .	1680	600	8,000,000	Chriftians, of various denominations, but moft of the North-American Indians are Pagans.

Copy of p. 55-56 from Carey's *Enquiry*.

that has been tried and demonstrated to be effective. But what we need in addition to methods is an approach to the entire task: first, an approach that helps us to understand what it is that we are called to accomplish; second, an approach that helps us evaluate the magnitude and character of the task; third, an approach that gives us a way of selecting those methods which are appropriate and effective; and fourth, a way by which we can discover and test new ways of accomplishing our task. It is our belief that there is a basic approach that can be used regardless of the magnitude of the task, an approach that is useful at the local as well as the national level.

Such an approach seeks to understand and describe the task from the inside of the situation rather than assume that "outsiders" have the answers. It uses all of the knowledge and data that is available to us and then seeks and depends on God's wisdom in planning for the future. Rather than stand outside the situation, we need an in-depth comprehension of the people we hope to reach from within their cultural setting, to understand the historical backdrop that brought them to where they are. The people of urban São Paulo will be dramatically different from the Indians of Amazonia. The needs of the rural worker will differ dramatically from those of the middle-class city-dweller.

This approach of examining the situation from the inside also seeks to understand that part of the Church - the force for evangelism - that is already at work or potentially able to proclaim Jesus Christ to the people to whom we feel called. Who is potentially available? Who is most likely to be effective? Such an approach poses an important question to the one doing the planning. Are we the ones that God has called to this place? Are we the ones who have become a part of the solution to the problem? Where do we fit? What makes us believe that we can have a positive influence in imparting God's love to this people?

This last point is most important. There is a mystical union that exists between the members of the Body all over the world. In one sense all men everywhere are objects of the evangelistic concern of all Christians everywhere. No part of the Church, the Body of Christ, should deny the right of another part of the Body, no matter how distant nor how foreign, to have a concern for each other. On the other hand, no part of that same Body should fail to take into account that part of the Church that already lives and attempts to minister among the people to whom the "outsider" feels called.

Steps to Understanding God's Strategy

There are some clearly defined steps which need to be considered as Christians in or outside Brazil seek to understand God's strategy and where they fit into God's great plans. Each of these steps will not be applicable in every situation. However, the data and statistics that have been gathered for this *Protestant Handbook* make it not only possible, but practical, for everyone from the local pastor to the national denominational leader, and from the foreign mission executive to the missionary on the scene, to discover the most effective ways of carrying out the evangelization of Brazil. It goes without saying that each of the steps that follow should be carried out in prayer and fellowship. "A man's mind plans his way, but the Lord directs his steps" (Proverbs 16:9) assumes that God is in the planning too! Pray your plans! And bring them under scrutiny of others in the Body of Christ so that the "whole body better joined together and compacted by that which every joint supplieth, according to the effectual working in the measure of every part" (Eph. 4:16) brings glory and honor to Jesus Christ.

1. Define the People to be Evangelized - Establish Boundaries

Few men are called to be responsible for an entire nation the size of Brazil. This does not mean that we should not attempt to formulate plans that will result in the eventual evangelization of the total country. But since there are so many different cultures and language groups to be considered, we have to select those natural groupings and lay out special strategy and plans for each group.

First, establish the boundaries of the group. Such boundaries might be geographical. We might decide to consider all of the people within the County of São Caetano do Sul, all of the people within micro-region #262, or all of the people within the State of São Paulo, or even all of the people within the Southeast region. In Brazil these are mainly geographic boundaries.

But we might also want to consider them from an ethnic viewpoint or a linguistic viewpoint i.e., the ten tribes speaking the Guarani language in Brazil. There are also large numbers of German speaking people, Japanese, Italian, and Chinese. If we define the purpose of our ministry to reach "all of the German speaking people within micro-region #313," the geographical limits of this micro-region in Rio Grande do Sul becomes the boundary for our ministry.

Again, people can be described socially. Those of the lower class have different needs and will respond to a different presentation of the Gospel than that needed to reach the middle and upper classes. Those living in a fairly stable rural environment will require a quite different message for favorable response than that which influences those living in the dynamic change of a growing urban center. Different strategies might be needed depending upon where people live. Thus, we might have a ministry to all of the people living in high-rise apartments within the County of Nova Iguaçu in the State of Rio de Janeiro.

However we define them, we need to be very clear as to the people that we are going to reach. This will not only help us to sharpen the focus of our evangelism, but at the same time will keep us from being diverted by attempting to adapt methods and programs for groups that may lie within the same geographical boundaries as the group we are working with when in fact such methods may be very inappropriate.*

2. Decide Where We Fit

It does not necessarily follow that because an individual Christian or a local body of Christians has a concern for another individual or another group that they are the ones who will be most effective in reaching those people. A simple example would be the difficulty of a lower class congregation reaching the elite or aristocracy of a particular city.

An early understanding of our own gifts and call may cause us to direct our attention to another group of people for whom we have more affinity, or they may lead us to search for other parts of the Body of Christ to do an effective job of evangelizing.

At this point in time we may be certain that we should be involved in the evangelization of a given people, but we should continually hold before ourselves the idea that there could be others more effective with these people even though we are part of the process. Every Christian should be willing to subjugate his own personal goals and desires to those of the larger Body. There may be others who can minister more effectively and achieve the goal set for certain people. The appendix lists the name and address of most of the missions and churches work-

---

*For an introduction to the concept of dividing populations by "unreached people" see Needham, Pentacost, Gilbert, *Unreached People: A Preliminary Survey*, MARC, 1973.

ing in Brazil; many of them are listed by the type of work in which they are specializing. The North American missions that have sent over 2500 missionaries to Brazil are broken down into ministries in *Mission Handbook: North American Protestant Ministries Overseas* tenth edition. Which of these might be useful?

The computerized data bank available at both MARC (in the U.S.) and CASE (in Brazil) permits one to examine the work in any county, micro-region, or state to find who is working there and what churches have been established (See Appendix 2).

NOTE: At every step of the process that is described below we need to ask again, "Where do I fit?" Planners are not necessarily leaders. Evangelists are not always good coordinators. You may play a different role at different times, a leader now, a follower later.

3. Break the Group Down into Workable Size Units

Establish smaller "boundaries." There is always a relationship between the potential force for evangelism and the size of the group being reached. This is why we have indicators of ratio of ministers to population or Christians to population, as was discussed in Chapter 6. But this does not mean that because we are one small local congregation that we should not consider, say, a total micro-region. The way to grasp a problem or task in its entirety is always to break it down into smaller problems or smaller tasks. Thus, if we believe that we are called to reach all of micro-region #268, we should break it down not only geographically but by the other types of boundaries mentioned in Step 1. These, then, may be dealt with as we carry out the tasks described below. Here again we can use the data in Appendix 2 and Appendix 3.

4. Estimating the Force for Evangelism

The force for evangelism includes local church members, local Christian leaders, major denominational leaders, the foreign missionary force already in Brazil, as well as all of the Church around the world that might in some way have an effective part in the evangelization of Brazil. But the kind of evangelism that needs to be done can be categorized in order of its <u>difficulty</u> as E-1, E-2, and E-3:

E-1 evangelism takes place when a Christian seeks to reach another person within his own group, usually his ethnic or social group. Few social or cultural barriers exist. An example would be lower class urban people speaking to those in their own apartment building.

E-2 evangelism takes place when an individual or local body attempts to move out beyond their primary group, and yet does not have to cross cultural and/or linguistic barriers. An example of this might be an individual group within a city that speaks only Portuguese reaching out to an ethnic group of German origin who are both Portuguese and German speakers.

E-3 evangelism takes place when an individual or group seeks to reach across cultural and/or linguistic barriers to another group. This is the most difficult form of evangelism and requires the greatest amount of preparation and training. This is what we have commonly referred to through the years as "foreign missions."

Who, then, are the E-1, E-2, and E-3 evangelists potentially available to reach the group we have selected? To know this, we would go to the church data for the county, micro-region, or state which we hope to reach. Here we would find data about all of the different Christians who are already in that particular locality.

We can measure the vitality of each one of these groups by noting its rate of growth or decline. As an example, look at the data given in Chapter 8 for the county of Santo André in micro-region #262. Here we see that the Baptist denomination is growing rapidly while the Methodist denomination is barely managing to keep up with the population growth. It would be quite appropriate to ask why this is so for this region. Are both denominations attempting to reach and/or attract the same group of people? Are they using different methods? How long have they been at it? And so forth.

A careful study of the micro-region and the denominations in the area will give us a good idea of the potential forces available for the evangelization of a given area. Of course, there will be differences between denominations. There will be those churches who will find themselves unable to cooperate directly with other churches. This is not the point. We are not advocating any one particular plan in which all churches must cooperate. Rather, we are suggesting that we need to take into account all of the members of the Church who are there so that we compliment each others' efforts and build on what the Holy Spirit is doing with other people. For example, in the illustration above, if the Baptists are doing well with some groups, are there others they are overlooking or are not attempting to reach or have discovered that they do not attract? If so, we can join forces merely by working alongside with a different group.

Make certain that you attempt to calculate and apply the indicators described in Chapter 6. These will give you another broad measure of the magnitude of the task.

5. Accept Measurable Goals

Having defined the group that we wish to reach, and having taken into account the force for evangelism that already exists within the target group, we now need to take the key step of setting a goal for evangelism and church growth.

There is a difference between a purpose and a goal.* The purpose is the grand reason for which we wish to move ahead; it may or may not be measurable. Purposes are the signal lights atop the mountains that lie ahead. They point us in the direction in which we wish to go.

Goals on the other hand, are the everyday working definitions that are so important if we are to make measurable spiritual progress. The basic elements of a usable goal are first, that we believe it is accomplishable; second, that we have set a date by which it will be accomplished; and third, that we will know when it has been accomplished. (We will have a way of measuring the fact that it has been accomplished.)

"To reach all of the people in Santo André with the Gospel of Jesus Christ" is a purpose. "To disciple 25 new believers and bring them into our congregation by January, 1976" is a goal.

Writing down measurable and accomplishable goals is not always easy. Many times the cause we are trying to achieve seems so far beyond us that it is difficult to know specifically what it is that God wants us to accomplish. It is here that the world of faith must not be ignored. Setting and writing a measurable and accomplishable goal is faith's response to God's imperative. It is risking our reputation, and betting our life, that this is what God wants us to do.

---

*For a further discussion on this see Dayton, Edward R., *God's Purpose/Man's Plans*, MARC, 1971.

Some people are afraid to set goals for fear of failure. Here it is important to recognize that as we move into the future, we will be faced continually with change. We will change. The situation will change. Those whom we are trying to reach will change. This means that we will have to continually reassess and reestablish our goals. How to do this will be covered below.

6. Analyze How the Force for Evangelism Might be Used to Accomplish This Goal.

Having defined the people we are going to reach, having set a goal for this particular people, and having made a first analysis of the force for evangelism that is potentially available to each of these people, the next question that comes about is how all or some of this force for evangelism might be used to accomplish the goal.

It is necessary from the very beginning to repeat that we are not speaking here of formal organic union between the different churches and/or missions within a locality. Nor are we excluding such a joint adventure. It may be recognized that in order to evangelize a given people we need a number of door-to-door witnesses who will be found within a local church, that we will need gospel literature that can be provided by a local representative of a foreign mission, that we will need Bibles that can be supplied by the Brazilian Bible Society, and that we will need the cooperation of a local Christian radio station.

In this first analysis of the force for evangelism we should attempt to identify the innovators and purveyors of change.* Which are the rapidly growing churches? These may be the ones with the social style most likely to reach out to the group in which we are interested. Are there some ministries that are being used in this area which are particularly effective with our group, such as ministries to young people? Are there outstanding church leaders whose influence and reputation can be used to unite the different members of the force for evangelism or who can communicate with others whose cooperation we need?

---

*Lyle Schaller does an excellent job of introducing the role of such people in his book, *The Change Agent: The Strategy of Innovative Leadership* (Abingdon, 1972).

7. Contact Key Individuals

We have previously pointed out how important it is that we consider all of the Christians working in an area. If we believe that any individual or local body part of Christ's Church potentially has an important function, then we must take them into account in our planning. To do this we should contact the individuals who will have an understanding of the goals and programs of other groups working in the same area. We may discover that what we feel called to do is already being done, or we may find that our plans and programs can greatly compliment those that are already underway. Here the Brazil 1980 Data Bank described in Appendix 2 will list names of churches in each county.

8. Describe the People to be Evangelized.

There are many ways of describing a group of people. We should make every attempt to see them in their total view. What is their religious background? What has been their previous contact and acceptance of Christianity? What are their social needs? What forces are at work which will tend to make them more open or more resistant to the Gospel?

Chapter 1, "The People of Brazil," is an illustration of the many factors that need to be considered. Chapter 8 on "Modernization" and Chapter 9 on the "Frontier Road System" are illustrations of the type of understanding that is needed if we are to be most effective for the Church.

Sources for such information are found in many places. The church growth statistics and other studies available for all of Brazil can be found in the Center for Advanced Studies in Evangelism (CASE), Rua Princesa Isabela, 109, São Paulo, Brazil. From such sources and other background material we locate, it will be possible to develop a "profile" of the people we are trying to reach. This should be the basis of our future planning.

9. Understand Methods

There have been many different methods that have been used to communicate the message of Christ. Door-to-door visitation, street corner witnessing, radio broadcasting, literature distribution, evangelistic meetings, church services, and a host of others. These need to be evaluated both as to their initial impact and their lasting results. CASE is now engaged in tabulating the results of a conversion survey. A copy of this survey is found in Appendix 1. The results will be published soon to further help us evaluate methods that are effective in different localities in Brazil. We need to exercise ingenuity to discover what methods God has used to reach what kind of people in what settings. We also need to understand what the lasting results of those methods of evangelism have been. As we examine and accept or reject various methods of evangelism or forge new ones from parts of others, we should be careful not to give the impression that we are making an overall value judgment about any of them. A method that works well in middle class U.S.A. may be completely out-of-place in middle class Brazil. Literature that was just right for lower class urbanites, may have no place in rural evangelism.

10. Select a Preliminary Target Group

A key step in planning a strategy for evangelism is to select a smaller target group with whom we can test our ability to communicate the Gospel.

This target group should be selected on the basis of apparent receptivity, the force for evangelism available to reach the group, and the ability of those reached to influence other people and resources. Example: Suppose we had set as our goal the evangelization of the people within ten different high-rise apartments all situated in the county of Santo André. Our preliminary examination reveals that one particular apartment complex has a number of Christians within it. Later, we discover that a number of individuals within this apartment complex have recently accepted Christ. We should obviously concentrate efforts on this apartment and discover which evangelistic methods have been greatly blessed, and also those which have not been effective. Attempt to multiply the force for evangelism so that the number of Christians within this apartment complex increases and reaches out to those in similar situations. Formulate a plan, then work the plan. Remember the indicators of Chapter 6.

11. Establish an Evaluation System

Many programs of evangelism needlessly fail because no effort was made to make an early evaluation of progress. An early evaluation might have uncovered situations where misunderstanding, lack of communication, and wrong methods of evangelism produced resistance rather than belief.

When planning any strategy, design an evaluation system that will quickly determine what direction we have taken and how effective we have been. If our goal is to disciple twenty-five new members into a local congregation, break this goal into smaller steps. Ten people discipled in six months may be a possible breakdown. If at the end of five months we find that only one or two have come to know Christ and have joined the church, there is obvious need to reevaluate to determine whether our goal is practical or whether we have laid out a plan which will help us to reach that goal. Many times the maintenance of an evaluation system spells success or defeat. Large evangelistic efforts require special individuals to take care of the task of evaluation and provide the solid orientation toward the goals that have been set down for the broader task. Evaluate in prayer. God's Spirit helps us in the ultimate evaluation of all we do!

12. Build a Communications System

Incorporate as many people as possible into the initial stage of goal setting and planning for any evangelistic endeavor. People who participate in the initial plans can become so involved that their motivation keeps them enthusiastically pressing forward, partners in the initial thrust. Keep them praying over the plans.

It is just as important that a good communications system be established within the total force. If an individual congregation is attempting an evangelistic task by itself, then it has a built-in communications system in the local life of the church. As the members gather each week, they can report progress to each other and the successes and the failures of different individuals or groups can be shared and prayed over. But as the size of the cooperating force grows larger, it is more and more important that ways be found to encourage all of the members of each church or organization to become involved with what is happening. Such a communication system might take the form of a newsletter, a local radio broadcast, visits between different members of the teams, reports back from the area being evangelized to the mother church, and many other forms.

Communication is also important to keep all of the different members apprised of what their task is. In order to respond to God's strategy each one of us needs adequate information on how we are to respond appropriately in a way that will let us "fit in" with all the others in this force for evangelism. One example of a communication tool that is being used among the Evangelicals of Brazil is the periodical newsletter published by the Center for Applied Studies in Evangelism (CASE) and distributed by different churches to local pastors all over the country.

13. Future Projections and Possible Results

Purposes point in direction toward which we are moving. Goals define objectives which we hope to reach. Plans are the step-by-step process by which we hope to reach our goals. However, since we are unable to predict the future with any certainty, we can be sure that changes in plans will be necessary. We can also be sure that many unexpected things will happen as a result of our efforts.

Many times in our planning we forget to plan for success! For example, suppose we plan that there will be 1,000 new Christians within such and such a county one year from now. What might this mean to the people of this county? What happens when 1,000 new converts accept Christ? What life-styles will be changed? What impact will this have on the total situation within which they are living?

Anything that can be done during the planning process or during the actual task of evangelization will help us recognize and accommodate any "unplanned" impact we will have upon the church or society in which we are working.

14. Recruit or Mobilize the Force for Evangelism

This is perhaps the most difficult and delicate step of all. Too often we come to this point having done too much planning and deciding! If we missed the key individuals of Step 7, we may have built resistance rather than cooperation. If we fail to include many people in our planning, they will not feel part of it.

So in one sense, the very process should have brought many people into the total program. But there will be many times when specialists or local groups must be carefully and prayerfully informed and motivated.

15. Carry Out the Plan

All the thinking, planning, and praying are now ready to be put into action. We know the people we want to reach. We have selected a target group. We have examined, and hopefully recruited, the force for evangelism most likely to reach the group. We have prayerfully selected or forged new methods of evangelism. Now to begin!

Of course, in practice things do not necessarily work in this step-by-step way. Many of these things will go on simultaneously or perhaps in a different order. The important thing for our approach is that we consider the usefulness of each step.

16. Be Ready to Replan

The future will no doubt be quite different than the one we imagine. Change continues to be upon us. Forces are at work in many directions which will both hinder and help our total objectives. Methods which were very useful five years ago will be out of date in the coming years. Changes in the government, plans for modernization, the economy, or world events may all work together to strengthen or impair our ability to reach the people or to make them more or less receptive to the Gospel. This means that we need to expect that our plans will have to be continually reset as we gain new understanding into God's total strategy for the day in which we are living. The Church is a marching army, not a fortress. It gathers members and momentum as it moves forward. It moves forward as it takes advantage of each new situation that arises and is ready to respond to God's will for that moment.

17. Share What is Learned With the Rest of the Church

As the evangelistic process takes place or as it is completed, what has been learned needs to be shared as widely as possible. If new evangelistic tools have been found to be successful, these need to be communicated to those who can use them. If great movements of the Spirit and ingatherings to the Church are taking place, the rest of the Body of Christ needs to know and be encouraged. As a greater understanding is obtained of a given people, this needs to be shared as widely as possible.

The results of such data gathering can be reported to CASE in São Paulo and will be widely shared via their pastors' newsletter.

The 17 steps that are outlined above are no magic formula for success. Many of them at times will be done in a reverse order or done so intuitively that we are not aware of them. Perhaps for some they will be nothing more than a series of items to consider. For others they may constitute a thoughtful procedure on how to move ahead.

The major point is this: The process of evangelism is as diverse as the cultures of the world. Each Human being is a sacred person before God. Each one deserves all the special consideration and attention to his need for Christ within his personhood that we can bring. By examining the need from <u>within</u> the situation and attempting to discover God's special plan for each group that is so special in God's eyes we will bring glory to God and be as effective as He would have us be.

11
Focus on the Future

SUMMARY

The outlook for the 1970's includes a larger Protestant church that will enjoy a continued and sustained growth and a gradual expansion into other parts of Brazil. Some of the obstacles and obstructions are considered under the topic of neglected chances, preoccupation with the Indians, and the problems connected with spiritual lethargy. Yet there is something new in the 1970's and this can be seen in the organizations, methods, and opportunities.

But what about the options open for the 1970's? Needed is a study around the facts that will become the prerequisites for a new strategy. This is now possible through CASE, the new information center for Protestants where all the findings of the Brazil 1980 effort are available. Out of these facts a whole new set of viable objectives for 1980 are possible for all who are open to the remarkable opportunities of the 1970's.

INTRODUCTION

In 1972, after traveling throughout Brazil and taking a good look at what was happening, a businessman voiced the opinion that he would like to be able to start all over and do it all in Brazil.

What the business man saw clearly was that in statistical terms Brazil was in the middle of an economic expansion that is unparalleled in the recent history of the world's developing nations. In 1971 Brazil's gross national product rose by 11.3 percent, and in 1972 it continued its rise at 10.9 percent. While this was happening, its industrial production increased 20 percent. Today Brazil has a higher economic growth rate than any nation in the world, with the possible exception of Japan. The present production of wealth in Brazil is equal to that of India, a nation having six times as many people.

Beyond mere statistics, what sets Brazil apart is its remarkable resource base. Brazil has five times as much land as Mexico and continues to discover new resources that are part of the inheritance handed down from the Portuguese colonial pioneers and settlers.

As Brazil begins to exploit its dormant resources, the times can be compared to the period of industrial expansion experienced in North America between the Civil and Spanish American wars. It is as though the future of the country had finally joined hands with the present. The opportunity is quite remarkable. What happens in Brazil in the next decade will certainly be important, and the destiny of the growth and development of Evangelical churches will be at stake.

The people of Brazil gladly received the message of the Gospel, and Protestant churches were planted in this great nation. These churches grew, and this growth has been brought into sharp focus by several chapters that presented and interpreted the latest church growth information. We have seen what happened in the 1960's, what happened regionally, what happened with the missionary force, and what happened in the different denominations. The term modernization was introduced and related to church growth. The frontier road system was described and presented as one of the outstanding opportunities for future growth and expansion. Indicators were discussed as a way of appraising the evangelistic task, and the last chapter attempted to show how all this data can be used to plan a strategy for future advance.

We now have the data and we have an approach to the problem of evangelization at all levels. What about the future? In this chapter we will attempt to focus on the future, dealing with the outlook and obstacles in the 1970's. Then we will consider the new things and options for the decade, and attempt to arrive at a new understanding of how to think about such a country in the days ahead in terms of evangelization and a well-rounded cycle of growth in the churches.

OUTLOOK FOR THE 1970's

A Larger Protestant Church in Brazil

In Membership. In 1900 the Protestant communicant membership in Brazil numbered 11,376 people. In 1970, this number had grown to a reported 2,623,600 communicants with an estimated Protestant community of almost 10 million Brazilians. In 1980 the MARC projection places this number at 5,477,000 communicants with a community of 16,529,000.

Protestant Churches Have Large Communities. There are dynamics that operate in certain denominations that cause them to have a "community" that is five times the number of communicant members. The size of the community, according to studies made by Frank A. Ineson, varies from two to five times the number of communicants.

In Brazil we can be safe in stating that the average community is three times the membership. Based on this formula for calculating community in Brazil, in 1970 there was a Protestant community of 9,528,738. In 1980 the Protestant community should number approximately 16,529,000. In 1970 this represented ten percent of the population and by 1980 this could rise to 12 percent of the population. This is the growing edge of the Church (Figure 11-1).

Evangelism has been a continual process in Brazil, a process that has been gathering momentum since the first foreign missionary arrived in 1837. These early missionaries and their converts were the first of a large Protestant community that was to grow out of their faithful, often feeble, witness to the grace and mercy of Jesus Christ to transform and redeem all who would put their trust and faith in Him, to redeem and transform their lives into that "new and living way." Missionaries and their converts taught leadership principles by example, indoctrination, and concept to eager, competent, enthusiastic Brazilians. Through the increase of their bold and courageous witness to Jesus Christ these Brazilian believers and their leaders enlisted members of their families, friends, and sought out neighbors to give them the opportunity to accept Jesus Christ and become responsible members in the young Protestant churches. Figure 11-1 indicates the way in which the door opened for thousands of believers to join with their new-found brothers and sisters in Christ to engage in the planting, establishment, and formation of local churches in all parts of Brazil.

Leadership Potential. In 1970 there were 16,800 ordained pastors and 47,840 deacons and elders, called lay leaders, who assisted these pastors in the local churches. This does not account for the other leaders, such as the Sunday school teachers and the leaders of different organizations in the church. If there was a total of 64,640 Brazilian leaders (all pastors, deacons, and elders) in 1970, we could probably double this number if we were to add the other leaders found in the local churches. This is a growing reservoir of dynamic leadership potential. Out of this pool of leadership and from young people will come the ministers and pastors needed for the churches that will be established in the decade of the 1970's.

FIGURE 11-1

GROWTH OF PROTESTANT COMMUNICANT MEMBERS IN BRAZIL 1900-1980

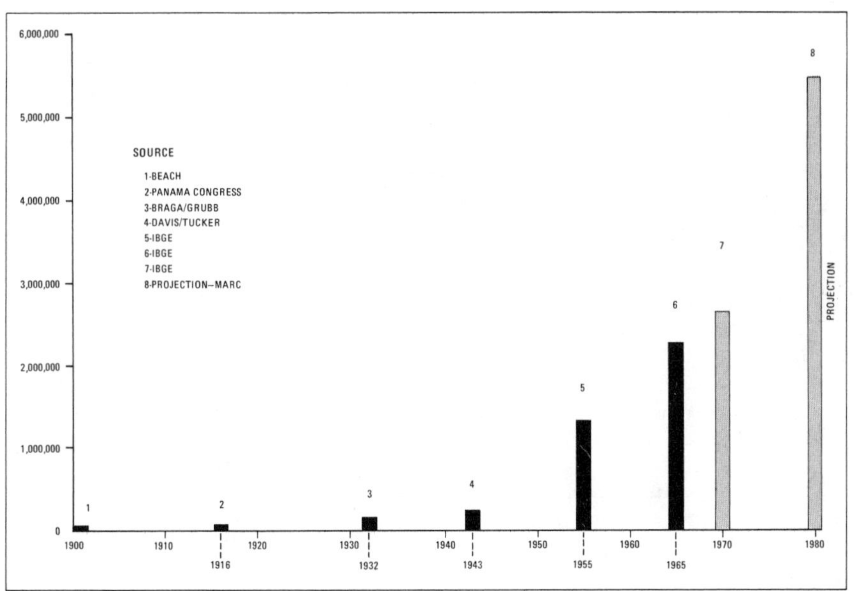

Many Brazilians have been gifted with leadership ability. They have a special capacity to inspire, an innate ability to speak, preach, and teach. Brazilian leaders often have an emotional makeup which, when set within a musical context, is very expressive, helping in the communication of the Gospel and attracting their fellow men to Christ. When Brazilians have a vital religious conviction that is expressed in a solid, enthusiastic, devotional type of faith. Such faith can catch fire not only in the immediate inner circle, but sparks from such fires have a way of spreading far and wide. Along with this, Brazilian leaders are able to inspire their members to high and noble undertakings for the Lord. But like Christian leaders everywhere, they need to be informed and to understand everything possible about God's strategy for Brazil today. If this can happen to the majority of the Brazilian leaders that are found in the Protestant churches, the accelerated growth of the churches in the future should be assured.

Continued and Sustained Growth. The accelerated growth of Protestant membership in Brazil since 1940 is quite pronounced (Figure 11-1). The sustained rate of growth from 1940 to 1970 is remarkable. The trends of growth that have been set in this 30-year period are forecasted to continue with a slight upswing into 1980. Brazilian leaders who were asked about the future of Evangelicals in Brazil in the 1970's revealed a real enthusiasm, believing that a new surge of evangelistic activity would be generated at the local church level. This is the decade of massive movement of rural populations into cities. Such mass movements of people increasingly trigger other types of change and adjustment throughout the entire social structure, creating a climate favorable for such evangelization. Antonio Elias, evangelist and president of the Burning Bush Evangelistic Association, anticipates in the decade of the 1970's a biblical revival that will sweep thousands into the Kingdom of God (Cunliffe 1971:13). If it were possible to visit in different Evangelical churches from Recife to Pôrto Alegre, from Rio de Janeiro to Brasília, it would be apparent that evangelistic thrusts in the local churches are being used to introduce many to Jesus Christ, and baptismal services are being scheduled with regularity to incorporate these new converts into churches in the steady process of sustained pattern of growth. But the MARC staff believes that the normal, sustained pattern of growth can be superceded by the rapid acceleration of evangelistic activity all up and down the line if the opportunities presented in this book are prayerfully utilized and the Divine intervention expected by the Brazilian leaders in the form of revival and renewal happen.

Gradual Wider Geographical Expansion

Protestants Reported in 55 Percent of the Counties of Brazil. In 1955, there were Protestants reported in 1,686 counties. By 1970 Protestant churches could be located in 2,500 of the 3,952 counties found in every part of Brazil. By 1980 it is reasonable that organized Evangelical churches and congregations will be found in more than 3,000 of these counties, or a

FIGURE 11-2

PROTESTANT MEMBERSHIP FOUND IN
MICRO-REGIONS IN 1955, 1960, 1965, 1970

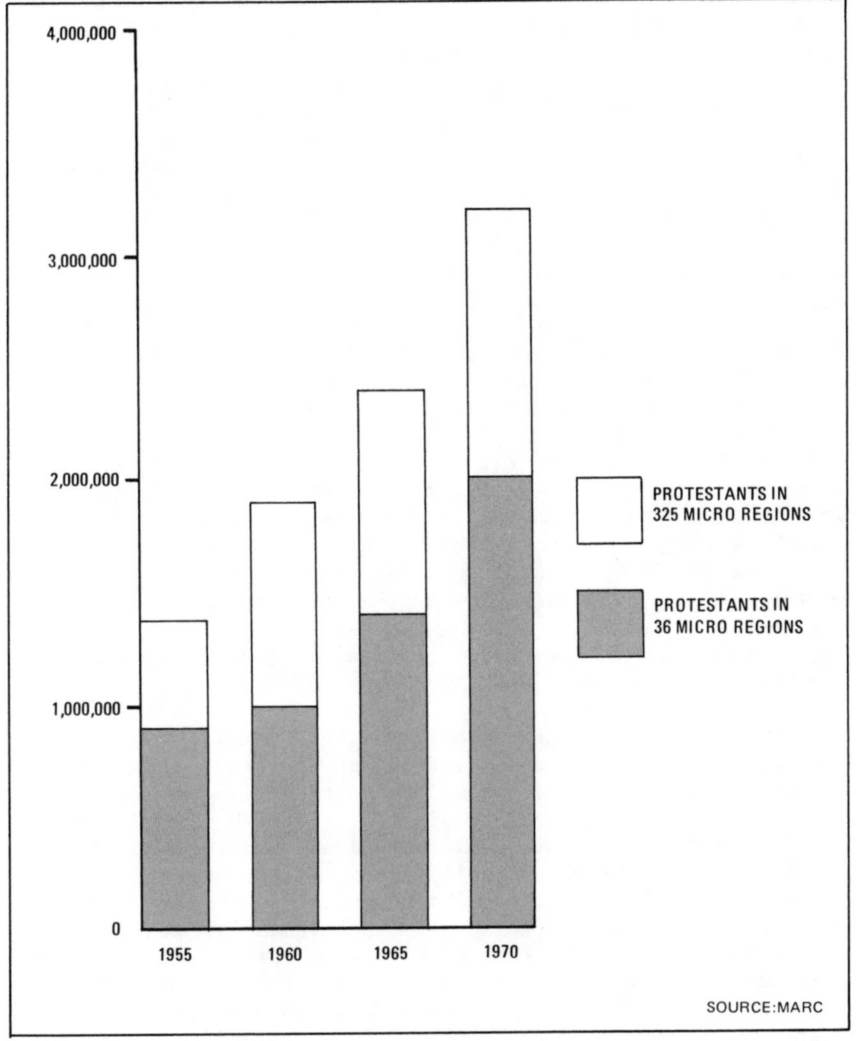

rise in occupance of 55 percent in 1970 to 75 percent in 1980 of the counties - the smallest socio-economic and political units to be found in this great country.

Protestants Reported in 99 Percent of the Micro-regions. These 4,010 counties have been distributed into 361 micro-regions, some micro-regions having as many as forty counties in them. In 1955 Protestants were reported in 346 of these micro-regions; however, Protestants are concentrated in only a few. When the total communicant membership found in each micro-region is calculated, sorted out, and made into a list of micro-regions that have the largest first, the second largest next, and so on in decreasing order, the largest concentration of Protestant membership is found in only 10 percent of these micro-regions - the first 36 to be exact. In 1955 these 36 micro-regions, having almost 30 percent of the total population accounted for 889,385 communicants or 65 percent of the country total of 1,394,727. Ten percent of the micro-regions accounted for 65 percent of all Protestant membership in Brazil! In 1960 believers found in the first 36 micro-regions totaled 1,091,233 out of the country total of 1,889,751. This was 58.8 percent of all Protestants, again 10 percent of the micro-regions accounted for almost 60 percent of all Protestants. This indicates that there are 36 areas, now called micro-regions, where Protestant growth is in rapid expansion. Ninety percent of the remaining micro-regions experience a slower, but gradual growth rate. In each five-year period the growth ratio appears to be the same (Figure 11-2). Evangelization and church planting in 326 micro-regions, or 90 percent of them, is still in the early stages of development, and the new opportunities for growth in these micro-regions are exceptional for the decade ahead.

Trends for Expansion and Projections. First, when the process of modernization was introduced in Chapter 8, a list of the micro-regions having the largest concentration of believers was given (Table 8-9). If the trends of the growth of membership continue for these 23 urban micro-regions, in 1980 more than 65 percent of all Evangelical believers in Brazil will be concentrated in 6 percent of the 361 micro-regions. Second, micro-regions that contained the new land settlement areas of the 1950's, 60's, and 70's will experience an index of growth almost without precedent in the past three decades, with the exception of regions like the Valley of the Rio Doce, northern Paraná, and micro-region #228 (Figure 8-14). The great land rush to the west is on in Brazil. In March 1972 land developers reproduced in a Londrina paper, a full size map that had been made after careful research in land offices of the counties of Diamantino and Pôrto dos Gauchos in the State of Mato Grosso. The counties are located north of Cuiabá, the capital of Mato Grosso, between the new road (BR-364) that has been completed from Cuiabá to Pôrto Velho, and the road now under construction (BR-165) from Cuiaba to Santarém on the Amazon River.

The greatest part of the new lands in these counties have been purchased by large corporations and associations of cattlemen who have taken advantage of the tax reductions and incentives offered by the Brazilian government program SUDAM (Development of the Amazon Basin). Eighty percent of these lands have been purchased by these different groups in the hope of realizing a large profit from the future sale of these choice pastoral and farming regions.

Anyone familiar with different companies in Brazil will recognize names like Mappen, Mercedes Benz, Vigor, Miramar Trust, Marape, etc. When such an initial wave of feverish land buying is in evidence, a second wave of settlement will follow within a few years. This is the prelude to the increase of this type of land investment in that part of Brazil that Brazilians call *Amazonia Legal*, the land area within the watershed of the Amazon River and its tributaries that is covered by SUDAM laws (Garland 1971:48).

The major areas of land that have already been affected and will be radically transformed with this type of land speculation and settlement in the 1970's are to be found within an area that looks like an inverted funnel whose base touches the Atlantic ocean in the north and is clearly displayed in Figure 11-3. This area includes four states, the Federal District, and the Territory of Rondônia. In 1950 these lands had a population of 5,472,695. By 1960 the population had grown to 9,866,163 and in 1970 the population had increased to 15,320,640. Since 1950 the attraction for these new lands in the west has increased. All the people living in this area in 1950 represented 10.5 percent of the population - in 1960, 13.8 percent, and in 1970, 16 percent. The entire State of Paraná is included in the area under consideration because it still remains one of the dynamic regions of frontier lands, especially the northern and western parts of the state. If the region of Amazonia were superimposed over these lands, it will be seen that the northeastern tip of Maranhão, the southeastern part of Goiás, southern Mato Grosso, and Paraná are not officially within the Amazon region being developed under SUDAM, but constitute the areas of approximation - a buffer zone of frontier lands in the West, extending in this funnel-like shape from north to south.

The growth of Protestant membership in these states, territories, and the Federal District has been remarkable. Table 11-1 is a record of the total for all of the Protestant denominational

FIGURE 11-3

LANDS AFFECTED BY LAND SPECULATION
AND SETTLEMENT IN THE 1970'S

membership within this geographical zone of the so-called frontier lands from 1955 to 1970 in five-year periods.

TABLE 11-1

PROTESTANT MEMBERSHIP IN FRONTIER LANDS IN WEST BRAZIL 1955-1970

	MEMBERSHIP IN FIVE-YEAR PERIODS			
STATE	1955	1960	1965	1970
Rondônia	1,807	3,136	3,759	4,913
Maranhão	19,477	32,234	35,757	54,800
Paraná	72,559	123,429	215,814	366,335
Mato Grosso	6,376	12,165	25,472	58,653
Goiás	18,319	29,774	40,971	56,794
Federal District	0	3,151	10,320	28,045
Totals	118,538	203,889	332,093	569,540

Source: MARC

The possibilities for expansion and growth of Protestant churches in these frontier areas for the 1970's are evident and can be seen by the remarkable gains of membership in each five-year period since 1955, shown in Figure 11-4. From 1960 to 1970 there has been an increase in Protestant believers in the churches of this region that exceeds 100 percent. If a 100 percent increase is recorded between 1970 and 1980 in these states, the total membership in frontier lands will soar beyond the million mark. Such projections are based on the rate of consistent growth that has been carefully recorded for every year since 1955.

These are important areas of high potential for church planting in the next decade. Because of the pioneer nature of the work, and the expenses involved in covering the vast distances, these areas constitute viable opportunities for foreign missionary activity. But this rugged evangelistic work in the hinterland should not be undertaken by foreign missionary agencies without a firm resolve to remain with the church planting task until vigorous churches have been established and strong Brazilian leadership has emerged to carry on the ministry of the churches.

FIGURE 11-4

GROWTH OF PROTESTANT MEMBERSHIP IN
FRONTIER LANDS - WEST BRAZIL 1955-1970

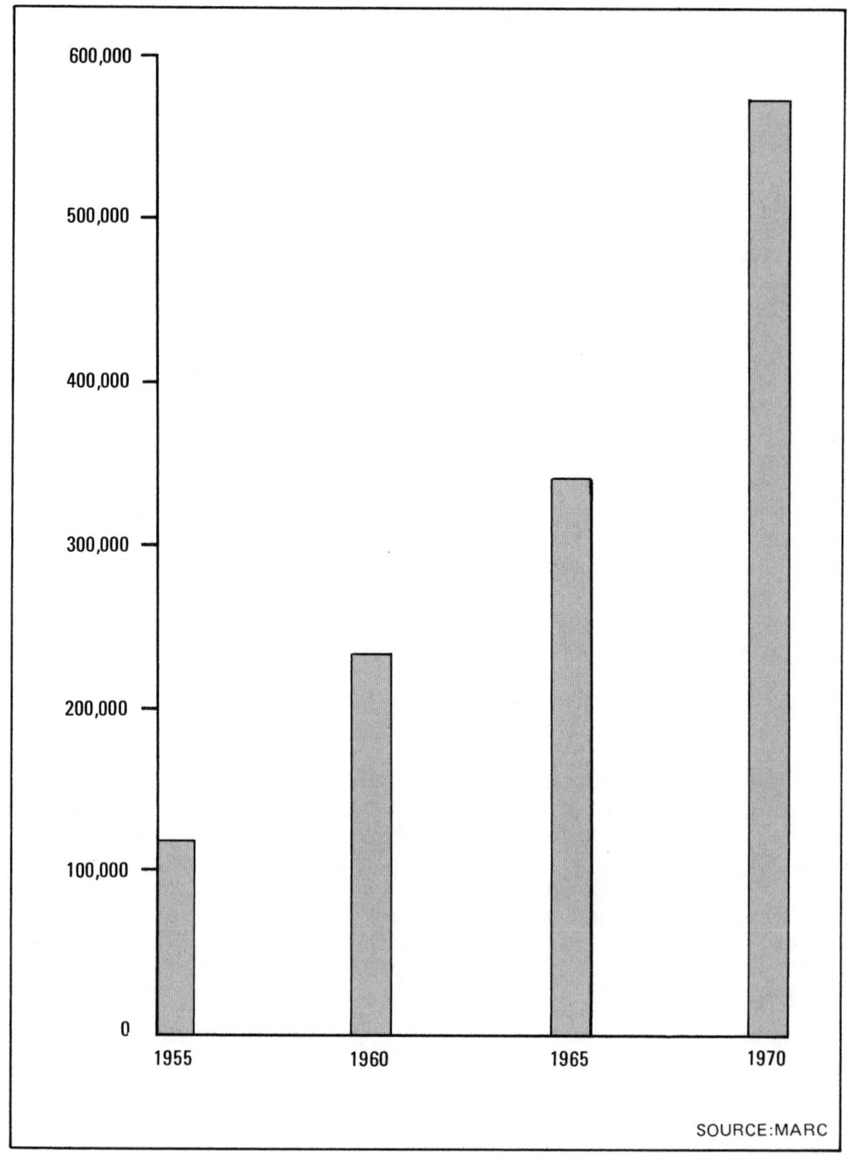

Concentration in Important Urban Centers and Areas of Outstanding Commercial and Economic Growth.

As was pointed out in the chapter "Modernization and Church Growth", the Protestant church grows in areas that have a healthy "money economy." To illustrate this, we have selected five different types of economic urban centers and displayed the manner in which the Protestant churches have been increasing their pattern of growth in these different locations. The following centers have been chosen and a brief description of their importance is given:

TOWN		DESCRIPTION
Campina Grande	--	Trade center for central Paraíba
Juiz de Fora	--	Textile manufacturing center
Volta Redonda	--	Steel manufacturing center
Nova Iguaçu	--	Small industries and commerce
Baurú	--	Rail and trade center for central São Paulo State

Each center has enjoyed a better than average index of growth, and the general increase has been 300 percent in each decade (Table 11-2).

TABLE 11-2

GROWTH OF PROTESTANT MEMBERSHIP IN SMALL URBAN CENTERS 1955-1970

LOCATION	1955	1960	1965	1970
Campina Grande PB	2,983	3,090	4,166	5,769
Juiz de Fora, MG	4,445	8,319	9,825	11,035
Volta Redonda, RJ	1,933	2,466	4,508	6,231
Nova Iguaçu, RJ	6,281	13,140	31,472	71,949
Baurú, SP	2,345	4,740	4,848	9,031
Totals	17,987	31,755	54,819	104,015

Campina Grande in Paraíba is the main trade center for the interior region of the State. It is one of the intermediate stop-overs for hundreds of immigrants from the interior that eventually migrate to other parts of Brazil. The turnover of believers is a constant problem to the pastors in this interior trading and commercial center.

Juiz de Fora, Minas Gerais, is located on the highway between Rio de Janeiro and Belo Horizonte. It is one of the oldest textile centers in Brazil and one of the largest trading and commercial centers located on the main railway and hard top roads in the state.

Volta Redonda is Brazil's best known center for the growing iron and steel industry. After Getulio Vargas took the initiative to establish this new industry in Brazil, and Volta Redonda was chosen, thousands of new people began to arrive seeking employment, a better life, and education for their children.

Nova Iguaçu is one of the bedroom communities outside of Rio de Janeiro, and as such is one of the fastest growing suburb areas close to Rio. The rapid growth of the Protestant churches here is a remarkable thing and needs to be investigated in more depth.

Baurú, São Paulo is the major trading and rail center in the central part of the state. It is the jumping-off place for most of the roads and railroads that serve the western part of the state and has become one of the important crossroad towns for this area.

Numbers of Believers Increase - Influence on Society and Politics Increase.

Hundreds of Evangelical believers occupy important jobs in national life, including a dozen or more who are Federal Deputies, one Senator, a Governor, a Vice Governor of one of the States, and a judge who is a member of Brazil's Supreme Court. At each election time the Protestants attempt to elect more of their number to serve in civil and political roles of great influence and importance. The implication of this is a wider acceptance of Protestants in the different positions of leadership in politics and other areas of public life. One Presbyterian pastor is the President of the Housing Development Commission for Guanabara. In this position he feels a personal responsibility to eliminate all of the shanty towns and slums in Rio de Janeiro by 1975 and provide adequate housing for the former slum-dwellers, an important responsibility.

Willems comments on the fact that Brazilian Presbyterianism has been successful in appealing to the middle sectors of society and to some extent to individuals in the upper class (Willems 1967:253). The fact that the historical churches in Brazil have succeeded in enlisting believers among the elite, indicates a remarkable opportunity for Gospel proclamation among the upper sectors of Brazilian society in the days ahead.

OBSTACLES AND OBSTRUCTIONS IN THE 1970's

Paradox of Membership Loss and Leakage

From 1956 to 1966 there were 2,535,767 additions registered on the rolls of Protestant churches in Brazil (Table 11-3). This included baptisms of adult communicant members, reaffirmation of faith for those who had been disciplined for moral conduct or had lapsed in their interest and attendance, transfers from other churches, and any other way in which new members might have been taken into the Protestant churches during this important decade.

TABLE 11-3

ADDITIONS, LOSSES, AND NET GAINS OF BRAZILIAN PROTESTANTISM 1956-1966

Year	Additions	Losses	Net Gains
1956	200,591	66,335	134,256
1957	206,815	84,814	122,001
1958	207,526	112,856	94,670
1959	220,782	114,366	106,416
1960	220,016	116,975	103,041
1961	206,718	123,798	82,920
1962	196,565	117,921	70,596
1963	207,657	125,469	81,688
1964	254,411	149,455	106,956
1965	317,179	129,137	188,042
1966	297,507	153,463	143,044
Totals	2,535,767	1,293,089	1,235,630

The column that registers the losses (1,293,089) in the same period accounts for more than 50 percent of these additions, leaving the net gain for the eleven years recorded of 1,233,630 members. What happened to the people who were registered in the "losses" column? Perhaps 10 percent could be accounted for as discipline cases whose lax moral conduct resulted in disciplinary action by their church officers, and they were suspended from the roles for one reason or another. Perhaps 12-13 percent of these "losses" were accounted for by death. Another two or three percent may have left to join other Protestant denominations or were attracted by "sects" considered by Evangelicals to be heretical. When these different losses are added up, this still leaves more than a million losses to Protestant churches between 1956 and 1966 that are not accounted for. This is the great paradox of membership loss and leakage that has not been studied, analyzed, or given sufficient research to be understood.

Many say that this can be explained by the "big backdoor" policy that operates in many Protestant churches that are free with their requirements for membership, receiving new members with little teaching and preparation at the "front door" only to have these members slip out the "back door" in large numbers when their enthusiasm wanes, and the impact of an emotional moment of affirmation in baptism is gone or cools down. There must be a substantial movement within the "losses" column through the back door but not as much as many estimate. A generous estimate would have 20 percent of these "losses" going out the back door of Evangelical churches.

A more plausible explanation must be sought in the "M" factor that was mentioned in the chapter on "Modernization." Let us cite a few examples.

> The church in Catoles, Bahia had a membership of 75 communicants. This church was a tight-knit homogeneous group of people whose main activity was agricultural work. Three or four families had accepted Jesus Christ simultaneously, and within two years their different family relations throughout the "family web" had made their decision for Christ and established this small Protestant church in the backlands of the State of Bahia. They heard about the new lands in Cáceres, Mato Grosso. Within six months family leaders had traveled to these new lands, made arrangements to move, returned, sold their lands in Bahia, and every member in this Presbyterian church climbed on the trucks that took them across the whole country of Brazil in fifteen days. That church ceased to exist in Bahia. The next year a new church was recorded in Mato Grosso, and in ten years it has grown to three or four times the original membership.
>
> The Congregational Church in Campina Grande, Paraíba. A letter from the pastor of this church discloses the constant turnover of the membership of his church. People from the *roça* (rural area) come into town, settle with friends, family, or just get along well enough to stay for six months or a year. When it is possible for them to move to Recife or south to Rio de Janeiro, São Paulo, or Paraná, they do so. In ten years this pastor's membership has turned over four or five times. This means that the church that now has

200 communicants would have had a membership of 800 communicant members if all of the transient *crentes* (believers) had remained in Campina Grande. There are fifty or more large interior towns throughout Brazil that have this role as a staging area where many believers as well as non-believers from the interior begin their move to the larger cities. Many encounter Jesus Christ in such stopovers and move from one place to another as believers that are not committed to any particular church. When they finally settle down at the end of their journey, these believers join Evangelical churches and leave the ranks of this great floating constituency of Protestants that is in constant motion and movement over the highways in all directions throughout Brazil.

Evangelical Church in Salinas, Minas Gerais. When Brasília was in the process of construction between 1958-1962, a church of 150 members in a countyseat town was shaken by the exodus of some of the top leadership. In this four-year period ten important leaders in the local church left taking their families to Brasília to settle in the satellite towns around the new capital. Ten communicant members left for Brasília taking twelve other people who were members of their families. Among those who left were an elder, a deacon, a Sunday school teacher, a teacher in the local Christian day school, and a young leader among the young people. They were losses from this Salinas church and were finally picked up three or four years later in other Evangelical churches in the bedroom cities adjacent to Brasília - lost for a few years in this stream of Protestants in the floating constituency.

Seventy to eighty percent of the *crentes* in the "losses" column may be on the move in Brazil, and it is safe to surmise that the majority will be picked up in two or three years on the roles of churches found in large urban or rural areas where there is economic opportunity, or in the churches that will be planted in the new frontier land areas. The patterns of church growth in Brazil cannot be understood without considering the magnitude of the "M" factor that is the force moving this floating constituency to different parts of Brazil.

Some of the statistical problems found in the religious census have their explanation in the "losses" column, and little or no research has been done in this area. When we say that there are more than three million communicants registered on the rolls of Protestant churches in Brazil, perhaps we can add another 700,000 members to this number and label them "in transit" for the past two or three years.

"In transit" can mean an eight-month stay for a small family in Montes Claros, another four months in the Nova Iguaçu area of Rio do Janeiro, five to ten months in northern Paraná, and then a definitive move to the suburbs of São Paulo. After eight months here, the family unites with a Protestant church of their choice. This family has been moving from place to place for more than two years. Any day of the year there will be more than 10,000 people taking buses to different parts of Brazil from the large bus depot in São Paulo. Another 10,000 arrive in São Paulo each day from different parts of Brazil. How many are Evangelical believers "in transit"? If we had a way of asking each one who leaves and each one who arrives on any given day, if they were Protestants, we might be amazed. Perhaps as many as 10 percent would answer that they were Protestant communicant members.

Neglected Areas and Groups of People

When mission and national church leaders look for opportunity areas to begin new Evangelical work, it is often done without sufficient planning and forethought. Some of these opportunities are lost because of insufficient information and data. The Trans-Amazonian road, previously mentioned, could alone trigger one of the largest planned movements of population Brazil has ever known. Protestant leaders cannot neglect this and, at the same time, cannot neglect some of the other areas and groups of people that present splendid opportunities in the 1970's. Six of these areas will be mentioned here to illustrate some of the opportunities that are found at the very doors of some of the Protestant churches in Brazil. To neglect these open doors would be tragic.

Valley of the Ribeira - a mini-Amazonia. The Ribeira River is located in the southern part of the State of São Paulo. In 1968 nine counties that lie within this hot, humid, tropical river valley situated along the coast, were brought together and made into micro-region #265 and given the name "Lowlands of the Ribeira." Before the Regis Betencourt highway (BR-116) and the Bandeirantes highway (BR-373) were engineered through the difficult, tropical terrain, this rich part of São Paulo was cut off from the rest of the state. The tropical jungle that exists along the Ribeira River is similar to the thick green junglelands of the Amazon River and remains intact, a home for the remaining Indians who still live in the jungles of Itariri. Within the past decade these highways were constructed through the region. Electricity and communication also arrived. In 1960 the population of these nine counties only included 85,000 people, but in 1970 the population had increased to 121,740 as the new roads opened into the region and electrical power lines entered.

The latest development is the construction of the coastal highway, BR-101, through the region. This highway is being cut from Natal in the north to Osário in the south along the coast, opening up the rich coastal lands for settlement and economic development. The part of the road from Salvador to Rio de Janeiro will be paved by early 1975, and the rest that is already completed in pieces from Rio to Osário in Rio Grande do Sul will be completed at about the same time. In 1960 there were 5,000 communicant members registered in the seven denominations found in this micro-region. In 1970 this amount had doubled and registered 10,792. With the new roads, the rich lands waiting to be developed, the increase of population, and a population open to the gospel presentation, by 1980 the ministries of the existing Protestant churches and all new denominations could account for a remarkable increase of believers. If by 1980 10 percent of the population in this micro-region were Evangelical, it could very well influence the future development of the region.

This is just one of these areas of Evangelical opportunity that exist along the new BR-101 coastal highway. Starting at Salvador in the north, Protestant leaders should travel down BR-101 and examine such places in Bahia as Gandu, Ubutu, Rio Branco, Itagimirem, Euriapolis, Itamaraju, São Gonçalo, and Helvecia. Similar opportunities will open along this highway as it moves down the coast through the States of Espirito Santo, Rio de Janeiro, São Paulo, Paraná, Santa Catarina, and Rio Grande do Sul.

<u>Paraîba Valley</u>. This is the region through which the Paraiba River flows and is that southeast protrusion of the state of São Paulo connecting with the state of Rio de Janeiro. All the major highways, railroads, and communication systems between the urban centers of São Paulo and Rio de Janeiro cut through this historical, fertile valley. This valley has passed through different cycles of development. First it was coffee; then it became a rich dairy farming region, and in the past decade its cities have been transformed by continued industrial development.

This valley has been divided into micro-region #259 containing 21 counties, and micro-region #263 containing 11 counties. Population of these 32 counties has grown in the following manner:

Years	Population
1940	143,118
1950	202,498
1960	345,603
1970	787,642
1980	Over one million (projection)

The region is a strong traditional Brazilian and Roman Catholic community, and the city of Aparecida is the principal religious center. The remarkable cathedral of Nossa Senhora Aparecida is located in the center of the valley, a historic shrine for all of the southeast of Brazil. Protestant churches have not grown rapidly in this region. In 1955 these 32 counties had only 7,136 Protestants registered. In 1965 this number had grown to more than 12,000 communicant members. With the rapid influx of people into the area and the new industrial activity, there should be a new climate in the valley for the acceptance of the biblical message of salvation through the transforming power of Jesus Christ. This valley should not be neglected by Protestant leaders in the 1970's. With the influx of new people, the industrial expansion, and the urban development in the valley a substantial surge of Protestant growth could result by 1980 if this opportunity was understood as a harvest field and properly worked.

Pato Branco in Southeast Paraná (Micro-region #289). In 1940 this region, with 21 counties, had a population of 23,000. After 1960, a large immigration of people from western Rio Grande do Sul and western Paraná occurred, and by 1970 there was a population of 446,969 people. The majority of the newcomers are farmers who have acquired small farms and are small landowners or minifundiarios. Three or four urban centers serve these settlers and only 80,109 people live in the small countyseat towns. Pato Branco is the largest town in the region with 1970 census data showing a population of 15,436. The urban development of the region is just beginning and by 1980 there should be close to 150,000 people living in the cities of this micro-region. This movement toward the cities is an opportunity that should not be neglected for planting churches in these growing urban centers. In 1955 there were only 323 Protestant communicant members registered in the entire micro-region. By 1960 this had increased to 4,200 communicants.

FIGURE 11-5

SPHERES OF URBAN INFLUENCE
AND ORGANIZATION IN BRAZIL, 1970

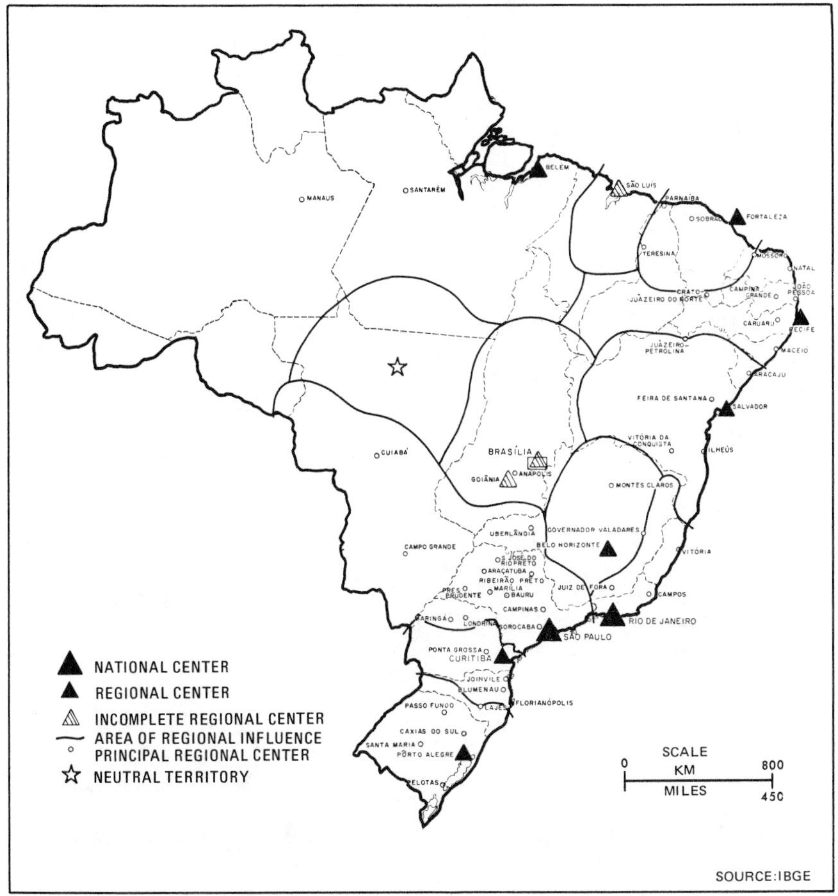

In 1965 there were 9,234 believers registered, and in 1970 there were 14,191.

The area is settled by hard working sons and daughters of German and Italian stock who originally immigrated from Europe to the southern states of Rio Grande do Sul and Santa Catarina. A pioneer spirit quite different from that found in northern Paraná pervades this area noted for its large grain crops, beef, and pork production. Seven to ten Protestant denominations are presently found here. Other denominations that can identify with the aspirations and the ethnic background of these people and adequately minister with humble people who work with the soil should not neglect this remarkable area.

Regional centers and the money economy. All over Brazil a network of urban regional centers is developing that will assume an increasingly important function in the decade of the 1970's. It is not possible to discuss at length here the urban organization that is going on in Brazil or the influence of these regional centers. In Figure 11-5, Brazil has been divided into different spheres of urban influence, each dominated by its metropolitan urban center.

Brazil is the only country in Latin America that has two large urban centers of national importance like Rio de Janeiro and São Paulo. Because of the increasing importance of São Paulo as an industrial and urban center, we are going to examine the hierarchy of urban organization under the jurisdiction of greater São Paulo (Figure 11-6) and relate this to the growth of Protestant churches.

The urban organization of Brazil is established around two major poles which have all of the functional equipment complete with all of the different types of industrial products and service and whose region of influence is the entire country. Below these two national poles other large cities appear that are also well equipped to distribute industrial products and services to large areas of Brazil. These are the regional centers that are subordinate to the two major urban centers. Below the regional centers are found smaller trade centers serving as sub-regional centers, each one dependent upon its regional center in one way or another. When the functions of these different categories of urban centers are studied in light of the money economy generated, they break down into a hierarchy of five different categories: first, the largest regional urban metropolis (11); second, the next important regional center (19); third, average regional centers (54); fourth, incomplete regional centers (30); and fifth, sub-regional centers (97).

FIGURE 11-6

HIERARCHY OF URBAN ORGANIZATION UNDER THE JURISDICTION OF GREATER SÃO PAULO, 1970

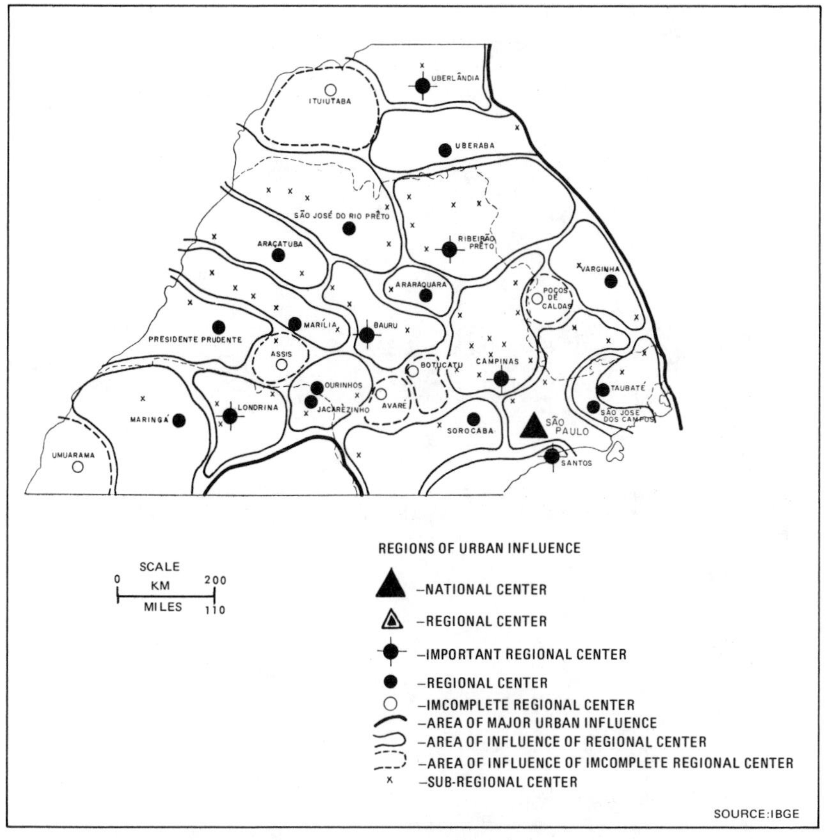

Protestant leaders in Brazil cannot afford to neglect these regional centers and the different parts of this remarkable urban network that is increasing in size so rapidly. The future of the Protestant church in Brazil could very well be decided in the large and small centers of this urban network by 1980.

Twenty of these regional centers within the sphere and jurisdiction of São Paulo (six important regional centers and fourteen average) have been brought together in Table 11-4 to show the increase in population and in Protestant membership that can occur in just one decade. In ten years

TABLE 11-4

GROWTH OF POPULATION AND PROTESTANT MEMBERSHIP
IN REGIONAL CENTERS OF SÃO PAULO, 1960-1970

	REGIONAL CENTERS	M/R	Population 1960	Population 1970	Protestants 1960	Protestants 1970
1.	Santos, S.P.	266	262,048	345,459	12,377	19,208
2.	Campinas, S.P.	248	179,797	333,947	6,221	17,218
3.	Ribeirão Prêto, S.P.	237	116,153	197,045	2,685	4,899
4.	Londrina, PR.	281	74,110	159,596	8,536	24,993
5.	Bauru, S.P.	241	85,237	123,267	4,740	9,031
6.	Uberlândia, M.G.	170	70,719	111,580	2,221	4,228
7.	Campo Grande, MT.	342	64,477	133,656	1,521	7,763
8.	São José Dos Campos, SP	259	55,349	132,374	1,480	1,517
9.	Uberaba, M.G.	178	72,053	110,341	1,704	2,363
10.	São José do Rio Prêto, S.P.	234	66,476	110,221	3,894	5,000
11.	Taubate, S.P.	259	64,863	100,701	2,252	4,120
12.	Presidente Prudente, SP	250	54,055	92,851	3,714	4,711
13.	Aracatuba, S.P.	231	53,563	86,970	2,139	6,732
14.	Araraquara, S.P.	242	78,775	86,389	3,285	12,624
15.	Cuiabá, Mt.	335	43,112	85,598	934	2,947
16.	Sorocaba, S.P.	256	58,076	84,399	12,921	15,222
17.	Marília, S.P.	245	51,789	75,139	3,376	4,650
18.	Maringá, PR	282	42,228	52,899	3,853	28,637
19.	Ourinhos, S.P.	252	34,292	40,733	1,473	1,512
20.	Varginha, M.G.	190	24,070	36,447	670	793
	TOTALS		1,551,245	2,499,612	79,996	179,168

the population of these centers increased by almost a million people or 60 percent. In the same period, the number of Evangelical believers more than doubled, an increase of 124 percent.

If this rate of growth continues, there will be more than 400,000 Protestant communicant members in these twenty regional centers in 1980. Brazilian leaders have an opportunity to double this "normal" rate of growth in such regional centers. If they can see the opportunity, plan to reap the harvest, work the plan assiduously, areas like this will exceed the normal trend growth projections.

Iron mountains of Minas Gerais. One of the richest deposits of high grade iron ore in the world is found in the center of the State of Minas Gerais in micro-regions #182, #183, #186, #187 that represent 81 counties in this mountainous country. In 1955 there were only 7,797 Protestants in these 81 counties. In 1960 there were 12,794 and by 1965 26,504 believers. In 1970 there were 68,764 communicants in the rapidly growing Protestant churches and it is only the beginning. People are coming into these iron ore producing counties, and with the new roads, the abundance of electrical energy, and the modern railroad that serves the iron fields so efficiently, this area is assuming the proportions of a boom area. It should not be neglected in the decade of the 1970's; the potential for growth is substantial.

Subsidized housing for Brazilian workers. In August, 1964, the National Housing Bank (*Banco Nacional de Habitação, BNH*) was organized and given the goal of lifting the standard of living for the masses and providing low-cost housing within the means of the Brazilian worker and shanty town dweller. By 1969 the BNH had financed the construction of 700,000 housing units in housing developments in every part of Brazil. These provided housing for an estimated 3,500,090 people. Beyond this, the goal to provide potable water and sanitation for millions was undertaken with such vigor in 1964, that by 1969 fourteen million people living in 280 different localities had a modern sanitation and the best water supply system available. At this writing, 644,000 new housing units are under construction and will be ready by the end of 1973.

Slum clearance is part of the long term BNH goals. In 1960, 1,360,000 people were living in these subnormal shanty towns. After ten years, 490,000 people still live in slums in the large cities, but the goal is to eliminate them completely by 1976.

Such a vast program of housing and slum clearance cannot be neglected by Protestant leaders. When so many people are being relocated into new housing, it is a splendid opportunity for evangelism and new Protestant churches to be established close by these new housing units. This is one of the remarkable challenges that is being offered to Protestant churches in Brazil in this decade, and little is being done to move into these prime opportunity areas in every part of Brazil.

Missionary Preoccupation With the Indians

Surveys show that close to 300 missionaries in Brazil, almost ten percent of the entire missionary force, are deployed in some way to evangelize and give the Gospel to the Indians of Brazil. Dale Kietzman, in his monumental work, *Indian Survival in Brazil,* locates and describes 130 surviving Indian tribes in Brazil. He refers to the published work of Darcy Ribeiro who was able to establish the identity of 230 surviving Indian tribes in 1900. By 1957, however, 87 of the tribes existing in 1900 were considered to be extinct (Kietzman 1972:71-72).

For many Indian tribes in Brazil the frontier road system described in Chapter 9 will constitute the ultimate threat. There are 50,000 to 90,000 Indians that remain in Amazonia and they face a struggle to survive in the decade ahead within the vast Amazon Basin as it is invaded by settlers from all parts of the country. The survival of the Indian culture, their civilization, their habitat is now threatened. The different faces of civilization will now accelerate its relentless confrontation and encroachment upon these diminishing Brazilian Indian tribes.

In 1968, more than 160 foreign missionary organizations were working in Brazil. A Missionary Information Bureau survey revealed that 15 percent of all missionaries from these different missionary agencies were situated in the North Region in Amazonia where the majority of all Indian tribes are located. A large number of these missionaries are associated with the Wycliffe Bible Translators who work among the different Indian tribes, studying their languages and providing portions of the Bible in readable form, but historically have not had as a goal the continuing effort to establish churches.

This is a time in the history of the evangelical church in Brazil, in which a new plan should emerge from responsible Protestant leaders about Indian work in the decade ahead. Goals could be set for the evangelization of specific target groups. Action is needed on this pressing problem by missionaries and national church leaders to see at firsthand what is happening to the Indian population, then read, digest, and carefully consider all literature that has been written. With all of this fresh information and data prepare a plan with an obtainable set of goals, both long and short term, for an effective effort in the 1970's and 1980's for evangelizing and planting churches among the remaining, receptive Indians in this largest of all frontier land areas of the world.

Spiritual Lags, Lethargy, and Stagnation in the Churches

Anyone who has a chance to travel in Brazil and visit a number of churches soon becomes aware of the large number of churches, some with second and third generation church members, that for one reason or another are no longer carrying on a vigorous ministry of Gospel proclamation, nor providing helpful services, nor have a vital ministry of identification with the essential problems and aspirations of their communities. Such a condition often could be diagnosed as a spiritual problem, a sickness that has given over to lethargy and results in a period of stagnation that causes people in a local church to be inner-directed, and inward looking. This is a worldwide problem, and often this disease is cured by evangelism that brings people like this into contact with new converts who have lives that have been radically transformed. The social pressure brought to bear by long-term ecclesiastical leadership, certain families, and the power blocks that form around groups in some churches have the tendency to limit, dissipate, and shut off any dynamic expression of the Christian faith. Only the influence and spiritual power found in changed lives can demonstrate the way God can transform and renew.

Such churches exist in Brazil and they need a strong ministry of revitalization to begin from within their ranks as well as a fresh touch of the revival power from God to touch them from the outside. This is a sickness unto death that must be fiercely fought, resisted, and treated in every possible way by the Protestant community in Brazil. The greatest antidote for this disease is to examine the available data on what other churches are doing with the same people in the same country. The challenge of Brazil church growth statistics lies right here.

Young People Do Not Feel At Home in the Churches (Loss of Youth)

Lethargy in the churches mentioned above is one of the reasons for the lamentable loss of the young people, many the children of believers, in the Protestant churches of Brazil. Young people are caught up in their respective peer groups and pass through a period of repugnance, retreat, and withdrawal from any activity and participation in the Protestant church that they might have grown up in. It would be a sad picture indeed, if all young people experienced this feeling, but happily it is not happening in every church. There are counties where Protestant churches are full of young people.

When the dynamic of the Christian life is working in a local church, when a challenge to the deepest needs of the human heart are presented to young people, when there is a variety of activities for young people that utilizes music, outings, conferences, social functions, spiritual retreats, and vacation camps to full advantage, the loss of young people can be minimized. With more than 50 percent of the population in Brazil under the age of 19, the problem of retaining young people is of first magnitude. Outstanding examples of successful incorporation of young people into the life and work of the churches should be widely publicized and circulated in the effort to encourage others to save this greatest resource of the Protestant churches today - its youth.

Part-time Pastoral Leadership

Some Protestant leaders are quick to blame a part-time pastoral relationship for the problems and obstructions to growth of the Church. Many pastors who have been prepared adequately in theology in the first class seminaries of their denominations continue to prepare themselves in law or in philosophy and later enter full time into teaching, a law practice, politics, or take a position in the business world and relegate what time that is left to the preaching and pastoral ministry. Some pastors take as many as three outside employments and organize a schedule that keeps them so much in motion that there is only a brief time left in a day when their church members can communicate spiritual needs to them.

The size of the church being served has a lot to do with this, and also the pattern of stewardship, education and promotion that has been taught in the local church. Churches with 200 or more communicant members need the leadership and full-time ministry of their pastor in order to fulfill the needs that such a ministry of reconciliation requires in such a congregation. Eight to ten hours a week cannot do justice to the ministerial calling, sermon preparation, counseling, and the ministry and its various responsibilities, especially for such churches in a country like Brazil.

SOMETHING NEW FOR THE SEVENTIES

New Organizations

The church in Brazil and all over the world is beginning to see itself as part of one Body. No part of the Body can say to another part, "I have no need of thee." This does not necessarily mean an organic relationship, but it does mean that each one of us does need to take into account what others are doing in God's plans. New concepts of "Body ministry," the mutual care and consideration of believers toward each other in a dual, earnest, supportive role, and the implication of ministry in, through, and from the Body to a lost world is beginning to take root in different ways in the Protestant community in Brazil.

Various service organizations now exist and are able to do special jobs to augment the capacity of the Protestant community in evangelistic know-how and to help the Brazilian church to rapidly and more effectively fulfill its ministry. These organizations can assist right now in the execution of plans for evangelism. Mention is made of a few of these such as: AETTE, ASTE, CAVE, CLEB, GLINT, MIB, SEPAL, CASE, and the Latin American Theological Fraternity.

AETTE, *Associação Evangélica para Treinamento Teológico por Extensão*, is an existing cooperative effort of a large number of evangelical groups. This movement grew out of the desire to accelerate the number of Brazilian leaders preparing to serve a rapidly expanding church. Brazilian and mission leaders from all sections of the country have prepared a basic set of uniform texts to teach potential national leaders already serving in the churches. This program has only begun to develop leadership for a continuing and expansive cycle of evangelism in Brazil.

ASTE, *Associação de Seminários Teológicos Evangélicos*, is a central organization coordinating the work of many of the theological seminaries.

CAVE, *Centro Audio-Visual Evangélico*, is a cooperative effort of about thirty evangelical groups in the area of radio/ television programming, slide and film strip presentations, and other audio-visual aids.

CLEB, *Camara de Literatura Evangélica Brasileira*, brings together the publishers and distributors of evangelical literature.

GLINT, Gospel Literature International, has prepared illustrated Sunday school materials used by numerous Evangelical groups.

MIB, *Missionary Information Bureau,* is a unique organization functioning on behalf of practically all mission agencies working in Brazil, and has, since 1968, been working with MARC in the BRAZIL 1980 project.

SEPAL, *Serviço de Evangelização para a América Latina,* is a unique team ministry that is a service to Brazilian churches in the areas of Christian education, youth work, pastoral support, Bible teaching, TV presentations, different types of evangelism, and a program of research through the CASE Center.

LATIN AMERICAN THEOLOGICAL FRATERNITY, has had two important consultations and Brazilians were present at both of these historic meetings to help lay a platform for dialogue among thinkers who confess Jesus Christ as Lord and who are willing to face the startling theological problems and debates from the point of view of evangelistic proclamation. The Bible is the unique Word of God, but theology - the study of God - is a continuous task of mankind so that he can adequately communicate Christ within various cultures and bring honor and glory to Him.

New Understanding About Effective Evangelistic Methods

We need to know more about the methods of evangelism that are being used, their dynamics, and the effectiveness of them. The MARC conversion survey and study entitled "Church Growth and Methods of Evangelism in Asia South Pacific" has been used to design a conversion survey for Brazil. It is now being used by CASE as a survey of individuals in different churches in an attempt to point out different ways in which people come to Jesus Christ. (See Appendix 1)

The Brazil conversion survey being undertaken by CASE is an effort to know more about the conversion experience of believers in Protestant churches. How were they led to Jesus Christ? CASE will publish a report on this recent survey in an attempt to better understand how God has been dealing with the people of Brazil as individuals.

This directly relates to the different methods of evangelism. It is basic information to place alongside literature, radio, personal witness, tracts, and all of the other things that God uses in the process of Gospel proclamation and communication in the evangelistic advance ever being planned and executed in Brazil.

Such a conversion survey points up the importance of understanding the people we are trying to reach. Protestant leaders in the churches are beginning to recognize the contribution, importance, and insights that sociology and social anthropology provide to enhance the task of communicating Christ in a culture that will augment, not hinder, the proclamation effort. The Gospel must be individual and must be interpreted into a culture as well as into a different language setting.

This survey can be used at all levels of Brazilian society and can help both the local pastor and the denominational leader.

New Opportunities

Understand the "M" factor and what it means for church growth. The great internal migrations in Brazil are bringing about a remarkable redistribution of Brazilian population and constitute an unparalleled opportunity.

Keep up with the new land areas opening for settlement in the 1970's. During the 50's and 60's the spread of São Paulo's coffee culture into Paraná was one of Brazil's remarkable chapters of spontaneous settlement on virgin lands. In the same ways the settlement of large areas within the Rio Doce Valley, the dramatic land rush to the central highlands of Goiás, and the movement of a quarter of a million migrants from northeast Brazil into north central Maranhão is a short review of the tremendous opportunity evangelical leaders will have in the 1970's.

Follow the development of the radial road system from Brasília to all parts of Brazil and keep awake to the magic these roads will perform in the isolated areas they will be opening up. Here is new opportunity for Protestant churches to grow up with these new communities if churches are planted in time.

Wake up to urbanization as an opportunity that will be ripe for this generation of Protestants. Afterward may be too late. Few countries in the world have undergone a transformation from a rural country to one where 60 percent of the population lives in the urban milieu as fast as Brazil, and the rules for city living have to be learned in one generation. While this is happening, Protestants can evangelize in a climate of acceptance and opportunity that has not existed in this way in any period of Brazilian history.

Be aware of Brazil's tremendous potential to send missionaries to other countries. In a recent survey of Third World nations, it was found that Brazil had more missionaries in other countries than any other Third World country.

OPTIONS FOR THE 70's

Data Bank of Church Growth Information Available to All Protestant Leaders

The MARC BRAZIL-1980 Project has transferred its computer analysis to Brazil, and it is available at the CASE offices in São Paulo.* All of this demonstrates clearly that the force for continuing evangelism of Brazil has a tool it can use to enhance the quantity and quality of its evangelistic task for the days ahead.

But this is only a beginning. Assuming that the numerical strength of the Evangelical church in Brazil is adequate for the task of carrying out the evangelization of Brazil, so much more work by every segment of the Protestant community remains to be done. Much enlistment, training, and pioneer efforts in church planting and evangelism await their proper times and seasons.

Information and Data Available for New Strategy Formulations

God works in mysterious ways His wonders to perform. He provides the needed technology for each generation, enabling them to communicate the message of the evangel in all of its spiritual dynamic and power. Each generation is called upon to understand God's great strategy for a nation and to take a vital part in performing God's sovereign mandate. The more we know about the people that we are to reach, the milieu in which we find them, and the force for evangelism God has placed in the churches, the greater is the probability that we will be able to honor God by instituting and carrying out biblically based evangelistic thrusts which fit within and meet the important cultural needs found in Brazil in these important years in the 70's.

Before all of this can happen we need to understand the role of research, the careful gathering and analysis of data that speak about the "mighty acts of God," in reality, what God has been doing.

Protestants in Brazil need a broad overview of every segment in the Church and the diverse ministries of various mission and service organizations that are now serving in this great country. A directory of missions and of the different churches and

---

*See Appendix 3.

denominations in Brazil, and of the other Christian organizations that are operating there, both Brazilian and non-Brazilian are found in the Directory section of this book, along with the Directory of the major theological training schools and other important related information. Information on what these different groups are doing, their capabilities, and their willingness to cooperate with others is valuable data. If each individual Protestant and each Protestant organization can begin to ascertain their proper place and function in the Body of Christ that is being formed in Brazil, this will transform and invigorate the Protestant community to achieve its noble destiny in service to the living Christ.

CASE - A Basic Information Center for Protestants in Brazil

We need to find ways of sharing information. One of the reasons that a great deal of the data in this handbook could be written can be traced to the fact that the government in Brazil produces census data on the Protestant church. A great deal of other information is available from the various groups and this book is an effort to bring as much of it together as possible. Much of this has been stored, correlated, and analyzed by the Missionary Information Bureau and by MARC. But the Center for Advanced Studies in Evangelism (CASE) in São Paulo has become the basic information center which will provide the data and information (and how to use and implement this data) which the mission and national church leaders need so desperately to get on with the task, and formulate the evangelistic plans for advance commensurate with the unusual openness and opportunity for the Gospel proclamation. A description of the data that is available is included in Appendix 2.

Leaders have expressed the need for a means to have a continuing consultation and fellowship around the facts. National church and mission leaders serve together on regional committees with the mandate to plan for regional congresses on evangelism in 1975. The original committees were made up from representatives who attended the Congress on Evangelism for Latin America in Bogotá, Colombia late in 1969. The objectives are clear to encourage cooperative efforts to assure the complete evangelization of Brazil during the 1970's. This mobilization effort will begin before the July 1974 World Congress on Evangelism in Lausanne. The CASE Center in São Paulo will have an important role to play in this great evangelistic effort.

Planning and Leadership

Sound principles of good planning and effective leadership will help to make a contribution in the development of effective strategy that will lead to an entirely new enlistment and deployment of men and resources in the different phases of evangelistic advance that are in motion. Modern techniques have made it possible for man to land on the moon and return safely to the earth. The same leadership principles that were used to put men on the moon can be applied to the planning of strategy, and the execution of these plans will help assure fulfillment of the goal of completely evangelizing Brazil during the 1970's. The MARC/ World Vision staff in tandem with MIB and CASE in Brazil is one of the ways God is "putting it all together" for a mighty harvest in Brazil. New training seminars are planned that will provide transferrable techniques needed for evangelism in the days ahead.

A Viable Objective for 1980

God wants every man and woman in Brazil to have a valid opportunity to say "yes" to Jesus Christ. This is an age in which God has provided His Church with unique communication tools to proclaim the Good News of Salvation in Jesus Christ. MARC of World Vision International has carried out a pilot program and demonstrated how much more effective churches and missions can become as they use the communication and research tools God has placed in our hands. Brazilian national church and mission leaders can use these different technical tools, management techniques, and principles in planning strategy for a continuing evangelism. This knowledge can be shared with one another in an environment of "fellowship around the facts," always attempting to ascertain God's strategy for Brazil for this present moment and paying the price to be a part of this great plan and strategy.

Ultimately, the goal should be for every church leader in Brazil to be a knowledgeable agent for a new understanding of how to think about approaching a county or a country and its people with an understanding of what is needed to win individuals to Christ in this generation and the next. May God help us to clearly understand who these people are and how they can be reached effectively with methods that are timely and adequate.

God is calling out a people for His Name in Brazil. Because of the large response to the Brazilian people to the proclamation of the Gospel, we should believe that God will honor and increase this work in Brazil and provide a growing evangelistic force that will move quickly throughout Brazil and into other parts of the world, participants in that advance for Gospel proclamation before the dawning of that great and notable Day of the Lord. Amen!

Directory of Missionary Agencies at Work in Brazil

DIRECTORY OF MISSIONARY AGENCIES

AT WORK IN BRAZIL, 1973

The Headquarters address appears first; the Brazilian address appears underneath.

I BRAZILIAN AGENCIES

1. Aliança Missionária Evangelística Mundial

   Caixa Postal 1206
   30.000 Belo Horizonte, M.G.

2. Assembléia Cristã

   Caixa Postal 5562
   São Paulo, S.P.

3. Assembléia Dos Irmãos

   R. Cel. Colares Moreira, 523
   65.000 São Luiz, Ma.

4. Associação Brás de Evangelização

   Caixa Postal 19.010
   01.000 São Paulo, S.P.

5. Associação Das Igrejas de Cristianismo Decidido

   Caixa Postal 2350
   80.000 Curitiba, Pr.

6. Associação Evangélica para o Desenvolvimento Missionario

   Caixa Postal 94
   89.230 São Francisco do Sul, S.C.

7. Avanço de Literatura Cristã

   Caixa Postal 2600
   01.000 São Paulo, S.P.

8. Brado da Hora Final

   Caixa Postal 30.623
   01.000 São Paulo, S.P.

9. Câmara de Literatura Evangélica do Brasil

   Caixa Postal 1061 ZC-00
   20.000 Rio de Janeiro, Gb.

10. Capela Metropolitana

    Caixa Postal 2600
    01.000 São Paulo, S.P.

11. Clubes Bíblicos

    Rua Barão de Bom Retiro, 2740
    Grajaú, R.J. ZC-11

12. Comunhão Dental Amazonica

    Caixa Postal 302
    69.000 Manaus, Am.

13. Comunicações Evangélicas

    Caixa Postal 13811
    01000 São Paulo, S.P.

14. Concílio Brasileiro da Comunhão Africana Evangélica

    Igreja Evangélica Fluminense
    Rua Alexandre Mackenzie 60
    20.000 Rio de Janeiro, Gb.

15. Confederação Evangélica Brasileira

    Rua Lusitana, 8
    13.100 Campinas, S.P.

16. Convenção Batista Nacional

    (A/C) Seminário Teológic
    Evangélico do Brasil
    30.000 Belo Horizonte, M.G.

17. Cristo Liberta

    Rua Teixeira de Freitas, 5
    Sala 201
    40.000 Salvador, Ba.

18. Cruzada da Nova Vida

    Caixa Postal 2734
    20.000 Rio de Janeiro, Gb.

19. Cruzada Estudantil e Profissional para Cristo

    Caixa Postal 20.822
    01.000 São Paulo, S.P.

20. Cruzada Mundial Evangélica

    Caixa Postal 10
    14.100 Ribeirão Prêto, S.P.

BRAZILIAN AGENCIES (CONTINUED)

21. Grupo Cristão de Estudantes e Profissionais

Travessa Otávio Correiz, 88
90.000 Pôrto Alegre, R.G.S.

22. Igreja Cristã Presbiteriana

Caixa Postal 445
09.500 São Caetano do Sol, S.P.

23. Igreja Evangélica da Confissão Luterana no Brasil

Caixa Postal 2876
90.000 Porto Alegre, R.G.S.

24. Igreja Evangélica Suiça

Caixa Postal 1071, ZC-07
20.000 Rio de Janeiro, AC-00, Gb.

25. Igreja Luterana Independente

Caixa Postal 44
87.300 Campo Mourão, Pr.

26. Igreja Reformada

Caixa Postal 2740
80.000 Curitiba, Pr.

27. Imprensa da Fé

Caixa Postal 30.421
01.000 São Paulo, S.P.

28. Irmãos

Caixa Postal 901 ZC-00
20.000 Rio de Janeiro, Gb.

29. Jovens da Verdade

Rua das Carmelitas, 166,
1.andar (Centro)
01.000 São Paulo, S.P.

30. Ministério da Vida

Caixa Postal 30.421
01.000 São Paulo, S.P.

31. Missão Cristã Brasileira

Caixa Postal 33
78.700 Cáceres, Mt.

32. Missão dos Indios Kaiuas

Caixa Postal 4
Dourados, Mt.

33. Missão do Vale do Paraná

85.980 Guaíra, Pr.

34. Missão Estrangeira Convenção Batista Brasileira

Rua Senador Furtado 56
20.000 Rio de Janeiro, Gb.

35. Missão Estrangeira Igreja Presbiteriana do Brasil

Caixa Postal 686
70.000 Brasília, D.F.

36. Missão Evangélica Amazonica

69.940 Sena Madureira, Acre

37. Missão Evangélica da Amazonia

Caixa Postal 154
69.800 Boa Vista, Rr.

38. Missão Evangélica da União Missionaria para América do Sul

Caixa Postal 1738
01.000 São Paulo, S.P.

39. Missão Evangélica do Interior do Brasil

Caixa Postal 35
Xanxerê, S.C.

40. Missão Informadora do Brasil

Caixa Postal 1498
01.000 São Paulo, S.P.

41. Missão Mundo para Cristo

Caixa Postal 48
69.000 Manaus, Am.

42. Obra Missionária Igreja de Cristo

Caixa Postal 30.217
01.000 São Paulo, S.P.

43. Os Ligados Instituto e Seminário Bíblico de Londrina

Caixa Postal 58
86.100 Londrina, Pr.

44. Pentecostal Independente

Caixa Postal 92
50.000 Recife, Pe.

BRAZILIAN AGENCIES (CONTINUED)

45. Publicações Cristãs Brasil

Caixa Postal 403
74.000 Goiânia, Go.

46. Sociedade Bíblica do Brasil

Caixa Postal 73 e 454
20.000 Rio de Janeiro, Gb.

47. Sociedade Evangélica Missionária

Caixa Postal 351
Guarapuava, Pr.

48. Sociedade Evangelizadora das Igrejas de Cristo

Caixa Postal 926
66.000 Belém, Pa.

49. Testemunho Batista para Israel de São Paulo

Caixa Postal 8614
01.000 São Paulo, S.P.

50. Vencedores Por Cristo

Caixa Postal 30.548
01.000 São Paulo, S.P.

51. Vida Abundante
Missão Conservadora do Brasil

Avenida dos Operários, 603
Caixa Postal 185
13.400 Piracicaba, S.P.

52. Voz-dos Andes

Caixa Postal 2612
01.000 São Paulo, S.P.

II NORTH AMERICAN AGENCIES

53. Agricultural Missions, Inc.

475 Riverside Drive
New York, New York 10027

54. Air Mail From God Mission, Inc.

4205 Santa Monica Boulevard
Los Angeles, California 90029

55. Amazon Mission, Inc.

P. O. Box 304
Gary, Indiana, 46406

Missão Amazonas
Caixa Postal 365
69.000 Manaus, Am.

56. American Leprosy Missions, Inc.

297 Park Avenue, South
New York, New York 10010

57. American Lutheran Church

Division of World Missions
422 South Fifth Street
Minneapolis, Minnesota 55415

Missão Evangélica Luterana
Caixa Postal 121
95.600 Taquara, R.G.S.

58. Apostolic Christian Church

P. O. Box 5233
Akron, Ohio 44313

59. Apostolic Christian Church in the United States

Francesville, Indiana 47946

60. Apostolic Christian Church in the United States

14726 Fox Road
Detroit, Michigan 75739

Igreja Evangélica Nazareno
Caixa Postal 208 74.000
12.200 Goiânia, Go.

61. Apostolic Churches of Jesus Christ

P. O. Box 158
Rochester, Michigan 55901

Igreja Evangélica Apostólica
Caixa Postal 2295 ZC-00
20.000 Rio de Janeiro, Gb.

62. Apostolic Church of Oklahoma

P. O. Box 9155
Tulsa, Oklahoma 74107

Instituto Apostólico do Brasil
Caixa Postal 592
13.100 Campinas, S.P.

63. Armenian Missionary Association of America, Inc.

156 Fifth Avenue
New York, New York 10010

II NORTH AMERICAN AGENCIES (CONTINUED)

64. Assemblies of God, General Council

1445 Boonville Avenue
Springfield, Missouri 65802

Conselho Geral das
Assembléias de Deus
Rua Henrique Fleiuss, 420
20.000 Tijuca, Gb

65. Association for Christian Literature

P. O. Box 50294
Dallas, Texas 75221

Rua Licinio Cardoso, 330
20.000 Rio de Janeiro, Gb.

66. Association of Baptists for World Evangelism, Inc.

1304 Schaff Building
1505 Race Street
Philadelphia, Pennsylvania 19102

Associação dos Batistas
Evangelismo Mundial
Caixa Postal 30045
01.000 São Paulo, S.P.

67. Baptist Bible Fellowship International

P.O. Box 106
Springfield, Missouri 65801

Missão Batista Bíblica
do Brasil
Caixa Postal 7701
01.000 São Paulo, S.P.

68. Baptist Faith Missions

975 E. Grand Blvd.
Detroit, Michigan 48207

69. Baptist General Conference

Board of Foreign Missions
5750 North Ashland Avenue
Chicago, Illinois 60626

União Batista Evangélica
Caixa Postal 30.259
01.000 Sao Paulo, S.P.

70. Baptist International Missions, Inc.

P. O. Box 696
Rossville, Georgia 30741

Caixa Postal 8324
01.000 São Paulo, S.P.

71. Baptist Mid-Missions

4205 Chester Avenue
Cleveland, Ohio 44103

Sociedade Evangelizadora
Baptist Mid-Missions
North - Caixa Postal 1012
60.000 Fortaleza, Ce.
South - Caixa Postal 2612
01.000 São Paulo, S.P.

72. Baptist Missionary Association of America

716 Main Street
Little Rock, Arkansas 72201

Caixa Postal 134
39.270 Pirapora, M.G.

73. Berean Mission, Inc.

3536 Russel Boulevard
St. Louis, Missouri 63104

Caixa Postal 187
Campo Grande, Mt.

74. Bethany Fellowship, Inc.

6820 Auto Club Road
Minneapolis, Minnesota 55431

Betânia do Brasil
Caixa Postal 10
87.550 Altonia, Pr.

Betânia do Brasil
Caixa Postal 10
Venda Nova, M.G.

75. Bethany Missionary Association

2201 East Sixth Street
Long Beach
California 90814

Sociedade Betânia
Caixa Postal 115
11.300 São Vicente, S.P.

76. Bethesda Missions, Inc.

2600 East 38th Street
Minneapolis, Minnesota 55406

Missão Betesda do Brasil
Caixa Postal 10
49.000 Aracaju, SE

77. Bible Conferences and Missions

Reeves
Louisiana 70658

Sociedade Bíblica Filadelfia
85.980 Guaíra, Pr.

II NORTH AMERICAN AGENCIES (CONTINUED)

78. Bible Literature International

P. O. Box 477
Columbus, Ohio 43216

79. Bible Meditation League

P. O. Box 477
Columbus, Ohio 43216

80. Bible Memory Association, International

Box 12000 Wellston Station
St. Louis, Missouri 63112

Memorizadores da Bíblia, Internacional
Caixa Postal 7966
01.000 São Paulo, S.P.

81. Bible Presbyterian Mission to Brazil

264 W. Walnut Lane
Philadelphia
Pennsylvania 19144

Missão Bíblica Presbiteriana do Brasil
Caixa Postal 9198
01.000 São Paulo, S.P.

82. Billy Graham Evangelistic Association

1300 Harmon Place
Minneapolis, Minnesota 55403

Associação Billy Graham
Caixa Postal 30.424
01.000 São Paulo, S.P.

83. Brazil Christian Mission

1664 Poplar
Denver, Colorado 80220

Missão Cristã do Brasil
Caixa Postal 201
74.000 Goiânia, Go.

84. Brazil Gospel Fellowship Mission, Inc.

121 North Glenwood
Springfield, Illinois 62702

Sociedade Evangelizadora
Caixa Postal 666
60.000 Fortaleza, Ce.

85. Brazil Inland Mission, Inc.

2507 West Malone Avenue
Peoria, Illinois 61605

57.500 Umuarama, Pr.

86. Brazil Mission, Inc.

Christian Church
Richmond, Indiana

Missão Brasileiras da Igreja de Cristo
Caixa Postal 11735
01.000 São Paulo, S.P.

87. Brazil Mission (Church of Christ)

P. O. Box 424
Glendora, California 91740

Caixa Postal 854
13.100 Campinas, S.P.

88. Brazilian Evangelistic Association

P. O. Box 14197
Dayton, Ohio 45414

ABRASE
Caixa Postal 19010
01.000 São Paulo, S.P.

Communicações Evangélicas
Caixa Postal 13891
01.000 São Paulo, S.P.

89. Brethren Church

Foreign Missionary Society
P. O. Box 588
Winona Lake, Indiana 46590

Missão da Igreja dos Irmãos
Caixa Postal 861
66.000 Belém, Pa.

90. Campus Crusade for Christ

Arrowhead Springs
San Bernardino, California
92414

91. Child Evangelism Fellowship, International

P. O. Box 1156
Grand Rapids, Michigan 49501

Aliança Pro-Evangelização das Crianças
Caixa Postal 1804
01.000 São Paulo, S.P.

92. Christian and Missionary Alliance

260 West 44th Street
New York, New York 10036

Aliança Cristã e Missionária
Caixa Postal 1590
70.000 Brasília, D.F.

II NORTH AMERICAN AGENCIES (CONTINUED)

93. Christian Baptist "World for Christ Missions"

Caixa Postal 48
69.000 Manaus, Am.

94. Christian Bible Mission

873 Scott Street
Muskegon, Michigan 49442

Caixa Postal 10
49.000 Aracaju, Se.

95. Christian Children's Fund

108 South Third Street
Richmond, Virginia 23204

Caixa Postal 2548
30.000 Belo Horizonte, M.G.

96. Christian Church World Missions

205 East Main Street
Enterprise, Oregon 97828

Christian Church World Missions
c/o Allan Brettel
Consulado Americano
Rua 15 de Novembro, 621 7°and.
80.000 Curitiba, Pr.

97. Christian Life Missions

P. O. Box 824
Wheaton, Illinois 60187

Editôra Mundo Cristão
Caixa Postal 6658
01.000 São Paulo, S.P.

98. Christian Literature Advance

Caixa Postal 30.421
01.000 São Paulo, S.P.

99. Christian Literature Crusade

P. O. Box 51
Fort Washington
Pennsylvania 19034

Cruzada de Literatura Evangélica do Brasil
Caixa Postal 758
50.000 Recife, Pe.

100. Christian Missionaries "Amazon Valley"

Caixa Postal 926
66.000 Belém, Pa.

101. Christian Missionary Fellowship

P. O. Box 26306
Lawrence, Indiana 46226

Comunidade Cristã Missionária do Brasil
Caixa Postal 487
13.100 Campinas, S.P.

102. Christian Missions in Many Lands

16 Hudson Street
New York, New York 10013

103. Christian Nationals Evangelism Commission, Inc.

321 Bradley Avenue
San Jose, California 95128

104. Christian Reformed Church

Board of Foreign Missions
2850 Kalamazoo Avenue S.E.
Grand Rapids
Michigan 49508

Caixa Postal 214
15.370 Pereira Barreto, S.P.

105. Christian Service Centers

Caixa Postal 631
13.100 Campinas, S.P.

106. Christian Service Corps

1329 - N Street N.W.
Washington, D.C. 2-005

107. Church of Christ (Christian Churches)

1711 Madison Avenue
Newport News, Virginia 23607

Igreja de Cristo
Caixa Postal 30.217
01.000 São Paulo, S.P.

108. Church of God

Missionary Board
P. O. Box 2498
Anderson, Indiana 46011

109. Church of God

World Missions Board
1080 Montgomery Avenue
Cleveland, Tennessee 37312

Igreja de Deus do Brasil
Caixa Postal 5409
20.000 Cidade Nova, Gb.

II NORTH AMERICAN AGENCIES (CONTINUED)

110. Church of God of Prophecy

World Mission Committee
Bible Place
Cleveland, Tennessee 37312

111. Church of the Nazarene

Department of Foreign Missions
6401 The Paseo
Kansas City, Missouri 64131

Igreja do Nazareno
Caixa Postal 1008
13.100 Campinas, S.P.

112. Church World Service

475 Riverside Drive
New York, New York 10027

113. Cleveland Hebrew Mission, Inc.

P. O. Box 18056
Cleveland Heights
Ohio 44118

Sociedade Brasileira
Amigos de Israel
Caixa Postal 3132
20.000 Rio de Janeiro, Gb.
ZC-00

114. Co-Laborers, Inc.

3027 Queen Avenue, North
Minneapolis, Minnesota 55411

Caixa Postal 290
87.500 Umuarama, Pr.

115. Colonia Evangélica Acailandia

Route 4, Box 232
Goshen Indiana 46526

Posto S.E.S.P.
A/C Sr. Carlos Gomes Amorim
65.900 Imperatriz, Ma.

116. Conservative Baptist Foreign Missionary Society

P. O. Box 5
Wheaton, Illinois 60188

Missão Batista Conservadora
North - Caixa Postal 2
64.800 Floriano, Pi.
South - Caixa Postal 995
13.100 Campinas, S.P.

117. Emmanuel Association

1108 East University
Mitchell, South Dakota 57301

Missão Missionária Emanuel
Caixa Postal 493
69.000 Manaus, Am.

118. Evangelical Enterprises

P. O. Box 1555
Topeka, Kansas 66601

Empresas Evangélicas
Caixa Postal 398
08.100 Mogi das Cruzes, S.P.

119. The Evangelical Lutheran Church of Canada

Board of World Missions
212 Wiggins Avenue
Saskatoon, Saskatchewan
Canada

120. Evangelical Mennonite Church

Board of Missions and Charities
P. O. Box 370
Elkhart, Indiana 46514

Associação Evangélica Menonita
Caixa Postal 1013
13.100 Campinas, S.P.

121. Evangelical Methodist Church

World Missions
3036 North Meridian
Wichita, Kansas 67204

122. Evangelical Union of South America

78 West Hudson Avenue
Englewood, New Jersey 07631

União Evangélica Sul-Americana
Caixa Postal 431
60.000 Fortaleza, Ce.

123. Evangelica United Brethren Church

Board of Missions
601 West Riverview Avenue
Dayton, Ohio 45406

124. Fellowship of Independent Missions

P. O. Box 1
York, Pennsylvania 17407

Caixa Postal 1665
40.000 Salvador, Ba.

II NORTH AMERICAN AGENCIES (CONTINUED)

125. Free Methodist Church of North America

General Missionary Board
Winona Lake, Indiana 46590

Caixa Postal 18.027
01.000 São Paulo, S.P.

126. Flying Missionaries, Inc.

Caixa Postal 435
69.000 Manaus, Am.

127. Free Will Baptists National Association

Board of Foreign Missions
P. O. Box 1088
Nashville, Tennessee 37202

Missão Batista Livre do Brasil
Caixa Postal 217
14.870 Jaboticabal, S.P.

128. Garr Memorial Church Carolina Evangelistic Association

P. O. Box 1936
Charlotte, North Carolina 28201

129. General Conference Mennonite Church Commission on Overseas Mission

P. O. Box 347
Newton, Kansas 67114

130. General Conference of Seventh-Day Adventists

6840 Eastern Avenue N.W.
Washington, D.C. 20012

131. General Conference of the Mennonite Brethren Church

Board of Missions and Services
315 S. Lincoln
Hillsboro, Kansas 67063

132. German United Christian Mission

146 Glendale Boulevard
Los Angeles, California 90025

Sociedade União Cristã
89.100 Blumenau, S.C.

133. Global Outreach, Inc.

Box 654
London 12, Ontario
Canada

Rua r. 17 - Setor Oeste
74.000 Goiânia, Go.

134. Gospel Crusades, Inc.

P. O. Box 12247
Sarasota, Florida 33578

Caixa Postal 46
15.990 Matão, S.P.

135. Gospel Fellowship Missions

Bob Jones University
Greenville
South Carolina 29614

Caixa Postal 2259
70.000 Brasília, D.F.

136. Gospel Light Publications

725 East Colorado Blvd.
Glendale, California 91209

Caixa Postal 20757
01.000 São Paulo, S.P.

137. Gospel Literature Outreach (Crusade)

Caixa Postal 28
17.100 Bauru, S.P.

138. Gospel Recordings, Inc.

122 Glendale Boulevard
Los Angeles, California 90026

139. Go-Ye Fellowship, Inc.

P. O. Box 26193
Los Angeles, California 90026

Go-Ye Fellowship do Brasil
Caixa Postal 231
96.100 Pelotas, R.G.S.

140. Hebrew Evangelization Society

P. O. Box 707
Los Angeles, California 90053

Esperança de Israel
Caixa Postal 9040
13.100 São Paulo, S.P.

141. Independent Bible Baptist

P. O. Box 48
Englewood, Colorado 80110

Caixa Postal 480
50.000 Recife, Pe.

142. Independent Board for Presbyterian Foreign Missions

246 Walnut Lane
Philadelphia, Pennsylvania
19144

II NORTH AMERICAN AGENCIES (CONTINUED)

143. Independent Faith Mission

3346 E. M. 36
Pinckney, Michigan 48169

Voz Bíblica Brasileira
Caixa Postal 267
12.200 São José dos Campos, S.P.

144. Independent Gospel Missions

P. O. Box 1507
New Castle
Pennsylvania 16103

Caixa Postal 267
12.200 São José dos Campos, S.P.

145. Inter-American Evangelistic Association

c/o Bethany Missionary Assn.
2201 East Sixth Street
Long Beach
California 90814

Caixa Postal 115
11.300 São Vicente, S.P.

146. Inter-American Missionary Society

P. O. Box A
Greenwood, Indiana 46142

Sociedade Missionária
Inter-Americana
Caixa Postal 58
86.100 Londrina, Pr.

147. International Board of Jewish Missions, Inc.

P. O. Box 1256
Atlanta, Georgia 30301

Caixa Postal 6318
01.000 São Paulo, S.P.

148. International Church of the Foursquare Gospel

1100 Glendale Boulevard
Los Angeles, California 90026

Igreja do Evangelho Quadrangular
Caixa Postal 3870
01.000 São Paulo, S.P.

149. International Committee of YMCA's of U.S. and Canada

291 Broadway
New York, New York 10007

150. International Fellowship of Evangelical Students

435 Rowell Boulevard
Fresno, California 93721

Aliança Bíblica Universitária
do Brazil
Caixa Postal 30505
01.000 São Paulo, S.P.

151. International Pentecostal Assemblies

Missions Department
892 Berne Street, S.E.
Atlanta, Georgia 30316

152. Japan Evangelical Mission

Box 640
Three Hills, Alberta
Calgary, Canada

153. Japanese Evangelical Missionary Society

112 No. San Pedro Street
Los Angeles, California 90012

Caixa Postal 9841
01.000 São Paulo, S.P.

154. Koinonia Foundation

Pikesville P.O. Box 5744
Baltimore, Maryland 21208

155. Laubach Literacy Fund, Inc.

P. O. Box 131
Syracuse, New York 13210

156. Laymen's Overseas Service, Inc. (Laos)

P. O. Box 5031
Jackson, Mississippi 39216

157. Lester Sumrall Evangelistic Association

P. O. Box 12
South Bend 46624

158. Life Mission

R. D. 1
Perkiomenville
Pennsylvania 18074

159. Literature Crusades

P. O. Box 203
Prospect Heights, Illinois
60070

II NORTH AMERICAN AGENCIES (CONTINUED)

160. Lutheran Church
Missouri Synod

Board of Missions
210 N. Broadway
St. Louis, Missouri 63102

Igreja Evangélica Luterana
do Brasil
Caixa Postal 166
92.000 Canoas, R.G.S.

161. Lutheran Church in America

Board of World Mission
231 Madison Avenue
New York, New York 10016

162. Lutheran World Relief, Inc.*

315 Park Avenue South
New York, New York 10010

163. Maranatha Baptist Mission, Inc.

P. O. Drawer 1425
Natchez, Mississippi 39120

164. Mennonite Board of Missions
and Services

315 Lincoln
Hillsboro, Kansas 67063

Missão Irmãos Menonitas
Caixa Postal 1640
80.000 Curitiba, Pr.

165. Mennonite Central Committee

21 South 12th Street
Akron, Pennsylvania 17501

Caixa Postal 15
13.000 Campinas, S.P.

166. Mennonite Church
General Conference

Board of Missions
P. O. Box 347
Newton, Kansas 67114

167. Mennonite Church
Board of Missions and Charities

P. O. Box 370
Elkhart, Indiana 46514

168. Methodist Church

World Division
Board of Missions
475 Riverside Drive
New York, New York 10027

Junta de Missões da Igreja
Metodista do Brasil
Caixa Postal 12.880
01.000 São Paulo, S.P.

169. Mission to Amazonia

P. O. Box 1145
Brookings, Oregon 97415

170. Missionary and Soul Winning

P. O. Box 7271
Long Beach
California 90807

Aliança Missionária do Brasil
Caixa Postal 402
50.000 Belo Horizonte, M.G.

171. Missionary Aviation Fellowship

P. O. Box 2828
Fullerton, California 92633

Asas do Socorro
Caixa Postal 184
77.100 Anápolis, Go.

172. Missionary Church

Overseas Missions Department
3901 S. Wayne Avenue
Fort Wayne, Indiana 46807

Caixa Postal 384
Maringá, Pr.

173. National Association Congregational

176 W. Wisconsin Avenue
Milwaukee, Wisconsin 53203

87.500 Umuarama, Pr.

174. National Baptist Convention
U.S.A., Inc.

Foreign Mission Board
701 S. 19th Street
Philadelphia
Pennsylvania 19146

175. Navigators, Inc.

P. O. Box 1659
Colorado Springs
Colorado 80901

Caixa Postal 2925
80.000 Curitiba, Pr.

176. New Testament
Missionary Union

256 Oak Street
Audubon, New Jersey 08106

Missão Neotestamentária
Caixa Postal 88
16.100 Araçatuba, S.P.

II NORTH AMERICAN AGENCIES (CONTINUED)

177. New Tribes Mission

Woodworth
Wisconsin 53194

Missão Novas Tribos do Brasil
Leste - Caixa Postal 7
76,870 Vianopolis, Go.
Oeste - Caixa Postal 221
69.000 Manaus, Am.

178. Next Towns Crusade, Inc.

3015 Gainesborough
San Antonio, Texas 78230

179. North American Baptists Association

716 Main Street
Little Rock, Arkansas 72201

Associação Batista Norte-Americana
Caixa Postal 269
13.100 Campinas, S.P.

180. North American Baptist General Missionary Society, Inc.

7308 Madison Street
Forest Park, Illinois 60130

Missão Batista Rio Grandense
Caixa Postal 78
95.100 Caxias do Sul, R.G.S.

181. Oriental Missionary Society

Box A - 1200 W. Fry Road
Greenwood, Indiana 46142

182. Overseas Crusades, Inc.

265 Lytton Avenue
Palo Alto, California 94301

Serviço de Evangelização
Para a América Latina (SEPAL)
Caixa Postal 30.548
01.000 São Paulo, S.P.

183. Pan American Christian Academy

Caixa Postal 30.874
01.000 São Paulo, S.P.

184. Pentecostal Assemblies of Canada

Overseas Missions Department
10 Overlea Boulevard
Toronto, 17, Ontario Canada

185. Pentecostal Church of Christ

P. O. Box 263
London, Ohio 43140

Igreja de Cristo Pentecostal
Caixa Postal 2016
50.000 Recife, Pe.

186. Pentecostal Church of God of America

Missions Board
P. O. Box 816
Joplin, Missouri 64802

Igreja de Deus Pentecostal
do Brasil
Caixa Postal 23
30.000 Belo Horizonte, M.G.

187. Pilgrim Fellowship, Inc.

1201 Chestnut Street
Philadelphia
Pennsylvania 19107

188. Pioneer Bible Mission

P. O. Box 21-4622
Sacramento
California 95821

Acampamento Bíblico Pioneiro
Caixa Postal 63
01.000 São Paulo, S.P.

189. Pocket Testament League, Inc.

49 Honeck Street
Englewood, New Jersey 07631

Liga do Testamento e Bolso
Caixa Postal 19068
01.000 São Paulo, S.P.

190. Presbyterian Church in the U.S.

Board of World Missions
P. O. Box 330
Nashville, Tennessee 37202

Missão Presbiteriana do Brasil
Caixa Postal 567
13.100 Campinas, S.P.

191. Presbyterian Foreign Missions Independent Board

246 W. Walnut Lane
Philadelphia, Pennsylvania 19144

Igreja Presbiteriana Independente
Caixa Postal 9198
01.000 São Paulo, S.P.

II NORTH AMERICAN AGENCIES (CONTINUED)

192. Protestant Episcopal Church in the U.S.A.

Domestic and Foreign Mission Society
815 Second Avenue
New York, New York 10017

Igreja Episcopal do Brasil
Caixa Postal 549
20.000 Rio de Janeiro ZC-00

193. Salvation Army

122 W. 14th Street
New York, New York 10011

Exército da Salvação
Caixa Postal 8631
01.000 São Paulo, S.P.

194. Scripture Union

239 Fairfield
Upper Darby
Pennsylvania 19082

195. Seventh Day Adventists

6840 Eastern Avenue NW
Tacoma Park
Washington, D.C. 20012

Adventistas do Sétimo Dia
Rua Chiberas, 20
01.000 São Paulo, S.P.

196. Slavic Gospel Association

2434 N. Kedzie Boulevard
Chicago, Illinois 60647

Caixa Postal 7296
01.000 São Paulo, S.P.

197. South American and World Mission

412 Laura Lee Avenue
Tallahassee, Florida 32301

198. South American Mission

P. O. Box 769
Lake Worth, Florida 33460

Caixa Postal 50
78.000 Cuiabá, Mt.

199. Southern Baptist Convention

Foreign Mission Board
P. O. Box 6597
Richmond, Virginia 23230

Missão Batista Equatorial
Caixa Postal 135
66.000 Belém, Pa.

North - Caixa Postal 221
50.000 Recife, Pe.
South - Caixa Postal 1982, ZC-00
20.000 Rio de Janeiro, Gb.

200. Southern Cross Scripture Mission

3030 Old Decatur Road
Apartment 303B
Atlanta, Georgia 30305

201. Spanish American Inland Mission, Inc.

P. O. Box 782
Joplin, Missouri 64802

Cruzada Interamericana do Brazil
85.890 Foz Do Iguaçu, Pr.

202. Things to Come Mission

P. O. Box 96
Cope, Colorado 80812

Caixa Postal 693
82.600 Campo Largo, Pr.

203. T. L. Osborn Evangelistic Association

Caixa Postal 2
Penha, ZC-22
20.000 Rio de Janeiro, Gb.

204. Trans World Missions

P. O. Box 2013
Los Angeles, California 90054

205. Trans World Radio

560 Main Street
Chatham, New Jersey 07928

Caixa Postal 18.300
01.000 São Paulo, S.P.

II NORTH AMERICAN AGENCIES (CONTINUED)

206. Unevangelized Fields Mission

P. O. Box 306
Bala-Cynwyd
Pennsylvania 19004

Missão Cristã Evangélica
do Brasil
Brazil Branch - Caixa Postal 243
66.000 Belém, Pa.
Poraima Branch - Caixa Postal 154
69.800 Boa Vista, Rr.

207. United Christian Missionary Society

222 S. Downey Avenue
Indianapolis, Indiana 46219

Federação Evangélica Japonesa
do Brasil
R. Paula Ney 381. Apt. ° 101
04.107 São Paulo, S.P.

208. United Church of Canada

Board of World Mission
85 St. Clair Avenue, East
Toronto 7, Ontario, Canada

Junta de Missões da Igreja
Metodista do Brasil
Caixa Postal 12.800
01.000 São Paulo, S.P.

209. United Evangelical Churches

P. O. Box 28
Monrovia, California 91016

Caixa Postal 29
37.590 Jacutinga, M.G.

210. United Church of Christ

Board for World Ministries
475 Riverside Drive
New York, New York 10027

211. United Missionary Society

1819 S. Main Street
Elkhart, Indiana 46514

Igreja Missionária Unida
Caixa Postal 384
87.100 Maringá, Pr.

212. United Mission Society

P. O. Box 21-4622
Sacramento, California 95812

213. United Missions

Alexander City
Alabama 35010

Caixa Postal 1506
50.000 Recife, Pe.

214. United Pentecostal Church

Foreign Missionary Department
3645 S. Grand Blvd.
St. Louis, Missouri 63118

Igreja Pentecostal
Unida do Brasil
Caixa Postal 5151
01.000 São Paulo, S.P.

215. United Presbyterian Church in the U.S.A.

Commission on Ecumenical
Mission and Relations
475 Riverside Drive, 9th Floor
New York, New York 10027

Missão Presbiteriana do
Brasil Central
Caixa Postal 1596
01.000 São Paulo, S.P.

216. United World Mission, Inc.

P. O. Box 8000
St. Petersburg, Florida 33738

217. The Wesleyan Church

Department of World Missions
P. O. Box 2000
Marion, Indiana 46952

Missão dos Wesleianos do Brasil
Caixa Postal 444
69.000 Manaus, Am.

218. West Indes Mission, Inc.

P. O. Box 39
Coral Gables, Florida 33134

Missão Pan-Americana
Caixa Postal 2350
90.000 Pôrto Alegre, R.G.S.

219. World of Life Fellowship, Inc.

91 Main Street
Orange, New Jersey 07050

Palavra da Vida
Caixa Postal 5649
01.000 São Paulo, S.P.

II NORTH AMERICAN AGENCIES (CONTINUED)

220. World Baptist Fellowship Mission Agency

3001 W. Division
Arlington, Texas 76010

69.190 Manaus, Am.

221. World Council of Churches

Commission on World
Mission and Evangelism
475 Riverside Drive Room 439
New York, New York 10027

222. World Gospel Crusades

P. O. Box 3
Upland, California 91786

Cruzada Mundial Evangélica
Caixa Postal 10
14.100 Ribeirão Prêto, S.P.

223. World Gospel Mission

P. O. Box 948
Marion, Indiana 46952

Caixa Postal 384
87.100 Maringá, Pr.

224. World Literature Crusade

10545 Burbank Blvd.
North Hollywood
California 91601

Cruzada Mundial de Literatura
Caixa Postal 187
01.000 São Paulo, S.P.

225. World Missionary Assistance Plan

P. O. Box A
Fontana, California 92335

226. World Missions, Inc.

P. O. Box 2611
Long Beach, California 90001

Caixa Postal 1947
30.000 Belo Horizonte, M.G.

227. World Missions to Children

P. O. Box 1048
Grants Pass, Oregon 97526

Missões Mundiais Para Crianças
Caixa Postal 699
50.000 Recife, Pe.

228. World Radio Missionary Fellowship, Inc.*

P. O. Box 691
Miami, Florida 33147

229. World Vision International

P. O. Box O
Pasadena, California 91109

230. World Wide Evangelization Crusade

P. O. Box A
Fort Washington
Pennsylvania 19034

Missão de Evangelização Mundial
Caixa Postal 1206
30.000 Belo Horizonte, M.G.

231. Wycliffe Bible Translators

P.O. Box 833
Calgary, Alberta, Canada

232. Wycliffe Bible Translators, Inc.

P. O. Box 1960
Santa Ana, California 92702

Summer Institute of Linguistics
Wycliffe Bible Translators
Caixa Postal 2221
70.000 Brasília, D.F.

233. Young Life Campaign

P. O. Box 520
Colorado Springs
Colorado 80901

Alvo da Mocidade
Caixa Postal 8568
01.000 São Paulo, S.P.

234. Youth for Christ, International

P. O. Box 419
Wheaton, Illinois 60187

Mocidade Para Cristo
Caixa Postal 1508
30.000 Belo Horizonte, M.G.

III EUROPEAN AGENCIES

235. Acre Gospel Mission

13 Willowbank Drive
Belfast 6, North Ireland

Cruzada de Evangelização
do Acre e Amazonas
Boca do Acre
69.320 Rio Purus, Am.

236. Allian - Mission - Barmen
56 Wuppertal - Vohwinkel
Falkenhaynstr. 11, Germany

Missão Evangélica
Independente do Brasil
Caixa Postal 222
85.900 Toledo, Pr.

237. Anglican Episcopal Church
The Church of England

London, England

Caixa Postal 21124
01.000 São Paulo, S.P.

238. Baptist Missionary Society

93 Gloucester Place
London, W.1, England

Caixa Postal 766
80.000 Curitiba, Pr.

239. Brazil Evangelistic Mission

7 Greenwood Avenue
Laverstock
Salisbury, Wilts, England

Missão Evangelistica Brasileira
Caixa Postal 119
39.800 Teófilo Otoni, M.G.

240. Brazilian Bible Mission

34 East Esk Road
Newport, Mon., England

Caixa Postal 19
36.400 Conselheiro Lafaiete
M. G.

241. Brazil Mission Within the
German Fellowship Deaconry, Inc.

335 Marburg (Lahn)
Friedrich-Naumann-Str. 15
Germany

242. Christian Literature Crusade

201 Church Road
London, S.E. 19, England

243. Christian Missions in Many Lands

Echoes of Service
1 Widcombe Cresc.
Bath, Somerset, England

Caixa Postal 2083
80.000 Curitiba, Pr.

244. Deutsche Indianer Pioneer Mission

Stuttgart-Gerlingen
Ganwiesenweg 37, Germany

Caixa Postal 4
79.800 Dourados, Mt.

245. Dutch Evangelical Reformed
Church Missions

Reformed Churches in the
Netherlands
Wilhelminalaam 3, Baarn
Holland

Missão da Igreja Evangélica
Reformada do Brasil
Caixa Postal 7315
01.000 São Paulo, S.P.

246. Dutch Pentecostal Missions

Rhoden 17
Steenbergen, Holland

Missionária Evangélica Pentecostal
Caixa Postal 76
08.700 Mogi Das Cruzes, S.P.

247. Elim Missionary Society

20 Clarence Avenue
Clapham Park
London S.W. 4, England

Igreja Pentecostal Elim
Rua Acari 372
Santo Amaro
01.000 São Paulo, S.P.

248. Escole Biblique

Le Roc. Cologny
Geneve, Suica

Acão Bíblica do Brasil
Caixa Postal 2353
01.000 São Paulo, S.P.

III EUROPEAN AGENCIES (CONTINUED)

249. Evangelical Union of South America

6 Novar Road
London S.E. 9 2 D.W.
England

União Evangélica Sul-Americana
(British)
Caixa Postal 5701
01.000 São Paulo, S.P.

250. Gnadauer Brazilian Mission

6306 Denkendorf
Dreis Esslingen a.M.
Locherhaldenstrasse 20
Germany

Sociedade União Cristã
89.100 Blumenau, S.C.

251. Kirchliches Assenamt der Evangelischen

6 Frankfurt, Main
Postfach 4025
Alemanha, Germany

Igreja Evangélica da Confissão
Luterana do Brasil
Caixa Postal 14
93.000 São Leopoldo, R.G.S.

252. Leipzig Evangelical Lutheran Mission

Paul-List-Str. 17/19
701 Leipzig 1, Germany

253. Marberger Mission

Marburg Hahn
Stressemannstr 22
Postfach 600 P.A. 2
Germany

Associação das Igrejas de
Cristianismo
Decidido
Caixa Postal 2350
80.000 Curitiba, Pr.

254. Methodisten-Kirche in Deutchland

6 Frank-Main-Ginhein
Hinnheimer-Landstr. 174
Alemanha, Germany

Junta de Missões da Igreja
Metodista do Brasil
Caixa Postal 12,880
01.000 São Paulo, S.P.

255. Missionary Centre of the Reformed Churches in the Netherlands

Wilhelminalaan 3
Baarn, Netherlands

256. Missionswerk Mitternachtsruf

Postfach 150, 8034
Zurich, Schweiz

Obra Missionária Brado
da Meia Noite
Caixa Postal 1516
90.000 Pôrto Alegre, R.G.S.

257. Orebro Missionen

Box 330
Orebro, Sweden

Sociedade Missionária
Batista Independente
Caixa Postal 1474
80.000 Curitiba, Pr.

258. Peniel Chapel Missionary Society

Kensington Park Road
North Kensington
London W.11, England

Sociedade Missionária
de Peniel
Caixa Postal 148
39.8000 Teófilo Otomi, M.G.

259. Salvation Army

101 Queen Victoria Street
London, E.C. 4, England

260. Society for Distributing the Holy Scriptures to the Jews

237 Shaftesbury Avenue
London, W.C. 2, England

Caixa Postal 2566
01.000 São Paulo, S.P.

261. Swedish Baptist Union of Finland

Radhusgat, 44
Vasa, Finland

262. Swedish Free Mission

Filadelfiaforsamlingen
Rorstrandsgatan 5
Stockholm 6, Sweden

263. Unevangelized Fields Mission

9 Gunnersbury Avenue
London W 5, England

III EUROPEAN AGENCIES (CONTINUED)

264. West Amazon Mission

18 Martens Close
Shrivenham
Berkshire, England

Missão da Amazonia Ocidental
Caixa Postal 462
69.000 Manaus, Am.

265. Worldwide Evangelization Crusade

Bulstrode
Gerrards, Cross, Bucks
England

266. Wycliffe Bible Translators, Inc.

Bletchingley Road
Merstham
Redhill, Surrey
England

IV ASIAN AGENCIES

267. Gospel of Jesus Church (IESU FUKUIN KYODAN)

c/o Rev. Yutaka Akichika
1548 Shimohoya
Tanashi P.O.
Tokyo-to, Japan

268. Japan Alliance Church

255 Itsukatchi-Matchi
Saeki Gun
Hiroshima Ken, Japan

269. Japan Baptist Convention

2-350 Nishiokubo
Shinjuku-Ku
Tokyo, Japan

Batista do Japão
Caixa Postal 338
86.100 Londrina, Pr.

270. Japan Evangelical Lutheran Church

303-3 Hyakunin-cho
Shinjuku-Ku
Tokyo, Japan

271. Japan Holiness Church

Megurita
Higashimurayama-shi
Tokyo, Japan

272. World Gospel Missionary Society

c/o Box 5
Ibaraki
Osaku Fu, Japan

V OTHER AGENCIES

273. Hospital Christian Fellowship

P. O. Box 353
Kempton Park, Transvaal
South Africa

União do Pessoal Médico e
Hospitalar Cristão
Caixa Postal 6617
01.000 São Paulo, S.P.

274. Open Bible Institute (Church)

Box 82 San Fernando
Trinidad, West Indies

Directory of Missionary Agencies and their Functions

	MISSIONARY AGENCIES AT WORK IN BRAZIL IN 1973	PRIMARY TASK OF MISSION AGENCIES											
		ADMINISTRATION	AGRICULTURE	AVIATION	CHURCH PLANTING	EDUCATION	EVANGELIZATION	LINGUISTICS	LITERATURE	MEDICAL	SERVE NAT'L CHURCH	TV & RADIO	OTHER
NO.	NAME	1	2	3	4	5	6	7	8	9	10	11	12
	I BRAZILIAN AGENCIES												
1	Alianca Missionária Evangelística Mundial						X						
2	Assembléia Cristã				X		X						
3	Assembléia Dos Irmãos				X		X						
4	Associação Bras de Evangelização						X						
5	Associação Das Igrejas de Cristianismo Decidido				X		X						
6	Associação Evangélica para o Desenvolvimento Missionário						X						
7	Avanço de Literatura Cristã								X				
8	Brado da Hora Final				X				X				
9	Câmara de Literatura Evangélica do Brasil								X		X		
10	Capela Metropolitana												X
11	Clubes Bíblicos						X				X		
12	Comunhão Dental Amazonica									X			
13	Comunicações Evangélicas										X	X	
14	Concilio Brasileiro da Comunhão Africana Evangélica										X		X
15	Confederação Evangélica Brasileira										X		
16	Convenção Batista Nacional				X	X	X		X				
17	Cristo Liberta						X						
18	Cruzada da Nova Vida				X		X					X	
19	Crusada Estudantil e Profissional para Cristo						X				X		
20	Cruzada Mundial Evangélica						X						
21	Grupo Cristão de Estudantes e Profissionais												X
22	Igreja Cristã Presbiteriana	X			X		X		X				
23	Igreja Evangélica da Confissão Luteriana no Brasil					X			X	X			
24	Igreja Evangélica Suica						X						
25	Igreja Luterana Independente						X						
26	Igreja Reformada						X						
27	Imprensa da Fé								X				
28	Irmãos				X				X				
29	Jovens da Verdade						X						
30	Ministério da Vida												X

MISSIONARY AGENCIES AT WORK IN BRAZIL IN 1973

BRAZILIAN AGENCIES - cont.

		PRIMARY TASK OF MISSION AGENCIES											
		ADMINISTRATION	AGRICULTURE	AVIATION	CHURCH PLANTING	EDUCATION	EVANGELIZATION	LINGUISTICS	LITERATURE	MEDICAL	SERVE NAT'L CHURCH	TV & RADIO	OTHER
NO.	NAME	1	2	3	4	5	6	7	8	9	10	11	12
31	Missão Cristã Brasileira						X						
32	Missão dos Indios Kaiuas						X						
33	Missão do Vale do Parana						X						
34	Missa Estrangeira Convenção Batista Brasileira				X		X						
35	Missão Estrangeira Igreja Presbiteriana do Brasil				X		X						
36	Missão Evangélica Amazonica						X						
37	Missão Evangélica da Amazonia						X						
38	Missão Evangelica da Uniao Missionária para America do Sol				X		X						
39	Missão Evangelico do Interior do Brasil						X						
40	Missão Informadora do Brasil	X									X		X
41	Missão Mundo para Cristo						X						
42	Obra Missionária Igreja de Cristo			X	X				X			X	
43	Os Ligados Instituto e Seminário Bíblico de Londrina						X						
44	Pentecostal Independente				X								
45	Publicações Cristã Brasil								X				
46	Sociedade Bíblica do Brasil								X		X		
47	Sociedade Evangélica Missionária						X						
48	Sociedade Evangelizadora das Igrejas de Cristo						X						
49	Testemunho Batista para Israel de São Paulo						X						
50	Vencedores Por Cristo										X		
51	Vida Abundante Missão Conservadora do Brasil						X						
52	Voz dos Andes											X	
	II NORTH AMERICAN AGENCIES												
53	Agricultural Missions, Inc.		X										
54	Air Mail From God Mission, Inc.						X		X				
55	Amazon Mission, Inc.						X	X					
56	American Leprosy Missions, Inc.	X				X				X	X		
57	American Lutheran Church				X	X	X		X	X	X		
58	Apostolic Christian Church				X		X						
59	Apostolic Christian Church in the United States - Indiana						X						

MISSIONARY AGENCIES AT WORK IN BRAZIL IN 1973

NORTH AMERICAN AGENCIES - cont.

PRIMARY TASK OF MISSION AGENCIES

NO.	NAME	1 ADMINISTRATION	2 AGRICULTURE	3 AVIATION	4 CHURCH PLANTING	5 EDUCATION	6 EVANGELIZATION	7 LINGUISTICS	8 LITERATURE	9 MEDICAL	10 SERVE NAT'L CHURCH	11 TV & RADIO	12 OTHER
60	Apostolic Christian Church in the United States - Michigan				X								
61	Apostolic Churches of Jesus Christ						X						
62	Apostolic Church of Oklahoma					X							
63	Armenian Missionary Association of America, Inc.	X				X			X	X			
64	Assemblies of God General Council	X			X	X	X		X	X	X	X	
65	Association for Christian Literature								X				
66	Association of Baptists for World Evangelism, Inc.				X		X				X		
67	Baptist Bible Fellowship International				X		X						
68	Baptist Faith Missions				X		X						
69	Baptist General Conference				X	X	X		X	X	X		
70	Baptist International Missions, Inc.				X		X						
71	Baptist Mid-Missions				X	X	X						
72	Baptist Missionary Association of America						X		X	X	X		
73	Berean Mission, Inc.				X		X			X		X	
74	Bethany Fellowship, Inc.				X	X	X		X	X	X		
75	Bethany Missionary Association				X								
76	Bethesda Missions, Inc.				X	X	X		X	X	X	X	
77	Bible Conferences and Missions					X							
78	Bible Literature International								X				
79	Bible Meditation League								X				
80	Bible Memory Association International					X			X		X		
81	Bible Presbyterian Mission to Brazil				X		X						
82	Billy Graham Evangelistic Association						X		X				
83	Brazil Christian Mission				X		X		X		X		
84	Brazil Gospel Fellowship Mission, Inc.				X						X		
85	Brazil Inland Mission, Inc.				X	X	X					X	
86	Brazil Mission, Inc.				X		X						
87	Brazil Mission (Church of Christ)				X		X						
88	Brazilian Evangelistic Association						X						
89	Brethren Church						X						
90	Campus Crusade for Christ						X				X		

MISSIONARY AGENCIES AT WORK IN BRAZIL IN 1973

NORTH AMERICAN AGENCIES - cont.

PRIMARY TASK OF MISSION AGENCIES

NO.	NAME	1 ADMINISTRATION	2 AGRICULTURE	3 AVIATION	4 CHURCH PLANTING	5 EDUCATION	6 EVANGELIZATION	7 LINGUISTICS	8 LITERATURE	9 MEDICAL	10 SERVE NAT'L CHURCH	11 TV & RADIO	12 OTHER
91	Child Evangelism Fellowship, International					X	X		X		X	X	X
92	Christian and Missionary Alliance				X	X	X		X		X		
93	Christian Baptist "World for Christ Missions"						X						
94	Christian Bible Mission								X				
95	Christian Children's Fund												X
96	Christian Church World Missions				X								
97	Christian Life Missions								X				
98	Christian Literature Advance								X				
99	Christian Literature Crusade								X				
100	Christian Missionaries "Amazon Valley"				X		X						
101	Christian Missionary Fellowship						X						
102	Christian Missions in Many Lands						X						X
103	Christian Nationals Evangelism Commission, Inc.					X	X		X	X			
104	Christian Reformed Church				X	X	X		X	X	X		
105	Christian Service Centers	X											X
106	Christian Service Corps					X							X
107	Church of Christ (Christian Churches)				X				X				
108	Church of God - Indiana				X	X	X		X	X	X		
109	Church of God - Tennessee						X						
110	Church of God of Prophecy				X				X			X	
111	Church of the Nazarene				X	X	X			X	X		
112	Church World Service										X		
113	Cleveland Hebrew Mission, Inc.						X						
114	Co-Laborers, Inc.	X	X						X				X
115	Colonia Evangelica Acailandia		X										
116	Conservative Baptist Foreign Missionary Society				X	X	X		X	X	X	X	
117	Emmanuel Association						X						
118	Evangelical Enterprises					X						X	
119	The Evangelical Lutheran Church of Canada				X		X					X	
120	Evangelical Mennonite Church				X	X							
121	Evangelical Methodist Church				X	X	X		X				

MISSIONARY AGENCIES AT WORK IN BRAZIL IN 1973

NORTH AMERICAN AGENCIES - cont.

		PRIMARY TASK OF MISSION AGENCIES											
		ADMINISTRATION	AGRICULTURE	AVIATION	CHURCH PLANTING	EDUCATION	EVANGELIZATION	LINGUISTICS	LITERATURE	MEDICAL	SERVE NAT'L CHURCH	TV & RADIO	OTHER
NO.	NAME	1	2	3	4	5	6	7	8	9	10	11	12
122	Evangelical Union of South America				X	X	X		X		X		
123	Evangelical United Brethren Church				X								
124	Fellowship of Independent Missions	X					X			X			X
125	Free Methodist Church of North America				X	X			X	X	X		
126	Flying Missionaries, Inc.			X									
127	Free Will Baptists National Association				X		X						
128	Garr Memorial Church Carolina Evangelistic Association						X						
129	General Conference Mennonite Church - Overseas Mission	X				X	X		X	X	X	X	
130	General Conference of Seventh-Day Adventists	X	X		X	X	X		X	X	X	X	
131	General Conference Mennonite Brethren Church				X	X		X	X	X	X		
132	German United Christian Mission	X											X
133	Global Outreach, Inc.						X						
134	Gospel Crusades, Inc.						X						
135	Gospel Fellowship Missions						X						
136	Gospel Light Publications								X		X		
137	Gospel Literature Outreach (Crusade)								X				
138	Gospel Recordings, Inc.						X					X	
139	Go-Ye Fellowship, Inc.						X		X		X		
140	Hebrew Evangelization Society	X					X		X			X	
141	Independent Bible Baptist Missions				X	X	X						
142	Independent Board for Presbyterian Foreign Missions				X	X	X		X	X	X		
143	Independent Faith Mission											X	
144	Independent Gospel Missions				X	X	X	X	X		X		
145	Inter-American Evangelistic Association						X						
146	Inter-American Missionary Society				X		X						
147	International Board of Jewish Missions, Inc.						X						
148	International Church of the Foursquare Gospel				X	X	X		X			X	
149	International Committee of YMCA's of U.S. and Canada												X
150	International Fellowship of Evangelical Students						X						
151	International Pentecostal Assemblies				X	X			X		X		
152	Japan Evangelical Mission				X		X						

MISSIONARY AGENCIES AT WORK IN BRAZIL IN 1973

NORTH AMERICAN AGENCIES - cont.

PRIMARY TASK OF MISSION AGENCIES

NO.	NAME	1 ADMINISTRATION	2 AGRICULTURE	3 AVIATION	4 CHURCH PLANTING	5 EDUCATION	6 EVANGELIZATION	7 LINGUISTICS	8 LITERATURE	9 MEDICAL	10 SERVE NAT'L CHURCH	11 TV & RADIO	12 OTHER
153	Japanese Evangelical Missionary Society	X									X	X	X
154	Koinonia Foundation					X							X
155	Laubach Literacy Fund, Inc.					X			X				
156	Laymen's Overseas Service, Inc. (Laos)												X
157	Lester Sumrall Evangelistic Association					X							
158	Life Mission					X							
159	Literature Crusades								X				
160	Lutheran Church-Missouri Synod				X	X	X		X	X	X	X	
161	Lutheran Church in America				X		X				X		
162	Lutheran World Relief, Inc.	X	X			X	X			X	X		
163	Maranatha Baptist Mission, Inc.						X						
164	Mennonite Board of Missions and Services		X				X						
165	Mennonite Central Committee	X	X				X			X			X
166	Mennonite Church General Conference						X						X
167	Mennonite Church Board of Missions and Charities		X		X	X	X		X	X	X		
168	Methodist Church					X			X		X		
169	Mission to Amazonia						X	X					
170	Missionary and Soul Winning Fellowship					X	X		X		X		
171	Missionary Aviation Fellowship	X		X							X		X
172	Missionary Church				X	X	X		X	X	X		
173	National Association Congregational Christian Churches of U.S.										X		
174	National Baptist Convention U.S.A., Inc.					X			X	X	X		
175	Navigators, Inc.					X	X						
176	New Testament Missionary Union				X	X	X	X					
177	New Tribes Mission				X	X	X		X				
178	Next Towns Crusade, Inc.	X			X	X	X		X		X		X
179	North American Baptists Association						X						
180	North American Baptist General Missionary Society, Inc.				X	X	X		X	X	X		
181	Oriental Missionary Society				X	X	X		X	X	X	X	
182	Overseas Crusades, Inc.	X									X		X
183	Pan American Christian Academy					X							

MISSIONARY AGENCIES AT WORK IN BRAZIL IN 1973 NORTH AMERICAN AGENCIES - cont.		PRIMARY TASK OF MISSION AGENCIES											
		ADMINISTRATION	AGRICULTURE	AVIATION	CHURCH PLANTING	EDUCATION	EVANGELIZATION	LINGUISTICS	LITERATURE	MEDICAL	SERVE NAT'L CHURCH	TV & RADIO	OTHER
NO.	NAME	1	2	3	4	5	6	7	8	9	10	11	12
184	Pentecostal Assemblies of Canada				X	X	X		X		X	X	
185	Pentecostal Church of Christ				X								
186	Pentecostal Church of God of America				X	X	X						
187	Pilgrim Fellowship, Inc.				X		X		X		X		
188	Pioneer Bible Mission						X						
189	Pocket Testament League, Inc.						X		X				
190	Presbyterian Church in the U.S.			X	X	X	X		X	X	X	X	
191	Presbyterian Foreign Missions Independent Board						X						
192	Protestant Episcopal Church in the U.S.A.					X				X	X		
193	Salvation Army		X		X	X	X		X	X	X		
194	Scripture Union								X				
195	Seventh-Day Adventists				X		X						
196	Slavic Gospel Association						X						
197	South American and World Mission								X			X	
198	South American Mission				X	X	X	X	X	X	X		
199	Southern Baptist Convention	X	X		X	X	X		X	X	X	X	X
200	Southern Cross Scripture Mission								X				
201	Spanish America Inland Mission, Inc.				X		X						
202	Things to Come Mission				X	X	X		X		X	X	
203	T. L. Osborn Evangelistic Association						X				X		
204	Trans World Missions			X			X		X			X	
205	Trans World Radio								X			X	
206	Unevangelized Fields Mission				X	X	X		X	X	X	X	
207	United Christian Missy. Society		X			X			X	X	X		
208	United Church of Canada	X	X		X	X				X	X	X	X
209	United Evangelical Churches				X								
210	United Church of Christ	X	X			X	X		X	X	X	X	
211	United Missionary Society				X	X			X			X	
212	United Mission Society	X											X
213	United Missions	X				X				X			
214	United Pentecostal Church				X	X	X						

MISSIONARY AGENCIES AT WORK IN BRAZIL IN 1973

NORTH AMERICAN AGENCIES - cont.

PRIMARY TASK OF MISSION AGENCIES

NO.	NAME	1 ADMINISTRATION	2 AGRICULTURE	3 AVIATION	4 CHURCH PLANTING	5 EDUCATION	6 EVANGELIZATION	7 LINGUISTICS	8 LITERATURE	9 MEDICAL	10 SERVE NAT'L CHURCH	11 TV & RADIO	12 OTHER
215	United Presbyterian Church in the U.S.A.	X			X	X	X		X	X		X	X
216	United World Mission, Inc.					X	X		X	X	X	X	
217	The Wesleyan Church				X	X	X		X	X	X		
218	West Indies Mission, Inc.				X	X	X		X	X	X	X	
219	Word of Life Fellowship, Inc.	X				X	X					X	
220	World Baptist Fellowship Mission Agency				X	X	X		X		X	X	
221	World Council of Churches	X									X		
222	World Gospel Crusades						X		X			X	
223	World Gospel Mission			X	X	X	X		X	X	X		
224	World Literature Crusade								X				
225	World Missionary Assistance Plan										X		X
226	World Missions, Inc.				X		X		X		X	X	
227	World Missions to Children												X
228	World Radio Missionary Fellowship											X	
229	World Vision International	X									X		X
230	Worldwide Evangelization Crusade		X	X	X	X	X		X		X	X	
231	Wycliffe Bible Translators-Canada							X					
232	Wycliffe Bible Translators-Calif.			X				X	X				
233	Young Life Campaign						X		X				
234	Youth for Christ International						X						
	III EUROPEAN AGENCIES												
235	Acre Gospel Mission						X						
236	Allian-Mission-Barmen										X		
237	Anglican Episcopal Church-England				X		X						
238	Baptist Missionary Society						X						
239	Brazil Evangelistic Mission						X						
240	Brazilian Bible Mission						X						
241	Brazil Mission Within the German Fellowship Deaconry, Inc.										X		
242	Christian Literature Crusade								X				
243	Christian Missions in Many Lands						X						

MISSIONARY AGENCIES AT WORK IN BRAZIL IN 1973

EUROPEAN AGENCIES - cont.

PRIMARY TASK OF MISSION AGENCIES

NO.	NAME	1 ADMINISTRATION	2 AGRICULTURE	3 AVIATION	4 CHURCH PLANTING	5 EDUCATION	6 EVANGELIZATION	7 LINGUISTICS	8 LITERATURE	9 MEDICAL	10 SERVE NAT'L CHURCH	11 TV & RADIO	12 OTHER
244	Deutsche Indianer Pioneer Mission						X	X					
245	Dutch Evangelical Reformed Church Missions				X								
246	Dutch Pentecostal Missions						X						
247	Elim Missionary Society						X						
248	Escole Biblique					X	X						
249	Evangelical Union of So. America					X	X						
250	Gnadauer Brazilian Mission										X		
251	Kirchliches Assenamt der Evangelischen										X		
252	Leipzig Evangelical Lutheran Mission										X		
253	Marberger Mission						X				X		
254	Methodisten-Kirche in Deutchland										X	X	
255	Missionary Centre of the Reformed Churches in the Netherlands										X		
256	Missionswerk Mitternachtsruf						X						
257	Orebro Missionen				X		X						
258	Peniel Chapel Missionary Society						X						
259	Salvation Army - England					X							
260	Society for Distributing the Holy Scriptures to the Jews								X				
261	Swedish Baptist Union of Finland				X		X				X		
262	Swedish Free Mission				X		X						
263	Unevangelized Fields Mission				X		X						
264	West Amazon Mission						X	X					
265	Worldwide Evangelization Crusade						X						
266	Wycliffe Bible Translators, Inc. England							X					
	IV ASIAN AGENCIES												
267	Gospel of Jesus Church (IESU FUKUIN DYODAN)						X					X	
268	Japan Alliance Church				X						X		
269	Japan Baptist Convention				X								
270	Japan Evangelical Lutheran Church				X								
271	Japan Holiness Church				X		X				X	X	
272	World Gospel Missionary Society						X					X	

MISSIONARY AGENCIES AT WORK IN BRAZIL IN 1973		PRIMARY TASK OF MISSION AGENCIES											
		ADMINISTRATION	AGRICULTURE	AVIATION	CHURCH PLANTING	EDUCATION	EVANGELIZATION	LINGUISTICS	LITERATURE	MEDICAL	SERVE NAT'L CHURCH	TV & RADIO	OTHER
NO.	NAME	1	2	3	4	5	6	7	8	9	10	11	12
	V OTHER AGENCIES												
273	Hospital Christian Fellowship									X			
274	Open Bible Institute (Church)				X								

Directory of Protestant Theological Institutions in Brazil

DIRECTORY OF PROTESTANT INSTITUTIONS IN BRAZIL PROVIDING THEOLOGICAL AND BIBLICAL PROGRAMS OF STUDY

NAME, ADDRESS & DIRECTOR OF SCHOOL	YEAR FOUNDED	NUMBER OF STUDENTS			LEVEL OF COURSE			FACULTY	
		Male	Female	Total	Advanced Seminary	Seminary Bible Institute	Bible Institute	Full Time	Part Time
1. CENTRO DE ESTUDOS DA IGREJA METODISTA DO BRASIL, Rua Junqueira, 344 (Santo Amaro), Caixa Postal 12.681, 01000 São Paulo Director: Rev. Myung C. Moon	1968						XX		XX
2. CENTRO DE ESTUDOS TEOLÓGICOS DA FECICS, Caixa Postal 855, 29000 Vitória, Espírito Santo Director: Dr. Claude E. Labrunie	1968	18		18	X			1	15
3. CENTRO TEOLÓGICO "ABECAR" Praça Firmina Santana, 21 sala 14, Caixa Postal 398, 08700 Mogi das Cruzes, São Paulo Director: Rev. Willis Stitt	1970	15		15	X	X	X	1	10
4. COLÉGIO DE CADETES, Caixa Postal 8641, 01000 São Paulo Director: Brigadeiro Suzie Uzzell	1959	5	5	10			X	3	6
5. ESCOLA BÍBLICA PENTECOSTAL E PROFISSIONAL DO NORDESTE, Rua Marechal Deodoro, 112, Caixa Postal 458 50000 Recife, Pernambuco Director: Rev. Harold Matson	1962	21	22	43		X	X	5	
6. FACULDADE ADVENTISTA DE TEOLOGIA Estrada do Itapecerica, Km 23, Caixa Postal 7258, 01000 São Paulo Director: Rev. Orlando Rubens Ritter	1915	102	2	104		X	X		17
7. FACULDADE DE TEOLOGIA DO EDUCANDÁRIO NORDESTINO ADVENTISTA Belém de Maria, 55.300 Catendo, Pernambuco Director: Rev. Robert Dean Davis	1964	30		30	X	X		1	6
8. FACULDADE DE TEOLOGIA DA IGREJA EVANGÉLICA DE CONFISSÃO LUTERANA NO BRASIL, Morro do Espelho, Caixa Postal 14, 93000 São Leopoldo, Rio Grande do Sul Director: Dr. Harm Alpers	1946	96	2	98	X			7	4
9. FACULDADE DE TEOLOGIA DA IGREJA METODISTA DO BRASIL, Rua Sacramento 230, Caixa Postal 2, 09720 Rudge Ramos, São Paulo Director: Rev. Reinaldo Brose	1938	37		37	X			5	5
10. FACULDADE DE TEOLOGIA METODISTA LIVRE, Rua Domingos de Morais, 2518 (Vila Mariana), 18600 São Paulo São Paulo Director: Dr. V. James Mannoia	1957	44	14	58	X	X	X	6	7
11. FACULDADE DE TEOLOGIA DA IGREJA PRESBITERIANA INDEPENDENTE, Rua Artur Prado, 331, Caixa Postal 300, 01000 São Paulo, São Paulo Director: Dr. Rubens Cintra Damião	1905	30		30	X			2	7

DIRECTORY OF PROTESTANT INSTITUTIONS IN BRAZIL PROVIDING THEOLOGICAL AND BIBLICAL PROGRAMS OF STUDY

NAME, ADDRESS & DIRECTOR OF SCHOOL	YEAR FOUNDED	NUMBER OF STUDENTS			LEVEL OF COURSE			FACULTY	
		Male	Female	Total	Advanced Seminary	Seminary Bible Institute	Bible Institute	Full Time	Part Time
12. FACULDADE TEOLÓGICA BATISTA DE SÃO PAULO, Rua João Ramalho, 466 (Perdizes), Caixa Postal 30.259, 01000 São Paulo, São Paulo Director Dr. Thurmon Bryant	1957	55	6	61	X			5	11
13. INSTITUTO BATISTA DE EDUCAÇÃO RELIGIOSA (IBER), Rua Uruguai, 514 20000 Rio de Janeiro, Guanabara Director: Mrs. Dorino Cobb Hawkins	1949		79	79		X		8	25
14. INSTITUTO BÍBLICO DE ABAETETUBA Caixa Postal 243, 66000 Belém, Pará Director: Rev. Leslie Jantz	1954	64	12	76		X		2	
15. INSTITUTO BÍBLICO DE ARAPONGAS Caixa Postal 612, 86700 Arapongas Paraná Director: Rev. Palmiro Francisco de Andrade	1962	22		22			X	2	4
16. INSTITUTO BÍBLICO DAS ASSEMBLÉIAS DE DEUS Rua João Bosco, 1114, 12400 Pindamonhangaba, São Paulo Director: Rev. João Kolenda Lemos	1959	13	11	24			X	3	2
17. INSTITUTO BÍBLICO BATISTA Caixa Postal 16, 44100 Feira de Santana, Bahia Director: Dr. Robert Elton Johnson	1960	22	11	33			X	9	
18. INSTITUTO BÍBLICO BATISTA A. B. DETER, Avenida Silva Jardim, 1859 Caixa Postal 66, 80000 Curitiba, Paraná Director: Rev. Richard T. Plampin	1940	38	38	76			X	6	12
19. INSTITUTO BÍBLICO BATISTA DE CAMPINAS, Caixa Postal 995, 13100 Campinas, São Paulo Director: Rev. George Hansen	1965	35	30	65			X	1	8
20. INSTITUTO BÍBLICO BATISTA DO ESTADO DE SÃO PAULO, Rua Azarias Leite, 20-43, Caixa Postal 428, 17100 Bauru, São Paulo Director: Rev. Paul W. Stouffer	1962	99		99			X		10
21. INSTITUTO BÍBLICO BATISTA INDE-PENDENTE, Caixa Postal 751, 13100 Campinas, São Paulo Director: Rev. Ragnbert W. Thorn	1952	12	5	17			X		5
22. INSTITUTO BÍBLICO BETÂNIA 87550 Guaíra, Paraná C.P. 10 Director: Rev. Allan H. McLeod	1966	14		14		X	X	4	

DIRECTORY OF PROTESTANT INSTITUTIONS IN BRAZIL PROVIDING THEOLOGICAL AND BIBLICAL PROGRAMS OF STUDY

NAME, ADDRESS & DIRECTOR OF SCHOOL	YEAR FOUNDED	NUMBER OF STUDENTS			LEVEL OF COURSE			FACULTY	
		Male	Female	Total	Advanced Seminary	Seminary Bible Institute	Bible Institute	Full Time	Part Time
23. INSTITUTO BÍBLICO BETEL BRASILEIRO Rua Profa. Maria Amélia Torres, 124, Caixa Postal 194, 58000 João Pessoa, Paraíba President: Profa. Lidia Almeida de Menezes	1935	18		18	X	X		2	4
24. INSTITUTO BÍBLICO DO BRASIL Rua Pires da Mota, 110 (Aclimação), Caixa Postal 18.078, 01000 São Paulo, São Paulo Director: Rev. John L. Griffin	1954	65	15	80		X	X	1	8
25. INSTITUTO BÍBLICO EDUARDO LANE Rua Governador Valadares, 629, Caixa Postal 12, 38740 Patrocínio, Minas Gerais Director: Rev. Donald W. Kaller	1933	24	54	78			X	8	5
26. INSTITUTO BÍBLICO EVANGÉLICO EMANUEL, Caixa Postal 10, 49000 Aracaju, Sergipe Director: Rev. Kenneth Mueller	1964	7	8	15		X	X	3	1
27. INSTITUTO BÍBLICO "IGREJA DE DEUS" Caixa Postal 367, 74000 Goiânia, Goiás Director: Rev. Phillip Shearer	1964	5	3	8			X	3	3
28. INSTITUTO BÍBLICO DE MARINGÁ Rua Teixeira Mendes, 810, Caixa Postal 384, 87100 Maringá, Paraná Director: Rev. Donald Granitz	1962	10	10	20		X	X	3	3
29. INSTITUTO BÍBLICO DO NORTE Caixa Postal 66, 55300 Garanhuns, Pernambuco Director: Mrs. Aretuza Gueiros Pessoa	1945	15		15		X	X		7
30. INSTITUTO BÍBLICO NOTURNO DE FORTALEZA, Rua 24 de Maio 272, 60000 Fortaleza, Ceará Director: Rev. Edward Knechtel	1949	5		5			X	2	
31. INSTITUTO BÍBLICO PALAVRA DA VIDA Caixa Postal 43, 01000 Atibaia, São Paulo Director: Rev. David N. Cox	1965	18	20	38	X	X		4	8
32. INSTITUTO BÍBLICO PARANAENSE Caixa Postal 1559, 80000 Curitiba, Paraná Director: Rev. João J. Klassen	1961	13	5	18		X	X	5	4
33. INSTITUTO BÍBLICO PENTECOSTAL Rua Carolina Machado, 88 (Cascadura) 20000 Rio de Janeiro, Guanabara Director: Rev. N. Lawrence Olson	1962	57	23	80			X		10

DIRECTORY OF PROTESTANT INSTITUTIONS IN BRAZIL PROVIDING THEOLOGICAL AND BIBLICAL PROGRAMS OF STUDY

NAME, ADDRESS & DIRECTOR OF SCHOOL	YEAR FOUNDED	NUMBER OF STUDENTS			LEVEL OF COURSE			FACULTY	
		Male	Female	Total	Advanced Seminary	Seminary Bible Institute	Bible Institute	Full Time	Part Time
34. INSTITUTO BÍBLICO PRESBITERIANO DE CIANORTE, Caixa Postal 142, 87200 Cianorte, Paraná Director: Rev. Décio de Azevedo	1965	34	21	55		X	X		7
35. INSTITUTO BÍBLICO QUADRANGULAR Praça Olavo Bilão, 90 (Santa Cecília) 01000 São Paulo, São Paulo Director: Ms. Dorothy M. Hawley	1957	30	10	40			X	6	3
36. INSTITUTO BÍBLICO UNIÃO (dades de 1966) Av. Assis Brasil, 1451, Caixa Postal 2647, 90000 Pôrto Alegre, Rio Grande do Sul Director: Paul M. Pugh	1961	16	7	23			X		12
37. INSTITUTO BRASILEIRO DE EVANGELISTAS E MISSIONÁRIOS, Caixa Postal 864, 87266 Araruna, Paraná Director: Rev. Paulo Guiley	1962	23	19	42		X	X	7	4
38. INSTITUTO EVANGÉLICO LUTERANO Av. Brasília (Jardim Shangri-lá, zona B), Caixa Postal 616, 86100 Londrina, Paraná Director: Rev. Jaime Hougen	1969	6	3	9			X	1	2
39. INSTITUTO EVANGÉLICO MISSIONÁRIO PENIEL, Caixa Postal 29, 37590 Jacutinga, Minas Gerais President: Rev. Philip B. Davis	1956	43	54	97			X	9	
40. INSTITUTO JOÃO WESLEY Rua Coronel Joaquim Pedro Salgado, 80, Caixa Postal 267, 90000 Pôrto Alegre Rio Grande do Sul Director: Rev. Erasmo V. Ungarotti	1963	11	4	15		X	X		12
41. INSTITUTO PRESBITERIANO NACIONAL DE EDUCAÇÃO SHI Sul, CH 1, lotes 13-18 (lago), Caixa Postal 1632, 70000 Brasília, Distrito Federal Director: Rev. Newton Serra	1964	2	29	31		X	X	2	18
42. INSTITUTO E SEMINÁRIO BÍBLICO DE LONDRINA, Rua Senador Souza Nevos, 880, Caixa Postal 58, 86100 Londrina, Paraná Director: Rev. Hubert K. Clevenger	1954	28	22	50	X	X	X	5	
43. INSTITUTO TÉCNICO E TEOLÓGICO Rua Nestor Pestana, 136, 01000 São Paulo, São Paulo Director: Dr. Rubens Cintra Damião	1969	7		7			X		7
44. INSTITUTO TEOLÓGICO BATISTA DE CAROLINA, Caixa Postal 5, 65000 Carolina, Maranhão Director: Rev. Wilson Pinto França	1944	13	14	27			X	7	2

DIRECTORY OF PROTESTANT INSTITUTIONS IN BRAZIL PROVIDING THEOLOGICAL AND BIBLICAL PROGRAMS OF STUDY

NAME, ADDRESS & DIRECTOR OF SCHOOL	YEAR FOUNDED	NUMBER OF STUDENTS			LEVEL OF COURSE			FACULTY	
		Male	Female	Total	Advanced Seminary	Seminary Bible Institute	Bible Institute	Full Time	Part Time
45. INSTITUTO TEÓLOGICO EVANGÉLICO Rua Amazonas, 1137, Caixa Postal 2445 80000 Curitiba, Paraná Director: Rev. Willy Janz	1956	21	18	39		X	X	4	
46. INSTITUTO TEOLÓGICO JOÃO RAMOS JR. Rua Indianópolis, 751 (Cachoeirinha) Caixa Postal 2561, 30000 Belo Horizonte Minas Gerais Director: Rev. Donald E. Cockrill	1969	3		3			X		9
47. INSTITUTO TEOLÓGICO DE VITÓRIA Rua Loren Reno, 17, 29000 Vitória Espírito Santo Director: Dr. Manoel de Farias	1967	18	3	21		X	X		14
48. INSTITUTO TEOLÓGICO W. C. HARRISON Caixa Postal 2875, 90000 Pôrto Alegre, Rio Grande do Sul Director: Rev. Peter Tcherneshoff	1956	13	12	25		X	X		2
49. SEMINÁRIO BATISTA DO AMAZONAS Rua Paraíba, 300, Caixa Postal 372 69000 Manaus, Amazonas Director: Dr. David Vernon Stowell	1947	10	4	14		X	X	7	2
50. SEMINÁRIO BATISTA BEREIANO Av. Hermes da Fonseca, 1596, Caixa Postal 246, 59000 Natal, Rio Grande do Norte Director: Rev. William P. Branda	1956	16	17	33		X	X		10
51. SEMINÁRIO BATISTA DO CARIRI Caixa Postal 51 63180 Juazeiro do Norte, Ceará Director: Rev. Jerry Leonard		16	10	26		X	X	2	5
52. SEMINÁRIO BÍBLICO GOIANO (dados de 1966), Caixa Postal 465, 77100 Anápolis, Goiás Director: Rev. Nicomedes Augusto da Silva	1937	23	19	42		X	X	4	
53. SEMINÁRIO BÍBLICO MINEIRO Caixa Postal 1814, 30000 Belo Horizonte, Minas Gerais Director: Rev. Tom E. Mac Intyre	1967	37	18	55	X	X	X	4	8
54. SEMINÁRIO BÍBLICO PRESBITERIANO INDEPENDENTE DO NORTE-NORDESTE, Rua Princesa Isabel, 290 Fortaleza, Ceará Director: Rev. Ezequiel Tamarozi	1965	7		7		X	X		5
55. SEMINÁRIO CONCÓRDIA DA IGREJA EVANGÉLICA LUTERANA DO BRASIL Rua Coronel Lucas de Oliveira, 894, Caixa Postal 911, 90000 Pôrto Alegre, Rio Grando do Sul Director: Rev. Arnaldo J. Schmidt	1903			85	X	X		8	1

DIRECTORY OF PROTESTANT INSTITUTIONS IN BRAZIL PROVIDING THEOLOGICAL AND BIBLICAL PROGRAMS OF STUDY

NAME, ADDRESS & DIRECTOR OF SCHOOL	YEAR FOUNDED	NUMBER OF STUDENTS			LEVEL OF COURSE			FACULTY	
		Male	Female	Total	Advanced Seminary	Seminary Bible Institute	Bible Institute	Full Time	Part Time
56. SEMINÁRIO CRISTÃO EVANGELICO DO NORTE, Caixa Postal 528, 65000 São Luis, Maranhão Director: Rev. Allan Stonsvad	1962	10	7	17		X	X	6	1
57. SEMINÁRIO DE EDUCADORAS CRISTÃS Rua do Padro Inglôs, 143 (Boa Vista), Caixa Postal 29, 50000 Recife, Pernambuco Director: Ms. Martha E. Hairston	1917		150	150	X	X		19	18
58. SEMINÁRIO E ESCOLA BÍBLICA CENTRAL DO BRASIL, Caixa Postal 23, 36000 Belo Horizonte, Minas Gerais Director: Rev. Jack J. Chinn	1964	13	3	16			X	3	5
59. SEMINÁRIO EVANGÉLICO CONGREGACIONAL DO BRASIL, Rua Arialva, 19 (Tejipió), 50000 Recife, Pernambuco Director: Rev. Antônio Sales de Oliveira	1969	13		13		X		2	2
60. SEMINÁRIO E INSTITUTO BÍBLICO BATISTA, Avenida Ipiranga, 877, conj. 75 01000 São Paulo, São Paulo Director: Rev. Donald Hare	1957	37	21	58	X	X	X	4	6
61. SEMINÁRIO E INSTITUTO BÍBLICO DA IGREJA DO NAZARENO, Avenida Francisco Glicório, 1355, Caixa Postal 1008 13100 Campinas, São Paulo Director: Rev. Charles W. Gates	1962	47	9	56	X	X	X	12	13
62. SEMINÁRIO METODISTA CÉSAR DACORSO FILHO, Rua Marquês de Abrantes, 55 (Catete) Rio de Janeiro, Guanabara Director: Rev. George C. Mogill	1958	17		17		X	X		15
63. SEMINÁRIO MISSIONÁRIO BATISTA BETEL (dados de 1966), Caixa Postal 2018, 50000 Recife, Pernambuco Director: Dr. Robert L. Carlton	1961	8	4	12		X	X	4	1
64. SEMINÁRIO DE PREGADORES Estrada de Araras, 1710 25600 Petrópolis, Rio de Janeiro Director: Rev. Rolf Dubbers	1969						X		
65. SEMINÁRIO PRESBITERIANO CONSERVADOR, Caixa Postal 332, 09700 São Bernardo do Campo, São Paulo Director: Rev. Carlos Pachoco	1953	24		24	X	X		1	5
66. SEMINÁRIO PRESBITERIANO FUNDAMENTALISTA DO BRASIL, Rua Dr. José Mariano, 186, Caixa Postal 115 50000 Recife, Pernambuco Director: Dr. Porfirio de Andrade Gueiros	1946	50		50		X	X		7

DIRECTORY OF PROTESTANT INSTITUTIONS IN BRAZIL PROVIDING THEOLOGICAL AND BIBLICAL PROGRAMS OF STUDY

NAME, ADDRESS & DIRECTOR OF SCHOOL	YEAR FOUNDED	NUMBER OF STUDENTS			LEVEL OF COURSE			FACULTY	
		Male	Female	Total	Advanced Seminary	Seminary Bible Institute	Bible Institute	Full Time	Part Time
67. SEMINÁRIO PRESBITERIANO DO NORTE Rua Demócrito de Souza Filho, 208 (Madalena), 50000 Recife, Pernambuco Director: Dr. Noé de Paula Ramos	1924	95	16	111	X	X	X	6	2
68. SEMINÁRIO TEOLÓGICO BATISTA BRASILEIRO, Rua São Miguel, 695 (Afogados), 56800 Recife, Pernambuco Director: Rev. José Domingues Figueiredo	1923	11	3	14		X	X		5
69. SEMINÁRIO TEOLÓGICO BATISTA EQUATORIAL, Caixa Postal 88, 66000 Belém, Pará Director: Dr. Jussiê Gonçalves de Souza	1955	25	14	39	X	X	X	2	14
70. SEMINÁRIO TEOLÓGICO BATISTA FLUMINENSE, Avenida Alberto Torres, 231, 28100 Campos, Rio de Janeiro Director: Dr. Ebenézer Soares Ferroira	1963	35	5	40	X	X	X	3	7
71. SEMINÁRIO TEOLÓGICO BATISTA DO NORDESTE, Avenida Eurípodos do Aguiar, 1200, Caixa Postal 2, 64800 Floriano, Piauí Director: Rev. Dewey Mulholland	1952	12	16	28	X	X	X	5	4
72. SEMINÁRIO TEOLÓGICO BATISTA DO NORTE, Rua do Padre Inglês, 243, Caixa Postal 221, 50000 Recife, Pernambuco Director: Dr. David Mein	1902	121	67	188	X	X		19	6
73. SEMINÁRIO TEOLÓGICO BATISTA DO SUL DO BRASIL, Rua José Higino, 416 (Tijuca), Caixa Postal 2541, 20000 Rio de Janeiro, Guanabara Director: Dr. João F. Soren	1908	131	64	195	X	X		7	22
74. SEMINÁRIO TEOLÓGICO BETEL Rua Marechal Rondon, 1020 (Rocha) 20000 Rio de Janeiro, Guanabara Director: Mrs. Tabita Miranda Pinto	1940	126	18	144	X	X		1	12
75. SEMINÁRIO TEOLÓGICO EVANGÉLICO DO BRASIL, Rua das Pedrinhas, 76 (Venda Nova), Caixa Postal 72, 30000 Belo Horizonte, Minas Gerais Director: Rev. Eneias Tognini	1966	58	10	68	X	X	X	1	14
76. SEMINÁRIO TEOLÓGICO DA IGREJA EPISCOPAL DO BRASIL, Avenida Adolfo Pinheiro, 1362 (Santo Amaro), Caixa Postal 30.928, 01000 São Paulo, São Paulo Director: Rev. Odilon Silva	1903	22	3	25	X		X	5	3
77. SEMINÁRIO TEOLÓGICO DO INSTITUTO EDUCACIONAL PIRACICABANO, Rua Boa Morto, 1257, Caixa Postal 68, 13400 Piracicaba, São Paulo Director: Rev. Colin B. Johnstone	1969	8	2	10		X	X		6

DIRECTORY OF PROTESTANT INSTITUTIONS IN BRAZIL PROVIDING THEOLOGICAL AND BIBLICAL PROGRAMS OF STUDY

NAME, ADDRESS & DIRECTOR OF SCHOOL	YEAR FOUNDED	NUMBER OF STUDENTS			LEVEL OF COURSE			FACULTY	
		Male	Female	Total	Advanced Seminary	Seminary Bible Institute	Bible Institute	Full Time	Part Time
78. SEMINÁRIO TEOLÓGICO PENTECOSTAL Rua São Bonto, 405, 218 andar, conj. 2123, 01000 São Paulo, São Paulo Director: Rev. José Almeida do Jesus	1969	191	55	246		X	X	1	9
79. SEMINÁRIO TEOLÓGICO PRESBITERIANO DE CAMPINAS, Avenida Brasil, 1200, Caixa Postal 133, 13100 Campinas, São Paulo Director: Dr. Eduardo Lano	1888	66	5	71	X	X		4	1
80. SEMINÁRIO TEOLÓGICO DO RIO DE JANEIRO, Rua Belchior da Fonseca, 151 Pedra do Guaratiba, Guanabara Director: Rev. João Arantes Costa	1945	22	5	27	X	X		2	8
81. AETTE Caixa Postal 30259 São Paulo, SP	DATA NOT AVAILABLE FOR NUMBERS 81 to 106								
82. ASTE Rua Rego Freitas, 530, -1o.and. s/13 01000 São Paulo, S.P.									
83. COMUNIDADE EVANGÉLICA LUTERANA Caixa Postal 113 89250 Jaraguá, SC									
84. CURSOS BÍBLICOS POR CORRESPONDÊNCIA, Caixa Postal 30498 01000 São Paulo, SP									
85. ESCOLA BÍBLICA EMAUS Phyllis Dunning, Caixa Postal 458 29000 Vitória, ES									
86. ESCOLA BÍBLICA EM COSMÓPOLIS Caixa Postal 2353 01000 São Paulo, SP									
87. ESCOLA BÍBLICA CENTRAL DO BRASIL Caixa Postal 1829 30000 Belo Horizonte, MG									
88. INSTITUTO BÍBLICO APÓSTOLO PAULO Caixa Postal 4, Via Carangola 36800 Fervedoura, MG									

DIRECTORY OF PROTESTANT INSTITUTIONS IN BRAZIL
PROVIDING THEOLOGICAL AND BIBLICAL PROGRAMS OF STUDY

NAME, ADDRESS & DIRECTOR OF SCHOOL	YEAR FOUNDED	NUMBER OF STUDENTS			LEVEL OF COURSE			FACULTY	
		Male	Female	Total	Advanced Seminary	Seminary Bible Institute	Bible Institute	Full Time	Part Time
89. INSTITUTO BÍBLICO BATISTA INDEPENDENTE, Caixa Postal 172 96200 Rio Grande, RGS									
90. INSTITUTO BÍBLICO BETEL Ac. Conde Francisco Matarazzo, 317 09500 São Caetano do Sul, SP									
91. INSTITUTO BÍBLICO LUTERANO LIVRE Caixa Postal 44 87300 Campo M urão, PR									
92. INSTITUTO BÍBLICO NAZARENO Caixa Postal 115 30000 Belo Horizonte, MG									
93. INSTITUTO BÍBLICO PEREGRINO Caixa Postal 444 69000 Manaus, AM									
94. INSTITUTO BÍBLICO PRESBITERIANO Caixa Postal 502 66000 Belém, Pará									
95. INSTITUTO CENTRAL DO POVO Caixa Postal 4102 20000 Rio de Janeiro, GB ZC05									
96 INSTITUTO DE TREINAMENRO CRISTÃO Rua Uruguai, 514 20000 Rio de Janeiro, GB									
97. INSTITUTE DE TREINAMENTO DA CONVENÇÃO BATISTA Caixa Postal 280 30000 Belo Horizonte, MG									
98. INSTITUTO MISSIONÁRIO E LINGUISTICO, Caixa Postal 53, 79130 Rio Brilhante, MT									
99. SEMINÁRIO E INSTITUTO BÍBLICO NAZARENO, Caixa Postal 560 70000 Brasília, DF									

DIRECTORY OF PROTESTANT INSTITUTIONS IN BRAZIL PROVIDING THEOLOGICAL AND BIBLICAL PROGRAMS OF STUDY

NAME, ADDRESS & DIRECTOR OF SCHOOL	YEAR FOUNDED	NUMBER OF STUDENTS			LEVEL OF COURSE			FACULTY	
		Male	Female	Total	Advanced Seminary	Seminary Bible Institute	Bible Institute	Full Time	Part Time
100. SEMINÁRIO E INSTITUTO BÍBLICO NAZARENO, Caixa Postal 102 06000 Osasco, SP									
101. SEMINÁRIO TEOLÓGICO BATISTA DA BAHIA, Rua Duarte Costa, 122 40000 Salvador, Bahia									
102. SEMINÁRIO TEOLÓGICO BATISTA DO ESTADO DO RIO, Rua Zezinho, 135 26500 Nilópolis, RJ									
103. SEMINÁRIO TEOLÓGICO PRESBITERIANO DO CENTENÁRIO, Caixa Postal 855 29000 Vitória, Espírito Santo									
104. S.I.B. BATISTA LIVRE Caixa Postal 217 14870 Jaboticabal, SP									
105. SOCIEDADE BÍBLICA EMAÚS POR CORRESPONDÊNCIA, Caixa Postal 30446 05073 Lapa, SP, SP									
106. % Theological Extension Courses COLÉGIO EVANGÉLICO DE BURITI Caixa Postal 41 78000 Cuiabá, MT Director: Rev. Gordon S. Trew									

Appendix 1: Conversion Survey

CONVERSION SURVEY

One of the primary aims of the church of Jesus Christ is to confront men with their need for repentance and salvation in Christ, and then to disciple them into the Church. The process through which the human being goes in becoming a Christian has typically been described as *conversion*, a turning about, a facing in a new direction, the beginning of a new life. The aim of every evangelist is to obtain *converts*.

During recent years more and more attention has been given to methods of evangelism. In general the "effectiveness" of evangelism has been measured by the numbers who have responded - the number of *converts*. Countrywide "evangelism-in-depth" campaigns, radio broadcasts, mass rallies, television programs, literature, congregational preaching and a multitude of other evangelistic methods have been used. Qualitatively the usefulness or effectiveness of the various methods has usually been dealt with quite pragmatically - "it works," and therefore must be an effective way. Unfortunately very little comparative study has been done from both the positive and negative aspects of evangelistic methods. For all we know, in many cases the most "successful" evangelistic method (the one that evidently produces the largest number of converts) may also be the one that produces the strongest negative reaction in those who do not accept the message - are not converted. Some studies have been done at mass evangelism campaigns on the background and motivation for conversion of those that have accepted Christ, but few if any studies have been done during the same mass campaigns on those who left the encounter without having made such a decision.

During this same period there has been a growing recognition that the number of "converts" that are claimed by all those in the business of proclaiming the Gospel far exceeds the numbers of those who are discipled into a local church body. Many theories have been advanced as to why this might be so. Some of these theories center around the means, methods, or circumstances of the conversion experience. Did the new converts really know what they were doing? Were they merely motivated by the emotional situation in which they found themselves? Were they manipulated by the people surrounding them, either through social pressure or psychological maneuvering? Others tend to focus on the "follow-up" and discipling that is recognized as being needful subsequent to a decision. What opportunities were given for the new convert to exercise his faith? Was he immediately incorporated into a body of believers? Was the environment of his home or work situation such that when he returned he could not stand the group pressure that was possibly applied to him? Still others believe that there is a strong correlation between the previous life of the individual and the conversion experience. His age, former religion, social setting, and other factors are all believed to have a major bearing on the efficacy of the conversion experience.

Another aspect which is less discussed, but which is of significant importance, is the question as to whether there is any correlation between the conversion experience and the subsequent maturing and discipleship of the believer. These are all very important questions.

It is probably safe to say that the only true measure of the advance of Christianity is the number of men and women who are folded into the Body of Christ and become church members. This is not to say that everyone who accepts membership in a Christian church is truly converted, but it does point out that the only real measure of evangelistic effectiveness is when the new convert has become a functioning part of the Body of Christ. In 1962 Presbyterian missionary, Dr. Roy Shearer, did a broad statistical study of conversion experience among Korean Christians. This first attempt at quantitative correlations was subject to a number of pitfalls. First, the sample was not controlled. Second, the results raised questions about the design of the instrument itself as it was discovered that the largest number of respondents believed that their family was the greatest influence in their becoming Christians, and this was the first answer on the multiple answer sheet. But Shearer had broken some good ground and opened some very real questions and possibilities.

In November, 1968, another opportunity arose for doing a similar study. A Congress on Evangelism was being held in Singapore with participants from 23 nations in the Asian-South Pacific area. A report was written in January of 1970 entitled "Church Growth and Methods of Evangelism in Asia-South Pacific" (MARC, Edward L. Gruman, editor). The report can speak for itself.

"It was recognized before the congress that the delegates who would come would have an unusual store of information about what God is doing through their churches in their countries. For this reason it was decided to attempt a series of surveys during the Congress. Four questionnaires were distributed at different times, and the delegates were asked to give information about the size and organization of their churches, and about methods of evangelism which are being used in these churches and the effectiveness of the different methods. They were also asked to evaluate their own conversion experiences so that others might see how God is working in the lives of men and women in other countries outside their own. Three of these questionnaires were used in constructing this report and they are reproduced in the appendix.

"As in the case of most surveys of this type, some caution is necessary in using the information presented. First, it should be recognized that not all of the delegates answered the questionnaires. Of the 938 delegates who registered, 225 to 287 of them took part in the three surveys. This means that in many cases an incomplete picture may have been given. Therefore, one should avoid making completely positive statements based upon the data. Instead, the data should be used as a guide and as a basis of discussion. In some countries a considerable amount of data is available; in others very little is available. We have attempted throughout the report that follows to always show how many people were responding in order to give the reader some indication of how authoritative the data may be.

"Some results are of special interest. First, the delegates sampled were mostly from Christian families, indicating the power of close kinship for producing evangelization. However, the question arises as to their understanding of their task as church leaders. One could draw either the conclusion that they have better insight into the non-Christians of their countries or that they have become somewhat isolated from non-Christian thought. In any event, the composition of the Christian leadership in each country merits study so that the effect it is having on the task of evangelizing that country is understood.

"Another result confirms what previous studies have indicated, that the most effective method of evangelism is person-to-person witness, and most particularly within a family. A life lived for Christ is more compelling than words about Him. Finally, it appears that those churches growing fastest are those that are doing the most, indicating the truth of Kenneth Strachen's theorem, that "the expansion of any movement is in direct proportion to its success in mobilizing its total membership in continuous propagation of its beliefs."

A departure was made from Shearer's survey and an attempt was made to differentiate between <u>people</u> who had an influence on the individual and experiences that related to the individual.

As was the case with the Shearer survey, the sample was not controlled and the best that can be said for the survey is it tended to confirm what the Shearer survey had already suggested.

It also pointed some directions which were useful. Perhaps the most notable and accurate indices that be drawn from the results are the negative correlations, means and methods which are apparently not significant. Also of considerable interest was the large variations between the data found in different countries.

A major difficulty with any probe into the personal conversion experience of the individual is the individual's changing perception of his past experience with the passing of time. William James was the first one to point out that we all select from our conversion experience those events which are acceptable to our peer group. This influence and the other circumstances that surround the passing years either diminish the individual's perception of his conversion experience, or tend to sharpen up certain aspects of it. What can be done to overcome this difficulty in subsequent testing remains to be seen.

Building on the effort at Singapore a new approach was attempted as part of the MARC/BRAZIL pilot study during 1971. The questionnaire that was used has been translated from Portuguese and is duplicated in Figure 1. Instead of merely asking for people and experiences that might have been involved in the Christian conversion experience, people, methods, events, and the content of the Gospel message were all explored. This instrument not only looked backward as to the person's history prior to his conversion experience, but also looked forward to his involvement in a local church subsequent to the conversion experience.

The instrument was designed to be carried out by a local pastor in a local church setting. Roger Schrage worked the instructions that were given to the pastor for its use, as well as the score sheet. These are reproduced in Figures 2 and 3. Note that the score sheet is designed to be placed physically next to the questionnaire. The pastor was also given a tabulation sheet (Figure 4) on which he could ascertain a general profile of his congregation. An attempt was made to present this to the local pastor in Brazil as a tool for his use, rather than as a research aid. In those churches where it was used, it was found to be quite helpful to both the pastor and to the congregation. By using the occasion of an evening service, most of the problems of having a controlled sample were overcome for the particular population (the individual congregation).

But for rural churches this method of testing proved to be somewhat too sophisticated, and a new instrument (translated into English in Figure 5) was designed for personal interview by Harmon Johnson of CASE. At the time of this writing the Center for Applied Study in Evangelism (CASE, Caixa Postal 30.548, São Paulo, S.P., Brazil) is planning to conduct 2300 interviews across

Brazil, both geographically and denominationally in January to August, 1974. By applying cross-correlation techniques in a computer study of the data, it is hoped that some new evidence will be uncovered.

For more information on the use of this survey in Portuguese, write to CASE.

FIGURE 2

INSTRUCTION SHEET

In the past decade the Evangelical Church doubled in the number of its members. How were these persons won for Christ? Who were the people that God used to reach them? Is it possible that our major efforts on behalf of evangelization have been the most efficient?

The answers to these questions are of primary importance to us in order to insure that evangelism in Brazil will continue to be as efficient as possible in this important decade. To be more efficient in our evangelism in the future, we must evaluate what we have done in the past.

With this in mind, and a desire to help your church and to make better plans for your entire program of evangelization, this survey has been prepared.

Instructions For This Survey

First, read the questionnaire to see if you understand it well, and be prepared to answer any questions that might be raised about it.

Some people use the term "conversion" in different ways. We use it because it is the best known term we have to explain what happens to one who "comes to Christ." If you want to substitute the word "conversion" by the term "accept Christ as personal Savior" or to "become a believer" or another expression that will be better understood by the church in which you are making this survey, feel free to do this without any problem. It is our aim for people to indicate the different factors that led them to a personal encounter with God, independently of the word used to describe the happening.

The survey should be done during a well attended worship service, so that the greatest number of people will fill in the questionnaire. It is well to announce it beforehand and ask the people to bring their pencils or pens.

Before the questionnaires are distributed, an explanation should be given of the value of the information they will provide. This will ultimately enhance the work of evangelization in the local church. If they understand this, people will probably feel a greater responsibility in filling in the different answers with care.

At the same time, it should be made clear that this is not a test with certain answers or answers that are right or wrong. The objective is to record on the survey forms the way those things happened in the life of each one and helped them to accept Christ as their Savior.

When the objective of the survey is explained, the survey sheets may be distributed and filled in without delay. If illiterate people are present, there should be a person by their side to help them. To validate the survey, all the people present in the service, regardless of age or social class, should fill in the questionnaire.

Before picking up the questionnaires, ask the people to verify the fact that they have put the No. 1 and No. 2 designations in their answers, especially in questions #5, 6, 7, 8, and 17. This is important for the survey to be consistent in all parts of Brazil.

Instructions For Compiling The Survey

Check to see if each sheet has been filled in correctly. If a person made their marks on the wrong side of the column, see that they are placed on the left between the parentheses where they should be.

Question #4 will have to be classified by someone before being compiled. Put to one side answers for questions #1, 2, 3, or 4, in accordance with the principal factor indicated in the answers. This should be done in the following manner: 1) If a specific person was indicated as the factor central in conversion. 2) If a specific way of evangelization was presented as the principal factor. 3) If a specific happening or experience led the person to accept Christ. 4) If it was a specific type of Gospel message that led the person to Christ. (Some examples follow of how they will be classified according to some answers.)

"My mother taught me to follow Christ." (PERSON-1)
"I read a tract and it helped me." (WAY-2)
"I was sick and God made me well and eventually I was converted to Christ." (HAPPENING-3)
"One day I saw that I was lost without help." (MESSAGE-4)

In question #25, if a person is of another denomination, mark that with an X to make it easier in the compiling.

Now, with all of the survey questionnaires in order, put them together in one pile. Take the tabulation form and fold it in the middle so it can be filled in vertically. Align the sheet in such a way that it will be easy to transcribe the result of the answers. When you finish a column on the left, turn the sheet and transcribe the answers of the right column.

Page Three

After doing the first side, turn the page and do the other side in the same way. Eventually, this will give you all of the different answers.

On the Tabulation Sheet in the column entitled, TOTAL, transcribe the totals for each answer. In questions #5, 6, 7, 8 and 17, write the order of the first five in the column at the left and the number of the indications for each one in the column of the total.

Soon we begin to see a general outline of evangelism emerge for our church. In order to better evaluate, and to be a little more efficient, we must divide the answers in diverse categories and begin to compare them. The growth of the church quantitatively can come from three different avenues:

1) Children of members of the church that grow and that become members of the church.

2) Members of other churches, that by moving or for some other motive have transferred to the church.

3) Persons from outside that are evangelized and come to take part in the church.

As important as the first two are, only when we find the third happening do we actually fulfill the great commission. In order to measure this, we suggest that you divide the sheets into piles accordingly with the question and the answer of #27, of those that were raised within the Gospel and of those that were not. After this subdivide each pile by six, according to the answers to the question #19.

Having done this, we now pass to do the tabulation of each pile by itself. We transcribe the results by columns as indicated in the sheet of tabulation.

Other comparisons are also possible. It would be interesting to know the difference between the diverse levels of instruction, or the age of conversion. In order to do any type of comparison like this, separate the piles into the proper category and do a comparative tabulation.

EXPEDITING THE SURVEY

The Survey can give you the answers to the following questions, and other questions that are similar that can be found in the facts that are being tabulated. In this way we can begin to plan an evangelism that is more efficient for the days ahead.

1) Which is the age group in which the largest number of converts have been recorded? Are we focalizing our evangelism in this age?

2) Which persons are most used in evangelization? Are they actually giving the proper attention to their ministry?

3) Which ways of evangelization are most efficient? Are we giving the proper attention to these? How can we increase this type of witness?

4) Are some methods unfruitful? Should we continue these methods?

5) Which Gospel messages convince and persuade persons to accept Jesus Christ?

6) Are we giving proper attention to the things that help people grow in the faith?

7) Which things that appear to be weak in the survey should be modified in order to obtain better results?

May God help us to be faithful servants and take advantage of all the resources that He has given and placed at our disposal for evangelization of those, who until now, do not know the peace of God in their hearts!

- - - - - - - - - - - -

When you finish the study of your church, please fill in the sheet describing your church and include it with the rest of the survey forms. Send them to the following address:

MARC - Rua Vigadeiro Tobias, 118 s-2507 - Sao Paulo,
Capital 01032

We want to put all of the information together with other churches in order to have a fuller picture of what God is doing in Brazil in the same way that you have done for your church.

Thank you very much for your cooperation and may God bless you richly.

FIGURE 14

HOW IS GOD BRINGING PEOPLE UNTO HIMSELF

God uses many manners and methods to bring people to Himself. Paul says that he used every possible way to save some (I Cor. 9:22). In the conversion of each one God can use different people, circumstances, methods, and even different aspects of His great Gospel. In order to be efficient testimonies, we need to understand better how God is working. Your help is needed in the response to these questions that deal with your own conversion.

1. Do you remember when you became a believer?
   ( ) Yes ( ) No

2. How long has it been? ______________________

3. What was your age?
   ( ) 12 years or less
   ( ) 13 to 17 years
   ( ) 18 to 30 years
   ( ) 31 years and above

4. Give in a few words a description of your conversion.

   ____

   ____

5. Of the people listed below, mark with an X those that were used by God in your conversion.
   ( ) Father
   ( ) Mother
   ( ) Neighbor
   ( ) Teacher in the Sunday School
   ( ) Brother or sister
   ( ) Colleague at work
   ( ) Pastor
   ( ) Wife or husband
   ( ) Teacher
   ( ) Missionary
   ( ) Official or leader in the church
   ( ) Whole family
   ( ) Old friend
   ( ) New friend
   ( ) Visiting preacher
   ( ) Boss or other benefactor
   ( ) Son or daughter
   ( ) ______________________

   Now return and mark with a #1 who was most important in your conversion and mark with a #2 the person who was second most important in your conversion. Fill in another if not found on the above list.

6. Of the ways listed below mark with an X those that were used by God in your conversion.
   ( ) Radio
   ( ) Sunday School
   ( ) Paper or Evangelical journal
   ( ) Service in the church
   ( ) Camp
   ( ) Service or Evangelistic Campaign
   ( ) Service in a home
   ( ) Bible reading
   ( ) Evangelical music
   ( ) Bible study
   ( ) Spiritual retreat
   ( ) Visitation campaign
   ( ) Open air services
   ( ) Evangelical film
   ( ) Evangelical hospital
   ( ) Gospel tract
   ( ) ______________________________

   Now return and mark with #1 the way most important in your conversion and with #2 the second in importance.

7. Of the happenings that are listed below, mark those that God used in your conversion.
   ( ) Death of a friend
   ( ) A reverse or a setback of some kind
   ( ) A promise made to God
   ( ) Friend who became a believer
   ( ) Miracle
   ( ) Death in the family
   ( ) A vision
   ( ) Difficulty in the life
   ( ) Blessing of some kind
   ( ) A cure
   ( ) Fellowship with believers
   ( ) Members of the family that became believers
   ( ) Sickness
   ( ) ______________________________

   Now return and mark with a #1 the happening most important in your conversion and with a #2 the second most important.

8. Of the message of the Gospel what aspects did God use to speak to your heart and finally terminated in your conversion?
   ( ) God loves me
   ( ) God is the Judge of the sinner
   ( ) God gives happiness
   ( ) God saves from Hell
   ( ) God sent His Son
   ( ) The penalty of my sin
   ( ) My need for God
   ( ) The blood of Christ purifies
   ( ) Christ crucified in my place

( ) Christ gives hope
( ) Christ will return
( ) Christ is the Friend of the humble
( ) Christ performs miracles
( ) Christ cures
( ) Christ gives peace
( ) Christ resurrected
( ) Christ liberates the sinner

Now return and mark with #1 the message that spoke the strongest to your heart and with #2 the second strongest and most important aspect of the message.

9. How many times a week do you attend worship services (average)
( ) Less than once a week
( ) One or two times a week
( ) More than two times a week

10. Are you an officer in your church?
( ) Yes ( ) No

11. Do you teach in the Sunday School?
( ) Yes ( ) No

12. Do you participate in the Choir or Band?
( ) Yes ( ) No

13. Do you preach in the church or in other activities?
( ) Yes ( ) No

14. Are you a tither?
( ) Yes ( ) No

15. Do you invite others to the Church?
( ) Yes ( ) No

16. Have you been used by God in the conversion of anyone to Christ?
( ) Yes ( ) No

17. In the items in the following list mark with an X those that have helped you most in your Christian growth and development.
( ) Worship services
( ) Camps
( ) Prayer meetings
( ) Sunday School
( ) Special conferences
( ) Meetings of young people
( ) Evangelistic meetings
( ) Bible studies
( ) Spiritual retreat
( ) Activities in the church
( ) Giving testimony
( ) Hearing the testimony of others

( ) Communion with the brothers
( ) Choir
( ) Band
( ) Personal evangelism
( ) Preaching
( ) Teach in the Sunday School
( ) Family devotions
( ) Bible reading
( ) Prayer
( ) Radio
( ) Evangelical literature
( ) Evangelical records
( ) Bible study courses
( ) ____

Now return and mark using a #1 that which contributed most to your Christian life and with a #2 second most important factor in your Christian life.

18. How old are you?
( ) 12 years or less
( ) 13 - 17 years
( ) 18 - 30 years
( ) 31 years or more

IMPORTANT - Have you marked with a #1 and a #2 the two answers most important in questions 5, 6, 7, 8, 9, and 17? If not, do so now.

19. Your sex?
( ) Masculine ( ) Feminine

20. You were raised in
( ) A large city
( ) A small city
( ) Rural sector

21. Were you born in the county where you live now?
( ) Yes ( ) No

22. Were you already a Christian when you arrived in the city where you are now living?
( ) Yes ( ) No

23. Were you converted soon after your arrival?
( ) Yes ( ) No

24. How long have you been living at your present residence?
( ) Less than a year
( ) 1 - 2 years
( ) 3 - 5 years
( ) 6 - 10 years
( ) 11 years or more

25. What is your denomination?

____

26. Have you attended regularly in another denomination?
( ) Yes ( ) No

If yes, which denomination?

____

27. In what religion were you raised?
( ) Evangelical
( ) Catholic
( ) Spiritist
( ) ______________________________

28. What is your level of education?
( ) None
( ) Primary
( ) Junior High
( ) High School
( ) University

29. What is the monthly salary of your family?
( ) Less than Cr$ 300,00
( ) Cr$ 300,00 to 600,00
( ) 600,00 to 1.000,00
( ) 1.000,00 to 2.000,00
( ) 2.000,00 to 4.000,00
( ) 4.000,00 and above

30. What do you think about Jesus Christ?

____

____

31. Would you like to comment more on this?

____

____

FIGURE 1B

FACTS OF THE CHURCH OR CONGREGATION STUDIED

Name ______________________________

Street ______________________________

City ______________________________

Denomination ______________________________

1. How long has the church or congregation existed?
   ( ) Less than 1 year
   ( ) 1 - 2 years
   ( ) 3 - 5 years
   ( ) 11 - 25 years
   ( ) 26 years or more

2. Actually - how many members does the church have?
   ( ) Up to 25
   ( ) 26 - 40
   ( ) 41 - 60
   ( ) 61 - 90
   ( ) 91 - 120
   ( ) 121 - 150
   ( ) 151 - 200
   ( ) 201 - 300
   ( ) 301 - 400
   ( ) More than 400 - how many? ______________

3. How many members does the church have more than it had last year?
   ( ) Doesn't have more members than it had last year
   ( ) Up to three members or more
   ( ) 4 - 6
   ( ) 7 - 10
   ( ) 11 - 20
   ( ) 21 - 30
   ( ) 31 - 40
   ( ) 41 - 50
   ( ) 51 - 70
   ( ) 71 - 90
   ( ) More than 90 members - how many? ______________

4. How many members did the church have five years ago?
   ( ) It doesn't have more members than it did five years ago
   ( ) Up to 5 members more
   ( ) 5 - 10
   ( ) 11 - 20
   ( ) 21 - 30
   ( ) 31 - 40
   ( ) 41 - 50
   ( ) 51 - 70

( ) 71 - 90
( ) More than 90 members, how many? ______________

5. In the last five years was there another church or congregation founded by the ministers of this church?
( ) No
( ) One church or congregation was established
( ) Two churches or congregations were established
( ) Three churches or congregations were established
( ) More than three churches or congregations were established

6. As to the buildings of the church.
( ) The church has its own building
( ) It is in construction
( ) It is being enlarged
( ) Building is only temporary
( ) None of the above

7. What is the monthly budget of the church?
( ) Up to Cr$ 500
( ) Cr$ 500 - 1.000
( ) 1.000 - 2.000
( ) 2.000 - 4.000
( ) 4.000 - 10.000
( ) More than 10.000

8. The pastor works
( ) Full time in the work of this church
( ) Full time in this church but responsibility for other churches
( ) Part time but only has the pastoral responsibilities of this church
( ) Part time and responsible for other churches
( ) The church does not have a pastor at the moment
( ) The system of government of the church does not have a pastor

9. How long has the pastor been working at this church?
( ) Less than 1 year
( ) 1 - 2 years
( ) 3 - 5 years
( ) 6 - 10 years
( ) 11 - 25 years
( ) 26 years or more

10. What is the educational level of the pastor?
( ) Primary
( ) High School
( ) College
( ) Bible Institute
( ) Seminary
( ) University
( ) ______________

11. Is the pastor taking special courses at the present?
    ( ) No
    ( ) High School
    ( ) College
    ( ) Bible Institute
    ( ) Seminary
    ( ) University
    ( ) ______________________________

12. What is the age of the pastor?
    ( ) Up to 24 years
    ( ) 25 - 30
    ( ) 31 - 40
    ( ) 41 - 50
    ( ) 51 - 60
    ( ) 61 years or more

FIGURE 3

TABULATION SHEET - 1

Category of people tabulated on this sheet ____________

Total number of people tabulated on this sheet ____________

3. Age of conversion

____________ - 12
____________ 13 - 17
____________ 18 - 30
____________ 31 -

4. The most important aspect of conversion

____________ people
____________ ways
____________ happening
____________ message

5. People indicated as the most important in the conversion

____________ father
____________ mother
____________ neighbor
____________ teacher in S.S.
____________ brother/sister
____________ colleague
____________ pastor
____________ wife/husband
____________ teacher
____________ missionary
____________ official
____________ family
____________ old friend
____________ new friend
____________ preacher
____________ boss
____________ son or daughter
____________ other

6. Ways indicated as the two most important in the conversion

____________ radio
____________ S. School
____________ magazine or journal
____________ service in church
____________ camp
____________ evangelistic campaign

- ________ house meeting
- ________ Bible reading
- ________ evangelical music
- ________ Bible study
- ________ retreat
- ________ visitation
- ________ open air meeting
- ________ film
- ________ hospital
- ________ tract
- ________ other

7. Happenings indicated as the most important in the conversion

- ________ death of friend
- ________ crisis in life
- ________ promise
- ________ friend turned believer
- ________ miracle
- ________ death in family
- ________ vision
- ________ difficulty
- ________ blessing
- ________ cure
- ________ Christian fellowship
- ________ family becoming Christian
- ________ sickness
- ________ other

8. Message of the Gospel - the two most important in conversion

- ________ God loves me
- ________ God the judge
- ________ gives happiness
- ________ saves from Hell
- ________ sent His Son
- ________ guilt removed
- ________ my necessity
- ________ blood purifies
- ________ Christ crucified
- ________ hope
- ________ Christ returning
- ________ friend of the humble
- ________ Christ miracle worker
- ________ Christ cures
- ________ Christ gives peace
- ________ Christ the Resurrection
- ________ Christ the Liberator
- ________ other

9. Attendance at services each week

____________________ - 1
____________________ 1 - 2
____________________ 2 -

10. Is an official in the church

____________________ Yes

11. Teaches in the Sunday School

____________________ Yes

12. Participates in the Choir or Band

____________________ Yes

13. Preaches in church or other services

____________________ Yes

14. Is a tither

____________________ Yes

15. Invites others to the church

____________________ Yes

16. Has been used by God to help someone else be converted

____________________ Yes

17. The two items that have most helped in Christian growth

____________________ No

____________________ worship service
____________________ camp
____________________ prayer meeting
____________________ Sunday School
____________________ conferences
____________________ Y.P. meetings
____________________ evangelistic service
____________________ Bible studies
____________________ retreat
____________________ activities
____________________ giving testimony
____________________ hearing testimonies
____________________ communion

______ choir
______ band
______ personal evangelism
______ preaching
______ teaching
______ family devotions
______ Bible reading
______ prayer
______ radio
______ literature
______ records
______ correspondence
______ other

18. Age

______ - 12
______ 13 - 17
______ 18 - 30
______ 31 -

19. Sex

______ masc.

20. Brought up in

______ large city
______ small city
______ rural area

21. Born where now living

______ Yes

22. Already was believer when arrived where actually live now

______ Yes

23. Was converted soon after arrival

______ Yes

24. Arrived where actually live

______ - 1
______ 1 - 2
______ 3 - 5
______ 6 - 10
______ 11 -

25. Of another denomination

____

26. Have attended another denomination

________________ Yes

27. Religion in which one was raised

________________ Evangelical
________________ Catholic
________________ Spiritist

28. Degree of instruction

________________ none
________________ Primary
________________ Junior High
________________ High School
________________ University

29. Monthly salary of the family

________________ - 300
________________ 300 - 600
________________ 600 - 1.000
________________ 1.000 - 2.000
________________ 2.000 - 4.000
________________ 4.000 -

FIGURE 4

TABULATION SHEET - 2

	TOTAL	WITHOUT EVANGELICAL BACKGROUND		WITH EVANGELICAL BACKGROUND			
		Masc.	Fem.	Masc.	Fem.		
TOTAL							
Age of conversion 12 years or less							
13 - 17 years							
18 - 30 years							
31 years and above							
Principal aspect Person							
Method							
Happenings							
Message							
Principal persons 1.							
2.							
3.							
4.							
5.							
Principal methods 1.							
2.							
3.							
4.							
5.							
Principal happenings 1.							
2.							
3.							
4.							
5.							
Principal Messages 1.							
2.							
3.							
4.							
5.							
Attend each week Less than one time							
One to two times							
More than two times							
Official of the church							
Teaches in the S. S.							
Choir or Band							
Preaches							

Tithes							
Invites others							
Used in the conversion							
Principal helps							
1.							
2.							
3.							
4.							
5.							
Age							
12 years or less							
13 - 17 years							
18 - 30 years							
31 years and above							
Sex							
Masculine							
Feminine							
Raised in large city							
Small city							
Rural section							
Migrants							
Believer on arrival							
Converted afterwards							
Arrived less than 1 year							
1 - 2 years							
3 - 5 years							
6 - 10 years							
11 years or more							
Of another denomination							
Attended another							
Was raised							
Evangelical							
Catholic							
Spiritist							
Other							
Degree of instruction							
None							
Primary							
Junior High							
High School							
University							
Monthly salary by family							
Up to Cr$ 300							
300 - 600							
600 - 1.000							
1.000 - 2.000							
2.000 - 4.000							
4.000 and above							

FIGURE 5

HOW GOD IS CALLING PERSONS TO HIMSELF

INTRODUCTION: God uses many ways and means to call men. Paul said that he sought by all means to save some (I Corinthians 9:22). In the conversion of each one, God can use different persons, circumstances, means, and even different aspects of His great gospel. To be more effective witnesses, we need to understand better how God is working. Please cooperate, answering these questions about your own conversion.

1. Do you remember when you were converted? ( ) Yes
( ) No

2. How long has it been? ______________________________

3. What was your age when you were converted?

( ) 12 years or less
( ) 13 - 17 years
( ) 18 - 30 years
( ) 31 or more

4. Describe in a few words your conversion ______________

____

____

____

5. Who were the PERSONS used of God in your conversion? (Indicate not by name but by category, e.g., FATHER, MOTHER, etc., according to LIST A in the order given by the informant).

1. ________ 2. ________ 3. ________ 4. ________

6. What were the MEANS he used? (Indicate by category according to LIST B, in the order given by the informant.)

1. ________ 2. ________ 3. ________ 4. ________

7. What events were used by God? (Indicate by category according to LIST C, in the order given by the informant.)

1. ________ 2. ________ 3. ________ 4. ________

8. Which aspects of the MESSAGE of the gospel did God use to speak to your heart that you might be converted? (Indicate by category according to LIST D, in the order given by the informant.)

   1. ________ 2. ________ 3. ________ 4. ________

9. Who was the first Evangelical in your family? (By category according to LIST A.)

   ____

10. Who was the second Evangelical in your family? (By category according to LIST A.)

    ____

11. Where were you living when you were converted?

    ____
    Township State

12. Before you were converted, what was your religion?

    ____

13. When you were born, what was the religion of your parents? (Indicate according to LIST E.)

    ____

14. In what religion were you raised? (Indicate according to LIST E.)

    ____

15. To what denomination do you belong?

    ____

16. Have you attended regularly some other denomination?

    ( ) Yes
    ( ) No

17. If so, which? ______________________________

18. On the average, how many times per week do you attend church services?

    Less than once per week ( )
    One or two times ( )
    Three or more times ( )

19. Do you teach in the Sunday School?

( ) Yes
( ) No

20. Do you have an official position in the church?

( ) Yes
( ) No

21. Do you participate in the church choir, band, or musical group?

( ) Yes
( ) No

22. Do you preach in the church or in its services?

( ) Yes
( ) No

23. Are you a member of the church?

( ) Yes
( ) No

24. Are you a tither?

( ) Yes
( ) No

25. Do you regularly invite people to go with you to church?

( ) Yes
( ) No

26. Have you, personally, already led someone to know Christ as Savior and Lord?

( ) Yes
( ) No

27. What things have helped most in your growth in the Christian life?
(Indicate according to LIST B; CAREFUL WITH THE HINTS)

1. ________ 2. ________ 3. ________ 4. ________

28. Name ______________________________

29. Date of Birth ______________________________

30. Place of birth ______________________

31. Marital status ______________________

32. Sex ______________________

33. Profession ______________________

34. Address ______________________

35. Distance from home to church ______________________

36. Type of house ______________________

37. Own ______________________

38. Rent ______________________

39. Maintain for owner ______________________

40. Number of persons in the house ______________________

41. Number of persons in the family ______________________

42. Number of employed persons in the household ____________

43. Source of income ______________________

44. How long have you lived at this address? ____________

45. Where did you live before that? ______________________

46. For how long? ______________________

47. And before that? ______________________

48. For how long? ______________________

49. Father's name ______________________

50. Mother's name ______________________

51. Are your parents believers? Father ______________________

Mother ______________________

52. What other members of your family are believers?

1. __________ 2. __________ 3. __________ 4. __________

53. What is your educational level?

Incomplete primary	( )
Complete primary	( )
Junior high	( )
High school	( )
University	( )

LIST A

a. Husband (wife)
b. Father
c. Mother
d. Son
e. Daughter
f. Older brother
g. Younger brother
h. Older sister
i. Younger sister
j. Godfather
l. Godmother
m. Godchild
n. Older relative (male)
o. Younger relative (male)
p. Older relative (female)
q. Younger relative (female)
r. Older non-relative (male)
s. Younger non-relative (male)
t. Older non-relative (female)
u. Younger non-relative (female)
v. Friend
x. Relative
z. Pastor
aa. Missionary
bb. Lay preacher
cc. Church worker
dd. Evangelist

LIST B

a. Bible
b. Preaching (hearing)
c. Testimonies
d. Example
e. Teaching
f. Radio program
g. Tract
h. Evangelistic church service
i. Evangelistic open air service
j. House meeting
l. Sunday school
m. Evangelical literature
n. Camp
o. Evangelistic campaign
p. Music
q. Spiritual retreat
r. Film
s. Prayer meeting
t. Special meetings
u. Youth meeting
v. Church activities
x. Testifying
z. Christian discipleship
aa. Fellowship with the brethren
bb. Choir
cc. Band
dd. Personal evangelism
ee. Preaching (doing)
ff. Teaching in the Sunday School (doing)
gg. Bible study course

LIST C

a. Personal crisis
b. Sickness
c. Family crisis
d. Vow
e. Dream
f. Vision
g. Friend who became a believer
h. Miracle
i. Death in the family
j. Personal blessing
l. Healing
m. Friendship with believers
n. Relatives who became believers.

LIST D

a. The guilt of my sin
b. God is the judge of the sinner
c. My need of God
d. God loves me
e. God gives joy
f. God saves from hell
g. God sent his Son
h. The blood of Christ cleanses
i. Christ crucified in my place
j. Christ gives hope
l. Christ will return
m. Christ the friend of the humble
n. Christ performs miracles
o. Christ heals
p. Christ gives peace
q. Christ rose from the dead
r. Christ frees the sinner

LIST E

a. Born in an Evangelical family
b. Raised in an Evangelical home
c. Catholic
d. Umbanda
e. Spiritism
f. Jehovah's Witnesses
g. Nominal Evangelical
h. Mormon
i. Buddhist
j. Indifferent
l. None

Appendix 2: Data Bank

INTRODUCTION

During the course of the BRAZIL 1980 Project, a tremendous amount of data about the membership and leadership of the Protestant churches in Brazil between 1955 and 1970 has been collected. The background of the computer programming that was done and the sources of the data are described in Appendix 3.

One of the difficulties of handling a mass of data like this is the data entry problem. Almost 100 denominations are covered by the Brazilian census, and these denominations are found in 3,997 counties which are in 361 micro-regions. If the researcher or inquirer were interested in learning about the activity of the Protestant church in a given geographical location in Brazil, he would want to look it up under a geographical heading. If, on the other hand, he was interested in information about the particular church or denomination, he would want to look it up under that name. If he looked in the geographical listing, he might have to go through more than 2,000 pages of computer print-out to find what he wanted.

The situation has been previously described in the introductions of Chapters 3, 4, and 5, where a geographical distribution versus denomination distribution chart was given. At the beginning of each one of these chapters the chart was used to explain which factors were being described. Figure 1 indicates the magnitude of the problem. Each one of the filled blocks represents a bank of data.

FIGURE 1

	GEOGRAPHICAL DISTRIBUTION						
DENOMINATIONAL DISTRIBUTION	**Country**	**Major Region (5)**	**State (27)**	**Urban Region (112)**	**Micro Region (361)**	**County (3,997)**	**District (15,000+)**
All Protestants	A B C		A D		A B E	A	
Categories					A		
Traditions					A		
Denominations	C		D		E	A	
Local Church							

In order to get around this data entry problem, a number of different computer-produced printouts were made, pages of which are reproduced in the figures which follow. Computer printouts which are available both at CASE and MARC include the following:

By Geography

A. Church Growth by Micro-regions. A 2,653 page report, dated January 31, 1973, which divides Brazil by states, counties and micro-regions. It lists the individual denominations within counties, and the traditions (groups), giving totals for each within the state.

B. Church Growth by Micro-regions. A 45 page report, dated March 23, 1973, which gives total Protestant church growth data for each micro-region.

By Denomination

C. Church Growth by Denomination. A 12-page report dated March 23, 1973, which gives country totals for each denomination.

D. Church Growth by State within the Denomination. A 131 page report, dated March 23, 1973, which gives the denominational totals within each state.

E. Church Growth by Micro-regions within Denomination. A 1,409 page report dated January 31, 1973, which gives denominational growth within Brazil, listed by micro-regions.

Figure 1 indicates by the letters within each block which of these reports covers what area.

CHURCH GROWTH BY MICRO-REGIONS

Two pages of the church growth by micro-region report are reproduced in Figure 2 and Figure 3.

Figure 2 indicates how one would go about analyzing a county *(municipio)* within Brazil. This figure gives the situation in county 17-Duque de Caxais. It indicates that eight denominations have work within the county. The headings at the top explain the three groups of data listed for each denomination. For example, in the first column we have three lines of data for denomination 1 (DEN 1) The Assemblies of God (ASSEM DE DEUS). The first entry, 3,023, is the government census data as of 1955. The second line, 3,582, is the census data for 1956. The third line ("CC") is the number of central churches, namely one.

The second column of data listed under "EXCL," "% GR," and "SC" is the number of exclusions - 140; percentage growth rate, using 3,023 and a growth to 3,582; and the number of satellite churches - 0. The same data is repeated for each of the years through 1965-1966. The far right-hand column - TOTAL %GR - is the total percentage of church growth between 1955 and 1966 for this particular denomination.

One of the reasons for giving the complete data for each of the 2-year periods is to check on reporting errors. For instance, looking at denomination 39, independent Presbyterians, we see an entry under 1965-1966 of 46 members with 19 exclusions. When the next reporting data is available for the following years from the census bureau, it will be interesting to see whether this was a reporting error or whether a new work was actually started by the independent Presbyterians during 1965. Another type of situation is shown in denomination 52, Congregational. Here we see a situation where no membership or exclusions were reported for 1965-1966. A number of things are possible. It could be there was just a failure on the part of the census taker, or that this local congregation switched its allegiance to another major group, or it might mean that the church was disbanded.

It should be noted that the name of individual churches is not listed within the county. However, by looking at the number of central churches ("CC") and satellite churches ("SC"), one is able to quickly ascertain how many congregations existed, and thus get a rough idea of the size of the individual churches as well as the proliferation of satellite churches.

Figure 3 is an eight-page report, "Church Growth by Categories and Denominational Groups." This figure indicates that if one were interested in looking at the growth of traditions within a state, he could look at the total situation for the state for Lutherans, Presbyterians, Methodists, Congregationalists, etc. You would also find under "CAT 1 TOTAL" the data for all of the traditional churches.

CHURCH GROWTH BY MICRO-REGIONS

Figure 4 gives the same data that we found in Figures 2 and 3, except the totals for micro-regions are conveniently put together along with the location of the micro-region within the s ate. Thus the first heading is Micro-region 1, which is found in state 1, Rôndonia.

In addition, on the basis of a compound percent curve, both projections have been made for the states for the years 1970, 1972, 1974, 1976, 1978, and 1980. Caution should be taken in using this projection data as anything more than what it is - a projection of the current growth rate. The fact that the church has been growing at this particular rate over a ten-year period is no guarantee that it will continue to grow at this rate. The research is encouraged to plot the data for each of the years given and to look at the shape of the resulting curve.

CHURCH GROWTH BY DENOMINATIONS

Figure 5 indicates the total church growth for each of the denominations in Brazil. In addition to the data that was given in Figures 2 and 3, the same kind of projection information that has been given on Figure 4 has been calculated. Again, the note of caution should be taken in the use of this data. (See above).

CHURCH GROWTH BY STATE WITHIN DENOMINATIONS

Figure 6 is the same type of data that was given in Figure 5, except this time each denomination is broken down by its figures within the state. Thus on Figure 6, we have denomination 1, the Assemblies of God, and an example of its state data for eight states. Subsequent pages of the report show all of the other states in which the Assemblies of God is found along with totals for the Assemblies of God.

Using this report, anyone interested in a particular denomination, would be able to trace its situation, state by state.

CHURCH GROWTH BY MICRO-REGIONS WITHIN DENOMINATIONS

Figure 7 has the same basic type of information as Figure 6. However, this time, those interested in searching data by micro-region for a denomination have the listing of every micro-region in which every denomination is found. State and country totals are also given.

USING THE DATA TOGETHER

From the information included in this BRAZIL 1980 Data Bank it is possible to analyze the situation almost to the total church level for any micro-regions. For instance, suppose that you were interested in a certain denomination's work within a given micro-region. By examining the report entitled, Church Growth by Micro-regions within Denominations, you could quickly look up the situation for your denomination within a given micro-region. Having found this, however, you might then be interested in knowing what other denominations were doing within the same micro-region. By turning to the report entitled Church Growth by Micro-regions, and looking up the micro-region in question, you would find a listing of what all of the other churches are doing in this area. Thus, we have data which is useful at both the national, state, micro-region and county level.

FIGURE 2

BRAZIL 1980; CG BY MICRO REGIONS — STATE OF RIO DE JANEIRO — COUNTRY PAGE 1108

REPORT DATE 1/31/73 — MICRO-REGION 221 — STATE PAGE 49

CHURCH GROWTH BY COUNTIES AND DENOMINATIONS — REPORT PAGE 1

STATE 18	1955- 1956 CC	EXCL % GR SC	1957- 1958 CC	EXCL % GR SC	1959- 1960 CC	EXCL % GR SC	1961- 1962 CC	EXCL % GR SC	1963- 1964 CC	EXCL % GR SC	1965- 1966 CC	EXCL % GR SC	TOTAL % GR
COUNTY 17-DUQUE DE CAXIAS													
DEN 1	3,023	140	3,986	233	5,711	344	7,293	560	8,978	227	11,530	502	
ASSEM DE DEUS	3,582	18.5	4,481	12.4	6,473	13.3	8,132	11.5	10,294	14.7	13,207	14.5	336.9
	1	0	1	1	2	9	2	10	2	16	2	19	
DEN 33	1,446	185	1,820	153	2,808	265	2,932	694	2,788	265	3,709	824	
BATISTA	1,684	16.5	2,065	13.5	3,298	17.5	2,871	2.1-	3,151	13.0	5,097	37.4	252.5
	10	0	12	14	13	18	13	18	12	18	29	36	
DEN 38	451	0	539	88	519	7	653	196	653	97	862	161	
PRESBITERIANA	494	9.5	527	2.2-	602	16.0	519	20.5-	661	1.2	1,011	17.3	124.2
	1	0	1	1	3	3	3	6	4	9	5	9	
DEN 39	0	0	0	0	0	0	0	0	0	0	0	19	
PRES INDEPENDENT	0	.0	0	.0	0	.0	0	.0	0	.0	46	.0	.0
	0	0	0	0	0	0	0	0	0	0	1	1	
DEN 43	0	0	0	5	196	0	215	6	314	157	550	4	
ADVENTISTA	0	.0	160	.0	199	1.5	259	20.5	307	2.2-	591	7.5	269.4
	0	0	1	1	1	1	1	1	1	1	1	7	
DEN 48	346	21	489	53	551	13	657	125	643	75	566	41	
METODISTA	414	19.7	546	11.7	605	9.8	600	8.7-	631	1.9-	636	12.4	83.8
	2	0	2	5	3	3	3	8	3	8	4	8	
DEN 52	97	9	125	14	125	22	114	14	144	16	0	0	
CONGREGACIONAL	94	3.1-	134	7.2	111	11.2-	125	9.6	137	4.9-	0	.0	41.2
	2	0	3	3	3	4	3	3	3	4	0	0	
DEN 66	0	0	0	0	0	0	0	0	0	0	97	6	
CASA DE ORACAO	0	.0	0	.0	0	.0	0	.0	0	.0	104	7.2	7.2
	0	0	0	0	0	0	0	0	0	0	2	3	
COUNTY 17 TOTAL	5,363	355	6,959	546	9,910	651	11,864	1,595	13,520	837	17,314	1,557	
	6,268	16.9	7,913	13.7	11,288	13.9	12,506	5.4	15,181	12.3	20,692	19.5	285.8
	16	0	20	25	25	38	25	46	25	56	44	83	
COUNTY 18-ITABORAI													
DEN 1	501	31	649	43	521	98	402	14	404	21	1,419	142	
ASSEM DE DEUS	579	15.6	542	16.5-	437	16.1-	410	2.0	500	23.8	1,542	8.7	207.8
	2	0	2	2	2	6	2	6	1	5	2	15	

FIGURE 3

BRAZIL 1980; CG BY MICRO REGIONS

REPORT DATE 1/31/73

STATE OF RIO DE JANEIRO
MICRO-REGION 221
CHURCH GROWTH BY CATEGORIES AND DENOMINATIONAL GROUPS

COUNTRY PAGE 1117
STATE PAGE 58
REPORT PAGE 1

STATE 18	1955- 1956 CC	EXCL % GR SC	1957- 1958 CC	EXCL % GR SC	1959- 1960 CC	EXCL % GR SC	1961- 1962 CC	EXCL % GR SC	1963- 1964 CC	EXCL % GR SC	1965- 1966 CC	EXCL % GR SC	TOTAL % GR
GRP 1	0	0	0	0	0	0	0	0	10	1	14	0	
LUTERANAS	0	.0	0	.0	0	.0	0	.0	12	20.0	14	.0	40.0
	0	0	0	0	0	0	0	0	1	1	1	1	
GRP 2	2.679	64	2.830	417	3.262	191	4.060	501	4.543	757	4.944	634	
PRESBITERANAS	2.945	9.9	2.591	8.4-	3.738	14.6	4.026	.8-	4.621	1.7	5.859	18.5	118.7
	14	0	14	21	17	28	19	34	25	46	32	57	
GRP 3	1.549	112	1.073	85	2.081	472	1.832	289	2.119	264	2.322	251	
METODISTAS	1.746	12.7	1.264	17.8	1.911	8.2-	1.861	1.6	2.390	12.8	2.498	7.6	61.3
	11	0	8	15	13	18	13	24	17	30	22	32	
GRP 4	3.350	284	3.225	431	3.631	182	3.490	346	3.404	587	3.057	251	
CONGREGACIONAIS	3.871	15.6	2.818	12.6-	3.786	4.3	3.386	3.0-	3.243	4.7-	3.433	12.3	2.5
	29	0	28	37	31	41	31	45	32	48	33	48	
GRP 5	257	0	287	28	292	46	285	48	228	1	0	0	
EPISCOPAIS	280	8.9	283	1.4-	281	3.8-	251	11.9-	277	21.5	0	.0	7.8
	1	0	1	1	1	1	1	1	1	1	0	0	
GRP 6	10.267	1.046	11.373	1.484	14.143	1.947	16.114	2.609	18.181	2.019	23.953	3.535	
BATISTAS	11.787	14.8	11.328	.4-	15.002	6.1	16.382	1.7	21.349	17.4	28.216	17.8	174.8
	73	0	75	101	81	116	89	138	132	198	176	289	
GRP 7	225	0	104	4	141	7	333	39	258	19	518	48	
OUTRAS TRAD	275	22.2	106	1.9	182	29.1	342	2.7	323	25.2	712	37.5	216.4
	3	0	1	1	2	2	4	5	5	5	7	12	
CAT 1 TOTAL	18.327	1.506	18.892	2.449	23.550	2.845	26.114	3.832	28.743	3.648	34.808	4.719	
IG TRADICIONAIS	20.904	14.1	18.390	2.7-	24.900	5.7	26.248	.5	32.215	12.1	40.732	17.0	122.3
	131	0	127	176	145	206	157	247	213	329	271	439	
GRP 8	12.450	685	17.235	1.571	21.788	1.095	26.876	1.874	33.318	1.483	49.214	3.011	
ASSEMBLEIAS	14.481	16.3	18.034	4.6	24.128	10.7	29.894	11.2	36.997	11.0	53.460	8.6	329.4
	30	0	28	49	22	161	21	168	20	206	32	308	
GRP 10	0	0	0	0	0	0	0	0	85	15	130	0	
OUTRAS PENT	0	.0	0	.0	0	.0	0	.0	85	.0	280	115.4	229.4
	0	0	1	1	1	1	0	0	1	2	1	3	
CAT 2 TOTAL	12.450	685	17.235	1.571	21.788	1.095	26.876	1.874	33.403	1.498	49.344	3.011	
IG PENTECOSTAIS	14.481	16.3	18.034	4.6	24.128	10.7	29.894	11.2	37.082	11.0	53.740	8.9	331.6
	30	0	29	50	23	162	21	168	21	208	33	311	

FIGURE 4

BRAZIL 1980; CG BY MICRO-REGION — COUNTRY PAGE 1

REPORT DATE 3/23/73

	1955- 1956 CC	EXCL % GR SC	1957- 1958 CC	EXCL % GR SC	1959- 1960 CC	EXCL % GR SC	1961- 1962 CC	EXCL % GR SC	1963- 1964 CC	EXCL % GR SC	1965- 1966 CC	EXCL % GR SC	TOTAL % GR
M/R 1	1.807	153	2.246	25	2.892	32	3.104	18	3.542	29	3.759	16	
STATE 1	2.003	10.8	2.637	17.4	3.136	8.4	3.202	3.2	3.646	2.9	3.996	6.3	121.1
RONDONIA	5	10	5	10	5	10	7	14	8	18	8	20	
PROJECTION PERCENTAGE	5.3												
GROWTH PROJECTIONS	1970-	4.913	1972-	5.448	1974-	6.041	1976-	6.698	1978-	7.427	1980-	8.235	
M/R 2	802	59	1.002	17	1.032	37	1.169	14	1.465	12	1.590	122	
STATE 2	849	5.9	1.058	5.6	1.017	1.5-	1.190	1.8	1.513	3.3	1.689	6.2	110.6
ACRE	5	0	5	9	5	17	6	19	6	17	6	18	
PROJECTION PERCENTAGE	7.5												
GROWTH PROJECTIONS	1970-	2.256	1972-	2.607	1974-	3.013	1976-	3.482	1978-	4.024	1980-	4.650	
M/R 3	1.677	28	2.294	39	1.066	5	2.564	20	3.314	37	3.533	20	
STATE 2	1.788	6.6	2.479	8.1	1.184	11.1	2.812	9.7	3.581	8.1	4.060	15.5	143.3
ACRE	5	0	5	9	5	10	6	8	7	13	10	19	
PROJECTION PERCENTAGE	9.7												
GROWTH PROJECTIONS	1970-	5.909	1972-	7.111	1974-	8.557	1976-	10.298	1978-	12.393	1980-	14.914	
M/R 4	251	0	214	2	388	3	420	6	1.574	11	1.245	152	
STATE 3	335	33.5	331	54.7	478	23.2	609	45.0	1.968	25.0	2.513	101.8	901.2
AMAZONAS	3	0	3	6	3	6	2	5	4	9	7	714	
PROJECTION PERCENTAGE	43.0												
GROWTH PROJECTIONS	1970-	10.508	1972-	21.488	1974-	43.941	1976-	89.355	1978-	183.744	1980-	375.738	
M/R 5	0	0	0	0	0	0	36	2	121	11	0	8	
STATE 3	0	.0	0	.0	0	.0	58	61.1	130	7.4	158	.0	338.9
AMAZONAS	0	0	0	0	0	0	1	2	2	2	2	144	
PROJECTION PERCENTAGE	34.4												
GROWTH PROJECTIONS	1970-	516	1972-	932	1974-	1.684	1976-	3.042	1978-	5.495	1980-	9.926	
M/R 6	212	3	531	11	767	8	1.466	40	406	4	0	9	
STATE 3	251	18.4	630	18.6	792	3.3	1.559	6.3	462	18.7	1.369	.0	545.8
AMAZONAS	3	0	4	4	4	9	4	7	4	11	5	1.302	
PROJECTION PERCENTAGE	.0												
GROWTH PROJECTIONS	1970-		1972-		1974-		1976-		1978-		1980-		
M/R 7	103	0	152	23	153	30	99	1	160	11	141	42	
STATE 3	116	12.6	149	2.0-	160	4.6	109	10.1	158	1.3-	176	24.8	70.9
AMAZONAS	2	0	2	3	3	4	2	5	2	2	3	73	
PROJECTION PERCENTAGE	12.2												
GROWTH PROJECTIONS	1970-	279	1972-	351	1974-	442	1976-	556	1978-	700	1980-	881	
M/R 8	0	0	0	0	0	0	199	10	204	3	0	1	
STATE 3	0	.0	0	.0	0	.0	204	2.5	239	17.2	312	.0	56.8
AMAZONAS	0	0	1	0	0	0	1	4	1	4	1	313	
PROJECTION PERCENTAGE	9.4												
GROWTH PROJECTIONS	1970-	447	1972-	535	1974-	640	1976-	766	1978-	917	1980-	1.097	

FIGURE 5

BRAZIL 1980; CG BY DENOMINATION

COUNTRY PAGE 1

REPORT DATE 3/23/73

	1955-1956 CC	EXCL % GR SC	1957-1958 CC	EXCL % GR SC	1959-1960 CC	EXCL % GR SC	1961-1962 CC	EXCL % GR SC	1963-1964 CC	EXCL % GR SC	1965-1966 CC	EXCL % GR SC	TOTAL % GR
DEN 1	255.954	13.074	323.042	22.168	386.879	24.526	426.197	23.416	511.812	29.666	579.653	35.382	
ASSEM DE DEUS	290.902	13.7	356.572	10.4	426.974	10.4	452.850	6.3	553.358	8.1	630.370	8.7	146.3
	1.100	26	1.003	2.620	1.083	3.687	1.168	4.336	1.245	5.332	1.291	9.399	
PROJECTION PERCENTAGE 8.1													
GROWTH PROJECTIONS	1970-	860.792	1972-	1005.888	1974-	1175.441	1976-	1373.575	1978-	1805.106	1980-	1875.664	
DEN 2	91.515	2.607	154.517	8.188	173.712	7.556	191.558	7.769	236.063	12.136	266.484	13.030	
CONG C NO BRASIL	123.195	34.6	172.073	11.4	186.547	7.4	205.415	7.2	255.827	8.4	282.233	5.9	208.4
	450	0	506	750	612	844	686	1.005	796	1.348	826	1.546	
PROJECTION PERCENTAGE 8.1													
GROWTH PROJECTIONS	1970-	385.399	1972-	450.362	1974-	526.275	1976-	614.984	1978-	718.646	1980-	839.782	
DEN 3	0	0	390	7	333	20	314	4	544	74	2.033	542	
O BRASIL PARA CR	0	.0	416	6.7	380	14.1	330	5.1	765	40.6	4.697	131.0	1104.4
	0	0	1	1	3	5	1	9	8	12	17	70	
PROJECTION PERCENTAGE 71.8													
GROWTH PROJECTIONS	1970-	40.918	1972-	120.770	1974-	356.456	1976-	1052.088	1978-	3105.263	1980-	9165.258	
DEN 4	1.577	48	2.605	488	6.187	291	11.956	463	14.528	1.183	20.869	769	
EV QUANDRANGULAR	2.080	31.9	3.310	27.1	10.209	65.0	12.842	7.4	16.341	12.5	25.071	20.1	1489.8
	7	0	9	21	20	41	29	66	39	72	57	127	
PROJECTION PERCENTAGE 15.9													
GROWTH PROJECTIONS	1970-	45.238	1972-	60.767	1974-	81.627	1976-	109.648	1978-	147.288	1980-	197.849	
DEN 5	0	0	1.576	50	2.081	249	2.418	220	2.633	125	3.624	372	
CRUZ N DE EVAN	0	.0	1.793	13.8	2.058	1.1-	2.540	5.0	2.982	13.3	4.912	35.5	211.7
	0	0	7	9	11	12	15	17	19	24	24	44	
PROJECTION PERCENTAGE 15.3													
GROWTH PROJECTIONS	1970-	8.681	1972-	11.541	1974-	15.343	1976-	20.397	1978-	27.116	1980-	36.048	
DEN 6	82	7	1.244	57	2.515	78	3.273	801	2.129	240	52	2	
EV DO AVIV BIB	111	35.4	1.454	16.9	3.162	25.7	1.672	48.9-	2.298	7.9	58	11.5	29.3-
	4	0	10	36	13	57	8	25	12	34	1	4	
PROJECTION PERCENTAGE .0													
GROWTH PROJECTIONS	1970-		1972-		1974-		1976-		1978-		1980-		
DEN 7	0	0	40	0	80	2	164	8	305	11	416	113	
CRUZ BIB SAGRADA	0	.0	50	25.0	106	32.5	181	10.4	344	12.8	309	25.7-	672.5
	0	0	2	3	1	1	4	4	6	7	3	3	
PROJECTION PERCENTAGE 13.4													
GROWTH PROJECTIONS	1970-	511	1972-	657	1974-	845	1976-	1.087	1978-	1.398	1980-	1.798	
DEN 8	1.735	75	289	50	703	50	68	2	500	26	0	0	
PENT INDEPEND	1.939	11.8	303	4.8	795	13.1	80	17.6	503	.6	0	.0	71.0-
	13	0	5	8	7	14	4	4	4	6	1	1	
PROJECTION PERCENTAGE 94.8													
GROWTH PROJECTIONS	1970-	27.485	1972-	104.297	1974-	395.776	1976-	1501.853	1978-	5699.088	1980-	2146.352	

FIGURE 6

BRAZIL 1980; CG BY STATE WITHIN DENOMINATION — COUNTRY PAGE 1

REPORT DATE 3/23/73 — DENOMINATION PAGE 1

DEN 1	1955-	EXCL	1957-	EXCL	1959-	EXCL	1961-	EXCL	1963-	EXCL	1965-	EXCL	TOTAL
ASSEM DE DEUS	1956	% GR	1958	% GR	1960	% GR	1962	% GR	1964	% GR	1966	% GR	% GR
	CC	SC	CC	SC	CC	SC	CC	SC	CC	SC	CC	SC	
STATE 1	1,672	133	2,099	22	2,720	16	2,750	8	3,096	3	3,394	11	
RONDONIA	1,865	11.5	2,475	17.9	2,953	8.6	2,822	2.6	3,168	2.3	3,475	2.4	107.8
	2	6	2	6	2	6	2	9	2	12	2	14	
PROJECTION PERCENTAGE 4.7													
GROWTH PROJECTIONS	1970- 4,176		1972- 4,578		1974- 5,018		1976- 5,501		1978- 6,030		1980- 6,610		
STATE 2	1,816	54	2,342	50	1,002	37	2,566	12	3,526	23	4,229	103	
ACRE	1,905	4.9	2,482	6.0	1,093	9.1	2,809	9.5	3,830	8.6	4,814	13.8	165.1
	5	0	5	10	5	12	6	12	7	14	9	20	
PROJECTION PERCENTAGE 13.4													
GROWTH PROJECTIONS	1970- 7,961		1972- 10,237		1974- 13,164		1976- 16,928		1978- 21,769		1980- 27,994		
STATE 3	1,563	96	2,366	55	3,244	63	4,404	52	3,587	53	3,546	55	
AMAZONAS	1,714	9.7	2,650	12.0	3,545	9.3	4,752	7.9	4,078	13.7	5,886	65.9	276.6
	5	0	5	13	5	17	6	17	6	21	10	1,970	
PROJECTION PERCENTAGE 5.9													
GROWTH PROJECTIONS	1970- 7,403		1972- 8,302		1974- 9,311		1976- 10,442		1978- 11,711		1980- 13,134		
STATE 4	250	4	332	3	472	0	494	1	781	2	1,292	15	
RORAIMA	300	20.0	426	28.3	474	.4	577	16.8	1,292	65.4	1,344	4.0	437.6
	1	0	1	1	1	4	1	4	1	5	1	9	
PROJECTION PERCENTAGE 22.2													
GROWTH PROJECTIONS	1970- 2,997		1972- 4,475		1974- 6,682		1976- 9,978		1978- 14,900		1980- 22,250		
STATE 5	21,879	1,017	25,615	1,784	27,212	605	32,983	1,967	30,556	1,403	33,523	1,420	
PARA	23,891	9.2	27,596	7.7	30,029	10.4	28,633	13.2-	32,773	7.3	37,937	13.2	73.4
	82	0	70	181	75	217	84	247	90	281	96	327	
PROJECTION PERCENTAGE 2.8													
GROWTH PROJECTIONS	1970- 42,368		1972- 44,774		1974- 47,318		1976- 50,003		1978- 52,842		1980- 55,843		
STATE 6	597	5	865	45	988	8	1,369	0	1,761	49	3,334	16	
AMAPA	771	29.1	1,226	41.7	1,199	21.4	1,652	20.7	2,338	32.8	3,519	5.5	489.4
	4	0	1	5	1	10	1	10	1	18	1	30	
PROJECTION PERCENTAGE 20.8													
GROWTH PROJECTIONS	1970- 7,494		1972- 10,936		1974- 15,959		1976- 23,288		1978- 33,983		1980- 49,590		
STATE 7	12,945	437	17,618	1,051	22,517	1,992	22,462	2,004	22,240	1,882	23,117	1,216	
MARANHAO	16,722	29.2	18,713	6.2	24,216	7.5	23,990	6.8	23,684	6.5	27,182	17.6	110.0
	62	0	56	119	63	171	69	220	56	240	60	266	
PROJECTION PERCENTAGE 3.8													
GROWTH PROJECTIONS	1970- 31,555		1972- 33,999		1974- 36,632		1976- 39,469		1978- 42,526		1980- 45,819		
STATE 8	1,268	301	1,127	296	1,219	132	1,167	65	2,590	403	5,199	247	
PIAUI	1,597	25.9	1,234	9.5	1,327	8.9	1,514	29.7	3,219	24.3	6,059	16.5	377.8
	17	C	11	20	12	22	13	27	18	46	23	85	
PROJECTION PERCENTAGE 39.1													
GROWTH PROJECTIONS	1970- 22,683		1972- 43,889		1974- 84,920		1976- 164,310		1978- 317,920		1980- 615,137		

FIGURE 7

BRAZIL 1980; CG BY MICRO-REGION WITHIN DENOMINATION 2 CONG C NO BRASIL

COUNTRY PAGE 75
DENOMINATION PAGE 19
STATE PAGE 2

REPORT DATE 3/23/73

STATE 20 PARANA	1955- 1956 CC	EXCL % GR SC	1957- 1958 CC	EXCL % GR SC	1959- 1960 CC	EXCL % GR SC	1961- 1962 CC	EXCL % GR SC	1963- 1964 CC	EXCL % GR SC	1965- 1966 CC	EXCL % GR SC	TOTAL % GR
M/R 279	4,374	82	4,272	599	5,523	301	5,944	502	5,947	430	6,508	439	
	5,287	20.9	4,743	11.0	5,876	6.4	5,996	.9	5,888	1.0-	6,855	5.3	56.7
	19	0	15	27	25	34	19	32	19	33	19	34	
PROJECTION PERCENTAGE 2.8													
GROWTH PROJECTIONS	1970-	7,656	1972-	8,091	1974-	8,550	1976-	9,036	1978-	9,549	1980-	10,091	
M/R 280	2,154	158	2,873	274	2,690	107	1,248	26	1,701	430	1,233	32	
	2,692	25.0	2,900	.9	2,662	1.0-	1,355	8.6	1,328	21.9-	1,803	46.2	16.3-
	19	0	13	20	23	23	10	12	11	11	9	29	
PROJECTION PERCENTAGE 7.5													
GROWTH PROJECTIONS	1970-	2,408	1972-	2,783	1974-	3,216	1976-	3,716	1978-	4,294	1980-	4,962	
M/R 281	4,593	77	6,953	592	7,880	698	8,266	663	11,122	911	15,362	962	
	5,808	26.5	8,337	19.9	8,690	10.3	8,591	3.9	12,836	15.4	16,897	10.0	267.9
	22	0	31	60	33	52	28	44	35	51	38	66	
PROJECTION PERCENTAGE 15.3													
GROWTH PROJECTIONS	1970-	29,863	1972-	39,700	1974-	52,778	1976-	70,164	1978-	93,277	1980-	124,003	
M/R 282	2,734	83	3,188	799	2,798	93	3,737	567	5,083	178	8,267	404	
	3,208	17.3	2,695	15.5-	2,829	1.1	4,451	19.1	5,512	8.4	8,444	2.1	208.9
	5	0	7	10	7	13	12	18	12	21	13	27	
PROJECTION PERCENTAGE 17.7													
GROWTH PROJECTIONS	1970-	16,205	1972-	22,449	1974-	31,099	1976-	43,082	1978-	59,683	1980-	82,681	
M/R 283	1,108	6	2,795	40	3,355	89	5,713	387	6,321	158	7,875	225	
	1,218	9.9	3,355	20.0	3,550	5.8	6,366	11.4	7,200	13.9	8,198	4.1	639.9
	5	0	10	11	12	17	12	28	15	39	18	42	
PROJECTION PERCENTAGE 7.5													
GROWTH PROJECTIONS	1970-	10,948	1972-	12,652	1974-	14,621	1976-	16,896	1978-	19,525	1980-	22,564	
M/R 284	2,082	26	2,246	128	1,997	115	2,487	113	6,472	172	7,666	501	
	2,100	.9	2,317	3.2	2,462	23.3	2,678	7.7	7,002	8.2	9,784	27.6	369.9
	9	0	9	15	11	18	8	23	8	48	9	67	
PROJECTION PERCENTAGE 31.6													
GROWTH PROJECTIONS	1970-	29,345	1972-	50,821	1974-	88,015	1976-	152,429	1978-	263,985	1980-	457,184	
M/R 285	512	15	1,374	3	1,924	13	3,054	47	5,495	327	7,567	1,231	
	583	13.9	1,780	29.5	2,232	16.0	3,494	14.4	6,809	23.9	7,840	3.6	1431.3
	4	0	4	9	5	11	5	13	9	39	12	52	
PROJECTION PERCENTAGE 20.8													
GROWTH PROJECTIONS	1970-	16,695	1972-	24,362	1974-	35,551	1976-	51,878	1978-	75,704	1980-	110,472	
M/R 286	397	1	551	0	1,086	8	887	12	2,510	120	4,684	628	
	583	46.9	820	48.8	1,347	24.0	1,152	29.9	3,408	35.8	4,907	4.8	1136.0
	6	0	3	7	6	11	3	3	4	36	5	34	
PROJECTION PERCENTAGE 40.8													
GROWTH PROJECTIONS	1970-	19,285	1972-	38,232	1974-	75,794	1976-	150,259	1978-	297,883	1980-	590,542	

Appendix 3: BRAZIL 1980 Project

USING THE COMPUTER FOR CHURCH GROWTH RESEARCH*

Experience with Brazilian church growth data in 1962 and 1963 convinced William Read that a tool was needed to handle large quantities of unique information and he set about to design such a tool. As the data grew year by year, the problem of how to handle it also grew. The amount of Brazilian religious census information that had to be gathered, stored, analyzed, and modified called for the use of the computer. [Read 1969:374]

The term "data processing" is used for different types of computer research. Several important steps are involved in the entire process from the time the data is gathered up to and including the period of analysis for the findings. Processing, by definition, consists in taking it in <u>one</u> form and changing it to <u>some other</u> form according to the directions of the person in charge of the operation. The essential stages in the process are recording, manipulating, compiling, analyzing, and printing out.

Recording for this present project has been a long process. More than 45,000 different sets of data have been transferred to 45,000 different sets of cards and punched. More than 100 people have been involved in this process for over four years.

The Religious Census Data for Brazil

A typical page is taken out of the 1963-1964 "Culto Protestante" and is reproduced here to show what the religious census data is. This page is divided into ten columns. Reading from left to right, the titles may be translated: (1) County, (2) Main Church, (3) Number of temples (congregations), (4) Membership (for one year as of December 31, 1963), (5) Admissions, (6) Exclusions (or losses), (7) Membership (as of December 31, 1964 for the following year), (8) Baptisms, (9) Marriages, (10) Deaths (Figure I-1).

---

*For a more detailed description see Chapter 2 of the doctoral dissertation of William R. Read entitled "Brazil 1980: A Tool for the Evangelization of Brazil." It can be obtained from Librarian, Fuller Theological Seminary, 135 North Oakland Avenue, Pasadena, California 91101.

FIGURE I-1

48 ESTATÍSTICA DO CULTO PROTESTANTE DO BRASIL - 1964

CULTO PROTESTANTE
ESTADO DO RIO DE JANEIRO

(1) MUNICÍPIOS	(2) TEMPLOS-SEDE	(3) NÚMERO DE TEMPLOS	(4) MEMBROS EXISTENTES EM 31-12-63	(5) ADMISSÕES	(6) EXCLUSÕES	(7) MEMBROS EXISTENTES EM 31-12-64	(8) BATIZADOS	(9) CASAMENTOS	(10) OFÍCIOS FÚNEBRES
Total 62	613	1.267	131.493	23.180	11.414	143.259	2.690	1.230	846
1. Angra dos Reis	1. Batista (Angra dos Reis)	5	81	13	2	92	6	-	2
	2. Evangélica Assembléia de Deus (Idem)	5	199	75	44	230	-	-	2
	3. Evangélica Assembléia de Deus (Idem-Praia de Provetá)	8	...	...	...	...	...	...	...
	4. Evangélica Congregacional (Idem)	1	70	6	3	73	6	2	-
2. Araruama	5. Batista (Araruama)	2	52	20	6	66	3	-	-
	6. Batista (Posse)	1	36	6	1	41	-	-	-
	7. Batista (São Vicente de Paulo)	1	111	17	18	110	15	-	1
	8. Evangélica Assembléia de Deus (Idem)	11	523	26	6	543	-	4	1
3. Barra do Piraí	9. Assembléia de Deus (Barra do Piraí)	6	513	80	27	566	85	4	1
	10. Batista (Idem)	1	250	60	45	265	-	3	1
	11. Cristã Presbiteriana (Idem)	1	230	7	4	233	2	-	-
	12. Metodista do Brasil (Idem)	1	89	16	10	95	5	3	1
4. Barra Mansa	13. Batista Central (Barra Mansa)	1	...	...	...	...	...	...	...
	14. Congregação Cristã no Brasil (Idem)	5	...	...	...	...	...	...	...
	15. Evangélica Assembléia de Deus (Idem)	13	408	160	68	500	-	5	1
	16. Metodista (Idem)	4	428	65	39	454	41	4	4
	17. Presbiteriana (Idem)	3	-	106	4	102	21	1	-
	18. Primeira Igreja Batista (Idem)	1	...	...	...	...	...	...	...
5. Bom Jardim	19. Batista (Bom Jardim)	2	80	3	3	80	3	-	-
	20. Presbiteriana (Barra Alegre)	3	135	14	28	121	13	-	1
	21. Presbiteriana (São José do Ribeirão)	1	172	10	14	168	7	-	-
6. Bom Jesus do Itabapoana	22. Batista (Bom Jesus do Itabapoana)	3	225	17	29	213	-	2	4
	23. Batista (Carabuçu)	1	197	14	17	194	-	5	1
	24. Presbiteriana (Bom Jesus do Itabapoana)	1	256	20	4	272	10	1	-
	25. Presbiteriana (Carabuçu)	2	79	5	6	78	-	1	-
	26. Presbiteriana (Rosal)	3	343	13	82	274	13	-	1
	27. Presbiteriana de Sacramento (Bom Jesus do Itabapoana)	2	215	4	3	216	1	-	-
7. Cabo Frio	28. Batista do Araça (Tamoios)	2	164	4	16	152	4	-	-
	29. Evangélica Assembléia de Deus (Cabo Frio)	19	4.200	116	76	4.240	69	38	17
	30. Evangélica Batista (Arraial do Cabo)	4	307	35	32	310	-	12	3
	31. Metodista do Brasil (Cabo Frio)	4	254	91	8	337	269	4	1
	32. Metodista do Brasil (Armação dos Búzios)	4	174	23	4	193	46	-	1
8. Cachoeiras de Macacu	33. Batista Central (Cachoeiras de Macacu)	1	103	11	8	106	-	-	2
	34. Evangélica Assembléia de Deus (Idem)	4	391	30	15	406	14	4	-
	35. Primeira Igreja Batista (Idem)	5	376	50	10	416	-	2	3
9. Cambuci	36. Batista (Cambuci)	1	100	8	1	107	-	1	1
	37. Batista (Monte Verde)	3	101	-	10	91	-	-	-
	38. Batista (São João do Paraiso)	2	113	-	2	111	-	2	-
	39. Batista (São José de Ubá)	1	186	21	9	198	20	1	1
	40. Batista (Três Irmãos)	1	25	-	-	25	-	-	-
	41. Batista Monte Sinai (São João do Paraiso)	1	105	-	-	105	-	-	-
10. Campos	42. Adventista do Sétimo Dia (Campos)	4	292	117	145	264	22	3	2
	43. Adventista do Sétimo Dia (Tocos)	1	23	-	1	22	-	-	-
	44. Apostolica Brasileira (Guarus)	1	300	100	-	400	100	-	-
	45. Batista (Campos - Parque Corrientes)	1	150	20	-	170	-	2	1
	46. Batista (Idem-Uraraí)	1	70	25	10	85	-	2	2
	47. Batista (Cardoso Moreira Cachoeiro)	1	390	28	36	382	-	4	2
	48. Batista (Cardoso Moreira Califórnia)	1	142	4	16	130	-	1	-
	49. Batista (Idem-Estação Dr. Matos)	1	200	6	26	180	-	-	-
	50. Batista (Idem-Palestina)	1	260	10	5	265	-	2	1
	51. Batista (Idem-Santa Catarina)	1	100	5	30	75	-	-	1
	52. Batista (Idem-Santa Helena)	1	160	30	10	180	-	1	-
	53. Batista (Idem-São Luis)	1	350	32	30	352	-	-	-
	54. Batista (Dores de Macabu)	1	90	-	30	60	-	-	-
	55. Batista (Goitacases)	1	195	20	25	190	-	2	2
	56. Batista (Guarus)	1	373	27	150	250	-	2	1
	57. Batista (Morro do Côco)	1	138	5	23	120	-	-	-
	58. Batista (Idem-Conselheiro Josino)	1	40	10	-	50	-	1	1
	59. Batista (Paciência)	1	65	-	20	45	-	1	1
	60. Batista (Santo Eduardo)	1	120	6	16	110	-	1	-

FIGURE I-2

ESTATÍSTICA DO CULTO PROTESTANTE DO BRASIL — 1958 1

CULTO PROTESTANTE

Número de templos e movimento verificado segundo as Unidades da Federação

UNIDADES DA FEDERAÇÃO	Templos-Sede	Número de templos	Membros existentes em 31-12-57	Admissões	Exclusões	Membros existentes em 31-12-58	Batizados	Casamentos	Ofícios fúnebres	Municípios informantes
Norte										
Rondônia	5	12	2 246	416	25	2 637	338	3	4	2
Acre	10	18	3 296	297	56	3 537	152	3	8	5
Amazonas	28	81	5 726	838	235	6 329	436	38	40	13
Rio Branco	4	7	479	123	9	593	79	3	4	1
Pará	105	225	29 849	4 545	2 104	32 290	2 363	128	153	43
Amapá	8	16	1 194	551	69	1 676	213	12	5	2
Nordeste										
Maranhão	139	237	24 962	3 254	1 738	26 478	1 062	162	114	58
Piauí	32	64	3 257	647	497	3 407	337	21	11	21
Ceará	81	183	23 477	2 795	1 679	24 593	1 612	68	64	42
Rio Grande do Norte	64	109	12 648	1 625	810	13 463	446	41	68	28
Paraíba	85	151	15 847	2 089	976	16 960	652	112	84	34
Pernambuco	277	434	51 487	8 780	5 559	54 708	3 853	436	355	69
Alagoas	55	101	15 927	1 945	697	17 175	566	66	49	24
Leste										
Sergipe	42	79	4 331	362	344	4 349	156	38	41	20
Bahia	278	490	36 594	5 027	2 251	39 370	2 573	195	106	111
Minas Gerais	508	1 279	115 662	20 967	11 366	125 263	7 120	1 757	539	188
Espírito Santo	285	615	80 653	11 632	7 557	84 728	4 495	575	459	34
Rio de Janeiro	461	675	74 140	10 349	7 429	77 060	3 741	517	374	58
Distrito Federal	233	374	62 710	10 145	8 384	64 471	2 780	595	375	1
Sul										
São Paulo	1 382	2 302	316 663	54 218	25 077	345 804	22 991	2 154	1 645	321
Paraná	531	947	98 296	19 940	9 434	108 802	6 753	827	713	132
Santa Catarina	174	621	192 581	12 327	7 557	197 351	6 769	1 321	1 267	52
Rio Grande do Sul	436	1 377	369 962	27 230	16 287	380 905	12 719	2 899	2 681	102
Centro-Oeste										
Mato Grosso	77	117	9 631	2 279	655	11 255	1 019	51	53	34
Goiás	169	311	22 915	5 145	2 061	25 999	2 198	197	115	83
BRASIL	**5 469**	**10 825**	**1 574 533**	**207 526**	**112 856**	**1 669 203**	**85 453**	**12 219**	**9 387**	**1 478**

The names of the counties are listed alphabetically and numbered in sequence. Under each county, the second column "Main Church" is listed by denomination, usually alphabetically and again in sequence. Other columns carry the church membership statistics for each individual church. Our sample happens to be the first page for the State of Rio de Janeiro. Note: The columnar totals for the state are recorded at the top of the columns on the first page. A glance across this top line gives one a feel for the magnitude of the church growth data and Protestant strength in each state.

The first part of the religious census publication has a recap of all data for the different states. Only the yearly totals are recorded on this first page, and it is an overview for the whole year. As a sample, Figure I-2 "Culto Protestante" for 1957-1958 is shown.

This page differs from the others in the first and last columns. Column #1, "Units of the Federation," contains the different states and territories of Brazil. Different regions, such as North, South, Central-West, etc., are recorded in this column also. The last column indicates the total number of counties in each state that provided church growth information. The total for the year is given in the last line of each column.

The religious census data is given by geographical location, state and county. To determine how many Baptists exist in one state is a painstaking effort if we have to extract such information on a page-by-page basis. The total number of Presbyterians in all of Brazil has to be extracted from more than 120 pages, and must be done for one year at a time. The task multiplies the difficulty when the other ten years of data are added. This is enough to indicate the impracticability of handling this data by any means other than a computer.

The pastor or leader of every Protestant church in Brazil is required to fill out a Religious Census Bureau form each year. This form is the basis for all of the data that is recorded on the pages of each year's publication. There is much more data on the form written in Portuguese than appears in the religious census report. More interesting comparisons could be made with information which is on file at the main offices of the Religious Census Department of Moral Law and Social Statistics in Rio de Janeiro. When research of the data that we have now in this religious census is finished, more is waiting in these offices.

What Do We Want to Know From the Data?

1. What church denomination is the largest? Where is it growing the most?

2. How many churches (congregations) are located in (a) rural areas? (b) urban areas?

3. What is the total size of all of the different denominations in any given year?

4. What areas in Brazil have the strongest concentration of Protestants? What denominations predominate in these high density areas?

5. How can a list of the top fifty churches in size be compiled? What is their growth per year? Was growth consistent, and regular, year by year?

6. What different patterns of growth are to be found in this data?

Before computerization was begun, answers to these questions had to be obtained by hand manipulation and on a limited sample basis. Many answers did come, but in the years that followed - up to 1965 - more and more questions arose.

1. What is the average percentage of growth by different denominations in different areas in Brazil? What is the percentage range of growth for these churches?

2. How are the different categories of churches growing? (Category I, the traditional, older denominations; Category II, the Pentecostal family of churches; and Category III, the different sects, sometimes called heretical, that are found in Brazil).

3. How have Protestant churches grown in different regions, areas, and in the 361 new micro-regions that have many counties within their boundaries?

4. How could one acquire a list of counties that have the largest concentration and density of Protestant members?

5. Which churches and denominations have had the greatest *growth dynamic,* that is, the highest percentage rates of increase for a ten-year period?

6. Is it possible to determine what church growth has occurred in the different economic areas of Brazil: industrial sectors, the coffee boom areas, certain urban areas, and the frontier land areas?

7. Can a series of comparative studies be made between Pentecostals and traditional churches?

8. Which areas have no Protestant churches reported?

9. What is the relationship between church growth patterns and road and railway systems?

10. What is the relationship between socio-economic factors and the growth or non-growth of churches?

11. Do the statistics suggest areas of receptivity and opportunity?

These questions were gradually incorporated into the thinking of how this data should be processed. In addition to these questions which the computer would answer, there were a great many questions of "why?" which other research methods would be required to answer. However, it seemed essential just to know the statistical facts, and this called for computer work. Until the statistical comparisons and contrasts are before you, one does not really know the "why" questions to ask.

What the Programmer Had to Know for Transcribing the Data

The data we had on hand set the limits for what we could do. Clearly, we would be able to construct a large, statistical, geographical grid for all of Brazil. By structuring our program on this grid, we filled in the data along the grid lines by county, micro-region, state, major region and country.

The first task was transcribing the data onto some kind of form which could be used for card punching. A data transcribing form was designed. It had eight horizontal columns and used 33 spaces for data on the basic IBM #26 rectangular card, measuring approximately 82 mm x 187 mm. This form had places for eleven different kinds of information and was designed by John Grove, our first programmer. It has been used for six years since transcribing began in 1967.

This form had eleven titles for the following kinds of information:

1.	State	The code number for the "state," (states were numbered from 1 to 28).
2.	County	The "county" code number is recorded in these three spaces. (No state had more than 999 counties.)
3.	Unit	"Unit" was a space provided to give each church its own unique continuing number.
4.	Den	The code for "Den" or denomination. (The number of denominations and churches did not exceed 100.)
5.	District	"District" occasionally occurred in the data to show the district of a town in which a local church is located. For larger urban centers this information was helpful.
6.	Satellite	"Satellite" represented the number of churches, congregations, or preaching points, each central church had recorded, and gave an indication of the magnitude of the outreach a central church had. It also provided a way for larger churches to list their associated churches.
7.	Year	"Year" was the first year of recorded data.
8.	Members	"Members" was the number of members recorded for this first year.
9.	Year	"Year" was the second year membership and was registered after a twelve-month period.
10.	Members	"Members" was the membership for this second year.
11.	Exclusions	"Exclusions" was the number of people that were lost to the church during the year for one reason or another.

Volunteers received these sheets and were asked to record the data accordingly. Each sheet represented data for eight individual churches. After these forms were checked, they were sent to a card punch operator and the information was punched on IBM #26 cards.

The List of Countries Had to Be Coded

A list of all the states in Brazil with their counties as they existed in 1957 was compiled. This list comprised 1,998 counties, and one IBM card had to be made for each and our master list of counties for Brazil was printed. These lists were given to each volunteer who did the work of transcribing this material onto the forms designed for card punching.

A Unit Number Was Given to Each Church

A unit number was given to each individual church (congregation) within each state. This number would become a permanent identification for each church. The computer may use this when sorting out comparative patterns of church growth for selected churches. A growth pattern of an individual church could be studied by using this number for pulling information from the computer data bank.

Instructions to Volunteers

Complete instructions had to be given to each person who worked on the transcribing task in order to obtain a normal level of accuracy. This instruction booklet and materials were put together for each person who was willing to serve as a volunteer. Transcribing work was assigned by states with the different years of data that had to be completed.

Six books of religious census data with all of their church growth information were transcribed in this way. Each book was larger than its predecessor and filled with new entries, so the task of transcribing data becomes more complex with each additional year of data. A decision was made early in the project to transcribe every other year of data. The same results could be obtained in this way with much less transcription, and these six books represented twelve years of membership statistics.

The Cards Had to Be Punched

After the transcribing task was done, all forms were keypunched on IBM cards, and each card had the following information listed in code form: (1) The state code number, (2) the county code number, (3) the unit church code number, (4) the denominational code number, (5) the number of satellite churches, (6) the first year of data, (7) membership in this first year, (8) the second year of data, (9) membership in the second year, and (10) the number of exclusions or losses. The computer calculated the item of data that was missing on each card, and the net number of additions to membership.

Computer Program Written

To organize this data that was transcribed and punched on cards, a program had to be written in FORTRAN, the basic computer language, which would give the data processing more versatility and permit our running it through different computers.

The first preliminary program was written in 1967 to test the data, but no comprehensive program could be written at that time until all the data had been transcribed. The first general program had 277 programming procedures. It was compiled and run on July 21, 1970 on a large Univac computer in Pasadena.

First Computer Printouts

The columns in this first computer format contained: (1) the different denominational groups by code number, listed in sequence (data for each denomination would read from left to right across the printout), (2) the data for the year, (3) the percent of membership of each denomination, (4) the membership for all of the denominations was listed on the left side, (5) the percentage of each denomination out of the whole membership for each state, (6) the number of churches reporting this membership, (7) the report of the average membership of each church in the denomination for that year, (8) average membership for that year per church, (9) the total of the different denominations that are considered to be the "traditional" churches that have been in Brazil for many years and represent the old line denominations, (10) the category of churches that represent the Pentecostal family of churches, and (11) the total of so called heretical sects.

Evolution of the Computer Program and Format

In 1972, another programmer, Joe Wood, began to help us with a new program. We began working toward the ultimate goal of a basic comprehensive program that would do everything we needed in one basic program. Joe Wood finally completed our "basic" program and then designed the present format in April, 1972. This latest program was a breakthrough because it produced a printout that permitted us, for the first time, to incorporate the dimension of micro-regions in the program. In 1968, the

Brazilian Census Bureau published the micro-region division for all of Brazil which had been approved officially as the way for tabulating all future census survey data. The 361 micro-regions now became important and had to be incorporated into our basic computer programming procedure. All of the work that had been done up to that time had to be radically reorganized according to the new list and placed in its proper geographic micro-region. When the computer project first began we were dealing with 2,000 county units. In 1968, there were more than 4,000 and these 4,000 counties were divided into 361 micro-regions. This new computer program was tried out on the state of São Paulo.

The BRAZIL 1980 Printout Format - The Basic Tool.

A sample of one section of this printout is reproduced in reduced form here. (Figure I-3). A basic format was now in hand that would produce a diversified, sophisticated, and practical analysis of the religious census church growth data of Brazil. The different arrows in Figure I-3 point out some of the improvements and indicate what new units of data have been included in this latest printout format. A brief explanation of the different arrows in sequence follows: (1) The title is BRAZIL 1980. (2) The date of the printout report. (3) The collection of a comprehensive unit of data for a reporting period. (A unit of data is reproduced in the same way in the box below it.) The church growth membership of Denomination #1 in 1955 was 34. In 1966 it was 54. "CC" means "Central Church." There is only one of these. "EXCL" is the abbreviation for exclusions or losses in Denomination. #1. "Assem. of Deus" is the Assemblies of God Church. "%GR" means the percentage of growth in a year period between 1955 and 1956. Denomination #1 had a 58.8% increase. "SC" means satellite church. In this particular year there was none. (4) The title of this particular section of the printout. (There are four sections in the printout and each has a title that appears on this line.) (5) The number of the micro-region being analyzed. (6) The name of the State being analyzed. (7) The page number of that section of the report, in this case, it is entitled "Church Growth by Counties and Denominations." (This entry is opposite the report title in the middle of the page.) (8) Page number for the state printout. (There is also a page number for the whole report from first to last page.) (9) "Total %GR" means total percentage of growth. (This is the figure that gives the total compounded percentage of growth for the period between 1955 to 1966). (10) "State 19" is the code number for the state. (In this case it was São Paulo.) (11) "County 148" is named IACANGA, and is one of the counties within Micro-region #241. (12) Total for the county in each one of the six areas that are included in Item 3, which is the collection of data in the rectangular box.

FIGURE I-3

[1] BRAZIL 1980; CG BY MICRO REGIONS

REPORT DATE 1/31/73 [2]

STATE OF SAO PAULO [6]
[5] MICRO-REGION 241
[4] CHURCH GROWTH BY COUNTIES AND DENOMINATIONS

[8] STATE PAGE 128
[7] REPORT PAGE 7

[10] STATE 19 [3]	1955- 1956 CC	EXCL % GR SC	1957- 1958 CC	EXCL % GR SC	1959- 1960 CC	EXCL % GR SC	1961- 1962 CC	EXCL % GR SC	1963- 1964 CC	EXCL % GR SC	1965- 1966 CC	EXCL % GR SC	TOTAL % GR [9]
[11] COUNTY 148-IACANGA													
DEN 1 ASSEM DE DEUS	34 54 1	3 58.8 0	77 84 1	16 9.1 2	0 0 0	0 .0 0	0 0 0	0 .0 0	0 0 0	0 .0 0	0 0 0	0 .0 0	147.1
DEN 2 CONG C NO BRASIL	21 32 1	0 52.4 0	0 0 0	0 .0 0	0 0 0	0 .0 0	0 0 0	0 .0 0	0 0 0	0 .0 0	61 69 1	2 13.1 1	228.6
DEN 38 PRESBITERIANA	269 161 1	112 40.1- 0	139 112 1	60 19.4- 2	120 71 1	54 40.8- 1	61 58 1	3 4.9- 1	63 20 1	6 68.3- 1	43 50 1	0 16.3 1	81.4-
DEN 40 PRES CONS DO BR	59 61 1	0 3.4 0	26 26 1	0 .0 2	21 22 1	0 4.8 1	22 22 1	0 .0 1	25 25 1	0 .0 1	20 22 1	0 10.0 1	62.7-
[12] COUNTY 148 TOTAL	383 308 4	115 19.6- 0	242 222 3	76 8.3- 6	141 93 2	54 34.0- 2	83 80 2	3 3.6- 2	88 45 2	6 48.9- 2	124 141 3	2 13.7 3	63.2-
COUNTY 203-JULIO MESQUITA													
DEN 1 ASSEM DE DEUS	0 0 0	0 .0 0	0 0 0	0 .0 0	50 45 1	13 10.0- 1	70 67 1	8 4.3- 1	77 120 1	19 55.8 1	62 80 1	2 29.0 1	60.0
DEN 2 CONG C NO BRASIL	0 0 0	0 .0 0	0 0 0	0 .0 0	0 0 0	0 .0 0	0 0 0	0 .0 0	70 90 1	12 28.6 1	96 104 1	3 8.3 1	48.6
COUNTY 203 TOTAL	0 0 0	0 .0 0	0 0 0	0 .0 0	50 45 1	13 10.0- 1	70 67 1	8 4.3- 1	147 210 2	31 42.9 2	158 184 2	5 16.5 2	268.0
COUNTY 212-LENCOIS PAULISTA													
DEN 1 ASSEM DE DEUS	66 75 1	0 13.6 0	37 41 1	4 10.8 1	0 0 0	0 .0 0	0 0 0	0 .0 0	0 0 0	0 .0 0	0 0 0	0 .0 0	37.9-
DEN 2 CONG C NO BRASIL	79 87 1	0 10.1 0	103 119 1	0 15.5 1	0 0 0	0 .0 0	184 231 1	5 25.5 1	233 249 1	2 6.9 1	273 297 1	3 8.8 1	275.9

This is a brief explanation of a printout format taken at random from a typical page from the church growth analysis. It merely serves as a model. The printout will show the composite way in which all of the data has been digested and placed on one page. When new church growth data arrives and is transcribed for later years, the first year of data will have to be omitted. The data will then be shifted in order to include the latest year of data when each new year is added to the printout.

The Structure of the BRAZIL 1980 Computer Printout.

The different sections of this latest computer format are listed below in the following order:

1. Church membership by micro-region (1 to 361).

   A. Church membership by counties and by denominations under the micro-regions.

   B. Church membership by categories and denominational groups (thirteen of these) under micro-regions.

   C. Church membership by categories (types of churches, three of these).

2. Church membership totals by states.

   A. Church membership totals for state by categories. and denominational groups (thirteen of these).

   B. Church membership totals for state by categories (three of these).

   C. Church membership totals for the state by micro-region totals.

3. Church membership totals for the country.

   A. Church membership totals for country (twenty-eight states and territories) by categories and denominational groups (thirteen of these).

   B. Church membership totals for country by categories (three of these).

   C. Church membership totals for country by micro-region totals.

   D. Grand total for all of country.

Variations in the Program

Various printouts are now available from this one basic computer printout format. Other variations of data can be adapted to the basic core program, and these different printouts can be produced at a later date when the time comes to manipulate the basic church growth data in different ways. Only seven variations are listed below and it is not possible to describe them in detail here.

1. The micro-region printout of church membership for all of Brazil.

2. The micro-region printout of church membership for all of Brazil with projections for 1970, '72, '74, '76, '78, and 1980.

3. Denominational group printout of church membership for Brazil (thirteen basic denominational families included in this) by micro-region.

4. Denominational group printout of church growth (thirteen basic denominational families included in this) by micro-region with projections for 1970, '72, '74, '76, '78, and 1980.

5. Church membership totals for each denomination in Brazil (less than 99 listed in major denominational code list) by micro-region.

These major printouts of the data are now available in their original form, as they came from the computer, in the CASE offices* in São Paulo, Brazil.

Use of the Data

For explanation on how to use the data in specific situations, see Appendix II.

* CASE, Caixa Postal 30.548, 01000 São Paulo, SP. Brazil, SA. Attention: Rev. Harmon Johnson.

Appendix 4: CASE

CASE: A NEW CHURCH GROWTH CENTER FOR BRAZIL

The New Center

In January, 1972, in response to the need for a Brazilian church growth research center which the data of this book has so forcefully demonstrated, SEPAL, the Brazilian division of Overseas Crusades, asked Harmon Johnson to join their team. Harmon Johnson is coauthor with William R. Read and Victor Monterroso, of *Latin American Church Growth,* published by Wm. B. Eerdmans. He is now Coordinator of Research for SEPAL and has been given the task of organizing a church growth center to serve all Evangelical churches of Brazil.

SEPAL's goal is a church growth research center staffed and administered by Brazilians and funded from within Brazil. The new center has been given the name of CASE (Center of Advanced Study for Evangelism) and will be known in Brazil as CEPE (Centro de Estudos Pró Evangelismo).

SEPAL Do Brasil

In attempting to reach this goal, CASE has a number of factors working in its favor. Not the least of these is the SEPAL team itself. The SEPAL team is a group of men committed to one another and to the task of edifying the whole body of Christ. Their idea is not to take the church's place or do the church's job for it, but to prepare the church technically and spiritually to do its own divinely appointed task. The members of the team have become servants of the churches, each member exercising his own ministry according to his gifts and abilities, always at the invitation of the church. Present SEPAL ministries include leadership training, religious education, theological training, pastors' retreats, youth ministries, and training in Christian discipleship. Team ministries are interrelated and all ministries are brought under the discipline of team orientation and interaction.

The Cooperation of MARC

Another major factor which helps SEPAL as it begins its research center is the BRAZIL 1980 Project of MARC/World Vision. This research effort has investigated missionary goals in Brazil in conjunction with the Missionary Information Bureau of Brazil. In addition, MARC has analyzed in depth the results of the government sponsored Brazilian religious census, storing all the information in computer usable form so it can later be used in multivariable analysis together with comparable socio-economic data which is already available. MARC has designed and tested a questionnaire to measure the conversion pattern of Brazilian Evangelicals and has requested CASE to serve as the repository for the data collected. MARC is now in the process of turning over to CASE/SEPAL the results of its five-year study of Brazil. MARC and SEPAL will be cooperating in various aspects of the research to be done as each finds convenient.

Evangelical Openness

Another positive factor is the openness of Evangelical leaders to the idea of a research center to serve all the churches. At a recent meeting of Evangelical leaders assembled at Caxambu, Brazil, at the invitation of MARC, all the leaders present expressed themselves as being in favor of the basic CASE approach as presented to them. The Rev. Karl Gottschald, president of the Brazilian Church of the Lutheran Confession, one of the largest denominations in Brazil, has asked CASE to train two researchers who have been appointed by the denomination. Other denominations, including the Wesleyan Methodist Church of Brazil, have expressed their desire for similar assistance. Denominations have volunteered to distribute newsletters which will be sent to 14,000 Brazilian pastors informing them of what is being done through the new center for church growth research.

An Association of Men

CASE aims to create an association of men who are committed to the concept of church related ministry advocated by CASE/SEPAL and to research dedicated to the service of the church and its growth and development. They will not leave their present employment but will cooperate with CASE in conducting research, in training researchers, and holding seminars for Brazilian churchmen. These CASEfellows will have a church growth point of view, background, experience, and interest in research, capacity for leadership, and executive experience or aptitude. They will have a SEPAL point of view, including the concept of teamwork, experience in Christian discipleship, and a strong commitment to the Church. CASEfellows will probably provide a major share of the financial support of the center, after the initial period of outside "seed" money.

Information Net Work

Since research is cumulative, the center will become a reservoir of information. The CASEfellows scattered all over Brazil, will form a natural information network. As information is shared, the churches will learn from one another's insights and experiences, and by their interaction will be drawn into a greater awareness of their essential unity in Christ.

CASE desires to serve as a catalytic agent to stimulate the Brazilian churches to greater church growth. By helping the churches to a more effective use of its human resources, and by educating the churches to see things through church-growth eyes, CASE can aid the church to accomplish its God given goal of evangelizing Brazil.

Work Completed Thus Far

1. Hundreds of Evangelical leaders and laymen interested in church growth research have requested that their names be included in the CASE Personnel Bank to be called when needed in future research projects.

2. Two important survey trips that covered north and south Brazil have been completed, permitting the CASE staff to get a good idea of what is happening in the Protestant churches of Brazil in 1973.

3. A series of newsletters designed to effectively communicate to Brazilian pastors the concerns for evangelistic advance in Brazil has been initiated.

4. An Association of Evangelical Researchers for Brazil, composed of people with background, training, and experience in the social sciences, communications, research, and administration is being formed.

5. Special work was performed to show the churches what they themselves can do in the area of research at the local level and this will become part of the regular outreach and communication through the newsletters.

6. The research seminar program that began in 1972 with a seminar for Lutheran pastors was well received and will be expanded in 1973-74.

7. The CASE team personnel served a number of times as consultant for research projects at the request of other Evangelical groups in Brazil who were trying to work out evaluation procedures for their own ministries.

8. The MARC/CASE *Conversion Survey* questionnaire was tested extensively and as a result has gone through a revision for the countywide sampling procedures.

9. An effort to develop an effective leadership profile for Brazilian Evangelicals was undertaken and has generated a whole battery of research instruments that are now being tested and adapted before being put into use.

Work Planned

1. A new training program is being designed that will be incorporated in the structure of CASE for the years ahead.

2. Development of adequate financial support base for the work of CASE is being sought within and without Brazil before any increase of the program and staff is finalized.

3. A CASE research involvement plan for the immediate six-month period is regularly brought together in the form of a PERT chart that serves to display the different research activities, training programs, and cooperative relationships with Brazilian churches, the Association of Brazilian Researchers, and other Evangelical groups working in the country.

DIRECTOR OF CASE: Rev. Harmon A. Johnson
ADDRESS: Center of Advanced Study for Evangelism
Caixa Postal 30.548
01000 São Paulo, S. P.
Brazil, S. A.

Appendix 5: Bible Translation for the Tribes of Brazil

BIBLE TRANSLATION FOR THE TRIBES OF BRAZIL

We cannot and we should not wait until every minority language group in Brazil learns Portuguese before we try to reach them with the Gospel!

What is needed? We need to translate enough of the Bible (or New Testament) to enable some from every unevangelized ethnic group to understand the Gospel <u>and</u> for them to be able to disciple others of their own language groups with the Scriptures in their own heart language.

The STIR (Scripture Translation Information Reports) program of FAST International is a project to collect and distribute information about the unreached language groups that still need Bible translation work.

Missionary volunteers or mission leaders who are planning strategy to evangelize unreached peoples may obtain further details on any language group from FAST. Data includes population, location, language family, interested agencies, and other ethnolinguistic information.

The following information has been compiled from the publications of the United Bible Societies and Summer Institute of Linguistics.

Alan Bergstedt
F.A.S.T. International
(Final Advance of
Scripture Translation)

STATUS OF BIBLE TRANSLATION IN BRAZIL

Work in progress - with some Scripture printed	30
- with no Scripture printed	41
Definite Need	12
Need Undetermined	52
May be Mutually Intelligible	10
Do Not Need Translation	18
Bible, New Testament or sufficient Scripture Portions Available	7
Total languages known at this time	170

Further translation work is not considered necessary for 25 languages as of the end of 1972. Work is in progress for 71 languages and there is a definite known need to do translation in 12 other languages. Some of the languages do not need translation because of bilingualism or mutual intelligibility. However, it is probable that up to 40 other languages may need some translation work - at least for initial evangelism and church planting work among these language groups.

LANGUAGES WITH SOME SCRIPTURES PUBLISHED

	Language	Scriptures Published
1.	Amahuaka=Amahuaca	Mark and I John (1963)
2.	Apalaí=Aparai, Apalay	Acts (1972)
3.	Apinayé=Apinaje	Mark (1967)
4.	Asurini=Assuriní	Mark (1973)
5.	Bakairí=Bacairi	1st book (1969);
6.	Baniwa=Baniua=Baniva do Icana	NT (1965)
7.	Guaraní	First book (1971)
8.	Hixkaryána=Hishkaryana, Parukoto-Charuma	Mark (1966); Genesis (1973)
9.	Kaingáng=Coroado, Guaiana	Titus (1967); Mark (1968)
10.	Kaiwá	Mark (1972)
11.	Karajá=Javae, Xambioa	Mark (1965); John
12.	Kobewa=Kubwa, Cubeo, Cuveo, Kobeua	20 Books (1958-1968)
13.	Kulina=Culina	Titus, I John (1967)
14.	Makuchi	John (1923)
15.	Maquiritaré=Maiongong	N.T. (1970)
16.	Mawe=Satere, Maue, Andira, Arapium	Mark (1968)
17.	Maxakalí=Caposho, Cumanasho, Macuni, Monaxo	Mark (1968); Acts, Genesis
18.	Mundurukú	Mark (1967); Acts (1968)
19.	Nambikuara	Acts, Luke (1973)
20.	Palikúr	First book (1971). Acts, Mark, Epistles
21.	Paresí=Paressí, Parecís	First book (1971). Mark
22.	Parintintín	Genesis and Mark. First book (1971)
23.	Paumari=Purupuru	Mark (1973)
24.	Piro, Manchineri	Mark (1960)
25.	Portuguese	Bible (1751)
26.	Shiriana=Xiriana	Mark

27. Terêna=Teréna, Tereno	John (1948); Luke (1964)
28. Tukana=Tucano, Daxsea	John (1967)
29. Tukuna=Tikuna, Ticuna	Mark (1964); I John (1968)
30. Tupí, Guajajára	Mark (1930); John, Acts, Romans, I Cor. (1931-1934)
31. Urubú	First book (1970)
32. Waiwai=Tapioca	John (1966); Mark (1967)
33. Wanana=Wanána, Guanano, Kotedia	Mark (1968)
34. Xavánte=Akuen	First book (1970)
35. Xerente	First book (1970)
36. Yanomamó/Guaica/	Mark, Titus (1961); 12 books (1966-1968)
37. Yeral=Nyengato, Nhengatu	Eleven books (1960); Luke (1967)

LANGUAGES WITH WORK IN PROGRESS

(* Indicates that some Scripture has been translated and printed.)

*1. Amahuaka=Amahuaca
*2. Apalaí=Aparai, Apalay
*3. Apinayé=Apinaje
4. Apurina=Ipurinan, Kangite
5. Aripaktsa
*6. Asurini=Assuriní
7. Bakairi=Bacairí
8. Borono=Bororo
9. Cinta Larga
10. Dani
11. Desana=Wina, Desano, Desaña
12. Galibib=Carib, Kalinya, Maraworno

37. Marubo=Maruba, Marova
* 38. Mawe=Sataré, Maue, Andira, Arapium
* 39. Maxakali=Caposho, Cumanasho, Macuni, Monaxo
40. Mayoruna
* 41. Munduruku
42. Mura-Piraha
* 43. Nambikuara
44. Pakaandvas=Jaru, Uomo
* 45. Palikur
46. Parakanan=Parakanán
* 47. Paresi=Paressí, Parecís

13. Gaviaó (Rondonia)
14. Gorotire
15. Guaja
*16. Guarani
*17. Hixkaryana=Hishkaryana, Parukoto-Charuma
18. Hupda=Maku
19. Jamamadi=Yamamadi
20. Juma
21. Kadiweu=Mbaya-Guaikuru, Caduveo, Ediu-Adig
*22. Kaingáng=Coroado, Guiana
*23. Kaiwá
24. Kapanawa=Capanahua
*25. Karaja=Javae, Xambioa
26. Karitiana
27. Katawian=Katwena
28. Katukina
29. Kaxinawa=Cashinahua
30. Kayabi=Kajabi
*31. Kobewa=Kubwa, Cubeo, Cuveo, Kobeua
32. Krikati=Karakati, Krikati
*33. Kulina=Culina
34. Makunabodo=Makunab: Od, Maku
35. Mamainde=Mamaindé
36. Marinawa=Marinahua

* 48. Parintintín
* 49. Paumari=Purupuru
50. Ramkokamekra=Canela
51. Sanuma
* 52. Shiriana=Xiriana
53. Surui
* 54. Terena=Teréna, Tereno
* 55. Tirio=Trio, Tirió
* 56. Tukana=Tucano, Daxsea
57. Tukuna=Tikuna, Ticuna
* 58. Tupi, Guajajara
59. Tuyuka=Tuyuca
60. Txukuhamai=Tuxukuhamae, Kayapo
* 61. Urubú
62. Waica=Guaica
63. Waikino=Pira-Tapuya
* 64. Waiwai=Tapioca
* 65. Wanana=Wanána, Guanano, Kotedia
66. Wapitxana=Wapitxana, Wapisiana, Vapioiana, Wapishana
67. Waura
68. Wayana=Oayana, Wayána
69. Witoto
* 70. Xavánte=Akuen
* 71. Xerente

LANGUAGE GROUPS THAT DO NOT NEED TRANSLATION

1. Amanaye
2. Anambe
3. Apiaka
4. Arikapu = Maxubi
5. Fulnio = Furnio, Carnijo, Iate, Fulnio
6. Irantxe = Iranxe, Iranche
7. Karipuna
8. Pakarara
9. Pankararu
10. Potiguara
11. Sabanes = Sabones
12. Tembe
13. Tuxa
14. Uamue = Aticum
15. Umotina = Barbados
16. Wakona
17. Xoko
18. Yeral = Geral, Nyengata, Waengatu, modern Tupi

Summary: Language groups that are sufficiently bilingual in Portuguese or another language are included here along with one or two groups where the use of the language is expected to "die out" within 10 years. The total population of these 18 groups who can be reached through Bible translation in another language is estimated to be 7,000 to 9,000.

LANGUAGE GROUPS WITH A DEFINITE NEED FOR TRANSLATION

1. Atruahi = Atroai
2. Emerillon = Emerilon, Mereo, Mereyo, Emerenon, Teco
3. Ingariko
4. Juruna = Yuruna
5. Kamayura
6. Kanamari = Kanamare
7. Kuikuro
8. Macushi = Makuxi
9. Mudjetire
10. Oyapi = Oyampi, Wayapi, Oyanpik
11. Tapirape
12. Urupa

Summary: No translation work has been done for any of these groups although linguistic analysis was started by SIL in 1965 on the Kuikuro language. The populations of these language groups range from 50 to 2000 according to present estimates. The largest group is the Macushi but the average population is about 400.

LANGUAGE GROUPS WITH NEED UNDETERMINED

1. Agavotokueng=Uaiaru
2. Aica
3. Arara=Tora
4. Ava=Canoeiros
5. Aweti
6. Barawaña
7. Boca Negra
8. Gaviao
9. Hohodene=Hohodena, Kadaupuritana
10. Huyan
11. Iawano=Iawavo
12. Ipewi
13. Jabuti=Yabuti
14. Kabixi=Cabishi
15. Kalapalo
16. Karutana
17. Katukina

LANGUAGE GROUPS WITH NEEDS UNDETERMINED, CONTINUED

18. Kaxuiana
19. Kreen-Akakore
20. Kuruaya
21. Macurapi
22. Mandawaka
23. Maopityan=Mapidian
24. Matipuhy=Nahukua
25. Monde=Sanamaika
26. Nukuini
27. Pakanawa
28. Paranawat=Paware, Majubin
29. Parikoto
30. Pianokoto=Marahtxo
31. Pokanga=Pakang, Pokanga-Tapuya, Bara
32. Poyanawa
33. Purubora=Puruba, Aura
34. Saluma
35. Sarare
36. Sikiana
37. Suya
38. Tapayuna=Tapanyuna, Tapañuma
39. Tariana
40. Taulipang=Jaricunas
41. Tukumanfed
42. Tupari
43. Tuxinawa
44. Txikao=Txikaó
45. Waimiri
46. Wayoro
47. Wirafed=Wirofed
48. Xipinawa
49. Xiriána
50. Xokleng=Aweikoma, Bugre, Botocudos
51. Yabaaña
52. Yaminawa=Yaminahua

LANGUAGES WHICH MAY BE MUTUALLY INTELLIGIBLE WITH ANOTHER LANGUAGE

Language	May Use Translation In
1. Diore	Txukuhamai
2. Galera	Nambikuara
3. Jaruara	Jamamadi
4. Kraho	Ramkokamekra
5. Kuben-Kragnotire	Txukuhamai
6. Kuben-Kran-Kegn= Cabeca', Pelada	Txukuhamai
7. Mehinaku	Waura
8. Menkragnotire= Mentuktire, Gente Preta	Txukuhamai
9. Xikrin=Xukru	Txukuhamai
10. Yawalpaiti=Yawalapiti	Waura

Summary: Scriptures have not been translated and printed for any of the above except for 2 books in the Nambikuara language which the Galera people may be able to use. SIL has done some linguistic analysis or survey work in these groups until it was learned that the languages are mutually intelligible.

Although Scripture translation may not be needed for each of these specific languages, these groups do represent 5000 people who need the Scriptures in the alternate language where translation work is in progress.

Association for the

FINAL ADVANCE OF SCRIPTURE TRANSLATION

Send us around the world with the news of your saving power and your eternal plan for mankind...and peoples from remotest lands will worship Him. Living Psalms 67:2, 7b.

In mid 1971, after several months of prayer and discussions, FAST was organized. FAST shares the convictions of many mission organizations that "all tongues and nations" should have the Scriptures in their own language in this generation.

Dan Piatt was elected President of this new missionary service project. He has been a key member of the Billy Graham Team for 20 years and has also served on the Board of Directors of Wycliffe Bible Translators along with Billy Graham for many years. Dr. Graham and Wycliffe both encouraged Dan in the formation of FAST.

FAST is a catalyst to the church-at-large for the completion of pioneer Bible translation work in this generation.

FAST is not a missionary sending organization but is urging the churches to set up their own linguistic programs to recruit, train and send their own translators.

FAST is seeking out the last unreached tribe by retrieving socio-linguistic data on all peoples of the world and immediately making it available to everyone from its Scripture Translation Information Bank.

For additional information contact:

F. A. S. T.
1740 Westminster Drive
Denton, Texas 76201

Phone: (817) 387-9531

Appendix 6: North American Missions

NAME	YEAR ENTERED	TOTAL NO. AMERICAN PERSONNEL IN BRAZIL, 1969*
Amazon Mission	1949	NA
American Leprosy Missions	1921	1
American Lutheran Church	1958	44
Apostolic Christian Church	1962	6
Armenian Missionary Association of America	1960	NA
Assemblies of God	1909	19
Association for Christian Literature	1961	NA
Association of Baptists for World Evangelism (ABWE)	1942	83 (1970)
Baptist Bible Fellowship International	1953	26
Baptist General Conference	1957	18
Baptist International Missions	NA	22
Baptist Mid-Missions	1936	89 (1970)
Baptist Missionary Association of America	1950	10
Berean Mission	1967	3
Bethany Fellowship Missions	1963	46
Bethany Missionary Association	NA	2
Bethesda Mission	NA	7
Bible Conferences and Missions	N NA	1
Bible Memory Association	1965	2
Brazil Christian Mission	1948	2
Brazil Gospel Fellowship Mission	1939	35
Brazil Inland Mission	1954	6
Brethren Assemblies	NA	13
Campus Crusade for Christ International	1968	NA
Child Evangelism Fellowship	1952	12
Christian and Missionary Alliance	1962	11
Christian Life Missions	1964	2
Christian Nationals Evangelism Commission	1969	2
Christian Reformed Church	1934	6
Christian Service Corps	NA	1
Church of God (Anderson, Indiana)	1970	2
Church of God of Prophecy	1965	1
Church of God World Missions	NA	10
Church of the Nazarene	1958	12
Churches of Christ	NA	129 (1970)
Churches of Christ (Christian Churches)	NA	62
Cleveland Hebrew Mission	NA	5
Co-Laborers	1958	NA
Conservative Baptist Foreign Mission Society	1946	58
Evangelical Enterprises	1959	13
Evangelical Lutheran Church of Canada	NA	2
Evangelical Methodist Church	1949	2
Evangelical Union of South America	1931	34
Fellowship of Independent Missions	NA	2
Free Methodist Church of North America	1936	9
Garr Memorial Church (Carolina Evangelistic Assoc.)	1961	2
Gen'l. Conf. Mennonite Church	1958	2
Go-Ye Fellowship	NA	6

NAME	YEAR ENTERED	TOTAL NO. AMERICAN PERSONNEL IN BRAZIL, 1969*
Hebrew Evangelization Society	NA	2
Independent Bible Baptist Missions	1955	5
Independent Board for Presbyterian Foreign Missions	1946	5
Independent Gospel Missions	NA	3
Int'l. Church of the Foursquare Gospel	1946	7 (1972)
Int'l. Pentecostal Assemblies	NA	1
Japanese Evangelical Missionary Society	1964	NA
Koinonia Foundation	1968	1
Lester Sumrall Evangelistic Association	1966	NA
Lutheran Church, Missouri Synod	1899	47
Lutheran World Relief	1961	1
Maranatha Baptist Mission	1969	2
Mennonite Brethren Churches	1944	30
Mennonite Central Committee	1964	17
Mennonite Church, Mennonite Bd. of Msns. & Charities	1954	37
Missionary and Soul Winning Fellowship	1958	6
Missionary Aviation Fellowship (MAF)	1955	28
Missionary Church	1955	39
National Association of Free Will Baptists	1958	28
National Baptist Convention USA	1950	10
National Fellowship of Brethren Churches	1949	20
Navigators	1963	6
New Testament Missionary Union	NA	6
New Tribes Mission	1949	152
Next Towns Crusade	1965	2
North American Baptist Gen'l. Miss'y Society	1966	6
Oriental Missionary Society	1950	27
Overseas Crusades	1963	10
Pentecostal Assemblies of Canada	1963	4
Pentecostal Church of Christ	1935	NA
Pentecostal Church of God of America	NA	6
Pilgrim Fellowship	1948	4
Pocket Testament League	1966	9
Presbyterian Church in the U.S.	1869	139
Protestant Episcopal Church in USA	1907	9
Seventh-day Adventists	NA	56
South America Mission	1914	22
South American and World Missions	1966	4
Southern Baptist Convention	1881	292
Spanish America Inland Mission	1962	NA
Things to Come Mission	1957	4
Trans World Mission	1965	4
Unevangelized Fields Mission	1931	138 (1970)
United Christian Missionary Society	1968	1
United Church of Canada	1961	16
United Church of Christ	1962	2
United Methodist Church	1880	83
United Missionary Fellowship	1948	5

NAME	YEAR ENTERED	TOTAL NO. AMERICAN PERSONNEL IN BRAZIL, 1969*
United Missions	1955	7
United Pentecostal Church	NA	4
United Presbyterian Church in USA (COEMAR)	1859	22 (1971)
United World Mission	1961	2
Wesleyan Church	NA	6
West Indies Mission	1957	12
Word of Life Fellowship	NA	NA
World Baptist Fellowship Mission Agency	1961	18
World Gospel Crusades	1963	1
World Gospel Mission	1966	2
World Missionary Assistance Plan	NA	NA
World Missions	1964	3
World Missions to Children	1957	9
World Vision International	1961	0
World-Wide Missions	1963	NA
Worldwide Evangelization Crusade	1957	32 (1971)
Wycliffe Bible Translators	1956	168
Young Life Campaign	1963	5
Youth for Christ International (YFC)	1950	4
TOTAL PROTESTANT		2,411
Roman Catholics (U.S. only, 1969)**		630

* From survey for 1970 North American Protestant Ministries Overseas. Data refers to 1969.

** From U.S. Catholics Overseas in Missionary Service. New York, N.Y.: The Society for the Propagation of the Faith, 1970.

NA Not applicable or not available. NA or 0 may indicate that ministries are carried on through national workers.

Glossary

GLOSSARY

Abbreviations, Terms, and Foreign Words

AETTE: Association in Brazil promoting Theological Extension (Associacão Evangéliços Para Treinãmento Teológico Par Extensão).

Agrovila: Name given villages planned by the government along the Trans-Amazonian highway.

Amazonia Legal: Area of Amazonia covered by SUDAM laws.

Anuário Estatístico: Annual Statistical Report of Census Bureau.

Areas Aristalenas: Sandy areas.

Arenito - basaltico: A special type of land in Brazil.

ASTE: Theological Association in Brazil (*Associacõa de Seminários Teológicos Evangélicos*).

BNH: National Housing Bank (*Banco Nacional de Habitacão*).

BR-14: Number given to the Belém Brasília highway.

BR-101: Number for highway that runs along the coast in Brazil from North to South.

BR-227: Number of road connecting Foz do Iguaçu with port city of Paranáguá in the State of Paraná.

Brasil Para Cristo: A large independent Pentecostal denomination

CASE: Center for Advanced Studies in Evangelism located in São Paulo, Brazil.

CAVE: Audio Visual Center in Brazil (*Centro Audio-Visual Evangélica*).

Central Churches (CC): Largest Churches of any denomination, usually located in large urban centers.

Charismatic Renewal: Growth of Pentecostal gifts among traditional denominations in Brazil.

CLEB: Literature clearing house for Evangelicals in Brazil (*Camera de Literatura Evangélica Brasileira*).

Congregação Cristã: Name of second largest Pentecostal denomination in Brazil.

Communicant Members: Members in good standing in the Protestant Churches in Brazil who have made their profession of faith, have been baptized, are usually adults and are eligible to partake regularly in Communion.

Crentes: Protestant believers.

Culto Protestante: Name for the Protestant Religious Census publication.

Denominational Family Groups*:* Protestant denominations were classified into thirteen "families."

Denominational Categories*:* Protestant denominations were classified into three categories.

DNER*:* National Department of Roads *(Departamento Nacional de Estradas de Rodagem)*.

EFMA*:* Evangelical Foreign Missions Association.

EXCL*:* Exclusion of Communicant Members from membership roles of denominations in Brazil.

Faith Missions*:* Independent missionary organizations who emphasize and exercise faith principals in missionary work.

Fazendas: Farms.

Fundaçao IBGE: Brazil Census Bureau.

GLINT: Gospel Literature International.

Green Inferno*:* Name given to the Amazon Jungles of Brazil by explorers.

IBGE*:* Census Department of Brazil.

IBM 360*:* Nomenclature to designate a type of computer used by World Vision in Monrovia, California.

IFMA*:* International Foreign Mission Association.

IPB*:* *(Igreja Presbiteriana do Brasil)* National Presbyterian Church in Brazil.

Industrial Triangle*:* Area circumscribed by the cities of São Paulo, Rio de Janeiro, and Belo Horizonte.

"M" Factor*:* The magnitude of internal migration and mobility of Brazilians in motion.

MARC*:* Missions Advanced Research and Communication Center.

MARC/CASE*:* When used in this way indicates the cooperative work arrangement between these two organizations.

MEMB*:* Membership.

MIB*:* Missionary Information Bureau.

Micro-region: A geographical unit of area that has one or more county units - a homogeneous region.

Minas Triangle: A geographical point of land in Minas Gerais, in the form of a triangle that is bordered by Goiás and São Paulo states.

Minifundiarios: Small landowners in rural Brazil.

MG: Minas Gerais State.

Modernization: Interaction of many factors involved in transition of society from traditional to modern aspects.

Mother Church: The large central churches located in urban centers of certain Protestant denominations.

M/R: Micro-region.

MT: Mato Grosso State.

Mulatto: Racial mixture between white and blacks of varying degree.

Others: Classification of small Protestant denominations in Brazil.

Paulista: One who lives in the State of São Paulo.

People's Movement: A mass movement of people incorporated into the membership of a denomination or local church.

PR: Paraná State.

RGS: Rio Grande do Sul - State in South Brazil.

Roça: Rural area in hinterland of Brazil.

Satellite Churches: These churches relatedly are under jurisdiction of the Central Church.

SC: Satellite Church.

Sects: Name given to religious groups usually not classified with ease as Protestant denominational groups for one reason or another.

SEPAL: Name for Overseas Crusade team in Brazil (*Servico de Evangelização para América Latina).*

SP: São Paulo state.

SUDAM: The Brazilian government's program for the development of the Amazon Basin.

UFM: Unevangelized Fields Mission.

Bibliography

Bibliography

GENERAL

AYRES, Sebastião Aquiar
1968 *Anuário Estatístico do Brasil.* Rio de Janeiro, GB, Brasil Fundação I.B.G.E., Instituto Brasileiro de Geografia.

AZEVEDO, Tales
1959 *Ensaios de Antropologia Social.* Salvador, BA, Brasil, S.A.

BAKLANOFF, Eric N., ed.
1966 *New Perspectives of Brazil.* Nashville, Vanderbilt University Press.
1969 *The Shaping of Modern Brazil.* Baton Rouge, Louisiana State University Press.

BARBOSA, Ignez Costa
1967 "Esboço de Uma Nova Divisão Regional do Paraná", *Revista Brasileira de Geografia*, Julho/Setembro 1967, pp. 83-102.

BEAVER, R. Pierce ed.
1973 *The Gospel and Frontier Peoples.* South Pasadena, William Carey Library.

BECK, Alexander
1973 "Brazil: A Giant Stirs" *Current*, March, 1973, pp. 51-59.

BECKER, Bertha K.
1968 "As Migrações Internas no Brasil, Reflexo de Uma Organização Do Espaço Desequilibrado", *Revista Brasileira de Geografia*, 2:3, Abril/Junho 1968, pp. 98-116.

BETTING, Joelmir
1971 *Brazil - The Take off is Now*. São Paulo, American Chamber of Commerce.

BINGLE, E. J., and GRUBB, Kenneth eds.
1952 *World Christian Handbook, 1952 Edition*. London, World Dominion Press.
1957 *World Christian Handbook, 1957 Edition*. London, World Dominion Press.

BRAZIL HERALD
1968 *National Housing Bank Mobilizes Private Initiatives*. April 28, 1968, pp. 6-7, 23.
1972 *The Important Role of the National Housing Bank*, February 29, 1972, pp. 5-6.

BRAZILIAN BULLETIN
1973 "Brazilian Tourism Push Is Under Way", April.

BRAZILIAN CENSUS, DEMOGRAPHIC
1970 *Resultados Preliminares, Tabulações Avançadas do Censo Demográfico*. Rio de Janeiro, IBGE.

BROOKS, Reuben Howard
1972 "Flight from Disaster: Drought Perception as a Force in Migration from Ceará Brasil." An unpublished PhD Dissertation. University of Colorado.

BURNQUIST, Boyd B.
1968 *São Paulo and its Geo-Economic Area*. São Paulo, American Chamber of Commerce for Brazil, Gráficos Brunner.

BURNS, E. Bradford
1970 *A History of Brazil*. New York, Columbia University Press.

CAVALCANTI, Flavio
1971 *Brasil em Dados.* Rio de Janeiro, Editoração de Indice--O Banco de Dados.

CLEARWATER SUN
1971 *São Paulo Growth Turning into Chaos,* June 21, 1971.

CONSELHO NACIONAL DE ESTATISTICA
1967 *Divisão Territorial do Brasil: Municipios Existentes 30-9-67.* Rio de Janeiro, IBGE.

CONSELHO REGIONAL DE GEOGRAFIA
1966 *Atlas do Brasil.* Rio de Janeiro. IBGE.

CORREA, P. H. da Rocha
1965 *Rumos do Brasil.* Catanduva, São Paulo, Edições IBEL.

COSTA, João Cruz
1964 *A History of Ideas In Brazil.* Los Angeles, University of California Press.

COXILL, H. Wakelin, and GRUBB, Kenneth, eds.
1962 *World Christian Handbook, 1962 Edition.* London, World Dominion Press.
1968 *World Christian Handbook, 1968 Edition.* London, World Dominion Press.

DAVIS, Kingsley
1969 *World Urbanization 1950-70, Volume I: Basic Data for Cities, Countries and Regions.* Berkeley, University of California Press.

DEAN, Warren
1969 *The Industrialization of São Paulo 1880-1945.* Austin. University of Texas Press.

DE ALCANTARA, Marco-Aurécia
1968 *Areas Metropolitanas: Grande Salvador, Grande Fortaleza, Grande Recife.* Recife, Fundinor.

DE AZEVEDO, Aroldo
1966 *As Regiões Brasileiras.* São Paulo, SP, Brasil, Companhia Editôra Nacional.

DE CARVALHO, Alceu Vicente W.
1960 *A População Brasileira: Estudo e Interpretação.* Rio de Janeiro IBGE Conselho Nacional de Estatística.

DE CASTRO, Marcos
1968 *"Baixo o Santo"*, October, 1968, p. 156, Rio de Janeiro, GB, Brasil, Editôra Abril.

DEPARTMENT OF CENSUS
1970 *Sinopse Preliminar Do Censo Demográfico*. São Paulo, VIII Recenseamento, Geral 1970, Rio de Janeiro, GB, Brasil, Fundação IBGE.

DOZIER, Craig L.
1971 "Geography and the Emergent Areas of Latin America", in *Lentnek, Barry (ed.)*.

ESTADO DE SÃO PAULO
1969 *O Paulistano*. São Paulo, SP, January 24, 1969.

FAISSOL, Sperdião
1970 "As Grandes Cidades Brasileiras: Dimensões Básicos de Diferenciação e Relações com O Desenvolvimento Economico, um Estudo de Analise Fatorial," *Revista Brasileira de Geografia*, October/December 1970, pp. 87-130.

FINAL ADVANCE OF SCRIPTURE TRANSLATION
1972 Scripture Translation Information Bank. Denton, Texas, F.A.S.T.

FONSECA, Luiz
1966 *Information Patterns and Practice Adoption Among Brazilian Farmers*. Research paper No. 20 Land Tenure Center. Madison, University of Wisconsin.

FREYRE, Gilberto
1956 *The Masters and the Slaves*. New York, Alfred A. Knopf.
1957 "Brazilian Melting Pot: The melting of races in Portuguese America." *Brazilian American Survey*, Rio de Janeiro.

FUNDACÃO IBGE
1968 *Divisão do Brasil em Micro-Regiões Homogênas*. Rio de Janeiro, Instituto Brasileiro de Geografia e Estatística.
1969 Distribuição Espacial da População do Brasil.

FURTADO, Celso
1968 *Um Projeto Para O Brasil*. Rio de Janeiro, GB, Brasil, Editôra Saga.

GALVÃO, Marillia Veloso
1968 *Subsidios ā Regionalização.* Rio de Janeiro, Fundação IBGE, Instituto Brasileiro de Geografia.

GALVÃO, Marillia Velosa et al.
1969 "Áreas de Pesquisa para Determinação de Áreas Metropolitanas," *Revista Brasileira de Geografia,* October/December 1969, pp. 53-128.

GEIGER, Pedro Pinchas
1967 "Esboço Preliminar de Divisão do Brasil nas Chamadas Regiões Homogênas," *Revista Brasileira de Geografia,* Abril/Junho, 1967.
1970 "Divisão Regional e Problema Regional," *Revista Brasileira de Geografia,* Abril/Junho 1970, pp. 157-170.

GRAHAM, Richard
1968 *Britain and the Onset of Modernization in Brazil 1850-1914.* New York, Cambridge University Press.

GREENWAY, Roger S.
1973 *An Urban Strategy for Latin America.* Grand Rapids, Baker Bank House.

GREENWOOD, Leonard
1970 "Fast Growing Latin Slums Gain Power." *Los Angeles Times,* March 22, 1970.

1973 "Progress, Indians Collide in Brazil." *Los Angeles Times,* April, 1973.

HARDOY, Jorge E.
1971 "The Problems of Urbanization in Latin America: A Future Perspective." *Anticipation* No. 8, September 1971, pp. 20-27.

HODGES, Melvin
1968 "A Pentecostal's View of Mission Strategy" *International Review of Missions* LVII:227 July, 1968, pp. 304-310.

INSTITUTO BRASILEIRO DE GEOGRAFIA E ESTATISTICA (IBGE)
1961-66 *Estatística do Culto Espirito.* Instituto Brasileiro de Geografia e Estatística, Rio de Janeiro, GB, Brasil.
1965 *Atlas Censitário Industrial do Brasil.* Rio de Janeiro, Serviço Nacional de Recenseamento.

INSTITUTO BRASILEIRO DE GEOGRAFIA E ESTATISTICA (IBGE)
1966-69 *Anuário do Brasil.* Instituto Brasileiro de Geografia e Estatística, Rio de Janeiro, GB, Brasil.
1968 *Religions of Brasil,* Estudo Sociográfico. Department of Statistics.

JAMES, Preston E.
1969 "Portuguese South America." *Latin America.* Fourth Edition. New York, The Odyssey Press.

JOHNSON, John J.
1959 *Political Change in Latin America: The Emergence of the Middle Sectors.* Stanford, Stanford University Press.

KAHL, Joseph A.
1968 *The Measurement of Modernism: A Study of Values in Brazil and Mexico,* Austin, University of Texas Press.

KLOPPENBURG, Boaventura
1966 "The Prevalence of Spiritism in Brazil," in Considine (ed.), *The Religions Dimension in the New Latin America,* pp. 77-87.

LANCELLOTTI, Sílvio
1973 *Communications in Brazil, Making Up For Lost Time* São Paulo, American Chamber of Commerce.

LANGENBUCH, Juergen Richard
1971 *A Estruturação da Grande São Paulo.* Rio de Janeiro, GB, Brasil, Fundação IBGE.

LEEDS, Anthony
1960 *Brazilian Careers and Social Structure:* (A Case History and Model In Contemporary Cultures and Societies of Latin America), Heath and Adams, (eds.) New York, Random House.

LIMA, Miguel Alves de
1968 *Novo Paisagens do Brasil.* Rio de Janeiro, GB, Brasil, Fundação IBGE, Instituto Brasileiro de Geografia.

LOETSCHER, Hugio
1971 "Sentenced to the Future" in Fulvio Roiter (ed.) *Brazil.* New York, Viking Press.

LOPES DA CRUZ MAGNANINI, Ruth
1971 "As Cidades de Santa Catarina: Base Econômica, Classificação Funcional," *Revista Brasileira de Geografia,* January/March 1971, pp. 86-122.

LOS ANGELES TIMES

1971 "São Paulo May Become World's Biggest City," October 19, 1971.

MAGALHÃES, Jose Cezar

1969 "Energia Eletrica: Fator de Desenvolvimento Industrial na Zona Metalurgica de Minas Gerais," *Revista Brasileira de Geografia,* January/March 1970, pp. 26-42.

MANGIN, William

1967 "Squatter Settlements." *Scientific American.* 219:4, pp. 3-12.

MATTOS, Rene de

1966 *Atlas Nacional do Brasil,* Instituto Brasileiro de Geografia e Estatística. Conselho Nacional de Geografia, Rio de Janeiro, GB, Brasil.

MCGAVRAN, Donald A.

1970 *Discipling Urban Populations.* Chapter 15 in Donald A. McGavran, *Understanding Church Growth.* Grand Rapids, Wm. B. Eerdmans Publishing Co. pp. 278-295.

MORAN, William E.

1969 "Brazil: A Prodigy of Growth." *Population Bulletin,* Vol. 25, pp. 89-90.

MULLER, Nice Lecoco

1969 *O Fato Urbano na Bácia do Rio Paraíba, Estado de São Paulo.* Rio de Janeiro. Biblioteca, Geografia Brasileira.

O.A.S. (Organization of American States)

1970 *Brazil.* American Republic Series No. 3. Washington, D.C. O.A.S. General Secretariat.

PINTO, Magalhães

1966 *Levantamento da População Favelada de Belo Horizonte,* Secretaria de Estado do Trabalho e Cultura Popular, Belo Horizonte, MG.

POPPINO, Rollie

1968 *Brazil, The Land and People.* New York, Oxford University Press.

POPULATION REFERENCE BUREAU

1970a *Brasil: Un Prodigio de Crescimento,* Boletin de Poblacion, Vol. 11, No. 3, May, 1970.

1970b *El Coloso del Sur,* Bogota, Colombia, May 1970.

READ, William R.
1973 "Church Growth as Modernization," *God, Man and Church Growth*. Grand Rapids. Wm. B. Eerdmans Publishing Co.

ROBOCK, Stefan
1968 *The Rural Push for Urbanization in Latin America: The Case for Northeast Brazil*. Occasional Paper No. 1., East Lansing, Michigan, Michigan State University.

RODRIGUES, Jose Honório
1967 *The Brazilians, Their Character and Aspirations*. Austin, Texas, University of Texas Press.

ROETT, Riordan, ed.
1972 *Brazil in the Sixties*. Nashville, Vanderbilt University Press.

ROGERS, Everett M.
1969 *Modernization Among Peasants: The Impact of Communication*. New York. Holt, Rinehart & Winston, Inc.

ROITER, Fulvio, ed.
1971 *Brazil*. New York. The Viking Press.

ROSTOW, W. W.
1967 *The Stages of Economic Growth*. New York, Cambridge University Press.

SAHOTA, Gian S.
1968 "An Economic Analysis of Internal Migrations in Brazil," *Journal of Political Economy*, 76:1, January/June 1968, pp. 218-245.

SAUNDERS, John, ed.
1971 *Modern Brazil: New Patterns and Development*. Gainesville, University of Florida Press.

SANDERS, Thomas G.
1970a *Japanese in Brazil*. Volume XIV, Number 3 of East Coast South American Series. Hanover, American Universities Field Staff.
1970b *Population Review 1970: Brazil*. Volume XIV, Number 6 of East Coast South America series, Hanover, American Universities Field Staff.

SAYERS, Raymond S.
1968 *Portugal and Brazil in Transition*. Minneapolis, Minnesota, University of Minnesota Press.

SCHALLER, Lyle
1972 *The Change Agent: The Strategy of Innovative Leadership* Nashville, Abingdon.

SEMPLE, R. Keith et al
1972 "Growth Poles in São Paulo, Brazil," *Annals of the Association of American Geographers.* 62:4, December, 1972, pp. 591-598.

SERVICO NACIONAL DE RECENSEAMENTO
1960 *VII Recenseamento Geral do Brasil - 1960.* Sinopse Preliminar do Censo Demográfico. Rio de Janeiro. IBGE.

SHIRLEY, Robert W.
1971 *The End of a Tradition: Culture Change and Development in the Município of Cunha, São Paulo, Brazil.* New York. Columbia University Press.

SIEGEL, Bernard J.
1971 "Migration Dynamics in the Interior of Ceará, Brazil." *Southwestern Journal of Anthropology* 27:3.

SIMONSEN, Mario Henrique
1969 *Brazil 2001.* Rio de Janeiro, APEC Editôra.

SINGER, Paul et. al.
1971 *Recursos Humanos na Granell São Paulo.* Two volumes. São Paulo, GREGAN, Órgão Da Secretaria De Economia E Planejamento Do Estado De São Paulo.

SOROKIN, Pitirim
1927 *Social Mobility.* New York, Harper and Brothers.

SLATER, Charles et. al.
1973 *Market Processes in the Recife Area of Northeast Brazil.* Research Report No. 2, East Lansing, Latin American Studies Center.

SMITH, T. Lynn
1970 *Studies of Latin American Societies.* New York, Doubleday & Company, Inc.
1973 *Brazil, People and Institutions.* Fourth Edition. Baton Rouge, Louisiana State University Press.

SPENCER, J. E., and THOMAS, Wm. L.
1969 *Cultural Geography, An Evolutionary Introduction To Our Humanized Earth.* New York, John Wesley & Sons.

STAR NEWS (Pasadena, California)
1972 "São Paulo Biggest City?" January 19, 1972

STATISTICAL SYNOPSIS OF BRAZIL
1971 *Sinopse Estatística do Brasil.* Rio de Janeiro, Ministério do Planejamento e Coordenação Geral.

STERNBERG, Hilgard O'Reilly
1966 "Reflections on the Brazilian Northeast," Monograph No. 2, Latin American Studies Center, Michigan State University.
1970 "A Geographer's View of Race and Class in Latin America." Berkeley, University of California.

TIPPETT, Alan R.
1967 *Solomon Islands Christianity: A Study in Growth and Obstruction.* New York. Friendship Press.

UNITED BIBLE SOCIETIES
1973 *Scriptures of the World.* New York, American Bible Society.

UNITED NATIONS
1968 *Urbanization:* Development Policies and Planning International Social Development, Review No. 1.

VALENTE, Waldemar
1955 *Sincretismo Religioso Afro-Brasileiro.* São Paulo. Campanhia Editôra Nacional.

VALVERDE, Orlando
1964 *Geografia Agrária do Brasil.* Rio de Janeiro, GB, Brazil, Ministério da Educação e Cultura.

VAN Es, J. C. et. al.
1968 "Rural Migrants in Central Brazil: A Study of Itumbiara, Goiás." Research paper No. 29. Land Tenure Center. Madison, University of Wisconsin.

VEJA
1969 As Grandes Cidades Estão Mundano. No. 31 April 9, 1969, pp. 34-48.
1970 *Censo: Quantos Somos, Como Vivemos, Para Dnde Vamos.* No. 104, September 2, 1970, pp. 42-49.

WAGLEY, Carles
1971 *An Introduction to Brazil.* Revised Edition. New York, Columbia University Press.

WEBB, Kempton E.
1969 "The Geography of Brazil's Modernization and Implications for the years 1980 and 2000 AD," in E. R. Baklanoff (ed.).

WEIL, Thomas E. et. al.
1971 *Area Handbook for Brazil*. Washington, D.C. DA PAM No. 550-200 U.S. Government Printing Office.

WILKENING, E. A.
1968 "Comparison of Migrants in Two Rural and an Urban Area of Central Brazil." Research Paper No. 35, Land Tenure Center, Madison, University of Wisconsin.

WINTER, Ralph D.
1973 "Existing Churches: Ends or Means?" *Christianity Today*. January 19, 1973, pp. 10-12.

BIBLIOGRAPHY (CONTINUED)

II THE AMAZONIA REGION

ANDERSON, Alan
1972 "Farming the Amazon: The Devastation Technique." *Saturday Review*. October, 1972, pp. 61-67.

BRAZIL EXPORT
1972 *The North*. São Paulo Comissariado da Feira Brasileira.

BRASIL PRESBITERIANO
1973 "Missão No Acre." ANO XV, No. 3, (Março).

BRAZILIAN BULLETIN
Brazilian Government Trade Bureau, New York, N.Y.
1969a (March) "Indians Preserve Tribal Way of Life in National Park."
1969b (December) "Should Indians Be Museum Pieces? Experts Say No."
1970a (April) "Background: Brazil's Tribal Indians."
1970b (October) "Vast Changes Seen Coming From Urubupunga Power."
1970c (March) "Indians Learn Needed Skills Fast."
1972a (January) "Finds Indians Friendly."
1972b (November) "2,500-Mile North Rim Road is Planned."
1973 (February) "Brazil-Venezuela: Two Presidents Agree."

BUSINESS WEEK
1970 "A Highway to Save the Stricken Northeast." *Business Week*, November 14, 1970.

DA ROCHA, Antônio.
1970 "Crítica Ao Lago Do Futuro" *O Estado De São Paulo*, (18-9-70).

DA SILVA, Guilherme Gomes
1973 "Na Amazônia: Itaituba," *Brasil Presbiteriano* XV:3, Março, 1973.

DENEVAN, William M.
1973 "Development and the Imminent Demise of the Amazon Rain Forest." *The Professional Geographer*. XXV:2, May 1973, pp. 130-135.

ELLETT, William H.
1972 "Pioneering the Amazon." *The Americas* 24:10, October 1972.

EMBAIXADA DO BRASIL
1970 Boletim Especial #129, July 17, *Transamazônica*. Washington, D.C.

EMPHASIS
1973 "The Last Frontier" *Emphasis*, March 15, pp. 12-13.

FALESI, Italo Cláudio; BASTOS, Therezinha Xavier; and MORAES, Vincente Haroldo Figueiredo
1972 *Zoneamento Agrícola Da Amazônia*. Boletim Technico do Instituto de Pesquisas Agro-pecuária do Norte. IPEAN. Belém Pará.

GREENWOOD, Leonard
1970a "Road Builders Battle Dense Brazil Jungle." *Los Angeles Times*, August, 1970.
1970b "For Pioneers, A New Wild West - The Amazon." *Think*, November/December 1970.
1972 Brazil Hacks Road Through Jungle to Open New Frontier *Los Angeles Times*, September 1972.
1973 Brazil Seeking Bids on Jungle - Circling Road. *Los Angeles Times*, April 1973.

HEGEN, Edmund E.
1971 "Geographic Studies in the Amazon Basin." *Annals of the Southwestern Conference on Latin American Studies*. Vol. 2. pp. 39-61.

HENRIQUES, Affonso
1972 "The Awakening Amazon Giant," *Americas*, 24:2 pp. 4-11.

HOWE, Marvine
1973 "Amazon Town, Focus of Colonization Effort, Suffers A Boom." *New York Times*, Thursday, January 4, 1973.

INTERNATIONAL REVIEW OF MISSIONS
1972 "The Church and its Missions Among the Indians of Latin America," (July 1972), pp. 252-256.

KIETZMAN, Dale Walter
1972 "Indian Survival in Brazil." An Unpublished PhD. Dissertation, University of Southern California.

LESLIE, Thomas M.
1973 *Population Growth Along the Brasília-Belém Highway*. California State University at Los Angeles. Department of Geography.

MCALLISTER, Doug
1972 "Personal Observations on Trip Along the Trans-Amazônia," *MIB Newsletter*, São Paulo.

McINTYRE, Loren
1972 "The Amazon, Untamed Titan of the World's Rivers," *National Geographic*, 142:4, October 1972 pp. 445-495.

MELD Ficho, Murilo
1972 "A Amazonia É Nossa" *Manchete* Vol # 1,068, October 14, 1972, pp. 16-17.

MINISTÉRIO DE TRANSPORTES
1970 *Carreteras Transamazônicas*. Rio de Janeiro, Governo Brasileiro.

MOLENAAR, Toby
1972 "On the Road: Hacking the Transamazonia Amid Leeches, Beans and Dreams of Glory." *Saturday Review*. September 1972, pp. 65-67.

NEVES, Jadar and TRINDADE, Antonio
1972 "Sinal Verde Para A Transamazônica." *Manchete*, Volume # 1069, October 14, 1972, pp. 4-15.

NEWSWEEK
1970 "Brazil: Taming the Amazon" *Newsweek*, November 2, 1970.

O. E. de S. P. (O ESTADO DE SÃO PAULO)
1972 "Hostilidade dos Indios." January 23, 1972, p. 14.

PAULSON, Belden
1967 *Some Observations on Policy for Developing Brazil's Interion Heartlands*. Current Developments in Brazil, Monograph Series No. 2, LAS Center, Michigan State University, Lansing.

PEREIRA, Osny Duarte
1971 *A Transamazônica: Pros E Contras*. Rio de Janeiro, Civilização Brasileira.

RAMOS, Rodrigo Otávio Jordão
1970 "A Amazônia, um Problem" *Jornal Da Tarde*, August 1970.

READ, William R.
1972a "Help Needed for Church Planters in the Amazon Basin." Fuller Theological Seminary, Pasadena, California.
1972b "The Road of the Century: What Does it Say to the Church?" *World Vision Magazine*, 16:9 October pp. 14-16.
1973 "Frontier Missions Needed for Brazil's Frontier Road System," *The Gospel to Frontier Peoples*, South Pasadena, Wm. Carey Library, p. 169.

REIS, Ferreira
1972 *O Impacto Amazônico Na Civilização Brasileira.* Rio de Janeiro, Editôra Paralelo.

SANDERS, Thomas G.
1971 *Brazilian Interior Migration: Three Frontier Cities on the Belém-Brasília Highway.* Volume XV, Number 2 of the East Coast South America Series, Hanover, American Universities Field Staff.
1973a *The Northeast and Amazonian Integration.* Volume XVII, Number 3 of the East Coast South America Series, Hanover, American Universities Field Staff.
1973b *Colonization on the Transamazonian Highway.* Volume XVII. Number 3 of the East Coast South America Series, Hanover, American Universities Series Field Staff.

SCHNEIDER, Arno Walter
1972 "Estes Colonos Já Estão Mudando A Face Da Amazonia. *Estensão Rural.* VII:75, Março.

SLOAT, Dale Lavern
1972 *Report on Transamazon Exploratory Trip.* Maringá Paraná, Igreja Missionária Unida. (Mimeographed).

THAYER, Yvonne
1972 "The Amazon Catches Up With the 20th Century."" *Brazilian Business.* July 1972, pp. 8-15.

TIME
1971 "Transamazonia: The Last Frontier." *Time*, September 13, 1971, pp. 36-37.

U. S. NEWS and WORLD REPORT
1972 "Unlocking a Rich Frontier: Report From the Amazon Basin." *U.S. News and World Report*, May 8, 1972, pp. 92-95.

VALVERDE, Orlando
1967 *A Rodovia Belém-Brasília.* Rio de Janeiro, Fundação IBGE.

VEJA
1970 "Indio no Caminho." *Veja*, August 18, 1970.
1972 "Meio Caminho Andado." *Veja*, Volume 213 April 10, 1972, pp. 18-19.

VILLAS BOAS, Orlando e Claudio
1968 "Saving Brazil's Stone Age Tribes from Extinction." *National Geographic*, 134:3 September, pp. 425-444.

BIBLIOGRAPHY (CONTINUED)

III THE ROMAN CATHOLIC CHURCH

ABBOTT, Walter (ed.)
1966 *The Documents of Vatican II.* New York, Guild Press.

AZEVEDO, Tales
1969 "Catolicismo no Brasil" *Vozes* 63:2, Fevereiro, 1969, pp. 117-124.

CONSIDINE, John
1958 *New Horizons In Latin America.* New York, Dodd, Mead and Co.
1966 *The Religious Dimension In The New Latin America.* Notre Dame, Fides Publishers, Inc.

CERIS
1965 *Anuário Católico Do Brasil.* Rio de Janeiro, GB, Brasil, Ceris.
1970 *Anuário Católico Do Brasil.* Rio de Janeiro, GB, Brasil, Ceris, Editôra Vozes Limitada.
1971 Informative Bulletin, (Supplement to Anuário Católico Do Brasil 1970), January/June 1971 #7, Rio de Janeiro, GB, Brasil, Editôra Vozes Limitada.

DAMBORIENA, Prudentia
1963 *El Protestantismo en América Latina.* Friboung, FERES.

GREGORY, Alfonso
1965 *A Igreja No Brasil.* Rio de Janeiro, GB, Brasil, Ceris.

I.B.G.E.
1958- *Estatística Do Culto Católico Romano do Brasil.*
1968 Instituto Brasileiro de Geografia e Estatística, Rio de Janeiro, GB, Brasil.

HOUTART, François et. al.
1965 "The Disintegration of Traditional Society." Chapter 6 in *The Church and the Latin American Revolution,* New York, Sheed and Ward.

RELIGIOUS NEWS SERVICE
1972 "Roman Catholic Church in Brazil" *RNS-Foreign Service,* January 11, 1972.

RIBEIRO DE OLIVEIRA, Paul A.
1970 *Catolicismo Popular No Brasil, 1970.* Rio de Janeiro, GB, Brasil, Ceris.

VAN STRAELEN, H.
1966 *The Catholic Encounter With World Religions.* Westminster, Maryland. The Newman Press.

VOZES
1969 *Catolicismo No Brasil.* Rio de Janeiro, Editôra Vozes Limitada, pp. 117-123.

BIBLIOGRAPHY (CONTINUED)

IV THE PROTESTANT CHURCH

A. General

ANDRADA, Laercio Caldeira
1947 *A Igreja Dos Fieis* (Coligny de Villegaignon). Rio de Janeiro, GB, Brasil, Centro Brasileiro de Publicidade LTDA.

BRAGA, Henriqueta Rosa Fernandes
1961 *Música Sacra Evangélica no Brasil.* São Paulo Livraria Kosmos Editôra.

BREWER, Earl D.C.
1973 "Social Indicators and Religions Indicators." *Review of Religions Research* 14:2 Winter '73 pp. 77-90.

DE MOURA, Abdalazig
1972 "O Pentecostalismo Como Fenômeno Religioso Popular No Brasil." *Revista Eclesiástica Brasileira* 31:121 pp. 78-94.

CAREY, William
1792 *An Enquiry Into the Obligation of Christians to Use Means for the Conversion of the Heathen.* London, Kingsgate Press.

CUNLIFFE, Peter
1971 "O Brasil Evangélico na Decada de 1970." *Mundo Cristão,* (January/February) pp. 12-15.

CURRY, Donald Edward
1969 "Lusiada: An Anthropological Study of the Growth of Protestantism in Brazil." An unpublished PhD Dissertation, University of Colombia. (m/f used).

DAVIS, J. Merle
1943 *How the Church Grows in Brasil.* International Missionary Council, New York City.

DAYTON, Edward R.
1971 *God's Purpose/Man's Plans, A Workbook.* Monrovia, M.A.R.C.

DE SOUZA, Beatrix Muniz
A Experiência Da Salvação: Pentecostals Em São Paulo. (Publisher N/A).

EDWARDS, Fred E.
1969 *The Role of the Faith Mission: A Brazilian Case Study.* South Pasadena, William Carey Library.

GAMMON, Samuel R.
1910 *The Evangelical Invasion of Brazil.* Richmond, Presbyterian Committee of Publication.

GATES, Charles W.
1972 *Industrialization: Brazil's Catalyst for Church Growth.* South Pasadena, William Carey Library.

GLASS, Frederick C.
1943 *Adventures With the Bible in Brazil.* New York, Loizeaux Brothers.

GODDARD, Bunton L. (ed.)
1967 *The Encyclopedia of Modern Christian Missions.* Camden, New Jersey, Thomas Nelson & Sons.

GUIMARÃES, Alberto Passo
1952 *O Quesito "Religião" No Censo Demográfico de 1950.* IBGE, Rio de Janeiro, GB, Brasil.

INSTITUTO BRASILEIRO DE GEOGRAFICA E STATÎSTICA (IBGE)
1955 *Estatistica do Culto Protestante do Brasil.*
-66 Instituto Brasileiro de Geografia e Estatística, Rio de Janeiro, GB, Brasil.

INTERNATIONAL REVIEW OF MISSIONS
1972 "The Church and its Mission Among the Indians of Latin America" from IRM, July 1972, pp. 252-256.

JOHNSON, Harmon A.
1967 "What is the Secret of the Growth of the Brazilian Church?" *Conviction,* 5:7, pp. 8-9.

KANE, Herbert J.
1971 "Brazil" First Section in Chapter XVII, *A Global View of Christian Missions.* Grand Rapids, Baker Book House, pp. 25-33.

KELLEY, Dean M.
1972 *Why Conservative Churches are Growing.* New York, Harper & Row Publishers.

LEONARD, Emile G.
1963 *O Protestantismo Brasileiro: Estudo de Eclesiologia e História Social.* São Paulo, SP, Brasil, Asociação de Seminários Teológicas Evangélicas.

MAKI, Mario
1972 *Relatório da Viagem A Transamazônica,* Igreja Missionária (ISBC), Londrina, Paraná.

MCGAVRAN, Donald A. (ed.)
1969 *Church Growth Bulletin.* Volumes I-V, South Pasadena, California, Wm. Carey Library. (Various references to Brazil).

MISSIONARY INFORMATION BUREAU
1973 *Directory of Missionaries in Brazil,* São Paulo, Brazil, M.I.B.

NEEDHAM, William L.; PENTECOST, Edward C.; and GILBERT, Ellen
1973 *Unreached Peoples: A Preliminary Compilation.* Monrovia, M.A.R.C./World Vision.

PENTECOST, Edward C.
1972 *Third World Missions Directory,* South Pasadena, Wm. Carey Library.

READ, William R.
1965 *New Patterns of Church Growth in Brazil,* Grand Rapids, Wm. B. Eerdmans's Publishing Company.
1966 *CGRILA Brazil Field Research Notes,* Vol. 12. Pasadena, California. Unpublished Notebook of Interviews, p. 38.
1968 "Scope of Strategy Planning for Latin America." *Evangelical Missions Quarterly,* June 1968, pp. 326-329.

READ, William R., MONTERROSO, Victor, and JOHNSON, Harmon
1969 *Latin American Church Growth.* Grand Rapids, Wm. E. Eerdmans.

RELIGIOUS NEWS SERVICE
1973 "Methodist Growth Cited in a Brazilian Area." *RNS - Foreign Service,* Thursday, May 17, 1973.

RIBEIRO, René
1969 "Pentecostalismo no Brasil." *Vozes* 63:2, Fevereiro, pp. 125-136.

B. Assemblies of God

CONDE, Emilio
1960 *História das Assembléias de Deus no Brasil.* Rio de Janeiro, GB, Brasil, Casa Publicadora das Assembléias de Deus.

BERG, Daniel
1957 *Enviado Por Deus.* São Paulo, SP, Brasil, Gráfica São José.

C. Baptists

CONVENÇÃO BATISTA INDEPENDENTE
1966 Quem Somos, O Que Fazemos, Em Que Crêmos, Santa Maria, RGS. Livraria Globo S/A.

CRABTREE, A. R.
1953 *Baptists in Brasil.* Rio de Janeiro, GB, Brasil, Baptist Publishing House.

Junta Executiva da Convenção Batista Brasileira
1967 *Atlas, Relatõrios, Paraceres e Outras Informações.* Da Quadragesima Nona Assémbleia Annual. Rio de Janeiro, GB, Brasil.

MESQUITA, A. N., and CRABTREE, A. R.
1937 *História da Igreja Batista do Brasil* (in two volumes). Rio de Janeiro, GB, Brasil, Casa Publicadora Batista.

D. O Brasil Para Cristo

CUNLIFFE, Peter
1970 "Homen Pequeno, Idêias Grandes." *Article in Mundo Cristã*, September, São Paulo, SP, Brasil.

LYRA, Jorge Buarque
1964 *O Movimento Pentecostal No Brasil: Profilaxia Cristã desse Movimento Em Defesa De "O Brasil Para Cristo."* Niteroi, RJ, Brasil.

E. Church of God

CONN, Charles W.
1959 *Where the Saints Have Trod: A History of the Church of God Missions.* Cleveland, Tennessee, Pathway Press.

SIMPOSIO
1966 *O Espirito Santo e O Movimento Pentecostal.* São Paulo, A.S.T.E.
1969 *O Movimento Pentecostal No Brasil.* São Paulo, A.S.T.E.

SOLTAU, Stanley T.
1954 *Missions at the Crossroads.* Wheaton, Van Kampen Press.

TAVARES, Levy
1965 *Minha Pátria Para Cristo.* São Paulo.

VASCONCELOS, A. P.
1967 *Correspondence with Wm. R. Read,* dated May 21, from Belém, Pará, Brasil.

VEJA
1972 "O Avanço dos Pentecostais." Number 219, 15-11-1972 pp. 58-61.

WILLEMS, Emilio
1966 "Religious Mass Movements and Social Change in Brazil." Eric N. Baklanoff (ed.), *New Perspectives of Brazil,* Nashville, Vanderbilt University Press.
1967 *Followers of the New Faith: Culture Change and the Rise of Protestantism in Brazil and Chile.* Nashville, Vanderbilt University Press.

WINTER, Ralph D.
1967 *Theological Education by Extension.* South Pasadena, Wm. Carey Library.

WONG, James
1973 *Missions from the Third World.* Singapore, Church Growth Study Center.

W.C.C. (WORLD COUNCIL OF CHURCHES)
1971 *"Declaration of Barbados."* Barbados Symposium, Program to Combat Racism, P.C.R. (1/71), W.C.C.

YUASA, Key
1967 "Churches in Minority Situation: The Brazilian Case." Document 68/49. Cuernavaca, CIDOC.

ZARA, Armando
1966 Correspondence with Wm. R. Reed, dated April 21, from Jundiai, São Paulo, Brazil.

CONN, Charles W.
1965 *Ensinos, Disciplina E Governo Da Igreja De Deus.* San Antonio, Texas. Editorial Evangélica.

F. Congregational

FRANCESCON, Louis
1960 (A testimony). 311 North Lombard Avenue, Oak Park, Illinois.

CONGREGACAO CRISTA NO BRASIL
1962 "Breve História, Fé, Doutrina e Estatutos." São Paulo, SP, Brasil.
1965 *Louvores e Súplicas a Deus.* São Paulo. Indústrias Reunidas Irmãos Spina, S/A.
1970 "Annual Relatório E Balanço." Sao Paulo, SP, Brasil.
-71 Assembléia Geral Ordinária.

G. Congregação Cristã no Brasil

SILVA, Ismael Junkor
1961 *Notas Históricas Sobre a Missão Evangelizadora do Brasil e Portugal* (in three volumes). Rio de Janeiro, Baptista de Souza & Cia. Editores.

TESTA, Michael D.
1963 *O Apóstolo da Madeira (Robert Reid Kalley).* Lisbon, Igreja Evangélica Presbiteriana de Portugal.

H. Episcopal

IGREJA EPISCOPAL DO BRASIL
1965a Atas E Outros Documentos da 67° Reunião do Concílio da Diocese Meridiunal da Igreja Episcopal do Brasil. Porto Alegre, RGS, Brasil.
1965b Atas e Outros Documentos da VIII Reunião do Sinodo da I.E.B. Porto Alegre, RGS, Brasil.

KRISCHKE, George Upton
1949 *História Da Igreja Episcopal Brasileira.* Rio de Janeiro. Gráfica Tupy Ltd.

PITHAN, Athalicio
1965 *Treze Anos Na Paroquia De Bagé.* Porto Alegre. Editôra Metrôpole.

I. Lutheran

SINODO RIOGRANDENSE
1961 *75 Anos de Existência do Sínodo Riograndense 1886-1961.* São Leopoldo, RGS, Editôra Sinodal São Leopoldo.

BACHMANN, Theodore E.
1970 *Lutherans in Brazil.* Minneapolis. Augsburg Publishing House.

PANKOW, Fred
1970 *Those Brazilian Lutherans.* Article in Lutheran Witness, June 1970.

REIMNITZ, Elmer
1970 *Mission Opportunities in Brazil for the Lutheran Church - Missouri Synod.* St. Louis, Board of Missions L.C. - M.S.

J. Methodist

LONG, Eula K.
1968 *Do Meu Velho Bau Metodista.* São Paulo, SP, Brasil, Junta Geral de Educação Cristã.

ROCHA, Isnard
1967a *Pioneiros e Bandeirantes do Metodismo no Brasil,* São Bernardo do Campo, SP, Imprensa Metodista.
1967b *Histórias da História do Metodismo no Brasil.* São Bernardo do Campo, SP, Imprensa Metodista.

K. Presbyterian

BEAR, James E.
1961 *Mission to Brazil.* Nashville, Tennessee, Presbyterian Church, U. S.

FERREIRA, J. Andrade
1952 *O Apõstolo De Caldas.* São Paulo, SP, Brasil, Edição da Gráfica Renacença.

Igreja Presbiteriana do Brasil
1967 *Boletim Oficial do Supremo Concilio.* São Paulo, SP, Brasil, Casa Editôra Presbiteriana.

MCINTYRE, Robert
First 50 Years (Unpublished doctoral dissertation, Princeton Theological Seminary, Princeton, N. J.).

NEVES, Mario
1950 *Digest Presbiteriano*. Resoluções do Supremo Concílio da Igreja Presbiteriana do Brasil, de 1888 a 1942. São Paulo, SP, Brasil, Casa Editôra Presbiteriana.

PIERSON, Paul Everett
1971 *A Younger Church in Search of Maturity, The History of the Presbyterian Church of Brazil from 1910 to 1959*. Princeton, New Jersey (Unpublished Doctoral Dissertation).

READ, William R.
1969 *A Presbyterian Church in Central Brazil*, Centro Intercultural de Documentation, Cuernavaca, Mexico.

RIBEIRO, Boanerges
1950 *O Padre Protestante*. São Paulo, SP, Brasil, Casa E Presbiteriana.

L. Wycliffe Bible Translators

WYCLIFFE BIBLE TRANSLATORS
1965 *Tribal Reports of the 1965 Brazil Branch of WBT*. Brasília, Brasil.
1967 *Brazil's Tribes*. Brasília. Summer Institute of Linguistics, Wycliffe Bible Translators.

BIBLIOGRAPHY (CONTINUED)

V THE BRAZIL 1980 PROJECT (MARC-MIB-CASE)

INESON, Frank A.

1968 "Brazil Impact Study, Protestant Summary Data." MARC/MIB, São Paulo Computer Printout Report 28 pages.

1969 *A Statistical Look at the Missionary Task in Brazil.* Occasional Bulletin #27, M.I.B., São Paulo, SP, Brasil.

1970 "CGRILA Brazil Computer Project." Inter-Office Communication, Monrovia, MARC.

1971a "Programming for Brazil Computer Project." Project Memo, Monrovia, MARC.

1971b "Brazil Computer Project Editing of Denominational Codes." Project Report, Monrovia, MARC.

1971c "Brazil Computer Project, Denominational Group Data by Micro-Region." Project Report, Monrovia, MARC.

1971d "Counts of Data Records by Years within States Versus Ecclesiastical Tradition." BRAZIL 1980 Computer Printout, Monrovia, MARC, 11-19-71.

1972 "List of Volunteers Who Worked on Brazil Project Since Inception." Monrovia, MARC.

JOHNSON, Harmon

1972 *A New Church Growth Research Center for Brazil.* São Paulo, SEPAL.

LATIN AMERICAN PULSE

1972 "Brazilian Research Center *Pulse.* Vol. VII, No. 3 October 1972, Wheaton, Evangelical Missions Information Service.

MARC

1967 "A Study of the Church at Work in Brazil." MIB/MARC Study. Monrovia, MARC/WV.

1970a *MARC Data Bank, Part I.* Monrovia, MARC/WV.

1970b *North American Protestant Ministers Overseas,* 9th Edition. Monrovia, Missionary Research Library/MARC.

1972 "Christianity in Brazil: A Preliminary Survey." Monrovia, MARC/WV

1972 *Status of Christianity in Brazil.* Country Profile Series, Monrovia, MARC/WV.

MARC/MIB

1971 *Continuing Evangelism in Brazil.* Monrovia, MARC/WV.

MIB-MARC
1968 *Protestant Missions in Brazil.* Directory of Non-Catholic Christian Missionary Groups. São Paulo, M.I.B.

READ, William R.
1967a *How to Transcribe the Religious Census Data.* Pasadena, Knox Presbyterian Church.
1967b "Breakthrough" *World Vision Magazine.* 11:9, October pp. 2-4.
1970 "Consultation with John Grove." Written report of Consultation, Monrovia, MARC.
1971 *A Historic Meeting in Brazil.* Monrovia, MARC.

Index